Elliott Carter Studies

Over the course of an astonishingly long career, Elliott Carter has engaged with many musical developments of the twentieth and now twenty-first centuries – from his early neoclassical music of the interwar period, to his modernist works of conflict and opposition in the 1960s and 1970s, to the reshaping of a modernist aesthetic in his latest compositions. *Elliott Carter Studies* throws new light on these many facets of Carter's extensive musical oeuvre. This collection of essays presents historical, philosophical, philological, and theoretical points of departure for in-depth investigations of individual compositions, stylistic periods in Carter's output, and his contributions to a variety of genres, including vocal music, the string quartet, and the concerto. The first multi-authored book to appear on Carter's music, it brings together new research from a distinguished team of leading international Carter scholars, providing the reader with a wide range of perspectives on an extraordinary musical life.

MARGUERITE BOLAND is a researcher in the College of Arts and Social Sciences at the Australian National University. Her scholarly interest is twentieth-century modernist music and aesthetics, particularly the music of Elliott Carter and of Johanna Beyer.

JOHN LINK is a composer and Professor in the Music Department of the William Paterson University of New Jersey. He is the author of *Elliott Carter: A Guide to Research* (2000), and co-editor, with Nicholas Hopkins, of Elliott Carter's *Harmony Book*.

Elliott Carter Studies

EDITED BY

Marguerite Boland

and

John Link

CAMBRIDGE
UNIVERSITY PRESS

CAMBRIDGE UNIVERSITY PRESS
Cambridge, New York, Melbourne, Madrid, Cape Town,
Singapore, São Paulo, Delhi, Mexico City

Cambridge University Press
The Edinburgh Building, Cambridge CB2 8RU, UK

Published in the United States of America by Cambridge University Press, New York

www.cambridge.org
Information on this title: www.cambridge.org/9780521113625

First published 2012

Printed in the United Kingdom by the MPG Books Group

A catalogue record for this publication is available from the British Library

Library of Congress Cataloguing in Publication data
Elliott Carter studies / edited by Marguerite Boland and John Link.
   p.   cm.
Includes bibliographical references and index.
ISBN 978-0-521-11362-5 (alk. paper)
1. Carter, Elliott, 1908– – Criticism and interpretation.   I. Boland, Marguerite.   II. Link, John F.
ML410.C3293E68   2012
780.92–dc23

2012013415

ISBN 978-0-521-11362-5 Hardback

Contents

Part IV   Music and text   [*251*]

Illustrations

All illustrations are from the Elliott Carter Collection at the Paul Sacher Foundation. Reproduced with kind permission of the Paul Sacher Foundation.

Contributors

Editors

MARGUERITE BOLAND, The Australian National University

JOHN LINK, The William Paterson University of New Jersey

Other contributors

JONATHAN W. BERNARD, University of Washington

GUY CAPUZZO, University of North Carolina, Greensboro

ANNETTE VAN DYCK-HEMMING, Kassel, Germany

STEPHEN HEINEMANN, Bradley University, Illinois

ANDREW MEAD, University of Michigan

FELIX MEYER, The Paul Sacher Foundation, Basel

MAX NOUBEL, University of Burgundy and CRAL-EHESS

BRENDA RAVENSCROFT, Queen's University, Canada

JOHN ROEDER, University of British Columbia

DÖRTE SCHMIDT, Universität der Künste Berlin

STEPHEN SODERBERG, Music Division, Library of Congress

ARNOLD WHITTALL, King's College, University of London

Preface

The study of Elliott Carter's music has entered a new phase. In the fourteen years since the publication of David Schiff's revised edition of *The Music of Elliott Carter*, new research and new resources have broadened the discourse and led to the reconsideration of many of the traditional narratives of Carter's music and his career. Major studies in German, French, and English have been published – Henning Eisenlohr's *Komponieren als Entscheidungsprozess*, Max Noubel's *Elliott Carter ou le temps fertile*, Felix Meyer's and Anne Shreffler's *Elliott Carter: A Centennial Portrait in Letters and Documents*, and James Wierzbicki's biography *Elliott Carter* – while articles and book chapters in many languages have appeared with increasing frequency and diversity of approaches. At the same time, the enormous body of work Carter has completed since his eightieth birthday has dramatically shifted the center of gravity of his career toward his later music, and prompted significant new scholarly activity. As an illustration of the reach of Carter studies today we may contrast Ève Poudrier's theoretical investigation of the perception of polymeter in Carter's music[1] and Anne Shreffler's study of "dramatic action" in Carter's opera *What Next?*.[2] As Carter's stature continues to grow and – most importantly – as an ever-widening audience discovers the pleasures of listening to his music, an inevitable and welcome diversification of viewpoints is taking place.

The celebrations surrounding Carter's centenary in 2008 provided a wonderful opportunity for just such musical discoveries, as festivals around the world, from Toronto to Ljubljana, were dedicated entirely to performances of his music. To mention but a few, the *Aspects des Musiques d'Aujourd'hui* festival in Caen (France) mounted an All-Carter program in 2005; the BBC Symphony Orchestra produced the *Get Carter!* showcase in 2006; the Saint Paul Chamber Orchestra in partnership with the University of Minnesota organized a week-long Carter festival in 2006; and the major Centennial event at Tanglewood's 2008 Festival of Contemporary Music featured no fewer than forty-seven of Carter's works. Many of the festivals included workshops, talks, and presentations offering audiences exposure not only to Carter's music but also to the perspectives and preoccupations of those performing and writing about it. The papers delivered at IRCAM's Carter Conference in 2008 were

[1] Poudrier, "Local Polymetric Structures in Elliott Carter's *90+* for Piano (1994)."

[2] Shreffler, "Instrumental dramaturgy as Humane Comedy: *What Next?* by Elliott Carter and Paul Griffiths."

even broadcast on *Radio France*. Importantly for Carter studies, these events also brought groups of geographically dispersed scholars together to exchange fresh ideas. The impetus for *Elliott Carter Studies* sprang out of the exchanges and connections that were made at a number of these events.

Not surprisingly, the increased attention to Carter's music has opened up a range of new perspectives. For many years a relatively small number of accepted narratives of Carter's music and career prevailed – mostly ones that were formed and propagated by Carter himself and by a close circle of friends and admirers to explain and promote the music and the musical aesthetic that brought Carter his first international recognition. *Elliott Carter Studies* offers a wider and more diverse set of viewpoints that both explore and question these well-known narratives: historical events and musical structures are reinterpreted, often revealing new points of connection between Carter's work and the milieu of twentieth-century Western art music in which he has played such a vibrant role. Whether American Neoclassicism of the 1930s and 1940s (see contributions by Jonathan Bernard, and Annette van Dyck-Hemming), the Second Viennese School (see chapters by Dörte Schmidt, Felix Meyer, and Stephen Soderberg), or the dramatic changes in musical styles and institutions at the end of the twentieth century (discussed in chapters by John Link, Arnold Whittall, Marguerite Boland, and Max Noubel), Carter has always explored and experimented with musical ideas of the time, adapting them to suit his own unique stylistic and aesthetic voice.

The narrative of disconnection and the divided ensemble has accompanied Carter's music and its early reception history from his First String Quartet onwards. With the benefit of much excellent work on Carter's techniques of individualizing harmonic and rhythmic materials, analytical studies are now seeking a better understanding of the integration and the sophisticated interaction of musical strands in Carter's music, both locally and at the formal level (see chapters by John Roeder, Andrew Mead, Stephen Heinemann, and Guy Capuzzo). At the same time, other work is recognizing that in much of Carter's music, the ensemble divisions are challenged by cooperative inter-action (see Heinemann and Boland), by a reconceived thematicism (see Whittall), and by the lyric perspective (see Link), all of which act as unifying elements and cut against the grain of the divided ensemble.

The lyricism of Carter's late music is very much tied up with the literary influences on his musical creativity, be it latently in instrumental pieces or directly in text settings (see chapters by Brenda Ravenscroft, Noubel, and Link). Although the triptych of American compositions that marked Carter's return to vocal writing dates from 1975–81, it was not until another twenty years later that Carter again turned his hand to vocal writing and since that time he has never stopped. With songs, song cycles, an opera, and a choral work all written in the last two decades, vocal composition – much of it based on the poetry of several generations of early twentieth-century modernists – is an essential aspect of Carter's late period.

Many of the new directions in Carter studies have been sparked by the archival resources now available to scholars. Since the mid-1990s, studies based on the collection of Carter's manuscript materials at the Paul Sacher Foundation, Basel, have appeared with increasing frequency.[3] More recently the digitization of the vast holdings of Carter manuscripts at the Library of Congress has made a wealth of resources instantly available to scholars around the world. Today sketches at both the Sacher Foundation and the Library of Congress are consulted almost as a matter of course in much analytical research (including here in Heinemann, Boland, and Schmidt). However, the chapters by Felix Meyer and by Stephen Soderberg represent major contributions to the small but growing field of Carter sketch studies, and what they uncover should entice scholars to delve deeper into the archives on both continents.

No deliberate attempt was made in this collection to cover the full span of Carter's musical career; however, the diversity of interests of the contributors has meant that representative pieces from all periods of Carter's creative output are discussed, whether historically, analytically, or philosophically. The chapters in this volume, written by an international cast of composers, theorists, and musicologists from seven countries and three continents, are evidence of the ongoing proliferation of voices in Carter scholarship, and a testament to the deep engagement that his music continues to inspire.

[3] Shreffler, "'Give the Music Room': Elliott Carters 'View of the Capitol from the Library of Congress' aus *A Mirror on Which to Dwell*"; Link, "The Composition of Carter's *Night Fantasies*"; Vermaelen, "Elliott Carter's Sketches: Spiritual Exercises and Craftsmanship."

Acknowledgments

We wish to express our thanks to Victoria Cooper for her support in making this volume a reality and to Rebecca Taylor for her invaluable advice and assistance throughout the editorial process. We are extremely grateful to the Paul Sacher Foundation and to its Director Felix Meyer for generously providing the manuscript images, including the cover image. Our thanks also to Sherrey Quinn for making the index. Our special thanks to Virgil Blackwell and James Kendrick, and to Elliott Carter for his enthusiasm and encouragement. We are very grateful to all of the contributors to *Elliott Carter Studies* and to the large and enthusiastic community of composers, performers, scholars, and Carter fans worldwide whose ideas helped to shape this book. We would also like to acknowledge the far-reaching influence of our collaboration, in no small part thanks to Skype™, which enabled us to meet "face-to-face" on a regular basis despite being continents apart. Our editorial conferences and wide-ranging conversations made the work a pleasure and improved this book in countless ways.

Finally, we would like to thank the people important to each of us in this project.

For Marguerite Boland: my special thanks to John McCaughey, Guy Capuzzo, and Kim Bastin for their advice and assistance; to Larry Sitsky, Jennifer Shaw, and both my parents for their support; and to the nurses at the Canberra Hospital, where much of the final manuscript was prepared during the few months leading up to the birth of Allan's and my daughter, Alice. My deepest gratitude is to Allan Walker, for introducing me to the music of Elliott Carter all those years ago, and for hours of discussion, support, and advice.

For John Link: I would like to thank the Amphion Foundation for a research grant, and William Paterson University for a sabbatical leave, a partial research leave, and assigned release time, all of which were essential for my work on this project. Thanks especially to Stephen Hahn. My most heartfelt thanks to my family, most of all to Anna Maria Schoenhammer Link, Eva Maria Schoenhammer Link, and Maria Schoenhammer.

This book was generously supported by publication grants from the Australian National University and the Society for Music Theory.

All examples of Elliott Carter's published music are reproduced by kind permission of Boosey & Hawkes Publishers Ltd., G. Schirmer Inc. & Associated Music Publishers Inc., and Theodore Presser Company, as follows:

Symphonia by Elliott Carter © Copyright by Hendon Music, Inc., a Boosey & Hawkes Company. Reprinted by permission.

Trilogy by Elliott Carter © Copyright 1992 by Hendon Music, Inc., a Boosey & Hawkes Company. Reprinted by permission.

"Under the Dome" by Elliott Carter © Copyright 1995 by Hendon Music, Inc., a Boosey & Hawkes Company. Reprinted by permission.

"End of a Chapter" by Elliott Carter © Copyright 1995 by Hendon Music, Inc., a Boosey & Hawkes Company. Reprinted by permission.

In Sleep, In Thunder by Elliott Carter © Copyright 1982 by Hendon Music, Inc., a Boosey & Hawkes Company. Reprinted by permission.

Flute Concerto by Elliott Carter © Copyright by Hendon Music, Inc., a Boosey & Hawkes Company. Reprinted by permission.

Oboe Concerto by Elliott Carter © Copyright 1988 by Hendon Music, Inc., a Boosey & Hawkes Company. Reprinted by permission.

Clarinet Concerto by Elliott Carter © Copyright 1996 by Hendon Music, Inc., a Boosey & Hawkes Company. Reprinted by permission.

Violin Concerto by Elliott Carter © Copyright 1990 by Hendon Music, Inc., a Boosey & Hawkes Company. Reprinted by permission.

String Quartet No. 5 by Elliott Carter © Copyright by Hendon Music, Inc., a Boosey & Hawkes Company. Reprinted by permission.

Esprit Rude/Esprit Doux by Elliott Carter © Copyright 1985 by Hendon Music, Inc., a Boosey & Hawkes Company. Reprinted by permission.

Riconoscenza per Goffredo Petrassi by Elliott Carter © Copyright 1985 by Hendon Music, Inc., a Boosey & Hawkes Company. Reprinted by permission.

Boston Concerto by Elliott Carter © Copyright by Hendon Music, Inc., a Boosey & Hawkes Company. Reprinted by permission.

Asko Concerto by Elliott Carter © Copyright by Hendon Music, Inc., a Boosey & Hawkes Company. Reprinted by permission.

A Celebration of Some 100 × 150 Notes by Elliott Carter © Copyright 1988 by Hendon Music, Inc., a Boosey & Hawkes Company. Reprinted by permission.

Horn Concerto by Elliott Carter © Copyright by Hendon Music, Inc., a Boosey & Hawkes Company. Reprinted by permission.

Permission for the reproduction of other materials is as follows:

Reproductions of Carter's sketch material are used with the kind permission of the Paul Sacher Foundation.

"End of a Chapter" from *Selected Poetry* by John Hollander, copyright © 1993 by John Hollander. Used by permission of Alfred A. Knopf, a division of Random House, Inc.

"Metamorphosis" from *The Collected Poems of Wallace Stevens* by Wallace Stevens, copyright 1954 by Wallace Stevens and renewed 1982 by Holly Stevens. Used by permission of Alfred A. Knopf, a division of Random House, Inc. Used in the UK by permission of Faber and Faber Ltd.

Abbreviations

CEL   Carter, Elliott. *Collected Essays and Lectures, 1937–1995*.
             Ed. Jonathan W. Bernard. Rochester: University of
             Rochester Press, 1997.

ECCP   Meyer, Felix and Anne C. Shreffler. *Elliott Carter: A
             Centennial Portrait in Letters and Documents*.
             Woodbridge: The Boydell Press, 2008.

ECGR   Link, John. *Elliott Carter: A Guide to Research*. New York
             and London: Garland, 2000.

FW   Edwards, Allen. *Flawed Words and Stubborn Sounds: A
             Conversation with Elliott Carter*. New York: W. W.
             Norton, 1971.

HB   Carter, Elliott. *Harmony Book*. Ed. Nicholas Hopkins and
             John F. Link. New York: Carl Fischer, 2002.

LTF   Noubel, Max. *Elliott Carter ou le temps fertile*. Geneva:
             Éditions Contrechamps, 2000.

MEC   Schiff, David. *The Music of Elliott Carter*, revised second
             edn. London: Faber; Ithaca: Cornell University Press,
             1998.

MEC, 1st edn Schiff, David. *The Music of Elliott Carter*, 1st edn. London:
             Eulenburg Books; New York: Da Capo Press, 1983.

WEC   Carter, Elliott. *The Writings of Elliott Carter*. Ed. Else Stone
             and Kurt Stone. Bloomington and London: Indiana
             University Press, 1977.

PART I

Overview: music early and late

1   The true significance of Elliott Carter's early music

Jonathan W. Bernard

> ... they come up to me at concerts when they hear my old pieces and say, "Why didn't you keep that up? You were doing it so well! It had such liveliness, such freshness of sound!" As if to imply that when I got into less tonal stuff my music went to pot.
>   *Well, I certainly don't think so. But I like your earlier music very much.*
> Well, so do I! I've come to like it a second time, for I didn't used to like it.[1]

Critical writing about Elliott Carter's early compositions has tended to treat them collectively as a kind of preparatory exercise to his music from the First String Quartet (1951) onward. This is understandable, since they were written in a basically neoclassical style that Carter firmly repudiated, with scarcely a glance back, over half a century ago. At most, it would seem, this earlier work – extending from the first acknowledged work in his catalogue, the *Tarantella* of 1936, to the Woodwind Quintet of 1948 – has been considered worth picking over for the occasional foreshadowing of one technique or another that would emerge in its definitive employment after 1950, far more extensively worked out and more fully integrated into a working method "advanced" enough to make use of its implications in a significant way. Moreover, the tendency of this earlier work, over the years since it was composed, to recede ever farther into insignificance has been encouraged by the sheer length of Carter's career. The first twelve years, after all, were one-fourth of its total span in 1984; today, a quarter century later, those same twelve years represent less than one-sixth.

After decades of listening to and writing about Carter's music, I have come around to thinking that the general lack of attention paid by Carter scholars (myself included) to the work of his first dozen years as a composer is unfortunate, for two reasons. One is that many of his pieces from the period 1936–48 are as well regarded by performers as any in the repertoire of the American neoclassical style, and are often programmed. Charting the Carter 100th birthday celebrations in 2008 and 2009, it would have been hard not to notice that, although the early works were almost completely neglected at some of the larger festivals (such as the annual Tanglewood Festival of Contemporary Music, wholly devoted to Carter in July 2008, which presented

[1] Bernard, "An Interview with Elliott Carter," 191.

only two works of this period among the forty-seven given in ten concerts), many of the commemorations of smaller scale held throughout the United States during that time tended to feature the early works. It's true that, by and large, they are easier to play than the later music; and no doubt they appeal more readily to the typical audience that has never heard any Carter at all. But such circumstances hardly need stand as a disincentive to those who study Carter's music to bring to the early pieces something approaching equal attention; rather the opposite, in fact, since in doing so one might be able to identify just what there is about Carter's notoriously formidable later music that the more "accessible" early music could clarify for a wider audience.[2]

Should such pragmatic considerations alone, however, not offer sufficient encouragement to undertake such an effort, one might be persuaded by Carter's altered attitude toward his own early work during the past thirty years or so, as indicated in the interview quotation above: coming "to like it a second time" has meant that he has been willing to take the time and trouble to orchestrate works such as the *Three Poems of Robert Frost*, *Pastoral*, and *Voyage*, and to make new arrangements of the *Elegy*. These changed circumstances suggest a second reason to regret the general critical disregard of the earlier music: that it impedes a proper appreciation of his formation as a composer. For Carter's later work is actually founded in the earlier, not simply foreshadowed; much of what makes him the composer he is today, and has been for the past sixty years, is already present in the first music he saw fit to bring to a public hearing.

The idea of the earlier music as *foundation* rests less on technique or style than on aesthetic. Although in the pages that follow it will be necessary to speak extensively of technical matters, the reader must keep in mind that such matters are, after all, only the outward manifestation of something else, less easy to specify or quantify yet in the end more significant. This stance is partly signaled by the topical organization of the present essay: my aim is not to present a chronology of Carter's stylistic development. More useful, it seems

[2] I should not like to give the impression that Carter's early music has been entirely disregarded in the critical literature. Schiff, *MEC*, 1st edn, which covered all the works up to 1979, devoted fifty-six pages – nearly a fourth of the main text – to the years 1936–48, and even found room for a few pages on the "student efforts" before 1936 (in Schiff's revision of 1998, which discards the chronological treatment of the first edition in favor of arrangement of Carter's works by genre, the early pieces, distributed as they are among those of all of Carter's other periods, register as a group much less prominently). Beck, "Elliott Carter's Tonal Practice in 'The Rose Family'," advocates fervently for closer attention to Carter's pre-1950 music (ironically, considering the title of the anthology in which the article was published), and engages in close analysis of one brief song, the second of Carter's *Three Poems by Robert Frost* (1942). And Meyer, "Left by the Wayside: Elliott Carter's Unfinished Sonatina for Oboe and Harpsichord," in this volume, examines an unfinished work from the 1940s, unknown until quite recently, pinpointing features that it holds in common both with other (complete) works of the same decade and the *Sonata for Flute, Oboe, Cello, and Harpsichord* of a few years later.

to me, is to show that certain fundamental preoccupations of Carter as composer were there from the start, even if expressed in quite different ways in the earlier music than in the later.

Within the necessarily limited confines of an essay like this, it would have been impossible to cover every work of the years 1936–48, even if I had wanted to do so. I do hope, though, that the five pieces from which I have drawn examples seem reasonably representative of the period as a whole. The choral music I have completely excluded, though in a way this may be justifiable: Carter has written no choral music since *Emblems* (1947). In compensation, one could say, the vocal work *Voyage* (1943), for voice and piano, is given extensive attention. The others are: *Canonic Suite* (1939); Symphony No. 1 (1942); *Holiday Overture* (1944); and the Piano Sonata (1946).

A love of complication

When Carter's early music is described as more accessible by comparison to his later, "difficult" work – as it sometimes is by newspaper critics, among others – the implication is often drawn that what has given the later work this forbidding quality are its intricate or complicated aspects: as if the tonal or tuneful qualities of the music of the 1930s and '40s made everything simpler, or at least more straightforward. This assessment, however, overlooks the fact that much of Carter's first professional work as a composer reflects the same complicating tendencies – something that may be more readily appreciated by comparing his music in a neoclassical style with that of other American composers from around the same time.

Carter, in fact, *was* trying to write in what he called "a deliberately restricted idiom" during this period, making "an effort to produce works that meant something to me as music" that would also "be understandable to the general musical public."[3] David Schiff has mentioned the close friendship between Carter and Aaron Copland during the 1940s, as well as Carter's admiration for the "directness" that Copland achieved especially in his works from *El Salón México* (1936) on.[4] And at first hearing, a piece like Carter's Symphony No. 1 (1942) seems to adopt much the same style. Yet closer scrutiny reveals how different it really is.

Example 1.1a reproduces mm. 1–41 of the first movement in short score. The first three measures are occupied by a sustained chord of ambiguous structure (B♭ thirteenth? G♭ ninth in inversion?), the contents of which are next arpeggiated, except for the G♭, in the clarinet and horn (mm. 4–12). At m. 13 the strings re-enter with a new chord, even more ambiguous than the

---

[3] Edwards, *FW*, pp. 57–58.   [4] Schiff, *MEC*, 1st edn, p. 114.

Ex. 1.1a Elliott Carter, Symphony No. 1, first movement, mm. 1–41, short score

Ex. 1.1b Carter, Symphony No. 1, first movement, mm. 62–69, short score

first, quite possibly best heard as a combination of Cb-major and F-minor triads (reading from low to high). The horn's subsequent arpeggiation of an F-minor seventh (mm. 14–16) suggests one way in which these two triads might be connected. This is followed directly by material offering a complete tonal and rhythmic contrast to what has been heard so far: a pizzicato figure in the strings, shifting irregularly between (eventually) just two different chords that collectively are almost but not quite in E minor. Its total extent (mm. 17–47) far outweighs that of the opening; it would entirely eclipse that opening were it not for the continuing presence of melodic lines in the woodwinds that bear a distinct similarity to the arpeggiative figures of mm. 4–16, adjusted to the tonal orientation newly sounded in the strings. After one sizeable stretch (mm. 27–35) in which the pizzicato material is heard alone, the clarinet and horn, now joined by flute and bassoon, re-enter in much the same vein in which they left off in m. 26. Just when the way seems prepared for the kind of stable thematic statement that one might normally expect in this style, another sudden tonal shift takes place (m. 65 ff., see Example 1.1b). And so on. The overall effect is restless, deliberately (it would seem) *unsimple*, thanks not only to the lack of a central tonal impression but also to its rhythmic qualities. As to the latter, both the irregular nature of the pizzicato material and the persistently syncopated melodic lines – especially as the counterpoint between them becomes more involved with the additional parts entering from m. 39 on – often counteract any strong sense of governance by the notated meter of $\frac{3}{4}$.

Comparison of this passage to other, roughly contemporaneous symphonic openings by Copland and Roy Harris is instructive. The first page of Harris's Third Symphony (1938) is reproduced as Example 1.2. This work,

Ex. 1.2 Roy Harris, Symphony No. 3, mm. 1–36

widely admired from the time of its premiere in early 1939 on,[5] could hardly be more different from Carter's symphony in the way it begins, in regular quarter-note motion occasionally interrupted, as it were cadentially, by longer notes; in its monophonic, then homophonic texture (polyphony in a limited sense develops eventually, but it takes a fairly long time to show up); and in its earnest concentration on a single mode of expression. The passage is not harmonically unadventurous, but its pacing in this regard is quite slow and regular.[6] Another useful foil to the Carter is Copland's Second Symphony (1933). This work belongs to the relatively brief period in which Copland favored a style rather angular and spare, not readily ingratiating, before he discovered his more "direct" mode of expression. Yet even in the opening of this symphony Copland keeps things simpler than Carter. The opening music (Example 1.3a), for all its spiky contours and (somewhat Stravinskian) rhythmic intricacy, is actually just one line, constantly splitting and recombining among the orchestral parts; its character persists throughout the first movement, thrown into relief only occasionally by alternation with or (eventually) fusion with the distinctly different gesture first heard at m. 14 (Example 1.3b). And of course Copland in the 1940s, having abandoned this style in the interests of trying, as he put it, to "say what I had to say in the simplest possible terms," composed works that, as it were, speak far more plainly, as becomes clear from a comparison of the Second Symphony's opening with that of *Appalachian Spring*, for example, or the Third Symphony.[7] One wonders whether the often-quoted remark attributed to him by Carter upon Copland's looking through the score of his *Holiday Overture* – that it was "just another one of those 'typical, complicated Carter scores'" – signals a view of Carter's work of the same period as an attempt, conscious or not, to bring back a mode of expression that Copland felt was not only passé but also socially irresponsible, since part of his stated intention in adopting his new style was to try to reconnect, on behalf of living composers in general, with the listening public.[8] Fortunately for us, Carter eventually realized that he would never be able to make things as simple as Copland had.

In the brief account given above of the opening passage in Carter's symphony, the contribution of contrapuntal intricacy to the overall impression of

[5] Among the admirers, eventually, was Carter himself, who essentially panned the work in his review of an early performance but later changed his mind. See Carter, "Season of Hindemith and the Americans" (1939) and "American Music in the New York Scene" (1940).
[6] See Hanson, *Harmonic Materials of Modern Music*, pp. 270–72, for an interesting analysis of this passage, in which the periodic harmonic changes are described in terms of systematic mutation of the "perfect-fifth hexad" into transpositionally equivalent forms, through the dropping of certain pitches and the addition of others.
[7] Copland, "Composer from Brooklyn: An Autobiographical Sketch," p. 229.
[8] Edwards, *FW*, p. 58.

Ex. 1.3a Aaron Copland, Symphony No. 2 ("Short Symphony"), mm. 1–8

Ex. 1.3b Copland, Symphony No. 2, mm. 14–22, short score

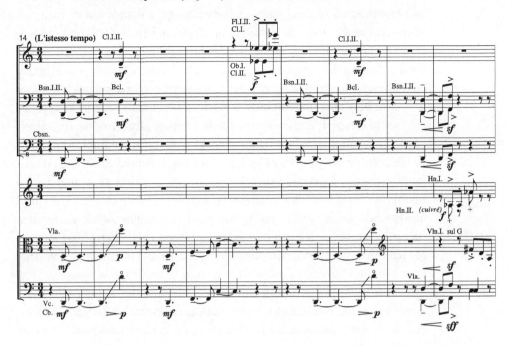

complication was mentioned. Carter came out of Nadia Boulanger's studio in 1935 well versed in the strictures of tonal counterpoint, something that must have helped him a good deal as he developed his later style, with its heavy reliance upon the simultaneous projection of two or more contrasting musical characters (see remarks below). It should not surprise us, then, that some of the works of his early period also demonstrate contrapuntal mastery, if in a more "traditional" sense. The *Canonic Suite* (1939), originally for four alto saxophones, is an outstanding example of this side of Carter in his tonal phase.[9]

Each of the three movements of this piece exploits a different type of canonic structure, with the intricacy increasing throughout, as each of the last two movements ups the ante from the previous movement. The first is relatively straightforward: a canon at the unison in all four parts, with entries one quarter-note value apart. This close succession, together with the largely arpeggiative course of the line, lends itself readily to harmonic combinations, although the successions of triads and seventh chords is not particularly

[9] The *Canonic Suite* was revised and transcribed for four clarinets, in which version it was published and remains best known. All references to the score in this essay are to this revised version. Also, all references to pitch level and chord labels are at "B♭ clarinet pitch": for instance, the first movement, with a key signature of four sharps, begins with arpeggiations of an E-major triad, as notated. This, of course, is "really" D major; however, since there are no C instruments in this score, it seems needless, and actually more cumbersome, to transpose back to concert pitch.

reminiscent of functional harmony in the common-practice sense. The second movement is of much more elaborate design: a double canon, each pair (clarinets 1 and 2, 3 and 4) in itself in inversion, in which the second canon is the retrograde of the first.[10] The first twenty-eight measures – almost exactly the first third of the movement – and, therefore, also the final twenty-eight are entirely diatonic within a signature of two sharps, projecting a quasi-B minor with definite pentatonic leanings; it is left to the middle section to offer the contrast of extensive chromaticism, the sudden appearance of which delivers quite a shock in this context. Here again, as with the initial impression made by the opening of Symphony No. 1, the seeming simplicity of surface (at least for two-thirds of the movement) is deceptive, masking as it does here a rigorously conceived, multi-leveled contrapuntal framework. The third movement's design strikes me as the most challenging of all: a canon in successive seconds, each new part entering a second higher and five measures of $\frac{6}{8}$ later than the previous (in the order 4, 3, 2, 1) and maintained with strict exactitude until breaking off for the cadence in the last few measures. The light-hearted character of this movement, almost in the manner of a *divertissement*, would not seem to require such contrapuntal feats – and, indeed, one might easily overlook the persistence of the canon throughout, although it would be hard to miss the imitative initial entrances.

A third example of deliberate complication is provided towards the end of the *Holiday Overture* (1944), in the form of a polyrhythmic canon. This, in a way, represents a culmination of the character of this piece, which for much of its length features distinctly different rhythmic layers moving along in parallel (see the next section of this chapter); but as a specific device, the polyrhythmic canon has not been encountered before, either earlier in the *Overture* or, for that matter, in Carter's previous compositions as far as I am aware.[11] There are actually two phases to this canon, the first of which is shown in Example 1.4a. Here I have extracted from the full orchestral texture just the parts that contribute to this canon. At Rehearsal 30 (m. 277), the canon begins, in the

---

[10] The canonic relationships preserve rhythm as well as pitch, with a very few exceptions where adjustments have evidently been made to fill out a triadic or seventh-chord harmony. See, for example, m. 28, where clarinet 2 should have a D5 on the second half of the second beat, tied into the first half of the third beat, but instead has an eighth rest, followed by an eighth-note B4, duplicating the next pitch in the line.

[11] Recently, as I was perusing some pages of comments that Carter had generated in handwritten form as he was looking over the texts being assembled for Meyer and Shreffler, *ECCP*, I came across his mention of this

canon, intended at that point in his comments to deflect the suggestion that he had gotten the whole idea of such procedures from looking later on at Conlon Nancarrow's scores, such as *Study No. 1* for player piano. Schiff, in *MEC*, mentions this canon, but his analysis is incomplete. In the first edition (pp. 122–23) he provides a musical example illustrating only part of the second phase; both phases are mentioned in the accompanying text, but are described as consisting of just four and five entries respectively. This description is repeated in the second edition (pp. 277–78), with the musical example omitted.

Ex. 1.4a Carter, *Holiday Overture*, mm. 277–82, partial score

lowest instruments and in the longest values of the canon (four quarters). Over this and the next five measures (mm. 277–82), a series of no fewer than eight entries unfolds, at ever shorter values (in quarters: 4, 3, 2½, 2, 1½, 1, ⅔, ½) and at transpositions that outline a series of ascending perfect fifths (with one entry, in quarter-note values on B♭ again, thus not conforming to this aspect of the overall design; in fact, it "should have" started on B♮ in order to be an exact transposition of the others). One obvious strategy that Carter might have pursued here would have been to arrange the entries such that all eight reached their final note at the same moment; this does not quite happen, as the example shows, although five do arrive on the downbeat of m. 282 together, and two others end together two beats earlier.

The second phase of the canon, beginning at Rehearsal 31 (mm. 284–90), is a good deal more elaborate in its design than the first one (see Example 1.4b). Again, there are eight entries, projecting eight different durational values and employing eight different transpositions of the same seven-note subject used in the first phase. Here, though, six of the eight enter as simultaneous pairs, flanked by first and last entries that occur singly. Carter begins with the line projecting durations of 3 quarter notes, then brings in 3½ and 2½ together, then 4 and 2, then 4½ and 1½, ending with 1: a slightly lopsided diverging wedge. The spacing of these five onset points gets steadily larger: in quarter notes, the successive distances are ½, 1, 1½, and 2. The outcome of this

Ex. 1.4b Carter, *Holiday Overture*, mm. 284–90, partial score.

manipulation is a staggered cascade of final notes of the eight strands, circled in the score to signal to the conductor the need to bring them out. This cascade is of interest both harmonically and rhythmically. As to harmony, the basic framework of pitches is a descending series of perfect fifths (compare the ascending fifths of the first canonic phase), two of which are split into thirds: C, A, F, B♭, E♭, C♭, A♭, D♭. As to rhythm, the cascade slows as it progresses downward, with durations in quarters between successive notes as follows: 1, 1, 1½, 2, 3, 3½, 4, "sweeping from top to bottom of the orchestra," as Schiff puts it, "and slowing the motion of the music to a tense halt."[12] Reflecting this slowdown is the order in which the cascade puts the eight canonic entries by last note: the 1-quarter entry ends first, followed by the 1½-quarter, and so on until 4½, the last. Granted, this polyrhythmic passage is of rather small scale, by comparison to the duration of the entire piece; yet there can be no doubt that Carter is already well disposed to engage at this point in his career in a certain kind of structural thinking that imbues much of his later work.

[12] Schiff, *MEC*, p. 278.

"Simultaneous streams of different things going on together"

This basic condition of much of Carter's music since 1950 has emerged in thoroughgoing, often spectacular deployment in works such as the Double Concerto (1961), with its array of ten distinct speeds accumulated, one by one, in the introduction, and the Third String Quartet (1971), in which the quartet ensemble is split into two duos that play utterly contrasting music at the same time for much of the work's duration. Part of the foundation for development of this practice was technical: as becomes clear from the study of pieces from the Cello Sonata (1948) on, the management of such intricate systems of simultaneity began with the systematic relating of different speeds by *succession*, in the form of the device known as metric modulation: one speed (or tempo) leading, gradually or abruptly, to another by assertion of a specific proportional relationship. Eventually, Carter figured out how to assemble such relationships into a grid, the contents of which could be used in whole or in part at any time.[13]

The other part of this foundation, however, was conceptual; and it is clear that thinking along such lines was already well in progress earlier in the 1940s than the Cello Sonata. Consider, for example, the first movement of the Piano Sonata (1946), usually thought of as a neoclassical work but possessing certain radical qualities not evident in contemporary works by (for instance) Copland or Barber. The movement begins *Maestoso*, with slowly changing sonorities (see Example 1.5). Twice within the first fourteen measures, a rapid arpeggio is interjected, which in this context registers at first as a momentary disturbance, a mere ripple on the broadly articulated surface. Upon its third occurrence, however, as the pickup to m. 15, the arpeggio turns out to be the springboard for an abrupt shift to fast passagework (*Legato scorrevole*), as movement in half-note or longer values is superseded completely by movement in sixteenths. The lack of transition is startling, as is the almost equally abrupt restoration of the *Maestoso* pulse in m. 24, followed by the sudden return to the *Legato scorrevole* in m. 33. One could call the faster music a "contrasting theme," but such classical (or neoclassical) terminology does not really suit this application. More appropriate to the case, perhaps, would be to call these different varieties of music *characters*, speaking their lines in alternation. The analogy to dramatic presentation also usefully brings into focus the effect of these abrupt shifts from one character to another: it is as if neither is really absent while the other is speaking, instead standing by mutely

[13] For further details, consult Bernard, "The Evolution of Elliott Carter's Rhythmic Practice."

for the time being. Another useful analogy invokes the montage techniques of filmmakers like Sergei Eisenstein, which (among other things) could portray the unfolding of different events simultaneously by cutting repeatedly from one to the other and back again. Among Carter's reading during the 1940s were several volumes of Eisenstein's essays on cinematographic theory and practice; these, together with his memory of having seen some of Eisenstein's films when they were first shown in New York during the 1920s, helped propel his then resurgent interest in Modernism and the change in his own compositional style that it would soon engender.[14]

The loquacious "discourse" of the *scorrevole* character, continued well beyond the extent of Example 1.5, at length gives way, first, to a brief interjection from *Maestoso* (mm. 79–82), and then to a third character, *Meno mosso*, starting in m. 83 (see Example 1.6). With the *Meno mosso*, we seem finally to have encountered a kind of mediator between the two extremes represented by the first two characters to have appeared on the scene, even though the dominant speed here (MM 144: eighths at ♩ = MM 72) is far from exactly splitting the difference between 66 (halves at 𝅗𝅥 = MM 66) and 528 (sixteenths at ♩ = MM 132). More precise quantification of speed relationships was still to come. One may be reminded of the traditional basis for this mediation by the fact that m. 83 is marked by the first real notation of a new tempo in this movement, since 𝅗𝅥 = MM 66 and ♩ = MM 132 are, quantitatively speaking, the same. But if on these grounds one expects this first movement of the Piano Sonata to conform to the so-called standard form of a sonata movement, further surprises are in store: the recapitulation, such as it is, restates the "themes" out of their original order, and not at the same pitch levels; in general, hardly any of the material harkening back to the opening pages of the movement is ever restated literally, even to within transposition;[15] and the movement as a whole, having begun in B, ends in B♭. Too much had happened in the history of Western music since the heyday of "classical" norms; the legacies of Liszt, Bartók, and Ives all obviously loomed large in Carter's musical conditioning.[16]

---

[14] Carter's debt to Eisenstein is discussed at length in Bernard, "Elliott Carter and the Modern Meaning of Time."

[15] As Hepokoski and Darcy note, "In a recapitulation ... the rhetorical materials of the exposition normally return in order" – although, even in the late eighteenth century, exceptions do occur (*Elements of Sonata Theory*, p. 233). Even as late as the 1840s and beyond, however, the expectation that the recapitulation would occur in original expository order remained in force, as we

know from the first music theorist to speak of "sonata form," Adolf Bernhard Marx (see Marx, *Die Lehre von der musikalischen Komposition, praktisch-theoretisch* [excerpts], esp. pp. 100–01).

[16] Rosen remarks: "[I]t is fairly obvious (at least to me, though, I hasten to say, probably not to Mr. Carter) that behind Carter's sonata there must have been a lingering memory of the Liszt Sonata in B Minor" (Rosen, "The Musical Languages of Elliott Carter," p. 3).

Ex. 1.5 Carter, Piano Sonata, first movement, mm. 1–27

Ex. 1.6 Carter, Piano Sonata, first movement, mm. 83–89

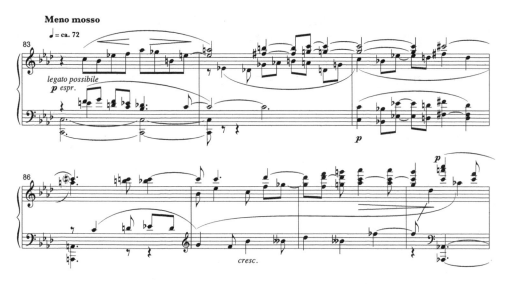

Even earlier in the 1940s, the *Holiday Overture* (1944) has been cited by
Carter himself as one of the first of his works in which his thinking about
"simultaneous streams of different things going on together" began to bear
fruit.[17] Here the approach is not so much the intercutting of different
characters as the literal projection of contrasting strata – most notably in
the extended passage beginning at m. 103 (see Example 1.7). For about twenty-
five measures, the woodwinds' rhythmically energetic line in eighths and
sixteenths, doubled at the unison and the octave, unfolds against a background
of string chords in longer, irregular values ranging from one beat to four and a
half beats' duration. Previous to this passage, the winds are heard alone with
similarly peppy material for about ten measures, preparing as it were for the
textural counterpoint of mm. 103–27. Granted, this example of simultaneous
streams, judged strictly from a technical standpoint, might not seem terribly
accomplished, especially when it is compared to Carter's achievements of later
years; yet it is worthy of more than passing notice, for several reasons.

One is the way in which the harmonic relationship between the two
instrumental groups is defined and maintained. Unlike the practice Carter
adopted in many works from the 1960s on, in which simultaneous strands of
the texture are distinguished not only by instrumentation and rhythmic
profile but also by pitch-interval and set-class content, in the *Holiday
Overture* passage the limited repertoire of set classes that comprises the
string chords is echoed for the most part in the woodwinds' music. The
correspondence, however, is closest on a global level (that of the entire

---

[17] Edwards, *FW*, p. 101.

Ex. 1.7 Carter, *Holiday Overture*, mm. 103–07, short score

passage); at any particular moment, the set-class types match up only fitfully, reflecting, perhaps, a substantial yet not exact duplication of pitch-class content between chord and line. The first few measures of Example 1.7 serve as an apt illustration. String chord 1 is (0257); its B, F♯, and C♯ are duplicated in the simultaneously heard segment of the woodwind line, which form a non-contiguous (0257) with the E and a contiguous (0257) with the E and the A (excluding C♯). Notice also that the upper three notes of the chord form (027), the lower three (025), both of which are also present in the woodwind line. Chords 2 and 3, however, are inversionally related forms of (0237). If this set class were to appear in the woodwind line, either C♯ and D or G♯ and A would have to occur fairly close together, but this does not happen while either of the chords is sounding; instead, further forms of (0257), (025), and (027) are spun out, as well as (037) and (0247), the latter also a component of the line with chord 1. At chord 4, (025), the matchup of set types improves again; at chord 5, (0135), there is another divergence; at chord 6, (0257), all four notes of the chord (E, A, B, D) are present in the woodwind line, plus F♯, which ensures the closest confluence of the two streams so far heard. It is not surprising, of course, to detect a *general* agreement between repertoires of set types in chords and line, since the entire passage is based, with few "chromatic" digressions, on the same large diatonic collection, G♯, A, B, C♯, D, E, F♯. But the sense of fluctuation, both in terms of set-class correspondence and in the degree of overlap between actual pitch classes in chord and line, seems to generate a good deal of the interest here, along with the other factors distinguishing these simultaneous streams from one another.

The second notable aspect of this passage is historical. At the same time as Carter was using what he had learned from Nadia Boulanger to establish himself professionally, and at the same time as ideas spurred by a renewed interest in Modernism were filtering their way into his work, he was also listening carefully to his American contemporaries. One pivotal passage in Roy Harris's Third Symphony involves simultaneity in the form of a kind of temporal overlap of movements. In this passage, which extends from the *Con moto* three measures before Rehearsal 57 (p. 82) to the downbeat of the section marked *Meno mosso, pesante*, six measures before Rehearsal 64 (p. 93), the previous, brass-dominated central section of the work ("Fugue–Dramatic") continues in the form of fanfare-like gestures, while sustained, slowly changing chords in the woodwinds and strings usher in, over this period of some fifty-five measures, the final, "Dramatic–Tragic" section.[18] The beginning of this passage is shown in Example 1.8. Really, the final movement has already begun in these fifty-five measures; so that at the *Meno mosso*, when the brass at length give up their fanfares, one understands that they are joining something already in progress. Harris employed this device to such striking effect that it could easily have made a strong impression on anyone – even Carter, although it is not necessary to know for sure that he was consciously (or unconsciously) influenced by it in order to notice the general resemblance between his usage and Harris's. In any case, in Carter's hands the device conveys a tone quite different from the neo-romantic cast it wears in Harris's symphony.

Collectional thinking in a pantonal environment

The word "pantonality" is generally understood in the meaning that Schoenberg assigned to it: composition with tones in a fully chromatic

---

[18] Page and rehearsal numbers are taken from the study score of the Third Symphony published by G. Schirmer, Inc., 1939. Section titles do not appear in this score, but Harris included them in his own program notes for the première of the work in 1939, which are quoted by Edward Downes in his sleeve notes for the LP recording by Leonard Bernstein and the New York Philharmonic issued by Columbia Records in the early 1960s (ML-5703 / MS-6303).

Ex. **1.8** Harris, Symphony No. 3, beginning of *Con moto* section (score, pp. 82–83)

environment, without any necessary articulation of a key or keys – in short, the word he preferred to "atonality." Readers of the literature on American neoclassical music will have encountered the word in a rather more specialized sense, referring to music that retains some of the (usually) harmonic or (sometimes) contrapuntal features of tonality, often articulating focal tones in the manner of "tonics" and even sounding as though it could be in a key for brief passages or moments but in fact able to move quickly from any pitch(-class) location to any other while creating this impression – in short, more globally than locally chromatic.

Not finding any overarching tonal organization to hold things together, whether in the form of a traditional key scheme or something more loosely (if still functionally) construed as tonal, music analysts may find their best alternative in a "collectional" approach, using pitch or pitch-class sets. Considered from this standpoint, however, composition in a neoclassical style imposes some obvious constraints from a sheerly technical standpoint, especially when one considers the extent to which Carter exploited, even exhausted, whole realms of the set-class repertoire in setting up the basic harmonic framework for many of his later works. Simply put, the realm of available collections in a largely diatonic environment is much smaller than it is in a truly *atonal* one. Was Carter in fact thinking collectionally at all in the works of his early period? Or, perhaps fairer to ask, is there anything about harmonic-contrapuntal organization in these works that would respond to a collectional approach to analysis?

While I am far from being able to provide a definitive or universal answer to the latter question, there is some evidence to suggest that the idea of collection has at least a limited relevance to pitch organization in the early music. *Voyage* (1943), a setting for voice and piano of a poem by Hart Crane, is one work that offers some traction for collectional analysis. The opening measures of this song are given in Example 1.9. The simple presence of a key signature in many of the early works, of course, always at least potentially implies that some pitch functions as a center; here, despite the four sharps, it appears to be B, with the A♮ first heard in m. 2 supplying a "Mixolydian" flavor. Perhaps more significant is that the outer voices of the piano part – at least an equal partner to the voice in this song – remain fixed at the interval of a (compound) major third during the excerpt shown, a feature that persists throughout the song as a whole; few measures, in fact, lack this boundary interval.

Besides the compound third, another important component is the opening gesture, <D♯, C♯, F♯, B, A♯, F♯>, readily divisible into two motivic trichords, (025) and (015). This gesture recurs often throughout *Voyage*, both at original pitch level (or an octave higher or lower) and transposed. In the latter case, however, the first trichord of the gesture tends to remain recognizable mainly

Ex. 1.9 Carter, *Voyage*, mm. 1–13

by virtue of its <102> contour (that is, a descending interval followed by a larger ascending interval); as a set class, it frequently turns into (027), as it does for example in m. 5, <C♯, G♯, D♯>, or mm. 6–7, <B, F♯, C♯>. By contrast, (015) is widely transposed without alteration; furthermore, it appears frequently on its own, split off from the beginning of the gesture. In fact, this trichord appears so frequently that the larger collections it forms in conjunction with the bracketing compound-third boundary interval account for an appreciable portion of the harmony of this song. Of equal interest are the restrictions that apply to the way in which boundary interval and (015) are juxtaposed: among all the possible combinations, only two composite set classes appear with appreciable frequency, with two others occurring much more rarely. Most common of all is the original juxtaposition of m. 2, (02347); next comes (0158), first heard in m. 3, a tetrachord because one of the pitch classes of the (015) is duplicated in the boundary interval; a third form is (01268), used repeatedly in one particular passage (mm. 26–31) but not much otherwise; scarcest of all is (0148), which does not turn up until mm. 36–37 (once) and otherwise is heard only a few more times near the end, where the basic identity of the gesture is moving toward its final dissolution anyway.

These four composite set classes together account for five of the twelve possible ways in which a trichord (015) may be combined with a boundary interval (04).[19] By avoiding the other seven, Carter has placed fairly stringent limits on this aspect of his palette, while allowing the component trichords of the main gesture a good deal of mobility: (015) appears at nine different transpositional levels in all. This tells us quite a bit about harmony in *Voyage*, though not of course everything. Another, broader route into the pantonality of this work flows from the observation that often, if not invariably, the boundary third is joined by another third sharing one of its pitches, such that one can readily hear the resultant harmonies as triads with added notes of various sorts. For instance, m. 1 consists of a B-major triad with added C♯, (0247). In m. 2, the interval A♮–C♯ forms an F♯-minor triad with the F♯; the additional A♯ and B produce the composite (02347). This set class was discussed earlier, as a composite of (04) and (015); here we gain a different perspective on it, for it is a superset of (0247) – as well, of course, as (037), the set class representing both the major and the minor triad.

Pursuit of analysis along this route reveals, as before, conditions that operate to restrict the repertoire of harmonies. Here, they are expressed as a preference for certain supersets of the triadic set class. Besides (0247) and (02347), tetrachordal set classes, (0158), (0237), and (0347) are frequently encountered; the second of these is a subset of (02347), while the third is the so-called major-minor tetrachord, a union of inversionally related (037)s. As for pentachords, (01237) is a superset of (0237), and (02479) is easily heard as an amalgamation of two inversionally related (0247)s.[20] Example 1.10

Ex. 1.10 Carter, *Voyage*, mm. 20–25

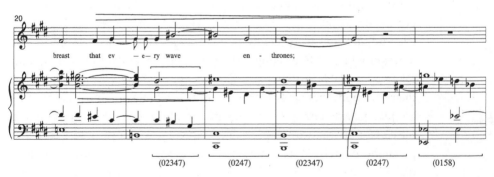

[19] (0148) can be formed two different ways; the others, only one each.

[20] Although this mode of analysis, focusing on harmony as it does, tends to privilege the piano part and to treat the voice simply as another component of that harmony, it is possible to analyze some of the vocal part alone using this limited repertoire of sets. For instance, in the opening measures, the first phrase, set to the words "Infinite consanguinity it bears," arpeggiates a (037); the second phrase ("This tendered theme of you that light") constitutes (0247); and the third phrase ("Retrieves from sea plains where the sky"), (01237).

Ex. 1.11 Carter, *Voyage*, subset/superset relationships abstractly summarized

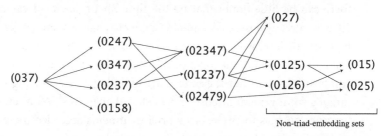

provides a sample excerpt (mm. 21–25) with analytical overlay, featuring some of these harmonies. Larger collections could be identified, but these would usually involve more than one of the boundary tenths, thus obscuring the vertical definition of the harmony. In the few places where the texture is sufficiently dense to produce hexachords (for instance) within a single pair of boundary pitches, such larger groups are perhaps best handled, analytically speaking, as combinations of smaller collections. On the other hand, smaller collections sometimes stand in place of larger ones in the repertoire so far enumerated, seemingly because of the occasional "failure" of the boundary tenth to complete a triad with another third. One plausible explanation for this would be an implied harmony of "incomplete" versions: subsets, in other words, analogous to dyads in common-practice harmony occasionally standing for complete triads. Thus we find (015) and (025), which also have motivic identities, as mentioned, as well as (0125) and (0126). These various relations are abstractly diagrammed in Example 1.11.

As this two-pronged approach to harmonic analysis of *Voyage* has shown, at least indirectly, the pantonal environment is a different kind of place for analysis by way of set classes than the unambiguously nontonal medium of Carter's later work. Yet given that Carter since 1950, even when he has worked with large repertoires of set classes, has often partitioned these repertoires into smaller "packets" for deployment within particular sections of a piece or regions of a texture, it is not surprising to see that the built-in restrictions on size of set-class repertoires in a generally diatonic context, and on the manipulation of their components, should have some bearing on the kinds of subset/superset relations that he began to develop on a much larger scale from the 1950s onward.

Text expression

As has often been pointed out, Carter majored in English, not music, at Harvard; and while this in itself was no guarantee that he would go on to display a keen sensitivity to literary texts in whatever walk of life he entered, there can be little doubt that by the time his professional career began, in 1936, he already possessed a notable ability to engage poetry, in particular, at a high artistic level when choosing texts and setting them to music. Much has been written about the relationship between music and text in Carter's compositions, whether these texts are literally present in sung form or not, ranging from general discussion to detailed analysis.[21] With few exceptions, however, such as the necessarily brief treatments accorded individual works in Schiff's *The Music of Elliott Carter*, scholars and critics have tended to concentrate on the works after 1950, lending the impression, if only by omission, that the earlier works, many of them short and for *a cappella* choral forces, are inferior – perhaps for that very reason.

One work from the early period featuring a sung text, which should leave no doubt as to its seriousness of purpose, is *Voyage*, the harmonic qualities of which were discussed above. For the publication of the score, Carter went to the special trouble of including a lengthy prefatory note in which he explained the meaning of Hart Crane's poem, line by line, as he understood it.[22] From reading this note, and eventually from listening to the piece, it becomes clear that, far from simple word painting, Carter's setting of Crane's text represents an attempt to engage the deeper meaning of the poem, almost in the way of (old-fashioned) literary criticism. Carter regards the poem as embodying the sea in (at least) a double sense: it is both Love and "an obstacle to be voyaged through to reach Love." Transferred to musical expression, the sea is both (1) symbolic of what the Poet wants to achieve – the poem's destination – and (2) the medium of the song – its carrier, if at times highly resistant to any headway being made. But these two senses are actually quite difficult to separate conceptually, which may explain why Carter represents them in musical terms as he does. What could be called the "Love theme" joins the

[21] Some representative examples: Kramer, "Song as Insight – John Ashbery, Elliott Carter, and Orpheus"; Bernard, "Poem as Non-Verbal Text"; Schwartz, "Elliott Carter and American Poetry"; Ravenscroft, "Setting the Pace: The Role of Speeds in Elliott Carter's *A Mirror on Which to Dwell*."

[22] This prefatory note and the Crane poem are reprinted in Meyer and Shreffler, *ECCP*, pp. 58–59. In their commentary, the editors mention that Carter wrote this note in response to a request from John Kirkpatrick, in his capacity as editor for Valley Music Press, the original publisher of *Voyage* in 1945, for "an explanatory note on the somewhat obscure poem." Further, they assert, "In preparation for his remarks,

Carter subjected the poem to another round of intense scrutiny that went far beyond what he had done while composing [*Voyage*]" (p. 56). While these circumstances might suggest that the prefatory note expresses insights into the poem that are not realized, at least not consciously, in Carter's setting of it, it seems unlikely that he would have put anything into his literary exegesis that contradicted the sense of that setting. Far more likely, in fact, is that the experience of setting the poem substantially influenced his later, perhaps more studied reading of it – despite his self-deprecating remarks on the subject in a letter to John Kirkpatrick of November 28, 1944 (see Meyer and Shreffler, *ECCP*, p. 60).

two principal motives discussed earlier (see Example 1.9, mm. 1–2) right at the outset into one rising/falling motion that might plausibly be taken as the medium of the sea: its placid side, abetted by the gentle, regular quarter-note pulsation of the piano part. The movement through this medium, on the other hand, is of more irregular, asymmetric aspect, assembling the rising/ falling of the Love theme into motions of larger scale, enacted several times in the first large part of the piece (mm. 1–52): a steady rise effected by the transposition upward of the small-scale rising/falling motives, followed by a more rapid falling off.

This happens first in mm. 1–8 and 9–10 respectively; then a second time in mm. 15–20 (to a slightly higher point than in the first large rise), and 20–22. The restatement of the opening music of the piece now occurs a whole step higher, and the third large rise reaches its zenith in mm. 28–31: sustained longer this time, and a half step higher than the previous highest point. The subsequent falling-off is more gradual; when the original pitch level of the opening music is reached again (m. 38), there is no exact repetition of mm. 1–2, rather a rocking motion derived from that opening that eventually moves a little lower. This feeling of dragging down seems intended to express lines 7–8 of the poem ("whereto this hour / The sea lifts, also, reliquary hands"), which Carter interprets as "a hint of the dangers lurking in the sea pictured as grasping at both swimmers with hand-like waves that could transform them into relics by disintegrating their bodies."

The second section (mm. 58–78), by contrast, "the ordeal that [the Poet] must undergo in order to come under the spell of love ... is represented metaphorically as a voyage into the depths, a rise to the surface and a swim over the waves." All of the elements mentioned here by Carter are present, symbolically, in his music: the great depths by the range of the chords spread out across all of this section, which themselves move from low to high and back again; the Love theme that seems to swim "Past whirling pillars and lithe pediments" from m. 61 on.

The third section (mm. 79–114) is cast as a kind of recapitulation that begins an octave lower than the opening of the piece and eventually rises (m. 93) to an octave *higher* than the opening, taking advantage of the great vertical space opened up in the second section and transcending the limits of the first ("Upon the steep floor flung from dawn to dawn"). This is plausibly in line with Carter's reading of Crane at this point: to pursue Love is also to risk death at the hands of the sea, "like the transformation of a poet's experience that suffers disintegration and reorganization into word-relics made into a poem ..." As the large rising motion unfolds, the motives seem to dissipate, preserving the up/down contour but with altered intervals, so that they are less distinct *as* motives. At m. 93, where the higher octave is reached, the motives reappear in their original pitch-class identity (in parallel

octaves), remaining as a kind of ostinato for six measures ("The silken trans-
memberment of song") before beginning, ever so gradually, to blur and
dissolve for the last time. In the coda (mm. 115–24), this dissolution is
complete, with only the barest trace of the second, (015) motive heard in
the D♯–B of m. 121.

Addressing text/music relationships in early works like this one is a different sort of task than doing so in the later song cycles, such as *A Mirror on
Which to Dwell* (Elizabeth Bishop) or *In Sleep, In Thunder* (Robert Lowell), or
in wholly instrumental works for which a specific text has proved suggestive
to Carter and in which some aspects of it are, in a way, interpreted, such as the
Concerto for Orchestra (St.-John Perse) or *A Symphony of Three Orchestras*
(Crane again). It is different, not only because these later works tend to be
much longer, but because there is so much more to talk about in terms of
sheer technique. These circumstances, however, cannot be allowed to obscure
the fact that, making perspectival adjustments for their rather more modest
scale and less technically virtuosic idiom, early works like *Voyage* or *The
Harmony of Morning* or *Emblems* are settings that reflect as much insight into
the literary qualities of the texts, and as much care and accomplishment in
their realization, as any of the later music.

The "long line"

Asked in an interview what lasting impact he thought that his years as a tonal
composer had left on his career as a whole, Carter saw fit to mention only one
specific feature that he had consciously retained: "a very strong feeling for
linear development."[23] Undoubtedly, he *could* have mentioned others, as the
foregoing parts of this essay have suggested; but it is clear that the idea of the
long line ("la grande ligne"), which he has mentioned more than once elsewhere as a quality that he learned to appreciate and to make part of his
working method under the tutelage of Nadia Boulanger, has remained in
place right up to the present day in his music.[24] The traditional roots
supporting linear development seem important, serving as a kind of bulwark
against the infiltration of ideas about time that Carter finds inimical, such as
the stasis of a work like Olivier Messiaen's *Mode de valeurs et d'intensités* or
Karlheinz Stockhausen's theory of moment form.[25] Small wonder, then, that
the ability to sustain the thread of linear continuity running through an entire

[23] Bernard, "An Interview with Elliott Carter,"
191.
[24] Carter, "'Elle est la musique en personne': A
Reminiscence of Nadia Boulanger" (1995),
esp. pp. 287–88.

[25] Bernard, "An Interview with Elliott Carter,"
196–97.

Ex. 1.12 Carter, Symphony No. 1, mm. 555–82 (beginning of second movement), principal line

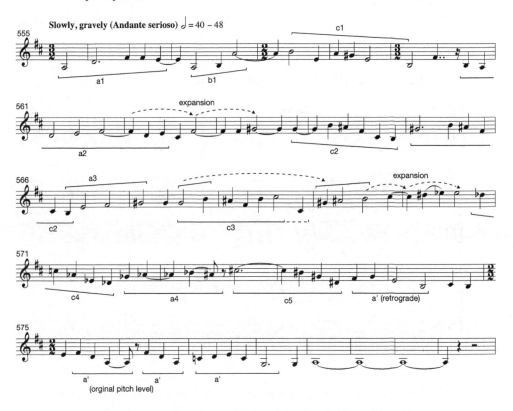

work or movement was already well developed in Carter's early years as a composer.

One particularly apposite illustration of the long line can be taken from the slow second movement of the Symphony No. 1. Limitations on space here will hardly permit a comprehensive view of this gloriously arching structure, but perhaps enough of an idea can be gained of its function from an examination of the opening period, which is rather long to begin with and describes an arch in itself. Example 1.12 displays just the melodic line of the first twenty-eight measures of the second movement (mm. 555–82), accompanied by analytical overlay that is intended to suggest how a kind of cumulative structure of motives is developed, with each continually finding new ways to connect to the others, all seamlessly unfolded over the time-span of this excerpt. The labels *a*, *b*, and so on are useful only to a limited extent in the attempt to trace this development, since much of the sense of flow in this music depends on constant small changes in both pitch and rhythm. For example, the initial *a1* "becomes" *a2* (mm. 560–62) by adding an initial quarter-note B (accommodated by shrinking the half-note A to a quarter note), by filling out the interval D–F♯ stepwise, and by elaborating the

Ex. 1.13a Carter, Symphony No. 1, mm. 583–89, principal line

Ex. 1.13b Carter, Symphony No. 1, mm. 600–03, strings

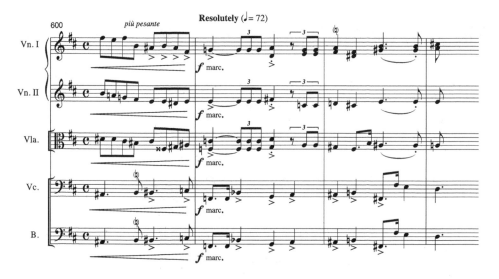

terminal interval F♯–E with an added D. The ascending stepwise gesture of *a2* is soon (m. 563) extended by another ascending step, to G♯, so that when a recognizable form of *a* next appears (mm. 566–67), as *a3*, it is a step higher than *a2*. This stepwise transposition in turn affects subsequent versions of the material initially labeled *c*, which changes in a slightly more complicated way as new forms flow from the original in mm. 558–60. Eventually, when near the end of this excerpt (mm. 573–74) the descending arpeggiation <G♯, E, B> is heard (followed by successive stepwise transpositions downward), it plausibly sounds both like a retrograde of the initial gesture <A, D, F♯> (the other end of the arch begun by *a1*) and like the descending arpeggiations that are integral to the *c* material. The recombinative, fluid nature of these motivic "particles" soon makes them sound less like distinctly different entities and more like different aspects of the same entity; there is just enough repetition to ensure continuity from gesture to gesture in this long line, but otherwise everything is in flux.

A few glimpses of what is to come in the second movement are provided in Example 1.13. The reader will have noticed that *b*, having been articulated in m. 557 of Example 1.12, is not invoked again. This aspect of the opening material is next taken up in mm. 585–86, transposed up a step to reflect the extension upwards of the *a* material in the previous two measures – which itself represents a compression of what took place across the first eight measures of the first period (see Example 1.13a). Next comes a further metamorphosis of *c*, which begins like a transposition of mm. 558–59 and ends at the same pitch level as the transformed *c* of m. 564. The unadorned ascending octave leap of m. 589 is *b* again, further transposed and simplified to a single interval. Jumping ahead just a bit (see Example 1.13b), to mm. 601–03, what seems as though it could be a "contrasting theme" turns out in fact to be another aspect of *a* – most closely resembling, at this point, *a3* by virtue of the way it is harmonized (its tendency, soon thereafter demonstrated, to expand upwards by step further improves the resemblance).

I must admit that it came as something of a shock, examining this melodic development closely for the first time, to realize how generically similar it was to the moment-to-moment continuity I was already intimately familiar with in the working out of Carter's long lines in much later pieces: the vocal part of "Anaphora," the first song of *A Mirror on Which to Dwell* (1975); the final long, steadily building progression to the cataclysm that ends the *Triple Duo* (1983); the inexorable and terrifying lament, stretching over some seventeen minutes, of the *Adagio tenebroso*, the middle movement of *Symphonia: Sum Fluxae Pretium Spei* (1993–96). The details of technique, naturally, are quite different; but the basic procedure and musical aims are much the same.[26] In both the earlier and the later examples of the long line, Carter has sought to project a musical organism that grows and changes constantly yet is at all times tightly integrated and interconnected in all its aspects.

This observation naturally raises the question: if Carter was doing this and other things so well in the basically neoclassical style of his early period, why indeed did he give it up? – and more or less simultaneously answers it. It seems clear that, in order to be able to *keep* doing the things that he had already decided were most important to him in composition – creating intricate and complicated textures and forms, in which multiple paths of continuity could be pursued simultaneously; further developing a nascently collectional approach to harmony; bringing the form and expressive content of his music to a level worthy of the great American poetry to which he was increasingly drawn from 1940 on; expanding the potential of the long line to organize musical movement and coherence in a significant way – he had to leave Neoclassicism behind. Carter's reconnection with Modernism turned out to be his vehicle for moving on. But in doing so, he certainly did not abandon what he had learned while composing in a neoclassical style.

[26] I am hardly the first to have noticed this kind of resemblance between works of Carter composed decades apart. See the brief remarks of Rosen on the Piano Sonata, *Night Fantasies*, *90+*, and *Dialogues* in "Elliott Carter: The Sustained Line."

From the statement quoted in the epigraph at the opening of this essay –
"I didn't used to like it" – one gets the definite impression that Carter did go
through a phase of conscious rejection of his earlier efforts, one which may
well have been necessary under the circumstances. But eventually he managed to rekindle his appreciation for music he had written in an older style,
even revisiting it from time to time, as mentioned, as an arranger. Coming to
understand this progression has made me wonder whether my own earlier
disinclination to study the earlier music was also a form of rejection. Not that
I ever *consciously* rejected it: when, sitting with Carter in front of a tape
recorder, I told him – for of course I am the interviewer in the epigraph
quotation – that I liked his earlier music very much, I was not merely being
polite. After all, my first exposure to his music, as a teenager, came in the form
of Beveridge Webster's recording of the Piano Sonata, on a Dover LP that I
distinctly remember playing over and over again. What I did not realize,
though, as I got to know Carter's work of the 1950s, the '60s, and so on
through the decades, was that my continued liking for the earlier music was
based on something more than affection or nostalgia. It has taken the writing
of the present essay to bring home to me just what it was.

2   Elliott Carter's late music

John Link

> The kind of music I am talking about does not grow in a desert.
>
> Elliott Carter[1]

With the celebrations of his centennial year behind us, perhaps it is now
reasonable to speak of Elliott Carter's "late music," but I wouldn't count on it.
The Double Concerto – commissioned when Eisenhower was President – was
once described as the culmination of Carter's mature style. And who could
have predicted that the Concerto for Orchestra – completed in 1969, when
Carter was sixty – would eventually join his Depression-era ballet *Pocahontas*
in the first quarter of his total output? Every piece that once seemed to be the
capstone of Carter's illustrious career has turned out instead to be a milestone
that marks the beginning of another new path. Not only has Carter continued
to compose into his second century, but the past decade and a half has been
the most fruitful period of his entire career: since reaching his eighty-fifth
birthday Carter has written more than a third of his life's work.

Beyond its abundance, Carter's recent music is more diverse than ever.
Densely textured and rhythmically elaborate pieces turn up alongside music
of the utmost transparency and economy. Miniatures lasting only a few
seconds rub shoulders with orchestral works of epic proportions. In addition
to an opera (*What Next?*) and a forty-minute orchestral triptych (*Symphonia:
Sum Fluxae Pretium Spei*), there are pieces for chamber ensembles both
familiar and odd, songs and song cycles (unaccompanied, chamber, and
orchestral), concertos small and large, and a bouquet of instrumental miniatures. With his bountiful and wide-ranging recent work Carter has left most
descriptions of his music far behind. Open a history of contemporary music
and you are likely to read that Carter is a standout representative of a
particularly abstruse brand of technically complex post-war American
Modernism. Encounter a recent piece of his in the concert hall and you are
likely to be dazzled and charmed. No calculator is necessary to enjoy the bold
colors, thrilling velocity, humor, and startling surprises of Carter's latest

[1] Carter, "The Composer's Viewpoint"
(1946), in *CEL*, p. 3.

music. When asked recently what he wanted the listener to walk away with after hearing a piece of his, Carter did not hesitate. "Happiness!" he said.[2]

This is not the Elliott Carter we thought we knew – the one who once said "to hell with the public and with the performers too" and set out to reinvent himself, sequestered in the Arizona desert.[3] In the proud battle over the legacy of Modernism, Carter is typically either praised for being "uncompromising" and refusing to follow fashion, or condemned as the quintessentially hermetic and antisocial "composer's composer."[4] Yet as the battle has raged in the press and in academic journals, Carter himself has moved on, achieving an unprecedented degree of popular success that his champions sometimes attribute to his sticking to his guns and his critics generally ignore. He has not turned away from his earlier style in the manner of Rochberg or Del Tredici, and his ambitions for music remain as high as ever. But neither has he held fast to an unchanging aesthetic, waiting for the rest of the world to see the light. On the contrary, his recent music is the result of an ongoing reevaluation of the expressive potential of post-war Modernism in a decidedly post-Modern age.

The changes in Carter's late music – prompted by both aesthetic and practical considerations – call into question the portrait of his style that has taken shape with remarkable consistency in the secondary literature and in Carter's own writings. Central to this view is the idea of the divided ensemble, in which instruments or instrumental groups interact and contend with each other somewhat like the characters on a stage.[5] Harmony, rhythm, form, and expression all reinforce the metaphor. Typically, Carter partitions the universe of possible intervals and chord-types among the characters, giving each one a unique harmonic identity; rhythmic behaviors (both gestural and global) are similarly partitioned. The clearly delineated characters, with their distinct simultaneous utterances, weave a captivating drama of separation and cross-purposes. As David Schiff puts it: "from the Cello Sonata onward, Carter's music sprang from a single idea: disconnection."[6] The sense of distance between the characters is heightened by the audience's perspective as an outside observer, witnessing the inexorable unfolding of dramatic events from safely beyond the fourth wall.[7]

---

[2] Carter, on-camera interview in Oteri, "Elliott Carter Centenary: Video Interview Podcast."
[3] The quote is from FW, p. 35. On the "desert myth," see Eisenlohr, Komponieren als Entscheidungsprozess, pp. 166–71.
[4] For the former attitude, see Barenboim, "Elliott Carter," and Boulez, on-camera interview in Scheffer, Elliott Carter: A Labyrinth of Time; for the latter attitude, see Taruskin, "Standoff (II)," pp. 304–06.
[5] The stage metaphor is ubiquitous in the Carter literature. See, for example, Carter, "Shop Talk

by an American Composer" (1960), in CEL, p. 221, quoted in Schiff, MEC, p. 26.
[6] Schiff, "The Carter-Messiaen Project," p. 2.
[7] See Herzfeld, "Carter, String Quartet, and the Idea of Musical Character," p. 5: "As a listener of his music, one is not invited to simply identify with one of the characters in play, but to join the composer in the role of a neutral spectator watching the interaction." Herzfeld also examines the political, philosophical, and sociological roots of Carter's idea of musical character.

Carter's late work destabilizes all of these premises. Not only are the interactions among the characters more sociable – with shared expression an essential and frequently realized goal – but the distinctive harmonic and rhythmic partitions on which the individualization of the characters is based have become more ambiguous, and in some cases have disappeared altogether. Perhaps most significantly, Carter has made his own retrospective engagement with his middle-period style the subject of his compositions, using the lyric viewpoint he developed in his vocal music of 1975–81 to represent human experience in a way that reframes the music's relationship with its audience.

Carter was already questioning the familiar elements of his middle-period style by the time of its greatest American success. In 1970, in a program note for a recording of the Second Quartet, he betrays a degree of dissatisfaction with the stylized nature of his instrumental characters:

> To a certain extent, the instruments [in the Second Quartet] are type-cast, for each fairly consistently invents its material out of its own special expressive attitude and its own repertory of musical speeds and intervals. In a certain sense each instrument is like a character in an opera made up of "quartets." The separation of the instrumental characters is kept quite distinct throughout the first half of the work but becomes increasingly homogenized up to the *Conclusion*, at which point the separation reemerges.[8]

As this quotation implies, the same strict partitions that define Carter's instrumental characters impose an important constraint on their expressive range. For to be "type-cast" (as Carter puts it) is to behave in narrowly determined and even predictable ways, without the contradictions and transformations that make the characters in Mann or Proust – to name two of Carter's formative literary influences – so fascinatingly real. The characters in the Second Quartet are closer to those of the *commedia dell'arte* that so inspired Schoenberg and Picasso's generation; the emphasis is less on the novelistic development of character and more on the interaction of fixed character types – capricious, meticulous, melancholic, and impetuous – in a wide variety of different situations. Carter was keenly aware of this aspect of his musical characterizations. In the Second Quartet, he abandoned his initial idea of maintaining the individualization of the instruments throughout the piece. Instead, they join together on a regular basis in expressively unified passages, and the dramatic tension between these two conceptions of instrumental writing is a key element of the piece's form. Carter uses similar strategies throughout his middle-period music – balancing the narrowly defined "behavior patterns" of the instruments or instrumental groups with

[8] Carter, "String Quartets Nos. 1, 1951, and 2, 1959" (1970), in *CEL*, p. 234.

highly varied and complex formal designs, such as the combinatorial "chain" forms in his larger instrumental works of the 1970s.[9]

Carter tried different ways of developing the instrumental characters in his music of this period. In the Brass Quintet, for example, the instruments add to their interval repertoires as a result of their interactions with each other. But the most significant development came with Carter's renewed interest in vocal music and the composition of *A Mirror on Which to Dwell*, *Syringa*, and *In Sleep, In Thunder*. By taking on the fully developed literary voices in the poetry of Elizabeth Bishop, John Ashbery, and Robert Lowell, Carter was challenging his earlier approach to the representation of character. The speakers in the works of these poets are both sophisticated and subtle, with changing perceptions and feelings that are frequently at odds with what they say. In order to faithfully represent their complex variability Carter first took care to choose poems that are well suited to the techniques he had developed in his divided ensemble music since the Second Quartet. In all of the poems in *A Mirror on Which to Dwell*, and many of those in *In Sleep, In Thunder*, the speaker reflects on the actions of a secondary character in a vivid setting, which Carter depicts in the music as a secondary layer of activity apart from the voice. More than just setting the scene – like the mill streams, hoof beats, and cuckoos of nineteenth-century lieder – the oboe-as-bird and strings-as-ocean in "Sandpiper," and the trumpet-as-soprano in "Across the Yard: La Ignota" act in counterpoint to the details of the texted vocal line to generate the form.[10] But Carter also made a crucial change of narrative point of view in his settings. In most of his earlier instrumental music, Carter shifts the focus of attention among the coequal layers of the divided ensemble, much as a film director focuses the camera on different groups of people within a crowded scene.[11] The shifts imply an omniscient point of view, shared with the audience, which is separate from the diegetic activity of the individual layers.[12] This omniscient perspective is a key element of Carter's middle-period style and of the literary models he favored at that time, such as Lucretius's *De rerum natura* and Pope's *Dunciad* "both of which

[9] Bayan Northcott gives equivocal support to a different view: that the complexity of Carter's middle-period works was meant "to compensate for his lack of 'simple gifts'," that is for his shortcomings (compared to Copland) as a composer of melodies. See Northcott, *The Way We Listen Now*, pp. 138–39.

[10] See Shreffler, "'Give the Music Room'," and Ravenscroft, "Layers of Meaning: Expression and Design in Carter's Songs," in this volume.

[11] This analogy is Carter's. See Rosen, "An Interview with Elliott Carter," p. 43, quoted in

Shreffler "'Give the Music Room'," p. 266. Carter describes Eisenstein's *The Battleship Potemkin* (1925) as an important influence in Meyer and Shreffler, *ECCP*, pp. 255–56, and acknowledges the influence of cinema in general in *FW*, p. 102. Also see Bernard, "Elliott Carter and the Modern Meaning of Time," 661–72, and Carter, "A List of Films for Frank Scheffer," in Meyer and Shreffler, *ECCP*, pp. 290–91.

[12] See Herzfeld, "Carter, String Quartet, and the Idea of Musical Character," 5.

erect a world from small beginnings and then destroy it," as Carter put it then.[13] In *A Mirror on Which to Dwell* and *In Sleep, In Thunder*, on the other hand, Carter maintains an unswerving focus on the vocal line. As David Schiff points out, "there are no interludes or parentheses indicating, in the debased romantic tradition, how the composer feels about the text"[14] – techniques that would interrupt the semantic continuity of the poetry but, more importantly, would suggest a point of view beyond that of the speaker. Instead, Carter's settings embody a first-person lyric perspective; the vocal line and the instruments create for the listener an image of the world from the speaker's point of view.[15] There is no omniscient narrator; the level of detail in the accompaniment and the relative prominence of the secondary characters vary as the speaker's attention shifts. Their activity is a musical conceit through which the conceit of the poem is developed – the speaker's strengthening identification with a creature able to ignore "The roaring alongside," or co-opting a once-youthful voice to carry the ebb and flow of middle-aged regret.

In *Syringa*, the specific external focus that is such a strong presence in Bishop's poems in *A Mirror on Which to Dwell* is deeply sublimated. The speaker in Ashbery's poem skirts the pain of an unnamed event by affecting the manner of a fairy-tale narrator telling the story of Orpheus and Eurydice.[16] Carter's setting restores the external focus in the form of a bass, singing ancient Greek fragments related to the Orpheus myth. In Carter's setting, the bass's impassioned laments expose the pain that Ashbery's speaker is trying to obscure.[17] From this perspective, Carter's added layer functions like a shadow play that slyly (and radically) contradicts the fairy tale it ostensibly is illustrating. But if Ashbery's speaker – embodied by the soprano – is trying to suppress the painful feelings that the bass represents, the bass is also earnestly asserting the validity and vivid specificity of Orpheus's pain, which is both co-opted and concealed by the Ashbery speaker's formulaic distancing ("Then one day everything changed"). It is precisely these conflicting claims of lyric predominance that make the narrative agency in *Syringa* so elusive. The soprano is as external to the bass's world as he is to hers.[18]

[13] Carter, Untitled program note to the recording of the Double Concerto and Duo for Violin and Piano. The passage containing the quotation was elaborated and the language changed when these notes were reprinted in *WEC*, pp. 326–30, and *CEL*, pp. 258–62.

[14] Schiff, "Carter in the Seventies," 4.

[15] See Griffiths, *Modern Music and After*, p. 58, and "'Its full choir of echoes'," p. 32, and cf. Danuser, in "Spätwerk als Lyrik," who identifies the principal lyric voice in the vocal works of 1975–81 as Carter's own.

[16] For a detailed analysis of the poetics of *Syringa*, see Kramer, "Song As Insight."

[17] For Daniel Albright, Carter's strategy "betrays the effect that Ashbery sought … where Ashbery frames an absence, Carter fills the hole with an opera." See Albright, "Elliott Carter and Poetry," p. 118.

[18] If the title of the piece, and the soprano's plain English and parlando style seem to give priority to Ashbery's speaker, then Carter's decision to begin with an extended aria for bass before the soprano's first entrance restores the ambiguous balance.

The reciprocal externality of the two voices in *Syringa* led Carter to represent their lyric perspectives somewhat differently than he did those in "Sandpiper" and "Across the Yard: La Ignota." With the function of ironic contrapuntal juxtaposition amply provided by the two poetic speakers, the instruments track and reinforce the linear development of the two sung texts. The accompaniment to Orpheus's grief at the loss of Eurydice is typical in its depiction of the speaker's train of thought and feelings, rather than his or her observation of something in the outside world. Carter takes this idea even further in songs like "Dolphin" and "Dies Irae" from his Lowell cycle *In Sleep, In Thunder* – internal monologues with only a metaphorical relationship to the world outside of the speaker's reflection. In these songs the voice and instruments have a common purpose – depicting the volatility of the lyric imagination as it weaves its uncertain and changeable course.[19]

Carter was quick to apply the techniques he developed in his vocal works of 1975–81 to other genres of music as well.[20] Given that his middle-period style involves the opposition of highly contrasting forces, it is not surprising that the etude-like pieces for timpani are the only solo compositions Carter wrote between 1948 and 1980. But solo pieces are an ideal vehicle for the lyric point of view and they have proliferated in Carter's more recent catalog. In *Riconoscenza per Goffredo Petrassi* (1984), three distinct behavior patterns are differentiated by strict partitions of intervals, rhythm and tempo, and even dynamics. But rather than developing simultaneously, the three types of music follow, overlap, or interrupt each other, to suggest (according to Carter) the sudden shifts of mood of a single lyric persona, in this case one modeled on the piece's dedicatee.[21]

As the preceding examples indicate, the lyric perspective joined, rather than replaced, the divided ensemble, and the two narrative modes coexist in a richly ambiguous and ironic relationship in much of Carter's late music. For most of *Triple Duo*, the three partitioned pairs interact antiphonally or contrapuntally, but they often come together for sections with a unified character and mood. In the last movement, in an outburst of "feverish lyrical expression,"[22] the six instruments contribute melodic fragments that connect via shared pitches to form a seamless long-line melody that carries through

---

[19] These songs come closer to presenting the nebulous and choric lyric voice proposed by Griffiths in "'Its full choir of echoes'."
[20] See Griffiths, *ibid.*, p. 26: "When the Bishop–Lowell–Ashbery trilogy was completed, even Carter's instruments began to sing."
[21] See Bons, Interview with Elliott Carter, p. 16: "I remember vividly that Petrassi – like many Italians – was somebody who could talk very seriously about important subjects and

suddenly burst into laughter or become terribly angry – then sometimes talk in a very exultant, quiet mood. I wrote *Riconoscenza* so that it has alternations of rather comically angry music, then lofty, slow and quiet sections." Also see Noubel, *LTF*, pp. 239–41, and Roeder, "'The Matter of Human Cooperation' in Carter's Mature Style," in this volume.
[22] Schiff, *MEC*, p. 123.

almost the entire last third of the piece. A similar ironic dichotomy between individual autonomy and collective effort is at work in the String Quartet No. 4. The instruments maintain unique partitions of intervals, rhythmic patterns, and characteristic behaviors, but their elaborate, often contentious interactions produce the four movements of a quasi-neoclassical string quartet: Allegro, Scherzando, Lento, Finale.

Carter has said quite frankly that, at the time he wrote the Second Quartet, maintaining the individualization of the instruments "was more difficult than I was able to carry on for a whole work," and that in the Third Quartet, "I was able to carry this particular conception through from beginning to end. … So that the Third Quartet was a realization of an idea that I'd had in the Second, which I didn't carry out completely and which I found another way of solving."[23] The implication that the homogeneous textures in the Second Quartet are a deviation from the goal of individualizing the instruments recurs in the piece's reception history. In Max Noubel's reading, "the dichotomy between the constraints of collective playing and the antagonisms exacerbated by strong individuals threatens to destroy the unity of the work."[24] In his music of the 1980s, Carter corrected this perceived shortcoming by using long-range polyrhythms to ensure the rhythmic differentiation of the parts through a wide variety of highly contrasted textures. This, in turn, allowed his instrumental characters to become more complex – like those of the poetry he set in the previous decade – developing and changing fluidly over the course of a piece in response to their changing situations and their interactions with each other, but without giving up their individual identities. As Noubel puts it, "an accord between the affirmation of identity … and the participation in a collective destiny is fully realized."[25]

Thus far I have tried to show how the traditional progress narrative of Carter's career, culminating in the divided ensemble works of the 1960s, distracts us from his ongoing refinement of the idea of musical characterization in his compositions of the 1970s and '80s. The argument suggests that lyricism is one of the primary strategies in Carter's music from 1975 on, and also shows how teleological thinking influenced Carter's compositional choices, his understanding of his own development, and the reception history of his music. Nevertheless, in tracking the lyric perspective I have replaced one progress narrative with another – substituting the instrumental music of the 1980s for the large-scale works of the 1960s as the goal of Carter's

[23] Porter "Interview with Elliott Carter."
[24] "la dichotomie entre les contraintes du jeu collectif et les antagonismes exacerbés des fortes individualités menaçait de détruire l'unité de l'oeuvre." Noubel, *LTF*, p. 213.

[25] "une adéquation entre l'affirmation de l'identité … et la participation à un destin collectif est pleinement réalisée." Noubel, *LTF*, p. 213. Also see Bernard's analysis of Carter's development in "The Evolution of Elliott Carter's Rhythmic Practice."

long-term efforts to develop techniques of musical characterization as rich and complex as those of contemporary literature. Such teleological accounts necessarily cast a composer's earlier works in the subordinate role of pre-cursors to the later ones. Describing the Second Quartet as the partial realization of a goal Carter fully achieved only in the Third or Fourth over-looks both the brilliance of the piece he did write, and its strong connections to his later music – connections unrelated to the linear narrative of progress toward the complete individualization of the instruments. In the Second Quartet, as we have seen, Carter juxtaposes two very different modes of instrumental writing. Episodes of clear differentiation by means of the tech-niques of the divided ensemble give way, often without warning, to those in which the four voices join in homogeneous textures based largely on the two all-interval tetrachords. Whereas the divided ensemble sections – build-ing on the examples of Ives and Crawford Seeger – point towards Carter's music of the 1960s, the sections of shared harmony are closer to the traditions of absolute music. Thus one can hear the Second Quartet as concerned less with the convergence and divergence of four instrumental personae than with the tenuousness of their existence within the eighteenth-century genre of the string quartet. When the four protagonists suddenly burst back into character after the turmoil of the climax, they gather their restored identities about them as though emerging from a bewildering dream. Understood as a remnant of Carter's pre-divided-ensemble thinking, the climax – with its dissolution of individual identities – is a way around a problem that Carter had not yet solved. But the Quartet's incommensurate rhetorical modes take on an entirely different value, and an entirely different relationship to Carter's other work, when understood as a fully realized example of the kind of sophisticated handling of point of view and ironic approach to musical characterization that similarly distinguishes his music since the mid-1990s.

The teleological narrative of Carter's development, centered on the divided ensemble and the related idea of disconnection, tends to define as non-normative both the middle-period compositions that lie outside of its bounds (like the *Sonata for Flute, Oboe, Cello, and Harpsichord* and the *Variations*), and the characteristics of those pieces that involve collaboration or shared expression. To do so is to risk obscuring one of the principal creative tensions in Carter's music.[26] A related weakness is the suggestion that Carter's devel-opment has remained largely free of outside influences. In the romanticized view of his career, Carter charts his own course, guided only by the strength of his inner vision, heroically resisting the siren's song of changing stylistic

[26] This tension is productively explored in Nichols, "Mistaken Identities in Carter's *Variations*," and Schiff, "Carter as Symphonist."

fashion and popular acclaim.[27] The attraction of this story has led even the most thoughtful critics to disregard the obvious signs of Carter's engagement with contemporary trends in intellectual history and compositional practice. His avid attention to the post-war avant-garde in Europe and the United States in the late 1940s and early 1950s is one example of this engagement, but it is equally characteristic of his later career. In *Night Fantasies*, the first of his late solo works, Carter sought to portray "the fleeting thoughts and feelings that pass through the mind during a period of wakefulness at night," in order "to capture the fanciful, changeable quality of our inner life at a time when it is not dominated by strong, directive intentions or desires."[28] That this scenario – with its nocturnal setting, altered state of consciousness, and projection of the lyric impulse onto a work for solo piano – consciously evokes the preoccupations of many composers in the early nineteenth century, reflects an interest in Romanticism that affected composers, artists, and writers of all stripes in the early 1980s.[29] In his preface to the score, Carter explicitly links the conceit of *Night Fantasies* to "the poetic moodiness that, in an earlier romantic context, I enjoy in works of Robert Schumann like *Kreisleriana*, *Carnaval*, and *Davidsbündlertänze*."[30] Edward Rothstein, in a prescient early review of *Night Fantasies*, recognized in Carter's declaration a significant aesthetic shift: "the creation of a musical universe out of a divided single voice, rather than out of a society divided by single voices" marks "a radical movement inward for Carter ... The articulation of mental life becomes central." But whereas most critics in the early 1980s hailed the New Romanticism for its appeal to non-specialist listeners (an appeal generally characterized as a moral imperative in much the same terms used by Boulez to advocate for serial music thirty years earlier), Rothstein seizes on a very different aspect of nineteenth-century aesthetics, interpreting Carter's lyric emphasis as indifference to the audience: "The public ... becomes a challenge to the individual voice, and finally becomes irrelevant to it."[31]

Rothstein's polemical reading of Carter's uses of Romanticism in *Night Fantasies* is an act of interpretational judo, leveraging the myth of the lone hero to redefine as reactionary arrogance Carter's interest in a notable contemporary trend. The argument is emblematic of a still-prevalent critical tendency to view the enormous changes taking place in contemporary concert music in the early 1980s as a proliferation of fresh new styles that swept

[27] For a recent example, see Rosen, "Happy Birthday Elliott Carter!," 31.

[28] Carter, "Preface," in *Night Fantasies* [score].

[29] See Alsen (ed.), *The New Romanticism*, and Straus, *Twelve-Tone Music in America*, pp. 202–06.

[30] Carter, "Preface," in *Night Fantasies* [score].

[31] Rothstein, "The Twilight Fantasies of Elliott Carter," 26. Also see Taruskin, "Standoff (II)."

away the hermetic narcissism of the post-war modernists. In addition to ignoring the aesthetic changes affecting modernist composers at the time, this narrative overlooks the importance of institutional changes that cut across stylistic boundaries. As resources became more limited, composers of all kinds had to find ways to write music that could be performed persuasively at a reasonable cost. For the New Romantics, the fact that their harmonic, gestural, and formal vocabularies were already familiar to performers steeped in the standard repertoire was economically beneficial as well as aesthetically attractive. For composers like Carter, who, throughout the 1960s, had enjoyed the patronage of large foundations eager to use Modernism to advance American geopolitical goals, the rehearsal time necessary for ensembles to come to grips with unconventional styles, playing techniques, and stage setups became increasingly difficult to come by. Techniques that were intended to expand the range of expressive possibility instead became obstacles to effective performance. In spite of Carter's reputation (at its pre-centennial zenith in the early 1970s), and a significant number of brilliant and expressive performances and recordings of his most complex works, his music was not widely played. His middle-period chamber music was beyond the reach of all but the most dedicated performers, and the larger works after the *Variations* were hard to program given the economic limitations of most orchestras. Nor were the difficulties of Carter's music limited to its performance. It was also extremely difficult and time-consuming to write, not least because Carter felt he had to "grope along like a blind man" as he painstakingly worked out the materials and techniques of his middle-period style.[32] As is widely noted, Carter completed only ten pieces in the twenty years between 1949 and 1969, a rate of production that must have seemed increasingly worrisome to him as he got older. Not long after signing a new contract with Boosey & Hawkes, Carter wondered aloud about whether the deal was a good one for the publisher: "Oh, I don't know if it's worth your while. I'm 73 and you might not get many pieces."[33]

In the popular mythology, Carter ignores all of these pressures and continues to compose "without compromise";[34] in fact, they prompted him to carefully rethink his work, and to simplify nearly every aspect of his style. In the early 1970s, just as he was assessing the nature of his characters in the Second Quartet, Carter was becoming frustrated with the generally poor performances his Concerto for Orchestra had thus far received (although he was careful to exempt those conducted by Boulez). "I realized at that point that if I wanted to compose for American orchestras, I would somehow have

[32] Johnson, "Elliott Carter at 100."
[33] Carter quoted in Wallace, *Boosey & Hawkes: The Publishing Story*, p. 168.

[34] Boulez, on-camera interview in Scheffer, *Elliott Carter: A Labyrinth of Time*.

to use a simpler structure, requiring less rehearsal time. [A] *Symphony of Three Orchestras* is the result of that decision ... "[35] And in 1975, before he accepted the commission for *A Mirror on Which to Dwell*, Carter arranged a meeting with the musicians of Speculum Musicae, who had asked him to write the piece. According to Fred Sherry, the group's cellist,

> the first thing [Carter] said was "Is my music too hard?" And everybody is looking around and we said "Uh ... No, no, no! It's really fine!" (Later on we compared notes and I wanted to say: "Yes! It's way too hard!") But then what came out was this very virtuosic piece.[36]

As Sherry points out, *A Mirror on Which to Dwell* is indeed a virtuosic piece, and Carter has continued to showcase the virtuosity of the performers in his more recent chamber music. And while the textures and rhythms played by each orchestra in *A Symphony of Three Orchestras* are simpler, coordinating the three ensembles and adjusting to the unorthodox seating plan remain formidable challenges.[37] But these initial steps encouraged Carter to further simplify the technical demands of his music in the years that followed (perhaps because he felt he had not gone far enough). When he next wrote for an American orchestra (in 1986), Carter thoroughly transformed his orchestral style, reducing the number of contrapuntal voices, and drastically simplifying his rhythmic notation. His chamber music, though still written for professional performers, has become less herculean in its demands, which in turn has led to more frequent performances and helped to fuel the widespread popularity of Carter's late music.

As Carter was making his music easier to play, he was also making it easier to write. By 1975 he had assembled a complete draft of his *Harmony Book* and streamlined his handling of the comprehensive harmonic partitions he used to write his music.[38] Not the least of the ironies in his remark (made almost thirty years ago) that he might not have many pieces left in him is that when he made it (in 1982) he had already doubled his rate of production over the preceding decade, an increase that did not go unnoticed at the time.[39] The years since 1980 have seen an even greater increase in Carter's productivity, due in no small part to a fundamental change in his attitude toward composition. For decades, Carter made the development of new materials and methods for each new piece a core element of his compositional practice, and a point of honor. He belittled the "journeyman['s]" reliance on "easily

---

[35] Restagno, *Elliott Carter in Conversation with Enzo Restagno*, p. 78.

[36] Sherry, Panel discussion, Tanglewood Music Center, July 21, 2008.

[37] Non-standard configurations are a consistent feature of the pieces Carter has composed for Pierre Boulez, whose critique of standard eighteenth- and nineteenth-century ensembles as poorly suited to the needs of post-tonal music is well known.

[38] See Link, "The Combinatorial Art of Elliott Carter's *Harmony Book*," in Carter, *HB*.

[39] See Schiff, "Carter in the Seventies," 2.

worn-out routines developed by others or even himself" as antithetical to "a musical imagination that has always prized a continuous exploration of musical means largely invented as various imaginative needs were felt."[40] This attitude is widely reflected in the secondary literature, in which the novelty of Carter's compositional methods is often taken as an indication of the quality of his music.[41]

Yet since the 1980s, Carter's avoidance of repetition has given way to an approach that might be called *reduce, reuse, recycle*. Although they are entirely dissimilar in genre and mood, *A Celebration of Some 100 × 150 Notes*, *Enchanted Preludes*, and *Anniversary* are all based on the same 56:45 poly-rhythm.[42] A small collection of core harmonies has replaced the elaborate harmonic partitions of his middle-period music in nearly every piece Carter has written in the past fifteen years.[43] In addition to a recurring harmonic vocabulary, there are recurring formal sections (like the ritornellos in *ASKO Concerto* and *Boston Concerto*)[44] and recurring titles to indicate new pieces in existing series, like the *Figments* (now numbering five), *Fragments* (*I* and *II*), and *Retracings* (*I, II,* and *III*). In the latter series Carter makes short pieces out of excerpts of longer ones, while in both *Réflexions* and *Luimen* he constructs a longer piece from the kernel of a shorter one.[45] Many of Carter's recent works, such as the *Three Occasions, Three Illusions, Tri-Tribute, Trilogy, Tre Duetti, Symphonia,* and *4 Lauds*, are suites whose movements may be performed as independent compositions. Perhaps most surprising – given his longstanding commitment to writing music that emerges from the character of the instruments that play it – Carter happily accepted and then published Benny Slucin's trombone transcription of the solo clarinet piece *Gra*.

Asked in 2001 about his Oboe Quartet, Carter reflected on the ways his compositional process had changed:

> When I was younger, I sometimes spent weeks putting these sorts of things in working order, but I'm tired of doing that now. I just write what's in my mind. In the old days I used to write them and then correct them to fit into the pattern. Now I don't correct.[46]

[40] Carter, Untitled program note to the recording of *Night Fantasies and Piano Sonata*.

[41] See, for example, Goldman, "Current Chronicle," 84; Skulsky, "Elliott Carter," 2; and Schiff, *MEC* 1st edn, p. 21.

[42] See Link, "Long-Range Polyrhythms in Elliott Carter's Recent Music," pp. 119–20.

[43] See Carter, *HB*, pp. 31–35, Boland, "'Linking' and 'Morphing'," and Capuzzo, "The Complement Union Property."

[44] See Boland, "Ritornello Form in Carter's *Boston* and *ASKO* Concertos," in this volume.

[45] *Retracing*, for solo bassoon, is excerpted from *ASKO Concerto*; *Retracing II* extracts an extended horn solo from its contrapuntal context in Quintet for Piano and Winds; and *Retracing III* is based on the trumpet solo from *A Symphony of Three Orchestras*. Carter set *Call* in *Réflexions* and built the last movement of *Luimen* around the solo guitar piece *Shard*.

[46] Meyer, "Elliott Carter in Conversation with Felix Meyer," p. 28.

The decision not to "correct" has further streamlined Carter's compositional process and palpably influenced his music. Even the most seamless of his middle-period works typically began as a series of discrete sections. For the String Quartet No. 3, Carter first made a large number of separate sketches that juxtapose two contrasting movements, one each for the quartet's two duos.[47] A second stage of composition then was required to revise and reorder the initial sketches and to connect and smooth out the transitions between them, usually via significant amounts of newly composed material. In his compositions of the 1980s and early '90s, Carter completely rewrote many sketches (sometimes more than once) to maintain their coordination with a long-range polyrhythm as he tried out different ways of ordering them.[48] Carter's process still involves considerable revision of his initial drafts, but the more labor-intensive methods described above have largely fallen by the wayside.

My historicist reading of Carter's late music as a response to the practical constraints of institutional change and advancing age challenges the myth of Carter as a romantic hero, stubbornly isolating himself from contemporary trends and practical limitations alike. But it also risks portraying Carter as a composer in the grip of irresistible forces, compromising his ideals to reduce his and his performers' workload and court popular acclaim. Such a portrayal is equally misleading, as the kinds of practical considerations I have described are a familiar part of every composer's working life, and are ultimately inseparable from the imaginative constraints all artists impose on themselves to focus their creative energies. In Carter's case, the developments I have grouped under the heading of simplification have been a powerful imaginative stimulus, both inspiring new aesthetic directions and placing his earlier achievements in a new context. This is especially true of Carter's simplified harmonic language. In his divided ensemble music, harmonic partitions define the instrumental characters in terms of their differences. When an ensemble is divided into groups of instruments, as in the Double Concerto and Third Quartet, each group consists of individuals who speak only the language of the tribe. Intervals are occasionally shared across the ensemble divisions, but in most cases the boundaries are reinforced, not bridged, by the harmony. In a well-known passage from the introduction of the Second Quartet, each of the instruments in turn makes a bold statement that reinterprets the same key pitches in the context of each instrument's own unique interval repertoire (see Example 2.1).

While the many reiterated pitches in this excerpt serve as points of contact among the instruments, their articulation via the instruments' clearly

---

[47] See Carter's sketches for the String Quartet No. 3 at the Library of Congress, Washington.

[48] See Link, "The Composition of Carter's *Night Fantasies*."

Ex. 2.1 Shared pitches in String Quartet No. 2, mm. 11–16

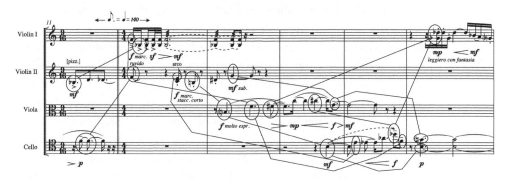

delineated intervallic vocabularies makes it difficult to hear these measures as a collaborative effort.[49] The emphatic repetitions sound more like corrections (whether polite or aggressive) or misunderstandings (whether willful or accidental) of the other instrument's point of view. In his recent compositions, on the other hand, Carter frequently loosens, or even dispenses with, the bonds between harmony, character, and instrumental grouping that are axiomatic in his divided ensemble music. Near the end of *A Celebration of Some 100 × 150 Notes*, there is a striking passage in which the energy of the climax gradually dissipates in the brass (see Example 2.2).[50] As indicated by the circled numbers, the instruments play the eleven fanfare motives – each articulating one of the eleven musical intervals – on which much of the piece is based.

Two aspects of the harmony in this passage distinguish it from that of Example 2.1. First, although the individual intervals have a motivic function, they are not fixed to a particular instrument or instrumental group. The jumble of short motives resembles the welter of stock phrases people shout at public gatherings, rather than the reasoned utterances of individuals in discourse. If there are characters here, they are radically reduced to an interval and a rudimentary rhythmic figure. In Carter's divided ensemble music of the 1960s, characters are constructed from combinations of musical raw materials; here the raw materials are treated as though they themselves were characters.[51] Second (and most unlike Example 2.1), the sound of the individual intervals is gradually subsumed in the sound of the seven-note

---

[49] For a different reading of the String Quartet No. 2 introduction, see Roeder, "'The Matter of Human Cooperation' in Carter's Mature Style," in this volume.

[50] The subsiding energy in the brass in this passage is offset by the gradual build-up of a sustained twenty-four-note chord in the strings (not shown).

[51] Carter uses a similar harmonic technique to create an entirely different effect in mm. 345–55 in *A Symphony of Three Orchestras*. There, a mosaic of repeated intervals, each fixed in pitch and rhythm, depicts a dystopian view of lifeless industrial mechanization. (See Noubel, *LTF*, pp. 181–87.)

Ex. 2.2 *A Celebration of Some 100 × 150 Notes*, mm. 128–39 (strings omitted)

fixed-register chord – E3, A3, C4, D4, E♭4, F♯4, C♯5 – from which all the intervals in this passage are drawn. That the overall sound of the harmony becomes the primary focus – reinforced even as it is variously articulated – is precisely the point Carter is making here about celebrations.[52]

The sectional forms that Carter has used in many recent works have similarly far-reaching consequences for his music, creating over-arching continuities no less evocative than the elaborate chain forms of the 1970s.[53] The first movement of Carter's Horn Concerto ends with the sudden interruption of a wedge-shaped flourish in the woodwinds at the peak of its crescendo and the extremes of its range (see Example 2.3).

The sudden cut-away from loud to soft – like the dominant pedals and elided cadences of an earlier age – is a familiar topos of modernist composition and Carter counts on us hearing it that way. The real surprise comes more than three dozen measures later, when the same woodwind flourish suddenly picks up where it left off, as though it had been frozen in time for the duration of the intervening slow movement (see Example 2.4).

This effect has its roots in the intercutting of multiple storylines in literature, and in cinema. If Carter's middle-period works resemble the

[52] The broken-off statement of the interval 8 motive in m. 139 is a marvelous comic touch – suggesting a moment of hesitation on the part of a celebrant, but also (because it is a unison) parodying the idea of combinatorial completion at work in this passage. In his later works, Carter typically uses the core harmonies and their derivatives in similar passages. (See, for example, mm. 212–25 of *Partita*, in which an irregular succession of trichords articulates a single fixed-register instance of the all-trichord hexachord.)

[53] See Boland, "Ritornello Form in Carter's *Boston* and *ASKO* Concertos," in this volume, and Dubiel, "Observations of Carter's Clarinet Concerto."

Ex. 2.3 Horn Concerto, mm. 64–70

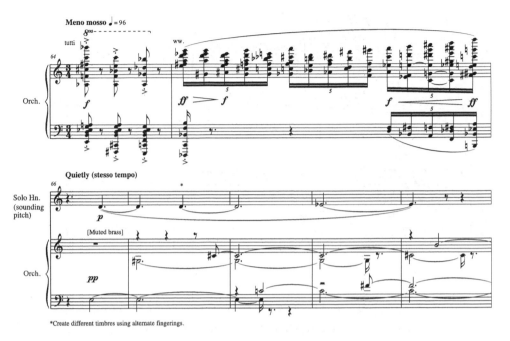

*Create different timbres using alternate fingerings.

Ex. 2.4 Horn Concerto, mm. 100–04

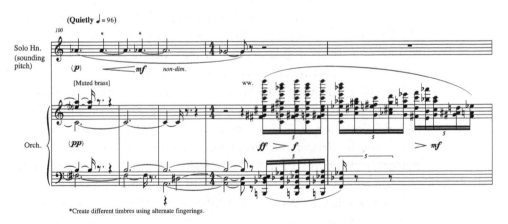

*Create different timbres using alternate fingerings.

"Odessa steps" sequence from Eisenstein's *The Battleship Potemkin* – a single large scene within which several overlapping narrative threads unfold simultaneously and the montage guides the audience's attention from one to another – the late works more often resemble a mode of cinematic story-telling in which discrete scenes that may or may not be synchronic are

cross-cut to form a linear sequence.[54] In the Horn Concerto, every movement after the first interrupts a transitional passage that continues where it
left off when the movement ends. Taken together, the transitions form a
continuous narrative frame that is successively interrupted by, and surrounds, the movements, creating a dramatic tension between the chronological sequence of events in the piece and the implied continuity of the
framing segments. This technique is typically associated with the framing
violin and cello solos in the First Quartet,[55] which Carter has said were
inspired by the famous interrupted shot of a brick chimney falling in
Cocteau's *Le Sang d'un Poète* (1930), but it is actually quite rare in
Carter's middle-period music. When the music associated with a particular
movement returns in a piece like the Third Quartet or Concerto for
Orchestra, it typically does so at a different point in its development, rather
than picking up where it left off. The explicit continuity between segments
separated by cross-cutting becomes a characteristic narrative mode only
when adapted to the lyric perspective, beginning with *Riconoscenza per
Goffredo Petrassi* in 1984. Carter explained his thinking in a 1994 interview:

> About ten years ago, while composing a piece in honor of a friend of mine
> [*Riconoscenza*], I thought of creating a work [*Partita*] … which would have the
> strings striving on throughout the composition while being interrupted by other
> instruments, not unlike how our lives are interrupted by unpredictable challenges and
> tragedies. That idea of a living struggle has permeated all my work since then.[56]

The struggle of the lyric voice to continue despite interruptions is a theme of
central importance in Carter's late music. It recurs in pieces large and small,
including (in addition to *Partita* and the Horn Concerto) the Cello Concerto,
Fons Juventatis, *Réflexions*, and *Interventions*.

The playfully ambiguous handling of character and motive that we
observed in *A Celebration of Some 100 × 150 Notes* is indicative of a broader
trend in Carter's late music toward revisiting and rethinking his middle-
period style. The prominence of memory in old age is a tempting explanation
for this trend, but age as a metaphor is of limited utility in surveying Carter's
recent music, which is no less vigorous than his music of forty years ago, and
is generally lighter on its feet. More useful is John Updike's reminder that
"What does haunt late works is the author's previous works: he is burden-
somely conscious that he has been cast, unlike his ingénue self, as an author
who writes in a certain way, with the inexorable consistency of his own

[54] For the influence of Eisenstein's conception
of montage on Carter's music, see Bernard,
"Elliott Carter and the Modern Meaning of
Time," 661–72.
[55] See Carter, "String Quartets Nos. 1, 1951,
and 2, 1959," in *CEL*, p. 233, and Lochhead,

"On the 'Framing' Music of Elliott Carter's
First String Quartet."
[56] See Carvin, "American Gothic: An
Interview with Elliot Carter."

handwriting."[57] The memorial cast of much of Carter's music since the mid-1990s – with its reflections, retracings, intermittences, fragments, and illusions – both interrogates and resists this "inexorable consistency," as Carter suggests by describing his Fifth Quartet as "a farewell to the previous four and an exploration of a new vision."[58]

As he does in the Horn Concerto, Carter explores this "new vision" in the Fifth Quartet by means of a sectional form. He proposes the scenario of a rehearsal to explain both the fragmentary nature of the quartet's discrete sections and the wrenching discontinuities that separate them: the musicians join together to rehearse the movements of a string quartet, breaking off in the interludes to try out bits and pieces of their parts individually. In an important sense, Carter's scenario is evasive. The movements are, of course, well prepared by the time the Fifth Quartet is actually performed, with only stylized breakdowns and restarts, and (in a good performance) free of the unselfconsciously ragged playing typical of actual rehearsals. Similarly, the interludes – with their isolated utterances divided by silence – lack the disorder and verbal debate that occurs when the members of a string quartet stop to discuss details of cueing and interpretation or practice their individual parts between run-throughs. There is also the matter of the movements themselves, which often recall signature textures from Carter's earlier quartets. All of this suggests that the Fifth Quartet enacts a memory as well as a rehearsal: a portrayal of the mind as it warily constructs and bids farewell to half-remembered echoes of its own past. But Carter's attempt to distract us from listening too hard to the Fifth Quartet's silences (by suggesting that they only signify a player counting rests or reviewing the score to locate an entrance) points to the underlying significance of his rehearsal scenario. As the memory of a life's art contends with the passage of time, perhaps the best hope is for that art to become its admirers (as W. H. Auden put it).[59] Rehearsal, in that sense, is the mirror image of decay – a gradual re-emergence of shared meaning from silence.

Carter's lifelong aversion to sentimentality suggests that it would be unwise to read too much pathos into the memorial aspects of his late work, and indeed, in late Carter, memory more often leads to a kind of self-deprecating irony, through which an unflinching realism is sometimes visible. In the coda of the Fourth Quartet, the pauses that characterize the instrumental writing have their apotheosis in an intense series of short fragments for the full ensemble separated by momentous silences. The fragments alternate with uncharacteristic regularity between explosive *forte* bursts and tranquil

[57] Updike, "Late Works," 69.
[58] Carter, "Composer's Note" from the Pacifica Quartet recording of String Quartets No. 1 and 5: n.p.

[59] Auden, "In Memory of W. B. Yeats" (1939), in *Collected Shorter Poems*, pp. 141–43.

sustained chords, so that the pattern – *forte* burst, [silence], tranquil chords, [silence] – quickly becomes predictable and its repetitiveness confirms the listener's expectations for far longer than any other passage in all of Carter's music. The pattern is broken only at the end, when a second quiet passage replaces the expected loud one, but the real surprise is the final gesture – a brief semi-coordinated flourish followed a moment later by a simple closely voiced staccato chord in rhythmic unison (marking the final coincidence point of the quartet's long-range polyrhythm) – made with such incongruous nonchalant playfulness that it completely obliterates the accumulated tension, and frames the intense drama of opposed musics in the coda, the final *presto*, and the quartet as a whole, with a mischievous wink.

The quiet, understated ending has been a favorite device of Carter's at least as far back as the Piano Sonata, but (as Felix Meyer and Anne C. Shreffler astutely point out) it has become "virtually a defining feature of Carter's late music."[60] Its effect (as in the Fourth Quartet) is to allude to the ephemeral, even illusory, nature of the preceding music. Carter has always emphasized the destruction of his carefully wrought universes as well as their creation, but in the later music he often seems intent on framing a piece for the audience by explicitly bursting the bubble of musical illusion so as to suggest a larger context. *Retracing III*, for solo trumpet, returns to the transcendent solo from the opening of *A Symphony of Three Orchestras* – a solo that carries the prophetic lyricism of Hart Crane's vision of a seagull circling New York harbor and the Brooklyn Bridge in the opening stanza of *The Bridge*. In spite of its brilliance, the solo has long bothered Carter. It was written for Gerard Schwartz (then the principal trumpet of the New York Philharmonic), but in spite of Schwartz's brilliant virtuosity (which may be heard on the Philharmonic's recording, conducted by Pierre Boulez) it has proven to be too demanding for many orchestral trumpet players due to its lack of pauses to allow the player to rest between soaring flights. Ostensibly, *Retracing III* was composed to address that problem, but the interpolations added to the original solo (which is otherwise unchanged) also subject the memory of its transcendence to fragmentation and ultimately to a kind of truncation far removed from the original context. The ending gradually draws the music back to the present (with which it is on a collision course), via the imperative of the ticking clock – a periodic staccato C♯4. (See Example 2.5.)

In the Fifth Quartet, the self-scrutiny that underlies Carter's retracings conveys a more far-reaching and sobering message. The Quartet's apparently simple premise of a rehearsal wreaks havoc with the idea of agency in the piece. The performers (members of a string quartet) play the roles of performers in a string quartet, whose shared purpose is to rehearse a piece, the actual

---

[60] Meyer and Shreffler, *ECCP*, p. 294.

Ex. 2.5 *Retracing III*, mm. 42–50

public performance of which the audience never hears. Or, to leave the human players out of it, the piece returns to the idea of four juxtaposed "character-continuities," like those of the Second and Fourth Quartets, but adds an additional layer beyond the self-contained world of the movements yet still bounded by the fourth wall. This multi-layered scenario – not the least significance of which is that it extends recursively to the audience and beyond – seems designed to question the very idea of "character-continuities" as dramatic characters, much the way the idea of dramatic characters as human beings is questioned in Beckett's *Waiting for Godot*, Pirandello's *Six Characters in Search of an Author*, and Stoppard's *Rosencrantz and Guildenstern are Dead*. This is especially true of the interludes, in which the four voices have only the limited vocabulary of their intervallic and rhythmic partitions with which to express themselves, and their limited utterances are bounded by silence.

Paul Griffiths well understood this aspect of Carter's late music when he wrote the libretto for their opera *What Next?*, the unspoken premise of which seems to be: What would happen if the instrumental character-continuities of Carter's middle-period music suddenly came alive as "real" stage characters?[61] (Griffiths even proposed an actual instrumental character "Horn" played by an on-stage horn player, although that idea was later dropped.[62]) With the significant exception of Kid, the characters that did make the cut – an aging hippie, an empirically minded astronomer, a clownish entertainer, a diva, and a flustered *mater familias* – are a *commedia* troupe for the twenty-first century: stock characters that embody clichéd oppositions (feeling vs.

[61] See Schiff, "Keeping up with Carter," Shreffler, "Instrumental Dramaturgy as Humane Comedy," and Capuzzo, "Text, Music, and Irony in *What Next?*," in this volume.

[62] See Shreffler, "Instrumental Dramaturgy as Humane Comedy," 159, note 15.

thinking; art vs. science; freedom vs. responsibility, and so on) in distinctly contemporary garb. The connection with Carter's definition of character in his middle-period music is reinforced by the percussion overture – a playful parody of the introduction to Carter's own Double Concerto with its quasi-mythological vision of the creation of a world from chaos.[63] And, as in the Fifth Quartet, there are multiple layers of perspective in the opera. As Guy Capuzzo points out, Carter uses the child's-eye view of Kid in *What Next?* to frame the delimited antic responses of the adult characters to the situation in which they find themselves.[64] Perhaps as a salvo in the perennial opera debate about the primacy of words or music, Carter adds a penultimate layer, carried by the extended wordless lyricism of an English horn solo in the episode Griffiths initially called "The Singing Stage," and Carter describes with a smile as "my *Swan of Tuonela*."[65]

In his discussions with Griffiths, Carter initially suggested that the ending of *What Next?* break the fourth wall – an indication, perhaps, that he was looking for a way to shatter the opera's self-contained universe, like those he so beautifully made and unmade in the Double Concerto and Concerto for Orchestra. In the end Carter and Griffiths found other subtler ways to extend the reach of their post-catastrophic world to encompass the audience, as Carter has in so many other recent works. It is this ardent ambition that lies beyond Carter's playful references to his earlier style in his music of the last two decades, and makes this most recent period of his career so much more than simply a late idyll.

Carter's vast and diverse body of late music poses significant challenges to critics long used to describing his life and work in terms of a small complex of settled and sanctioned narratives. Carter's insight into the implications for his style of the simplified harmonic language and sectional forms he has lately favored, and his remarkable uses of memory and his own earlier work as subject matter for his compositions suggest that Carter's Modernism remains finely tuned to the dramatic changes in the history of ideas that have taken place over the last forty years. Some, like the development of minimalism, he has rejected in no uncertain terms (and, as in the coda of *A Symphony of Three Orchestras*, fiercely mocked), but others he has embraced, or – more accurately – turned to his own ends. Given his reputation as an uncompromising loner, it is ironic that Carter's skill at navigating the currents of stylistic fashion through more than six decades of the twentieth century is precisely

---

[63] A similar self-parody may be heard in Carter's use of percussion and polyrhythm to represent the cold mechanization of *More's Utopia*. See Noubel, "*Three Illusions . . .* and Maybe a Fourth," in this volume, and Link, *Elliott Carter's Late Music.*

[64] See Capuzzo, "Text, Music, and Irony in *What Next?*," in this volume.

[65] Quoted in Schiff, "Keeping up with Carter," 4.

what has led to his being fixed in the twenty-first either as a chilly (or heroic) modernist holdout, or – as David Levine's cartoon would have it – as a cheerful mad scientist (hair à la Einstein), conducting atop an upside-down metronome. Carter's highly publicized transformation from a patriotic American populist to a virtuoso of highly specialized post-war Modernism may have encouraged this view, but that transformation is only one of the many ways that he has applied the principle of change in his life and work, a process that continues to this day. Now that the midpoint of Carter's catalog is advancing rapidly toward the 1990s, the stories we tell about his development and about the ways his music reflects the end of the modernist period need to be rethought. Carter's recent music is far too rich and varied to be dismissed as a pendant to his compositions of the 1960s and '70s, or marginalized in historiographical narratives that no longer fit the times nor the compositions they originally were meant to contain. With its ongoing vitality and mutability, the music resists such treatment, even as it reminds us of Carter's greatest strength as a chronicler of the human journey.

PART II

Analysis and aesthetics

3   The search for order: Carter's *Symphonia* and late-modern thematicism

Arnold Whittall

As far as I am aware, Elliott Carter has never referred to something called "late-modern thematicism." But in one of his most penetrating pieces of self-analysis, a discussion with Stuart Liebman (1973), he said that "I see the motion of music as a kind of analogue to the processes of our inner life. It must present not merely the patterns of feeling, but also the patterns of logical thought and of the stream-of-consciousness. I've tried to develop patterns which include all these ways of thinking in any given work and which also attempt to motivate these types of thought. For instance, the dreams of systematic logical thought as opposed to the flux of the dream world."[1] Given the familiar association of "pattern" with model, and as "a design or figure repeated indefinitely" (*The Chambers Dictionary*, "pattern"), it is worth noting the implications for order and recurrence in Carter's form of words. Whether or not "pattern" and "theme" are literally synonymous, their close contiguity is surely undeniable.

No less significantly, Carter sought to give the vision of music outlined to Liebman a specifically human and therefore social connotation: "human beings, I think, come to expect more from music than entertaining patterns of tone-colors. Mine uses a large variety of these but, I hope, always to transcend the medium of sound completely and present a more significant human message."[2] These comments build on the kind of thinking Carter displayed in a letter to Peter Yates back in 1959: "my music has sought mainly two things – to deal with vertical and horizontal dimensions in a more varied way than is usually done – I try to find continuities that gain meaning, change, and operate in time on a level that is parallel to our present experience of living."[3] The conclusion is that, for Carter, the search for meaning, for that "more significant human message," is best pursued not by way of structural abstractions but by characterizing musical thought in terms of analogies between "the processes of our inner life" and those musical patterns and processes which best represent them. As I understand it, Modernism defines itself in opposition to Classicism, and "Late Modernism" indicates a third

---

[1] Meyer and Shreffler, *ECCP*, p. 216.   [3] *Ibid.*, p. 155.
[2] *Ibid.*

phase – after Early and High Modernisms – which came into focus during the later twentieth century. Late Modernism is no less diverse and unstable than High Modernism: it too reacts strongly against Classicism, while nevertheless showing a greater capacity for recognizing and exploiting points of contact with it. It follows that "late-modern (or late-modernist) thematicism" has a paradoxical quality: on the one hand, it resists the predominantly invariant pitch orderings of classical thematicism, where there are clear distinctions between the principal version of a theme and any identifiable transformation, variation, or development of that theme, in favor of more varied relations to a basic shape which is more likely to be defined as an unordered collection of pitch classes than as an ordered presentation of pitches: on the other hand, it retains degrees of association with classical thematicism's flexibly invariant qualities, of character and content – its capacity for distinguishing constituent motives from overall trajectory. But in late-modern thematicism it is the musical character associated with an unordered collection that determines content, and it is not inappropriate that the only entry in David Schiff's technical glossary for Carter's music that pertains directly to such issues chooses the term "character-patterns" in preference to "thematic elements" or "motivic processes."[4]

Post-tonal choices

Since Carter is not just a modernist composer but also a post-tonal composer, his music represents a particular challenge to the categorizing, systematizing theorist. When tonal composers devise thematic material, the resulting shapes and lines use pitches which, as scale degrees, have a range of identities and functions whose realization has much to do with the harmonic character and structure of the composition within which they appear and evolve. That thematic process is therefore constrained by harmonic possibilities, and by the voice-leading procedures that all tonal compositions employ. By contrast, post-tonal composers can use as many or as few constraints as they desire, and the ways in which their choices are presented tell us much about their aesthetic objectives and technical preferences. For Carter, the all-triad (or all-trichord) hexachord (ATH) – [012478] – became one such constraining construct (the two all-interval tetrachords were another) and its place in the melodic dimension of his music is illustrated here by three examples, one from each of the movements of his magnum opus from the 1990s, *Symphonia: Sum Fluxae Pretium Spei* (Example 3.1).

[4] Schiff, *MEC*, p. 36.

Ex. 3.1a *Symphonia,* I. *Partita,* mm. 124–26, English horn only

Ex. 3.1b *Symphonia,* II. *Adagio tenebroso,* mm. 52–53, oboe only

Ex. 3.1c *Symphonia,* III. *Allegro scorrevole,* mm. 235–39, piccolo only

Example 3.1a, from *Partita,* uses the hexachord in a version whose prime form ascends from G; Example 3.1b from *Adagio tenebroso* uses a version ascending from A♭; and Example 3.1c from *Allegro scorrevole* an inversion descending from C: all three are, therefore, related. Yet they are not different versions of the same "theme": nor, as thematic statements, do they tell us anything about the functional capacity of their common source hexachord to generate versions of all twelve trichords as subsets. If they respond in any direct sense to the hexachord's special comprehensiveness, it is simply in being significantly different from each other. It could also be argued that these statements involve an interaction between that comprehensiveness, when the collection is regarded as unordered, and the constraint provided by regarding the interval-class succession of that unordered prime as ordered intervals. That interval-class succession is [11231], and all three of the melodic statements quoted in Example 3.1 have some degree of ordered-interval constraint, which is seen clearly if represented as a succession of semitone totals, modulo 12: <72237>, <96586>, <21513>. Each set gains further

distinctiveness when inflected for interval direction, ascending or descending, and compound intervals, like the tritone plus octave shown as '6' in the second collection. But Carter's use of such hexachords, as lines and as chords, is a mark of identity in his musical language, a source or resource which has come to signify for him the plenitude and freedom inherent in post-tonal composition. To repeat: the hexachords do not come with a set of functions and procedures attached, after the model of tonal scales. But the materials which Carter derives from them, and from all the pitch- and interval-class collections codified in his *Harmony Book*, can nevertheless acquire qualities, by shaping, emphasis and other compositional procedures, that make it difficult if not impossible to detach them from all association with concepts, like thematicism, which have a long history in music composed before the era of post-tonal Modernism.

Thematicism in theory and practice

"Theme" is such common currency in music writing that the latest *Grove* allots much less space to the term than to other fundamental theoretical concepts. Nevertheless, William Drabkin makes a clear distinction between thematic materials and processes found in music before the modern era and a situation whereby "in much contemporary music it is difficult to draw a line between what is proposed (i.e. the theme) and what is worked out from the proposal."[5] Implicit here is the perception that one possible attribute of musical Modernism is the difficulty of distinguishing between "athematicism" and "all-thematicism," and the issue becomes even more challenging when Modernism's problems with balancing textural, harmonic tendencies to converge on or diverge from centers or points of focus are acknowledged. One way in which the historical process leading from Early Modernism (beginning in late Beethoven) to High Modernism (initiated by the earliest post-tonal work of the twentieth century's first decade) and Late Modernism (a quality associated with the ultra-pluralism of music since c.1970) can be characterized has to do with different attitudes to thematicism, and one reason for proposing the notion of "late-modern thematicism" was suggested by Pierre Boulez in 1997: "in my youth, I thought that music could be athematic. In the end, however, I am now convinced that music must be based on recognizable musical objects. These are not 'themes' in the classical sense, but rather entities which, even though they constantly change their form, have certain characteristics which are so identifiable that they cannot be confused with any other entity."[6]

---

[5] Drabkin, "Theme," p. 352.   [6] Boulez, "Conférence sur *Anthèmes 2*," p. 79.

Boulez's reliance on the form-building functions of exactly repeated or, more commonly, varied recurrences of small-scale pitch and rhythmic patterns in works from the mid-1970s onwards (most explicitly, at first, in *Rituel* and *Messagesquisse*) reinforces his perception that "recognizable musical objects" are not incompatible with a viably contemporary idiom. Yet his reluctance to define this "retreat" from the radicalism of his earlier music is understandable, since he has remained resistant to what he has seen as Schoenbergian motivic practice, at least as Schoenberg defined it in his pedagogical writings.[7] Like Carter, Boulez has had much less time for Schoenberg's "neoclassical" twelve-tone compositions than for the ostensibly freer and more genuinely progressive pieces of 1908–14. Nevertheless, Boulez's verbal formulation is not so unlike an impressionistic version of Schoenberg's description of the *Gestalt* in the *Gedanke* manuscript: "a *Gestalt* usually consists of more than one statement of the motive," and will have "a characteristic feature to justify its name; a striking interval or interval progression or a striking rhythm or rhythmic progression. A *Gestalt* need not necessarily have more than local significance."[8] Schoenberg's talk of "characteristic" or "striking" features seems far from dissonant with Boulez's "recognizable musical objects": and, in turn, Boulez's formulation is far from dissonant with what Carter has termed "character-continuities," when referring to the materials deployed in his second string quartet.[9]

As the tendency for dictionaries to conflate definitions of "theme" and "motif" shows, it is not easy to make plausibly absolute distinctions between a whole range of verbal terms – element, entity, theme, motive, motif, object – especially when the possibility of pitch material moving between linear and vertical, melodic and chordal, arises. But this does not mean that "late-modern thematicism" cannot embrace the application of another Schoenbergian concept – developing variation: especially in relation to a particular *Gestalt* which, in Schoenberg's phrase, "need not have more than local significance." Nevertheless, without some use of "recognizable musical objects" – however subjective the process of identifying such usage might be – the possibility of "athematicism," as distinct from the suspension of traditional thematicism, must remain part of the modernist technical armory.

---

[7] See Whittall, "Boulez et le classicisme moderne (Schoenberg, Berg)."
[8] Schoenberg, *The Musical Idea*, p. 169.
[9] Carter, "String Quartets Nos. 1, 1951, and 2, 1959" (1970), in *CEL*, p. 232. For

Boulez's most extensive discussion of "envelope" as a formal principle, see his *Leçons de musique*.

Promoting "focused attention": Carter's sources

That Carter has thought of his materials primarily in terms of chords that are linearly deployed and at the same time characterized by rhythm, shape, dynamics, and phrasing has long been obvious, and is confirmed when he comments in the *Harmony Book* that "I'm really writing contrapuntal music so that these chords are seldom notes played at the same time."[10] Commentators therefore tend to use terms like "materials" or "gestures" to suggest the difference between Carter's methods and traditional thematicism, and to acknowledge the modernist reality of the degree to which, as John Link observes, "stability is ephemeral or uneasy, and the musical argument constantly surges in new and unexpected directions."[11] As will be argued below, what brings particular power to Carter's music is the way he uses small-scale repetitions of patterns of pitch and rhythm to provide a core of thematic stability which the music then challenges, plays with, but never entirely escapes. And this seems to be his way of working out a response to the cultural situation which he defined with unusual sarcasm, even bitterness, in a discussion in Banff in 1984. Picking up on Adorno's remarks about the "regression of listening ability," he diagnosed "a loss of the wish to pay attention to music" as "one of the many types of breakdown of communication we are faced with at a time when focused attention [is] needed more than ever in our democratic and highly complex society, where choices of citizens are so important for their own welfare." At the same time he declared that for him "music that is mechanically ordered like some minimalist or some popular music seems to me pointless as it does not give any sense of being alive."[12] To be alive to the creation and recognition of patterns as they evolve, without shunning complexity yet at the same time acknowledging the need to match human experience and feeling: this might seem a dangerously ambitious, if not utopian aim. But it represents the ethical core of Carter's motivation as a composer, and suggests some of the ways in which thematicism remains an essential part of his creativity.

In 1953 Carter wrote revealingly about his efforts to extend the scope of what he calls "my musical flow," and he contended that the most important features of Second Viennese School composers were not twelve-tone routines (or, we might infer, the relatively neoclassical formal qualities that soon became attached to them), but those that had already been established in their earlier, expressionist post-tonal works:

---

[10] Link, "Elliott Carter Talks about his *Harmony Book*," in *HB*, p. 33.
[11] Link, "The Combinatorial Art of Elliott Carter's *Harmony Book*," in *HB*, p. 9.

[12] Meyer and Shreffler, *ECCP*, pp. 253, 256.

the high degree of concentration, lending itself to rapid change and the quick, intense making of points. The use of equally intense melodic shapes, often broken up into short, dramatic fragments, joins with a very varied rubato rhythmic technique to produce a new kind of what might be called instrumental recitative. The rapid increases and decreases of harmonic tension, quick changes of register, and fragmented, non-imitative counterpoint are also worthy of note. This all adds up to a style of remarkable fluidity which seems to have been derived from the late works of Debussy but seen through the expressive extremes that characterise late Romantic German music, particularly Mahler and Richard Strauss.[13]

Among the works by these composers mentioned elsewhere by Carter are *La Mer*, and his description of it as moving "in a shimmering buzz of elegant and mysterious sounds"[14] can be linked to many of his own orchestral tapestries, not least the capriciously flowing finale of *Symphonia*.[15] But Carter also noted that Debussy's music, with the considerable exception of *Pelléas*, had not greatly affected the "emotional tone" of later progressive music. *Pelléas* apart, "there never seems to be any kind of darkness in it":[16] and this is where his Viennese examples – Schoenberg's Five Pieces for Orchestra and *Pierrot lunaire*, Berg's Four Pieces for clarinet and piano and Three Pieces for Orchestra, and Webern's *Bagatelles* for String Quartet – become significant. With these, Carter implies, we get an "emancipated discourse" whose darker tone of voice is the perfect complement to Debussian elegance and mystery. It is these core components, where intense melodic shapes move between fragments and more extended lines, and recitative-like shaping is preferred to tuneful periodicity, to which his late-modern thematicism alludes: and in his concern with "our present experience of living," Carter needs to shape his materials to engage in dialogues, not just to project a sequence of separate identities.

Carter was giving expression to a view of a turbulent half-century of musical history that evidently has much in common with the thinking of the European avant-garde. At the same time, however, he was able to avoid the kind of intransigent Boulezian rhetoric that helped to impede appreciation of European attempts to build constructively and systematically on the foundations of post-tonal expressionism. The polemics of Boulez, Stockhausen and others during the 1950s were emblematic of a well-nigh totalitarian determination to make music new at all costs – an understandable exasperation with the sins of the fathers which had the no less understandable consequence of leaving the sons with the time and the eventual need to

[13] Carter, "To Be a Composer in America" (1953/94), in *CEL*, p. 207.
[14] *Ibid.*, p. 123.
[15] Carter's Latin title comes from "Bulla" (Bubble) by the seventeenth-century metaphysical poet Richard Crashaw. The complete poem, with translations, can be found in the booklet with the 1999 recording of *Symphonia: Sum Fluxae Pretium Spei* (Deutsche Grammophon 459 660–2).
[16] Carter, "The Three Late Sonatas of Debussy" (1959/94), in *CEL*, p. 123.

contemplate how to effect viable accommodations with the attempts of the fathers to "make it new" half a century before. The nature of this "Cold War" mentality in both Europe and the United States has been fully explored in recent musicological and music-theoretical work, one of the most interesting results of which is the different understandings of musical identity to be found in the exceptionally iconic figures of Milton Babbitt and Pierre Boulez respectively.[17] There is a revealing and instructive contrast between what can be thought of as Babbitt's faithfulness to the fundamentals of the serial principle as he saw them – fundamentals which take the style and structure of the music beyond Schoenbergian precepts – and Boulez's more troubled, more history-conscious attempts to devise ways of working with musical materials which depend ultimately on conformity with the Schoenbergian concept of "suspension," whether of tonal identity, thematic recurrence, or formal symmetry. As I argue here, it is with Boulez (and, through Boulez, Schoenberg) that Carter might best be aligned, rather than with Babbitt.

Thematic process and suspended tonality: a context for Carter

Schoenberg studies, and with them our understanding of the cultural as well as the technical elements which served to forge the evolution of musical Modernism, continue to unfold in gratifyingly rich and thought-provoking ways. Most challenging of all, at the time of writing, is the manner in which ways of theorizing extensions and enrichments of diatonic tonality have remained in the forefront of scholarly enterprise, partly in response to convictions about how to answer, and not just dismiss, Schenker's anti-modernist ideology, partly to test the relevance of one non-Schenkerian theory of tonality, Hugo Riemann's, to music which is highly valued but to which Schenker himself gave little or no attention.[18]

The wealth of Riemann-based theoretical studies has not so far been matched where Schoenberg's theoretical work is concerned. Although there were early forays into the kind of "Schenker and Schoenberg" comparisons which the passing, polemical engagements of the theorists themselves served to encourage,[19] there has been rather more emphasis on providing editions and translations of Schoenberg's theoretical works, finished and unfinished, than on working with his theoretical ideas, at least as far as tonality is

[17] For an outline discussion with extensive references, see Whittall, *Serialism*, esp. pp. 122–34 and 171–81.
[18] For introductory discussions, see Klumpenhouwer, "Dualist Tonal Space"; and Bernstein, "Nineteenth-century Harmonic Theory."
[19] See Dahlhaus, "Schoenberg and Schenker."

concerned. That this has begun to change can be seen in the work of Richard Kurth, which introduces an ambitious attempt not only to elucidate such difficult Schoenbergian concepts as fluctuating (*schwebende*) and suspended (*aufgehobene*) tonality, but to build bridges between Schoenberg's earlier and later compositions in the light of these notions. Noting that "the concepts of *schwebende* and *aufgehobene Tonalität* were first described in Schoenberg's 1911 *Harmonielehre*," Kurth observes that "the twelve-tone method which took shape a decade later constitutes … a synthetic extension of both. … While the total abandonment of tonality may have become a basic assumption for some later composers … for Schoenberg the twelve-tone method was not a way to abandon tonality, but instead a systematic way to achieve a complete suspension of tonality: *aufgehobene Tonalität* in the fullest Hegelian sense."[20] The implication is that one reason why "post-tonal" is a preferable blanket term to "atonal" is in leaving open the possibility of "what comes after" retaining certain points of contact with "what went before," rather than requiring the rejection of any such points of contact. But Kurth's ambitions extend beyond the redefining of something basic about the evolving musical language of Schoenberg and those who think like him. He is effectively making the case for a fully functional theory of suspended tonality (or pantonality, or *unvorstellbare* [imperceptible] *Tonalität*: the terminological plurality is rightly endemic) whose long-term legitimacy can be suggested by analogies not only with Hegel but also with Derrida. This is because, as Kurth sees it, the one thing suspended tonality is *not* is some kind of straightforward musical reality. With it, he argues, we enter a "strange utopia … where only the imperceptible can actually bear witness. Schoenberg's argument enacts exactly the kind of paradoxical and supplementary interplay of absence and presence that is analyzed in Derrida's early writings. More important, Schoenberg's concept of an imperceptible tonality also bears deep connections with ideas expressed in *Moses und Aron* and in the second of the Op. 27 Choruses."[21]

But it is another terminological weapon in Kurth's theoretical armory – *Scheintonalitätsmomente* – that resonates most strongly with Carter's late-modern thematicism. Seeking to go beyond what he believes to be the unsatisfactory notion of "tonal reminiscences" in Schoenberg's twelve-tone works, Kurth aims to pin down how "the sense of tonal agency" in such passages as the ending of the Fourth Quartet's first movement

> often has an illusory quality, and it often arises more from mere appearance [*Schein*] than from actual structural function. If we conceive of Schoenberg's twelve-tone

[20] Kurth, "Suspended Tonalities in Schoenberg's Twelve-tone Compositions," 241.

[21] *Ibid.*, 244.

practice as extending *aufgehobene Tonalität* to the point of *Unvorstellbarkeit*, then *Scheintonalitätsmomente* can be understood as fragmentary and supplementary artefacts that reveal how the twelve-tone method suspends tonality. Because Schoenberg's music involves the interplay of balance and imbalance, *Scheintonalitätsmomente* can be understood to result from temporary imbalances in the twelve-tone system's abstract counterbalance of multiple tonal relationships. They are fissures in the twelve-tone structure, and they reveal the suspension of tonality antithetically, in a momentary impression of tonal function that appears as a (Derridean) supplement to the twelve-tone method.[22]

In categorizing the significance of *Scheintonalitätsmomente* as "liminal – if not deconstructive – rather than structural," Kurth does not literally set the systematic (the "classical") against the unsystematic (the "modernist"): nor does he use the point to argue that *unvorstellbare Tonalität* is the fulfillment of Schoenberg's modernist aesthetic. Yet he does claim that *Scheintonalitätsmomente* "reveal in a fleeting tonal representation how Schoenberg's twelve-tone music generally suspends tonality through the abstract counterbalancing of numerous tonal forces."[23] This claim seems to pinpoint that fundamental resistance to synthesis which is at the heart of Modernism. And if that fundamental resistance to synthesis applies in the sphere of chord, harmony, simultaneity where Kurth places it, can it not also migrate to the sphere of musical material shaped into lines that suggest some kind of thematic identity? Might not *Scheinmotive* or *Scheinthemen* be just as important a facet of modernist music as *Scheintonalitätsmomente*? And might it not be the case that it is a useful strategy to think of thematicism (in the traditional sense) as suspended – not eliminated – by the "abstract counterbalancing" of diverse motivic elements – especially if "abstract" can carry with it the idea of ordered materials deriving from unordered materials which imperceptibly control – up to a point – the process and progress of the music?

At the very least, the possibility of conceiving such a kind of thematicism might serve to counter the kind of claim, found in Adorno and reiterated more recently by Gary Tomlinson, that "the specific musical-historical tradition behind Schoenberg, of which he saw himself as the culmination, offered him no access to an unintegrated musical language – a musical language of difference."[24] This is not the place to pursue the problems with an understanding of *Moses und Aron* as excessively unified and organic; still less is it the place to trace in detail the travails of post-tonal analysis which fails to respond sufficiently to the roots of post-tonal initiatives in the Wagnerian balance – sometimes even, often uneven – between the opposing poles of as-smooth-as-possible transition and the fracturing incisions defined

---

[22] *Ibid.*, 247.
[23] *Ibid.*

[24] Tomlinson, *Metaphysical Song: An Essay on Opera*, p. 151.

by Wagner himself as "rhetorical dialectics [*rhetorische Dialectik*]."[25] But if it is to be claimed, for Carter, that he occupies a specially privileged place in the history of Late Modernism on grounds which transcend his mere longevity, the notion of late-modern thematicism could have a useful role to play.

Symphonia I: *Partita* (1993)

Even if, as suggested earlier, Carter's thinking about music has more in common with Boulez's than Babbitt's, his compositions have never sought obvious rapprochements with those of his French *confrère*. Principally, there is far less evidence of centricity as a harmonic and formal principle in the mature Carter than in the later Boulez. Is it therefore equally futile to search Carter's works for "recognizable musical objects" equivalent to Boulez's late modern thematicism? Might Carter's practice after all be closer to Babbitt's non-thematic contextuality? The complexity of this topic can be hinted at by way of the suggestion that (in my terms) Babbitt himself is actually more of a modern classicist than a late modernist: that is, he resists those elements that challenge integrative and connective strategies which late modernists – including Carter – are happy to embrace. Nevertheless, David Schiff, for one, seems to find persuasive evidence of "Classicism" in the later Carter, even if this is defined more in terms of the spirit of the music than of its techniques.[26] This "Classicism" does not require the exclusion of Modernism, as is clear from Schiff's pungent characterization of *Symphonia*'s first movement, *Partita* (1993), as music in which the composer might have "wanted to give the younger generation a lesson in the pleasures of Modernism; the music is angular, brash, chaotic, unpredictable, violent and exhilarating: Carter compared its rapidly changing landscape to the view of the world from a jet plane." And Schiff caps his argument with the terse assertion that "there are no themes and no 'form'. The only formal pattern that the listener may notice is a gradual movement in register," a "narrowing wedge-shaped motion" which, however, "is not carried out continuously."[27]

Yet Schiff finds it difficult to avoid all sense of the systematic controlling the spontaneous and the improvisatory: he notes that the music has "rules" which are rhythmic and harmonic. Rhythmically, the form is underpinned by the binary grid of a large-scale polyrhythm (a sequence of notional attacks every 35th sixteenth note set against another every 34th triplet eighth note). Harmonically, the basis is an all-interval twelve-tone series or "Link" chord;

[25] Wagner used this term in his 1879 essay *On the Application of Music to the Drama.*

[26] For Schiff's initial formulation of this argument, see his "Carter's New Classicism."

[27] Schiff, *MEC*, p. 318.

Ex. 3.2 *Partita*, mm. 120–35, English horn only

		0	1	2	4	7	8
(i)		G♮	G♯	A	B	D	D♯
(ii)		G♮	G♯	A	B	D	D♯
(iii)		E♭	D	C♯	B	G♯	G♮
(iv)	(A)	B♭	B♮	C	D	F	F♯

and the hexachord deriving from the first half of this series (Carter's favored all-triad hexachord [012478]) appears to have a role in the four woodwind solos which are prominent features of the music's design as well as in "the chords that surround them."[28]

Those solos emerge only after other forms of characterization have underlined the general turbulence and lack of sustained melody that Schiff describes. That their function is not simply to provide contrast but a degree of stability is suggested by the way the first, English horn, solo, with its frequent pitch repetitions, gradually assembles the ATH statement quoted in Example 3.1a, and then reinforces the background identity of that collection in several further statements. But the invariant elements of the first half of the line (Example 3.2) never suggest that this recitative is likely to turn into a motivically unified aria. The object which is recognizable here is not so much a particular melodic statement but the process whereby the melody is gradually built up by "recovering" its successive intervals. As Example 3.2

[28] *Ibid.*, p. 319.

Ex. 3.3 *Partita*, mm. 466–72, vln 1 only

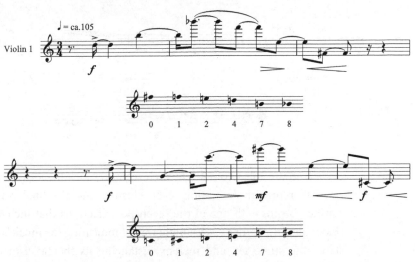

shows, the melody first assembles a particular ordering of the ATH, with a single note, then a trichord, finally the complete hexachord (i): next comes a different permutation of the same hexachord, with more repeated pitches (ii), followed by an inversion sharing all but one of its pcs with the original (iii): the A♭/G dyad which begins the last measure of the third system could of course "belong" to either hexachord (ii) or hexachord (iii). Finally (iv) a transposition of the original ascending version adds an extra, initial pitch (A) to underline the developmental process of expansion involved.

In classical terms, Schiff might be correct: "there are no themes." But there is certainly a process which suggests associations with the kind of connected thinking originally thought of as "thematic," and it serves here to bring the music's modernist dialogues into the clearest relief, as something to be heard as well as felt. Crucially, the phases of *Partita* in which such melodic shapes are not present to the same extent can increasingly be heard in terms of a positive resistance to or suspension of the relatively explicit identities provided by the woodwind solos. The game Carter plays, involving most elementally a shifting between relatively regular and relatively irregular types of material, must aspire to something more than demonstrating the protean capacity of all-trichord hexachords to generate ever-new ideas, something that would risk appearing as negative as the mental condition of having no memory, no capacity of anticipation, and therefore unrelated to "our present experience of living."

At the same time, a comparison of the first solo with its various successors indicates that the latter are more "recognizable" as offshoots or responses to the former than as returns to its ordered pitch-interval materials. There is a particularly forceful, almost motto-like pair of statements in the first violins of versions of the ATH which give prominence to "D-scale" components (Example 3.3) as the movement approaches a startling climax of boldly

Ex. 3.4 *Partita*, mm. 553–56, E♭ clarinet only

declaimed unisons (from 481) which seem to mock the idea that such effects can still represent resolution, even closure: and the final solo, in the E♭ clarinet, begins with one of the seven-pc collections that includes the ATH (Example 3.4), perhaps as a simple way of indicating the music's resistance to stabilizing strategies, and thereby distancing its thematicism further from classical models. Thus, it risks over-simplification for Schiff to claim that the "'bubble' theme" which Carter attaches to *Symphonia* by way of Richard Crashaw's poem "is emblematic not programmatic."[29] The two qualities can and surely do overlap, and one of *Symphonia*'s concerns is to suggest ways of signifying ephemerality by suspending motion even as it appears to be most active, most propulsive. The interval repetitions and the phrasal relations in *Partita* thematicize this process most provocatively, and also most memorably, not least by building possible bridges to comparable processes in the work's remaining movements.

From *Trilogy* for oboe and harp (1992) to *Symphonia* II: *Adagio tenebroso* (1994)

Since the mid-1990s Carter has remained faithful to his preferred modes of characterization, while making less use of polyrhythmic frameworks and form-governing twelve-tone chords. The "new Classicism" has itself begun to age. Yet broader aesthetic associations between Classicism and the Apollonian, as opposed to the Dionysian, spirit, were part of Schiff's initial frame of reference: and they linked in with the perception that Carter's late period was turning out to be less turbulent, less expressionistic, than what had preceded it. The essence of the aging composer's wry, playful approach can be found at the end of the *Trilogy* for oboe and harp, written just before *Partita*: the third movement is called *Immer Neu*, alluding to Rainer Maria

Ex. 3.5a *Trilogy* for oboe and harp, III. *Immer Neu*, ending

Ex. 3.5b String Quartet No. 2, ending, vln 2 only

Ex. 3.5c *What Next?*, mm. 932–34, vocal line only

Rilke's grandly poetic image of music as something which, "ever new, builds out of the most unstable stones her divinely consecrated house in unexploitable space." The ending of *Immer Neu* (Example 3.5a) is certainly fragile, the two instruments converging onto barely audible, rhythmically fragmented common ground. At the same time, however, that common ground falls back for its pitch content on something old and familiar: Carter's favorite all-interval tetrachord [0146] provides closure by appearing in its unordered (or pre-ordered) essence as F♯–G–B♭–C, perhaps shadowing the ending of the Second String Quartet, where the second violin has the last word with D♭–D–F–G (Example 3.5b). An even more explicitly witty, or possibly just sarcastic, allusion of this kind crops up near the end of a work written soon after *Symphonia*, the opera *What Next?*, where a character sings the words "it's only a game" to a particular ordering of the alternative all-interval tetrachord [0137]: in this case G–E♭–B♭–G again, and A, ordering the unordered {B♭, A, G, E♭} (Example 3.5c).

That the special features of Carter's late style need not be seen as contradicting all that had gone before is confirmed by Roger Scruton's 1997 view of Carter's large-scale score from the late 1960s, the Concerto for Orchestra. As the scourge of "antisocial" atonality, Scruton might be expected to give short shrift to this demanding and intricate work. All the more notable, then, is his verdict, that it succeeds "in turning an uncompromising Modernism to the service of joy."[30] Scruton even goes a step further than Schiff's 1998 claim that "the music of the last quarter of the Concerto is perhaps the most exhilarating Carter has ever written."[31] The alleged conjunction between High Modernism – uncompromising Modernism – and exhilaration, even joy, is striking indeed, since it seems to run directly counter to the claim that Modernism, if it is to be authentic, should somehow suggest or reflect a sense of alienation, of endemic melancholia, as composers contemplate the professional and personal challenges which arise as they attempt to live and work within communities that have little understanding of and even less time for their activities. If this represents one's yardstick for "modernist authenticity," then Carter would seem to conform only if it can be accepted that such alienation need not invariably find expression in songs of sorrow and despair.

The later Carter comes closest to such a darker, sorrowful spirit in the central movement of *Symphonia*, *Adagio tenebroso*. Schiff observes that, while Carter has never written religious music, and belongs to no church, the *Adagio tenebroso* embodies "both a solemn ritual and an anguished medi-tation": and he suggests that the music's "desolate, pain-filled landscape" relates to Carter's memories of being taken on a tour of First World War battlefields in the early 1920s. In addition, Schiff proposes that recurrent rising major sixths, C to A, in the movement's melodic material are a deliberate allusion to Beethoven's "heiliger Dankgesang" from the String Quartet, Op. 132 – an expression of hope and confidence that is then dismissed by Carter as no longer possible in a post-tonal, post-classical age; until, that is, a more hopeful, confident mood ("neue Kraft fühlend"?) returns in *Symphonia*'s finale.[32]

Schiff's particular intertextual association – Carter with Beethoven – is by no means implausible. Nevertheless, one should not ignore the degree to which the central movement of *Symphonia* stands in the shadow of its immediate predecessor, the central movement of the *Trilogy* for oboe and harp, *Inner Song*. Just as the *Adagio tenebroso*'s rising sixth C to A, often in the oboe (see Example 3.1b), provides a "recognizable musical object" quite independently of its membership of various unordered collections, so the same interval provides the focus for the most stable, most explicitly invariant stages of *Inner Song* (Example 3.6). That these occur at its center shows Carter's instinct for giving musical life to the primordial familiar post-tonal image of symmetrical pivoting, while the music at the outer extremes of the form is more exploratory, less stable, less connected. Alternatively, one could associate the pitches C and A with Carter's own name, and see his emphasis

---

[30] Scruton, *The Aesthetics of Music*, p. 494.   [32] *Ibid.*, p. 319.
[31] Schiff, *MEC*, p. 299.

Ex. 3.6 *Trilogy* for oboe and harp, II. *Inner Song*, mm. 56–70, oboe only

on them as evidence of self-projection rather than of dialogue with
Beethoven. I have not trawled through Carter's complete works looking for
instances of C–A emphasis in association with the pair of all-interval tetrachords and the single all-trichord hexachord: but I have been struck by the
point in the song collection *Of Challenge and of Love* where the word "echoes"
is allocated the pitches E and C in the vocal line: these pitches are then echoed
in the piano as the composer allows his presence, his identity, to make itself
felt (Example 3.7). After all, *Of Challenge and of Love* was written in 1994,
very much around the time that Carter was also using pitch collections drawn
from a particularly august pair of names in celebratory compositions – Pierre
Boulez in *Esprit Rude / Esprit Doux II*, and Paul Sacher in *A Six-Letter Letter*.

Symphonia III: *Allegro scorrevole* (1996)

Whereas *Partita* and *Adagio tenebroso* were written in fairly close proximity –
only the short piano piece *90+* comes between them in Carter's official work-
list – several compositions separate *Adagio tenebroso* from *Allegro scorrevole*,
including *Of Challenge and of Love* and the String Quartet No. 5. While the
possibility of significant connections between these different pieces cannot be
ruled out, I am concerned here only with the continuing relevance of the
Trilogy for oboe and harp, completed just before *Symphonia* was begun. Like
Inner Song, the *Trilogy*'s finale *Immer Neu* contains plentiful instances of the
trichord [014]: more significant, however, from the criterion of musical
character, of what is audible and memorable, is the extension of this trichord
to generate the tetrachord [0347]. This is not only symmetrical, with the same

Ex. 3.7 *Of Challenge and of Love*, 'Under the Dome' (No. 2), mm. 8–16

[313] interval-class sequence ascending or descending, forwards or back-wards: it embodies the shadow of major/minor triadic combination which often attracts post-tonal composers for the possibilities of hinting at the old cadential, closural stabilities while countering if not entirely contradicting those stabilities (Richard Kurth's *Scheintonalitätsmomente*). In *Immer Neu*

Ex. 3.8 *Allegro scorrevole*, mm. 5–10, vln 1 only

Carter makes particularly pointed use of forms of those trichords and tetrachords in which a kind of broken-chord effect brings a strong eloquence to his
melodic writing. And it is this eloquence, at times seeming to echo, or shadow,
the late-romantic lyricism of Mahler or Berg, which re-emerges with particular
pointedness in *Symphonia*'s *Allegro scorrevole*.

Allegro scorrevole is regarded by Carter as, generically, a scherzo: indeed, a
"Queen Mab scherzo," after Berlioz's in the *Roméo et Juliette* symphony. But
Schiff (who also offers Scriabin's piano piece *Vers la flamme* as a relevant
precursor) implies a more Germanic perspective in noting that Carter's
scherzo is "more dialectical in its form" than Berlioz's, with an initially
"light, fast motion" which is "opposed by a more traditional lyricism which
is finally overcome."[33] Carter's own note does not labor analogies with the
floating, aimless, ungraspable – "charming … inconstant" – image of the
bubble. Rather, he allows for the degree to which even the "flow of soft, rapid
passages that move over the entire range of the sound spectrum" occasionally
"form into thematic material" – implying by this a degree of definition and
stability consistent with thematic identity. As for the "lyrical idea," this is
"developed throughout," which also suggests a process in which initial, basic
elements are extended or elaborated.[34] What (contrasting significantly with
the more fragmented lines of *Partita*) is in some respects an "endless melody,"
with the crucial initial marking "cantabile" (from m. 5), uncoils in ways which
allow for both pitch and interval repetition as a means of off-setting the all-
inclusiveness of the all-interval hexachord.

Example 3.8, from near the beginning of the piece, offers a simple indication of how this process functions: there are eight different pitches (excluding

---

[33] *Ibid.*, p. 322.   [34] Carter, cited in Schiff, *MEC*, p. 322.

immediate repetitions) before a pitch (F) is repeated, but the succession of intervals includes two perfect fifths (one descending, one ascending in compound form). Thus far, difference is much more evident than similarity. But the phrase's continuation, from m. 8, begins with one of those small-scale quasi-sequential repetitions which have become Carter's principal agent of melodic stability – F–A–F♯; A–F♯–A♯ (as RI of the initial [014] trichord). A complex process is therefore set up in which different orderings and transpositions of the [014] trichord provide audible stability in a line which can be interpreted hexachordally but also in relation to F as focal pitch. Above all, the concept of something relatively inchoate forming into "thematic material" and dissolving out again suggests an "organic" mechanism whose capacity for interpretation in terms of either freedom or fixity is entirely open-ended.[35] For example, the complete pc content of the movement's final piccolo line, including F♯ and G as well as the ATH discussed earlier (Example 3.1c), can be parsed abstractly as two [014] trichords – F♯–G–B♭ and E–F–G♯ – spanned by and finally converging into a third – C–B–G♯. That is, assuredly, not the only way in which the pitch-structure of the line might be interpreted. But it is at least one plausible way of understanding the line's thematic relationship to other lines in the movement. While it "suspends" traditional thematic emphasis on literal repetition, it still allows for consistency and connection, and a role, in providing conclusion and closure, which is not merely arbitrary or accidental.

Of course, to attempt to map unordered pitch-class collections onto lines and harmonic sequences as volatile as Carter's is to provide a stark illustration of the apparent mismatch between compositional intuition and analytical systematization. I say "apparent" because it is undeniable that invariants first observed visually can often play a leading role in one's subsequent aural experience of the music, and the potential for deriving exact or related versions of that prominent melodic trichord from Carter's favored all-interval collections is undoubtedly put to work throughout *Allegro scorrevole*. Carter himself mentions the contrast between the continuous, unstable flow of soft, rapid material and a more melodic "idea" that moves between separation and connection but involves consistent development. In turn, Schiff describes the two types of material as "light and heavy," and he sketches a three-section form with coda, as in the ABA' model.[36] The tripartite scheme is fair enough, but the implication of ternary symmetry is less satisfactory. As Schiff's own analysis indicates, it is really a case of three distinct phases in the dialogue between bubbling "passages" and flowing "ideas." In the first phase, flowing

[35] A similar idea is explored in Boland, "'Linking' and 'Morphing'."

[36] Schiff, *MEC*, pp. 322–23.

keeps bubbling in check: in the second phase, the bubbling material itself aspires to more lyric status: in the third phase, bubbling and flowing are more consistently superimposed, the buoyant interaction intensifying as the music flows upwards to disappear on the piccolo's highest G♯. You could even sense that part of Carter's strategy is to play with a degree of recapitulation, since the shapes of the violin melody in Section 3 echo some aspects of the shapes heard in the first section. In effect, the subordination of accompanimental figuration to lyric-melodic development – the placement of such figuration in a complementary, context-creating role – prevents harmony from exercising any kind of determining control. In particular, what Schiff describes as the lyrical idea's "climactic phrase" achieves its most expansive, post-Mahlerian, post-Bergian projection of aspiring optimism (as opposed to despairing melancholia): and it does this without its positive spirit being challenged by harmonic counterweights, still less by any strategy to drag it down to a depressively rooted substructure. So although the coda begins in a spirit of crisis, as if the abandonment of lyricism opens up the possibility of chaotic disintegration, the bubbling figures survive to float free and to fly away into eternal, blissful silence, on the breath of that final all-trichord hexachord.

Epilogue

In a recent essay, Fred Lerdahl argues that "Carter's … musical characters [speaking through the kind of strongly contrasted polyphonic discourse whose origins are found in Ives] are intensely social … In his music, individual behaviours are understood only in the context of other behaviours … Carter projects interacting personalities in lively and often conflicting conversations. The resulting music is vividly dramatic yet non-programmatic." From this, Lerdahl proceeds to the even bolder contention that "Carter creates original forms that are integral to the musical materials yet intelligible in their overall shapes." For Lerdahl it is the "unfolding dramas" of Carter's compositions that "carry the listener through their technical intricacies": and although Lerdahl's main focus of attention is the Second String Quartet of 1959, he is careful to add that "in later works, such as the Concerto for Orchestra and the Fifth Quartet, Carter dispenses with traditional formal references and freely creates intricate formal discourses that nevertheless remain intelligible."[37]

To revert to *Symphonia*, and to *Allegro scorrevole* in particular, in the light of Lerdahl's ideas about formal freedom and dramatic meaning is

---

[37] Lerdahl, "On Carter's Influence," p. 19.

illuminating. For his examples of "emancipated discourse" in an essay from 1958, Carter gave pride of place to Schoenberg's Five Orchestral Pieces, Op. 16:[38] and in praising second Viennese post-tonal music for its production of "what might be called a new kind of instrumental recitative" he clearly had the last of those pieces, "Das obligate Rezitativ," in mind.

Perhaps because that title is so notoriously oblique, "Das obligate Rezitativ" has tended to inspire uncharacteristic degrees of brevity in musicological commentaries. One of the best, by Bryan Simms, makes four useful points: first, that the parent genre of the music is the waltz rather than recitative as a declamatory, relatively fragmented design: second, that sectional divisions are notable for their absence, and that continuity is further enhanced by evident if small-scale motivic recurrences. Simms's third point is that a single leading voice (with the *Hauptstimme* indication) runs throughout the piece, and is "passed every few notes to a different instrument." Fourth, that leading voice is accompanied by "a complex web of fleeting subsidiary lines, creating a texture that Schoenberg later called 'semi-counterpoint'."[39]

Most of these points can also be made about *Allegro scorrevole*, and are indeed given special attractiveness and vitality by the change of genre from waltz to scherzo. What Simms defines as "motives" can equally well be regarded as patterns, or even "recognizable musical objects." But it is also possible that Carter was stimulated by the darker, more expressionistic aspect of Schoenbergian Modernism to transfer Schoenbergian techniques into his own very different, more exuberant, less melancholic world. I am mindful here of Alan Street's discussion of how the Op. 16 Pieces "come to register a double trauma: mourning and melancholia,"[40] in response, that is, to the composer's recent (1908) marital problems and the suicide of his wife's lover, the painter Richard Gerstl. Street argues that, "as the apotheosis of this narrative sequence, the 'Obbligato' or endless 'Recitative' transmits meaning across possibly two discursive fields. Most vitally it represents the cathartic refusal of ending as extinction" (that is, it offers a religious affirmation): in Schoenberg's own words, "if death does mark the end of tragedy, it is still not the end of everything."[41]

In these terms, Street characterizes the creative burden of Schoenberg's early twentieth-century engagement with the transcendent, which would soon lead him to wrestle with the never-to-be-finished oratorio *Die Jakobsleiter* and a range of religious works that are among the modern era's most intense: they are also at an immense remove from Carter's secular ethos. Even so, few have had the opportunity to respond as resourcefully as Carter

---

[38] Carter, "A Further Step" (1958), in *CEL*, p. 6.
[39] Simms, *The Atonal Music of Arnold Schoenberg*, p. 81.

[40] Street, "The Obbligato Recitative," pp. 179–80.
[41] *Ibid.*, 180, citing Schoenberg, *Theory of Harmony*, p. 126.

has to the implications of Schoenberg's early twentieth-century initiatives, which took shape at a stage when the primary impulse behind them was probably more personal, and social, than religious. Carter's cheerfully eloquent acknowledgment of ephemerality and dissolution, while striving to observe his self-declared aim of being neither oblique nor resigned, represents heroic humanism: always vulnerable, always determined to relish the irony of executing complex designs that ultimately vanish into nothingness, at least until the next time (which could always be the last time) they are heard. Placing *Symphonia: Sum Fluxae Pretium Spei* in such late-modern contexts might dilute its strangeness but might also enhance its distinctiveness and humanity. That, in essence, defines the ultimate objective of this essay.

4   Ritornello form in Carter's *Boston* and *ASKO* concertos

Marguerite Boland

Pierre Boulez's 1960 Darmstadt lecture entitled "Form" opens with an important orientation to the modernist reconception of possibilities for large-scale musical organization:

> [In the past] the composer was working in a universe clearly defined by general laws that already existed before he embarked on his composition. From this it followed that all "abstract" relationships implicit in the idea of form could be defined a priori, and this gave rise to a certain number of schemes or archetypes that existed ideally before being realized in any actual work ... This whole scaffolding of "schemes" had eventually to make way for a new conception of form as something that could be changed from one moment to the next. Each work had to originate its own form, a form essentially and irreversibly linked to its "content."[1]

For Elliott Carter, form conceived as a process linked to musical content has been a long-held aesthetic principle of his composition. Be it a large-scale polyrhythmic frame that generates the basic rhythmic material of a piece, textural divisions in the music that derive from exhausting all possible combinations of individual musical characters, or a harmonic structure built out of the coordination of individualized intervallic strands, Carter's compositions have emphatically *originated their own forms*, to borrow Boulez's expression.[2]

In his own essay "A Further Step," written two years before Boulez's lecture, Carter discusses the break with what he called "pre-established patterns" in the twentieth century and explores his idea of an "emancipated musical discourse" in which new music must re-examine musical continuity from the premise that "no item, no unifying principle or method of continuity is self-evident or considered a given part of musical process ..."[3] Carter's own emancipated musical discourse developed in his mature music from his

---

[1] Boulez, *Orientations*, pp. 90–91. For an interesting discussion of other composers' and theorists' presentations at the 1965 Darmstadt symposium "Form in the New Music," see Williams, "New Music, Late Style," 193–97.

[2] For some important studies of Carter's formal processes, see Schiff, "Musical Time: Rhythm and Form," in *MEC*, 1st edn, pp. 23–51; Bernard, "Poem as Non-Verbal Text"; and Bernard, "Elliott Carter and the Modern Meaning of Time."

[3] Carter, "A Further Step" (1958), in *CEL*, p. 5.

interest in the compositional manipulation of musical time. It resulted in a "polyvocal" music where a constant flow of multiple interacting and overlapping streams created an experience of temporal unfolding that was not about traditional thematic *development* but rather about, as Carter puts it, "very vivid moments" and "the process by which these moments came into being and by which they disappeared and turned into other moments."[4]

The idea of form as self-originating and developing out of a process of constantly changing moments seems, at least on the surface, very much at odds with Carter's recent use of ritornello form in the *ASKO Concerto* (2000) and *Boston Concerto* (2002). Not only is ritornello form an archetype that would have earned Carter's designation of "pre-established pattern" in the 1950s, it is also a form to which the continual return of previously heard material is intrinsic – it contains a kind of "self-evident continuity" contrary to Carter's ideal of an "emancipated musical discourse." And yet, while the appearance of ritornello form in Carter's music could never have been predicted, two established aspects of his formal approach make its appearance less incongruous with his overall compositional aesthetic than one might initially suspect. Firstly, in contrast to a composer such as Boulez, Carter has, on more than one occasion, constructed his complex and novel formal processes in a delicate shadow of more traditional formal schemes, as for example David Schiff points out in relation to the Double Concerto (1961) and the Fourth String Quartet (1986).[5] Secondly, it is important not to forget that Carter's interest in the Baroque principle of ensemble contrasts – fundamental to ritornello form – goes back a long time, particularly in his concerto writing. The Double Concerto was the first to employ soloists each accompanied by their own contrasting concertino. This principle was later realized in various ways in the Piano Concerto (1965), Oboe Concerto (1986–87), and Clarinet Concerto (1996). However, it is not until the Clarinet Concerto that the idea of a regular alternation of tuttis and subsections of the ensemble appears as a formal device. In the Clarinet Concerto, the tuttis function more as transitional passages, rather than full-blown formal sections, although they do recur between each of the solo sections, hinting at what is to come in later pieces. Marrying the Baroque principle of ensemble contrasts with the formal ritornello patterning, as Carter does in the *ASKO* and *Boston* concertos, could be seen as a logical extension of this compositional interest.

Nevertheless, what remains surprising is Carter's choice to work so explicitly with a traditional form principally characterized by the repetition of

---

[4] *FW*, p. 99. See also Schiff's discussion of "epiphanic development," *MEC*, 1st edn, pp. 37–40. Compare *FW*, pp. 74–78, for Carter's critique of "moment-form." See also Hasty, "Broken Sequences," 155–73, for an interesting comparison with Wolpe's "ever-advancing moment."
[5] On the Double Concerto, see Schiff, *MEC*, p. 245; on the Fourth Quartet, see *MEC*, p. 86.

previously heard material – something the modernist aesthetic has always eschewed. It is particularly surprising in Carter's music since, throughout most of his career, Carter has been an outspoken critic of repetition and obvious formal structures in contemporary music, especially as found in post-modern musical styles such as Minimalism and Neo-Romanticism. Importantly, however, these views were not developed in response to the rise of a post-modern aesthetic but rather have had a much longer history in the development of Carter's aesthetic stance. As Eisenlohr points out,[6] already in 1938, when Carter was still composing in an American neoclassical style, he had articulated his criticism of the passive listener and his views on the responsibility of composers to compose a "living message" about the world around them, which should be communicated to an "intelligent listener," who in turn is responsible for actively listening to grasp this message.[7] Excessive repetition of musical ideas and musical forms that rely on classical or romantic models are clearly experienced as anathema to these aims and are mostly the target of Carter's earlier critiques.[8] Carter's views echo his modernist predecessors, particularly Schoenberg and later Adorno. Carter's intelligent and "active listener," for example, has resonances with Schoenberg's ideal listener who must have "an alert and well-trained mind."[9] While his early critiques seem to be motivated by a desire to promote the humanist and reflective values of new music,[10] Carter's later criticisms also have definite parallels with Adorno's concern not only with the effect on the listener but with the features of repetitive music that facilitate capitalist production and marketability. Carter cites Adorno's "regression of listening"[11] and, like Adorno, he targets the effects of repetitive music that mimic negative influences on the development of a civilized society – advertising, consumerism, passive engagement, conformism, propaganda and, at its extreme, fascism.[12] In interviews over the last decade, Carter has maintained

---

[6] Eisenlohr, *Komponieren als Entscheidungsprozess*, p. 210.

[7] Carter, "Orchestras and Audiences; Winter, 1938," in *WEC*, pp. 28–31. For further references to Carter's writing on the active listener, see Eisenlohr, *ibid.*, pp. 208–12. See also Schmidt, "'I try to write music that will appeal to an intelligent listener's ear.' On Elliott Carter's String Quartets," in this volume.

[8] See many of Carter's reviews for *Modern Music* in the 1930s; for example his critique in 1937 of Chavez's *Sinfonia India* (*WEC*, p. 17); in 1939 of Harris's Second Symphony (*WEC*, p. 61) and Sibelius's music (*WEC*, pp. 64–65). See also Carter's "Music of the 20th Century," p. 18, cited in Eisenlohr, *Komponieren als Entscheidungsprozess*, p. 225.

[9] Schoenberg, *Style and Idea*, pp. 401 and 102–04. See also the discussion in Garcia, "On and On."

[10] For example Carter, "Music as a Liberal Art" (1944), in *CEL*, pp. 309–13.

[11] Johnston, "Elliott Carter's Imagery Drawn from Modern Life," cited in Eisenlohr, *Komponieren als Entscheidungsprozess*, pp. 201, 225. An earlier transcript of this interview with Carter is published in *ECCP*, quote on p. 253.

[12] See Johnston, "Elliott Carter's Imagery"; Kerner, "Creators on Creating: Elliott Carter," cited in van Dyck-Hemming, "Diskurse zur 'Musik Elliott Carters'", p. 154 (see also pp. 154–57 for a discussion of parallels between Carter's comments and the thinking of the Frankfurt school); Restagno, *Elliott Carter in Conversation with Enzo Restagno,*

this position toward repetition, particularly as it is manifest in Minimalism in the arts.[13]

Yet neither Schoenberg, Adorno nor Carter ignore the fact that ridding music of repetition altogether threatens comprehensibility, continuity, and logical coherence.[14] The modernist avoidance of repetition is thus not a question of the presence or absence of repetition *per se*, but rather a question of what is repeated, what is changed, and how this is done. In addressing these questions, Carter approaches the perception of musical similarity and difference as something more complex than the mere recognition of the literal or varied repetition of musical shapes. Instead he brings into play the coordination of a whole range of musical characteristics that cue various sorts of repetitions. In *Flawed Words and Stubborn Sounds* (1971), Carter cites the many coloristic, rhythmic, and textural effects that assist the listener to recognize important structural and thematic returns in Beethoven's music – without the listener necessarily following the underlying tonal harmonic structure. He parallels this with his own practice, in which there are no themes or formal returns but in which many different parameters are coordinated "in order to produce a noticeable and meaningful effect." The coordination of "harmonic sounds … [with] tempos and rhythmic ideas … form[s] characteristic kinds of events that are distinct and follow-able, not only because of their pitch-structure but because of their other coordinated aspects."[15] In a discussion of his Third Quartet (1971) with Charles Rosen, Carter also addresses the question of repetition and formal coherence:

> What may be interesting about the form is that none of the material ever repeats literally, and this is characteristic of many of my pieces ever since the First Quartet. They never actually repeat the same theme, but they are always improvizing [*sic*] on a basic piece of material that holds together all the various things that are being played. There will sometimes be repetitions of certain speeds and textures that dominate different sections … but the form is not a form in which there is literal repetition, only a constant repetition of a general principle … Maybe you can find one chord that is the same from beginning to end, but the main thing is the sense of constant growth and change.[16]

p. 58; Scheffer, *A Labyrinth of Time*, 6′15″. See also Fink, *Repeating Ourselves*, pp. 62–64. For a discussion of Carter's views on music and politics, see Eisenlohr, *Komponieren als Entscheidungsprozess*, pp. 226–40.

[13] For example, Tusa, Interview with Elliott Carter; Oteri, "In the First Person: Elliott Carter"; Norris, "Minimalism is Death."

[14] Paddison, *Adorno's Aesthetics of Music*, pp. 176–79, esp. p. 179; Schoenberg, *Style and Idea*, p. 399; also Haimo, "Developing Variation and Schoenberg's Serial Music," 349–65, esp. 350–51.

[15] *FW*, p. 109. See also Carter, "Shop Talk by an American Composer" (1960), in *CEL*, pp. 218–19.

[16] Rosen, "An Interview with Elliott Carter," p. 39.

The need to create coherence through consistent and related musical material is balanced with a constant flow of changing musical shapes. Carter's "constant growth and change" is not Schoenbergian developing variation, since there is no gradual transformation of material from one shape to the next. Nor are Carter's "very vivid moments" completely block-like in a Stravinskian sense; instead there is a flow and elasticity to the motion from texture to texture. Carter himself refers to the influence of late Debussy on this aspect of his formal thinking.[17] Debussy's non-systematic and discontinuous presentation of distinct musical ideas is more akin to a stream-of-consciousness approach to musical time, neither developmental nor consisting of a collage or moment-form approach.[18] Indeed, the "constant change and growth" of Carter's forms and his belief that "music should be continuously surprising, [but] it should be so in a sense that whatever happens should continue an already-perceived ongoing process or pattern"[19] resonates with Richard Parks's discussion of "kinetic form" in Debussy's music: "Kinetic form arises from the organization of discontinuities and imparts the sense of motion that is such an important aspect of musical experience ... Kinetic form derives coherence from a consistent pattern of *change* of a particular type ..."[20]

Compositionally, the question at issue here is how to establish a coherent vocabulary of musical shapes and ideas – which requires a certain amount of reinforcement (that is, repetition) – while at the same time creating constant musical motion through change, and avoiding any sense of stagnation associated with repetition or sectional return. In his music from the Second String Quartet onwards, Carter's well-known techniques of defining musical character types – by way of a range of individual "behavior patterns" determined by fixing parameters such as interval, rhythmic pattern, speed, expressive style – avoided a musical logic based on thematic or motivic repetition; in other words, pitch could essentially change freely, while other coordinated parameters created a perceptible musical coherence.[21] Presenting these character types as distinct but simultaneous musical streams – and giving each its own discontinuous unfolding over the course of a piece – has resulted in

[17] *FW*, p. 98.

[18] Carter sees himself as having developed this aspect of Debussy's music further in his own music. See Carter, "The Three Late Sonatas of Debussy" (1959/94), in *CEL*, pp. 122–33; Schiff, *MEC*, p. 39; and also Eisenlohr, *Komponieren als Entscheidungsprozess*, pp. 251–52. On form in Debussy, see Parks, *The Music of Claude Debussy*, pp. 201–55. For some other relevant perspectives on Debussy's forms, see Wheeldon, "Interpreting Discontinuity in the Late Works of Debussy,"

97–115; and Greenbaum, "Debussy, Wolpe, and Dialectical Form," 343–59.

[19] *FW*, pp. 87–88.

[20] Parks, *The Music of Claude Debussy*, p. 233. My thanks to John McCaughey for making me aware of this reference.

[21] See Heinemann, "Composition with Intervals: Melodic Invention in Elliott Carter's Recent Concertos," in this volume for a discussion of restrictions on pitch choice resulting from Carter's instrumental interval repertoires.

many and varied "combinatorial" forms, which avoid sectional and repetitious structures.[22]

Noticeably different – in light of this treatment of form and repetition particularly characteristic of Carter's middle-period music – is the ease with which the sectional ritornello structures in the *ASKO* and *Boston* concertos are grasped on first listening.[23] Unlike the Baroque concerto grosso, where the ritornellos were an important structural means of stabilizing tonal regions, reinforcing themes, and providing a coherence to the (still novel) virtuosic escapades of the instrumental solos,[24] here the ritornellos get their identity not from any traditional thematic return or harmonic stability but because of the memorable tutti *textures*. In the *Boston Concerto*, the pizzicato/staccato texture is so unusual and striking that Charles Rosen's observation about the solo classical concerto – "[t]he most important fact about concerto form is that the audience waits for the soloist to enter, and when he stops playing they wait for him to begin"[25] – could be applied here in reverse: when the tutti gives way to the soloists, we wait for the tutti to return. This surprisingly light yet energetic orchestral sound creates an effect of shimmering movement with its frequent repetition of short single pitches and pitch intervals in individual instruments. The allusion to the "rain" in the lines of the William Carlos Williams poem accompanying the concerto is inescapable, and the listener is undoubtedly expected to make the association. By contrast, the *ASKO* ritornellos' loud sustained tutti chords, spread across a consistently wide registral space, appear as static monolithic objects periodically interposed between the flowing counterpoint of the smaller concertino sections. While Carter has not identified any poetic or textual association with the *ASKO Concerto*, the orchestral sonority and static rhythmic treatment of the tutti chords are reminiscent of Varèse's chord masses and what Jonathan Bernard has termed Varèse's "frozen music" – particularly in *Intégrales*.[26]

These are not pieces that Carter could have written in the 1960s, when the self-evidence of the form and the repetitive structure would have grated with an avant-garde aesthetic. Yet the treatment of repetition here is decidedly modernist. In fact, it can be read – without necessarily implying intentionality on the part of the composer – as containing a critical engagement with postmodern stylistic trends, particularly of minimalist repetition and the adoption of traditional forms. In these pieces, however, the engagement is unlike the

[22] Schiff outlines many such forms in *MEC*. See also Bernard's analysis of the Concerto for Orchestra in "Poem as Non-verbal Text," pp. 169–204.

[23] Link argues that, since the 1980s, Carter's avoidance of repetition has given way to an approach allowing for the "recycling" of compositional materials (see "Elliott Carter's Late Music," in this volume).

[24] Talbot, "The Italian Concerto," p. 45.

[25] Rosen, *The Classical Style*, p. 196.

[26] Bernard, "Varèse's Space, Varèse's Time," pp. 149–55.

deliberate symbolic critique of pitch repetition at the end of *A Symphony of Three Orchestras*, where Carter seems to be implying, through the latent program of the piece, that minimalist repetition represents a kind of death.[27] Instead, these pieces might be heard as an ironic commentary on repetition: it is quite surprising to discover the myriad of ways in which Carter creates the effect of return when in fact very little is actually being repeated and there are certainly no literal repetitions. The unavoidable ease with which the ear makes connections between similar sounds means that only very little need stay exactly the same in order for the listener to associate sonic events, thus allowing for the "constant growth and change" in musical content that Carter prizes so highly, without losing the effect of return.

The traditional ritornello form would appear, on the surface at least, to have been adopted less critically in these two concertos. However, a detailed listening to Carter's particular adaptation of ritornello form reveals a more complex formal design. In both pieces, a secondary linear formal process extends across the sectional boundaries and pattern of return, one determined by the discontinuous unfolding of the musical content. In each piece, there is a clear division of basic musical content between the ritornellos and the contrasting concertino sections with which they alternate. Broadly speaking the ritornellos, with their focus on whole ensemble playing, emphasize the vertical pitch dimension by way of vertically ordered twelve-tone chords prolonged in various ways. By contrast, the concertinos – each very different from the other – unfurl long contrapuntal melodies that emphasize the movement and interplay of lines over time. Line and chord are in a sense treated as distinct musical entities and partitioned between the two sections, giving them contrasting characters similar to the partitioning of interval repertoires, speeds, and "behavior patterns" in previous compositions. However, if this characterization of sections holds true in a general sense, it is also precisely the chord–line distinction that begins to blur and change over the course of both pieces, and this process, as we shall see, provides a subtle yet powerful overarching linear continuity overlaid onto the cyclic ritornello form. This reading posits a more complex and ambiguous continuity to the *ASKO* and *Boston* concertos than the term ritornello form implies. In creating a new kind of multi-layered formal design, the manner of Carter's engage-ment with the "pre-established" ritornello form represents less a departure from, and more a new facet of, his continuing aesthetic concern for an "emancipated musical discourse."

---

[27] Carter: "one repeated pattern is like death." In Kerner, "Creators on Creating: Elliott Carter," cited in van Dyck-Hemming, "Diskurse zur 'Musik Elliott Carters'," p. 156. See Noubel's interpretation of the static repetition in this passage in *LTF*, pp. 181–85, particularly p. 185. Thanks to John Link for bringing this to my attention.

Boston Concerto ritornellos: the "rain" texture and its transformation

The *Boston Concerto*[28] is in essence Carter's second concerto for orchestra and these two concertos are a good illustration of the contrasts between what are now considered Carter's middle-period and his late-period styles.[29] The earlier Concerto for Orchestra (1969) has as a literary model St. John Perse's epic poem *Winds* that "describes winds blowing over the American plains destroying old dried-up forms and sweeping in the new."[30] Bernard has shown many parallels between the "cosmic character" of the poem and the "grand scale" on which Carter's music is conceived, particularly with respect to the density of ideas and the complexity of formal conception.[31] By contrast, the lighter and more transparent *Boston Concerto* suggests parallels with the intimacy of William Carlos Williams's poem *Rain*, the opening lines of which are quoted in the score. In *Rain*, the outside – where the rain ("the spring wash / of your love") falls freely, cleansing and transforming everything it touches – is juxtaposed with the inside – where "the priceless dry / rooms" hide material riches, secrets and desires ("all the whorishness of our delight"). Inside, the rain can only be heard and seen but its "drips," "drops," and "unworldly love" which, by their very nature, will "bathe every / open / object of the world" and transform it, are kept at a protective distance.[32] Just as the ritornellos suggest a parallel with the outside rain of the poem, so the concertinos evoke the more emotionally intense and closed inner spaces, with the accompanying bursts of *staccatissimo* chords from other sections of the orchestra alluding to the perception of the rain that continues to fall outside. Formally, the concertinos can be heard as a series of tableaux each enacting a self-contained scene in a gradually unfolding drama.[33]

While the ritornellos continually repeat the "rain" texture, the returns are never static; each ritornello, in fact, presents a very different kind of rain. To begin with, the instrumentation of the tuttis is constantly changing. The ritornellos, which Carter first labeled "interlude" but later "tutti" in his sketches, are in fact only true tuttis in the opening and closing ritornellos (see Table 4.1). In the remaining ritornellos, the lower-sounding instruments are generally excluded (except in the occasional full tutti chords), which helps to keep the sound very light; and

---

[28] *Boston Concerto* is dedicated to Carter's wife Helen and written as a "thank-you" piece for the Boston Symphony Orchestra. See Meyer and Shreffler, *ECCP*, p. 323.

[29] See Link, "Elliott Carter's 'Late Music'?," 2–3.

[30] Schiff, *MEC*, p. 291.

[31] Bernard, "Poem as Non-Verbal Text," pp. 169–204; quotes on p. 180.

[32] Williams, *Asphodel*, pp. 43–46.

[33] Others have also noted a dramatic trajectory across the concertinos, for example Link, "Elliott Carter's 'Late Music'?"; Lister, "Boston, Symphony Hall: Harbison's *Requiem* and Carter's *Boston Concerto*," 38.

Table 4.1 Formal sections in the *Boston Concerto*

Section	mm.	Orchestration	Expressive marking	Tempo
Ritornello 1	1	**tutti** (full)	***Allegro staccatissimo***	♩ = 90
Concertino 1	29	flutes/clarinets	*Lento, teneramente*	𝅗𝅥 = 54
Ritornello 2	74	**tutti** (no fl/cl in 1st half) (no pf/hrp/vibs)	***Tempo primo***	♩ = 90
Concertino 2	91	piano/harp/vibs	*Meno mosso*	♩ = 72
Ritornello 3	119	**tutti** (no pf/hrp/vib) (no basses)	***Tempo primo***	♩ = 90
Concertino 3	141	violas/basses	*Meno mosso*	♩ = 60
Ritornello 4	164	**tutti** (no brass)	***Tempo primo***	♩ = 90
Concertino 4	190	brass	*Lento, sostenuto*	𝅗𝅥 = 36
Ritornello 5	221	**tutti** (strings only)	***Tempo primo***	♩ = 90
Concertino 5	244	oboes/English horn/bassoon	*Più mosso*	♩ = 120
Ritornello 6	281	**tutti** (no strings)	***Tempo primo***	♩ = 90
Concertino 6	305	violins/cellos	*Maestoso – molto espr.*	♩ = 72
Ritornello 7	344–58	**tutti** (full)	***Tempo primo***	♩ = 90

the piano only makes an appearance in ritornello 6 (Rit.6). Furthermore, each set of concertino instruments is withheld from either the preceding or following ritornello (or sometimes from both, as for concertino 2 and 4). This orchestration may be read metaphorically: just as the rain cannot enter the internal spaces, so each of the internal spaces is in turn excluded from the touch of the falling rain.

In addition to instrumentation, textural differentiation is crucial to the piece's form and to the process of change across the ritornellos. In the main, the concertinos consist of a polyphony of instrumental lines (the chordal brass chorale at the center being the most significant exception), while the hallmark of the ritornellos is the fast, reiterated, and oscillating notes that form chords of varying densities. This is most strikingly illustrated by the opening ritornello: a *forte* attack on the down beat of m. 1 consisting of strummed quadruple stops in the strings with guiro and wood chimes (whose sound is left to decay gradually), and fast staccato sextuplets in flutes and clarinets oscillating on a major second (see Example 4.1). On beat two, strings reiterate two pizzicato notes each, introducing the familiar all-interval tetrachord 18 (AIT 18 – [0146]) and all-trichord hexachord (ATH) in a fragmented 4 against 3 pattern that leads to a second strummed chord across mm. 2–3.[34] All the notes in these

[34] This opening was only added after many of the tutti sections had been composed, as evidenced from a renumbering of measure numbers during the composition of the piece. Initially Carter began the piece not with the declamatory down-beat chord but with an up-beat gesture similar to the final score's mm. 3.3–4. *Boston Concerto* folder, Elliott Carter Collection, Paul Sacher Foundation. All sketch material referred to in this chapter was viewed with the kind permission and generous financial support of the Paul Sacher Foundation.

Ex. 4.1 *Boston Concerto*, mm. 1–3

measures are part of a single fixed-register twelve-tone chord (TTC). With the exception of a few denser measures following the opening (mm. 3–6),[35] this first ritornello realizes the rain texture using the repertoire of AITs, ATH, and TTC chord types arranged to encompass the wide registral span of the orchestra. These spatially ordered chords are shaped into a variety of gestures and mostly rhythmically activated over one to three measures by way of reiterated staccato and pizzicato pitches and pitch intervals.

The next time such a clear chordal texture returns, however, is not until the final ritornello of the piece, and in quite a different form. The final ritornello in fact intensifies the chordal texture, doing away with any varied gestures and having the entire orchestra reiterate gentle patters and sprinkles of single

---

[35] Here five-note chords and three-note chains of ATHs change on every subdivision of the beat.

notes across four TTCs (none of them repeated from Rit.1). These chords gradually fade out over a sequence of ATHs and finally end with the strings playing a single pizzicato B3 (suggesting a reference to the piece's title). The effect is like the petering out of raindrops at the end of a rain shower. However, the sound is not one of static repetition, but rather one of subtle change and movement of pitch and harmony. Carter achieves this effect by using a sequence of chord transformations that produce a number of pitch and interval "reflections" from the first to the last chord. On a sketch page for the final ritornello (reproduced on staff (i) in Example 4.2 with my annotations below), Carter notates four TTCs in a sequence that also shows common tones between the first three chords (asterisked below in the example).[36] The four chords are vertical realizations of a single all-interval (AI) row class of the QI-type,[37] built from two chromatic hexachords. The transpositional relationship between the rows is given at (iii) in Example 4.2 and the chord progression across the final ritornello is shown on the analytical staff (ii). As the example shows, firstly the interval order from low to high of chord I is reversed in chord II, while the boundary pitches F1 and B6 are maintained. Chord III then changes boundary pitches to C♯1 and D7 and inverts all of chord II's intervals; however, the pcs of its adjacent chromatic hexachords remain the same as those of chord II (bottom pcset {456789}, top pcset {te0123}). Finally, chord IV reverses chord III's interval ordering while maintaining boundary pitches C♯1 and D7, mirroring the relationship of chords I and II. The end result of this transpositional sequence is that the pcs of chord I's two hexachords swap registral positions in chord IV while each maintains their interval ordering (shown on the right of staff [ii]). The harmonic progression can be heard as a kind of "prolongation" of the cadential harmony. Chords II and III occupy a mere two measures but, because of common tones and interval structure, nonetheless facilitate a subtle transition from chord I to chord IV, creating a sense of motion that breaks up what would otherwise be a static repetition.

The intervening ritornellos – Rit.2 to 6 – all unmistakably return to the rain soundscape. However, none of the material is ever repeated. What remains unchanged is the shared *Allegro staccatissimo* character always expressed by

---

[36] In the sketch, chord IV is notated a few staves down the page and includes an additional C7 that is part of chord III rather than chord IV. The 8ve signs shown in brackets are not included in the sketch but from the score and sketches are clearly intended. In chord III, Carter's accidental omission of a ledger line means the notated B♮1 should instead be G♯1 as in the score (and notated here in parentheses).

[37] In QI-type rows "the interval-class sequences of their two hexachords are identical, projected as complementary intervals." Koivisto, "Syntactical Space and Registral Spacing in Elliott Carter's *Remembrance*," 159. On the Q-operation, see Morris and Starr, "The Structure of All-Interval Series."

Ex. 4.2 *Boston Concerto*, final ritornello (i) transcription of Carter's sketch; (ii) pitch and interval relationships between chords; (iii) row transformations

(i)

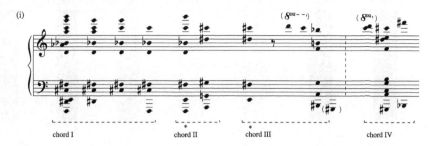

chord I   chord II   chord III   chord IV

(ii)

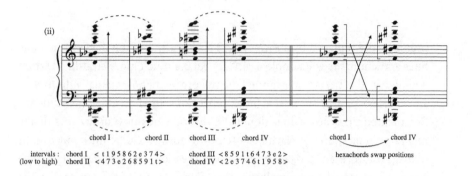

chord I   chord II   chord III   chord IV   chord I   chord IV

intervals :   chord I   < t 1 9 5 8 6 2 e 3 7 4 >   chord III < 8 5 9 1 t 6 4 7 3 e 2 >   hexachords swap positions
(low to high)   chord II < 4 7 3 e 2 6 8 5 9 1 t >   chord IV < 2 e 3 7 4 6 t 1 9 5 8 >

(iii)

row A = {5, 3, 4, 1, 6, 2} {8, t, 9, 0, 7, e} realized as chord I
RT4I(A) = {5, 9, 4, 7, 6, 8} {2, t, 3, 0, 1, e}   chord II
RT9(A) = {8, 4, 9, 6, 7, 5} {e, 3, t, 1, 0, 2}   chord III
T1I (A) = {8, t, 9, 0, 7, e} {5, 3, 4, 1, 6, 2}   chord IV

way of the same articulation (pizzicato in the strings, staccato in the rest of the orchestra) and the same rhythmic layering (beat subdivisions of 6 and 3 against 4 at a tempo of MM 90). However, the pitch reiterations and chordal textures that characterize the first and last ritornellos are transformed into much more rapidly changing pitch successions and more stratified, contrapuntal textures. And while recognizable musical gestures, harmonies, and rhythmic figures recur, they nevertheless always do so in a transformed and unique musical context.

This textural transformation underpins a secondary formal process that shapes the discontinuous succession of ritornello sections across the piece. As can be seen in Example 4.3, the chordal texture gradually moves to a single melodic line at the center of the piece and back again to the exclusively chordal ending. Melodic fragments which are first introduced in the opening ritornello – with a short trumpet call and a response from the horns at mm. 14–18 – become more extended in Rit.2. Here the clear TTCs of Rit.1 are

Ex. 4.3 Textural transformation across *Boston Concerto* ritornellos

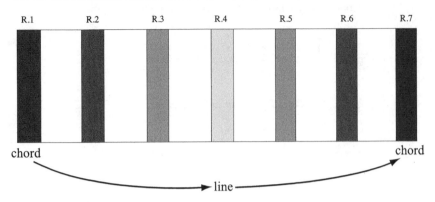

momentarily replaced by a series of ATHs rapidly shifting between melodic lines and chords (see Example 4.4).[38] By Rit.3 a much more stratified texture emerges: as the TTCs that spanned the full orchestra now virtually disappear, so do most of the successive note repetitions in individual instruments. Fragmented pizzicato strings doubled by woodwinds now only occasionally reiterate pitches; erratic clarinets attempt to form melodic lines but cannot manage more than a dyad or two in succession (see Example 4.5). The harmonic materials are equally layered. Each strand of the texture has its own linear motion and lacks the clear coordination of the TTCs and ATHs that previously unified the orchestral sound. At the midpoint of the piece, Rit.4, the texture makes a final transformation away from a chordal texture to a linear one. This ritornello presents a continuous melodic line built of ATH and AIT collections that weaves its way through the whole section (an extract of this line can be seen in Example 4.6). However the line is divided between (primarily) piccolo, xylophone, and pizzicato first violins, as indicated by the *Hauptstimme* brackets in the score. The melody maintains the rhythmic values of the rain texture – beats are divided into sixteenths against sextuplet sixteenths – making for a very fast and intense line, with the high register of the piccolo and xylophone dominating. The accompaniment also retains the pizzicato/staccato character of the rain texture, but the instruments move quite independently with little harmonic coordination. Only towards the end of the ritornello do strings and woodwinds combine more frequently to articulate irregular pulses of AIT and ATH chord attacks. Following the melodic texture of this central section, Rit.5 (for strings alone) and Rit.6 (largely without strings) each in their own way reintroduce the reiterated

---

[38] ATHs and AITs are indicated using Carter's set class numbering. Transposition levels indicated on Examples 4.4 and 4.6 refer to transpositions of the prime form of the set class.

Ex. 4.4 *Boston Concerto,* ritornello 2, mm. 74–77

notes and chords of the rain texture, finally leading back to the full tutti *staccatissimo* chords of the piece's closure.

This transformation of the rain texture across the piece, from chordal to melodic back to chordal texture, creates a dynamic process of change that lends an arch-shaped trajectory to the otherwise repetitive ritornello form. Within this process, certain musical parameters (especially tempo, rhythm, and articulation) are coordinated to create "distinct and followable events" while other parameters (pitch, harmony, instrumentation, texture) are constantly altered to create change and movement from moment to moment while also contributing to an over-arching continuity. Parks's description of "kinetic form" is once again useful in thinking about this process of change and continuity. According to Parks, kinetic form manifests itself through "tendencies," for example:

Ex. 4.5 *Boston Concerto*, ritornello 3, mm. 132–34

a series of entrances separated by ever-shorter durations; [a series] of ever-expanding register extremes across a fluctuant register-field; or of ever contracting formal units …; a coordinated series of any type, even embracing several parameters at once. Kinetic formal units are defined by the boundaries of tendencies of increase or decrease in any musical parameter and may be perceived as a sense of motion towards or receding from these boundaries. A kinetic tendency may interact with other organizing features to capture the listener's attention and induce a sense of activity which has, as its object, a goal or goals.[39]

The motion across the *Boston Concerto* ritornellos can be understood as being driven by such a kinetic tendency, operating across the immediately obvious sectional divisions and providing the *Boston Concerto* with a secondary layer of formal unfolding that is more temporally directed. "Kinetic tendency" is also a powerful way of understanding the secondary formal process in the *ASKO Concerto*, as we will see next.

---

[39] Parks, *The Music of Claude Debussy*, p. 233.

Ex. 4.6 *Boston Concerto*, ritornello 4, mm. 167–71

"Thematic" return in the *ASKO Concerto* ritornellos

Carter's *ASKO Concerto* for chamber ensemble was commissioned by the Dutch ASKO ensemble, a sixteen-member group consisting of five woodwinds, three brass, five strings, harp, piano, and percussion.[40] Table 4.2 lays out the pattern of alternation between ritornello and concertino material. The concertinos have a unique expressive character and instrumental grouping, with each instrument appearing in only one concertino. The concertinos start out alternating between duos and trios, but this pattern is broken toward the end with a quintet followed by a bassoon solo.[41] The tutti ensemble, on the other hand, plays predominantly *Quasi maestoso*; even in the last two ritornellos, where the indication is not explicitly given in the score, the *maestoso* character is maintained. Before addressing the question of large-scale form in the *ASKO Concerto*, we will look at how repetition manifests itself in the ritornellos and how the first ritornello sets up elements of the piece's larger formal processes.

Like the *Boston Concerto*, the *ASKO Concerto* divides line and chord between concertinos and ritornellos: the concertinos consist of a counterpoint

---

[40] Since 2008 the ASKO and Schoenberg ensembles have merged into a group of larger forces. See http://www.askoschoenberg.nl/.

[41] Carter later extracted the bassoon line and turned it into a free-standing piece for solo bassoon entitled *Retracing*.

Table 4.2 Formal sections in the *ASKO Concerto*

Section	mm.	Orchestration	Expressive marking	Tempo
Ritornello 1	**1**	**tutti**	*Quasi maestoso*	♩**= 96**
Concertino 1	20	trio: oboe/horn/viola	*Giocoso*	♩= 96
Ritornello 2	**56**	**tutti**	*Quasi maestoso*	♩= 96
Concertino 2	73	duo: clarinet/double bass	*Allegretto lyrico*	♩= 115+
Ritornello 3	**112**	**tutti**	*Quasi maestoso*	♩= 96
Concertino 3	125	trio: bass clarinet/ trombone/cello	*Tranquillo*	♩= 60
Ritornello 4	**162**	**tutti**	*Agitato*	♩= 90
Concertino 4	169	duo: trumpet/violin 1	*con intensitá*	♩= 54
Ritornello 5	**213**	**tutti**	*Quasi maestoso*	♩=54
Concertino 5	221	quintet: piccolo/xylophone/ celeste/harp/violin2	*Leggierissimo*	♩= 144
Ritornello 6	**262**	**tutti**	*ff–f*	♩= 144
Concertino 6	268	solo: bassoon	*con umóre*	♩= 96
Ritornello 7	**292–96**	**tutti**	*ff–f*	♩=96

of melodic lines while the ritornellos continually return to widely spaced tutti chords. Unlike the *Boston Concerto*, however, the chords in the *ASKO Concerto* form loud, sustained tutti gestures that might be mistaken for literal repetitions on first listening because of their similarity. One of the prominent shared features of these chords is their harmonic content. The vast majority of the tutti chords are "Link" chords – the subset of the all-interval (AI) twelve-tone series which has the ATH as adjacent notes.[42] While Carter does not appear to give special attention to the ATH property of these "Link" chords, he does consistently highlight a five-note subset of the ATH, pentad 31 ([01367]),[43] which, together with pentad 36 ([02368]) and their aggregate forming partners, septad 31 ([0123679)] and 36 ([0135679]),[44] are singled out as principal harmonies for the *ASKO Concerto* in a number of Carter's pre-compositional sketch pages.[45] Pentad 36 is a subset of the ATH complementary hexachord 36 ([012568]). Both pentads and septads 31 and 36 contain the two all-interval tetrachords (AITs) – tetrachords 18 ([0146]) and 23 ([0137]).[46] In a succinct sketch, transcribed in Example 4.7, Carter shows the shared AIT pitch-class content for the two pentads and septads by adding single pitches and trichords respectively to the initial AIT collections (Carter labels the sets above the staff; the labels below are my addition). Thus while focusing on five- and seven-note collections, Carter's favored ATH and AITs remain the foundation of his pitch

---

[42] Carter, *HB*, pp. 358–61.
[43] It should be noted that the pitches of the pentads 31 extracted from the AI chords are only very occasionally contiguous.
[44] After the first reference, I will refer to set classes using only Carter's numbering. For a full correspondence of Carter's numbering with Forte's, see Carter, *HB*, pp. 23–26.
[45] *ASKO Concerto* folder, Elliott Carter Collection, Paul Sacher Foundation.
[46] Pentads 31 and 36 are in fact the only two pentads to contain both AITs.

Ex. 4.7 *ASKO Concerto*, transcription of Carter's sketch

language for the piece. These five- and seven-note collections are made explicit in the orchestration of the first tutti chords of each ritornello (see Example 4.8). After each full tutti attack of an AI chord, a smaller group of instruments sustains one of these pentad/septad subsets. Pitches are principally kept in fixed register thus maintaining a static harmonic field with changing instrumental color. This is particularly clear at the opening of the piece where the same AI chord is reiterated three times. The opening gestures of each ritornello are also orchestrated in the same way: the woodwind and string families are not blended but always used as alternating sonorities, creating a coloristic distinction between the complementary harmonies.

While the opening gesture of each ritornello has a common harmonic sound, instrumental color, and rhythmic realization – forming a kind of abstracted thematic material – the succession of the subsequent AI chords in each ritornello is unique (see Example 4.9). In the first three ritornellos, chords are connected by melodic lines that use pitch material external to the chords (not shown in the example but to which I will return below); however, from Rit.4 onwards the chords represent the section's entire pitch material. While the succession in each ritornello is unique, chords do reappear – most notably the first chord of the piece also begins Rit.2. It is as if Carter wishes to establish the "ritornello" idea clearly at the beginning, if only to be able to then diverge from it. Furthermore, the chord succession over Rit.3 and 4 (labeled W, X, Y, Y′, Z in Example 4.9) can also be read as returning in varied form across Rit.5 and 6 (as $T_{10}(W)$, X, $T_4I(Z)$, $T_8(Y)$), thus connecting the harmonic material over larger stretches of music.

The AI chords and highlighted instances of pentad 31 and septad 31 are not the only feature of the ritornellos to return. As already mentioned, the first three ritornellos have melodic lines unfolding between AI chords. Each line (doubled by various instruments) moves at its own speed, articulated by regularly spaced note attacks, together creating a polyrhythmic counterpoint which will be discussed below in more detail. These lines do not draw on the pitches of the AI chords but, as we will see shortly, they do share harmonic

Ex. 4.8 *ASKO Concerto*, opening chords of ritornellos 1–7

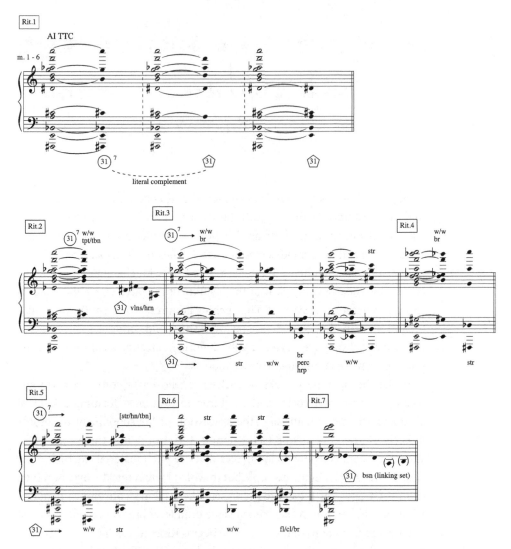

features with the chords. The trumpet line (mostly doubled by the oboe) makes a particularly clear return in all three ritornellos. Its line stands out each time because of the dynamics and timbre which project it out above the tutti texture, and also because of its more active rhythm and the way it leads each time into the closing chords of the section. Example 4.10 shows the trumpet line in Rit.1, Rit.2, and Rit.3. The phrases have a strong rhythmic congruence (attacks every 4 quintuplet-eighth notes at ♩ = 96, with faster single quintuplet eighths at the beginning or end of the phrase) and they also share contour similarities (or inversions) and pitch boundaries – D4, E4, and F4 are the lowest pitches in phrase one and two; A♮5 the highest pitch of

Ex. 4.9 *ASKO Concerto*, ritornellos 1–7, twelve-tone chords

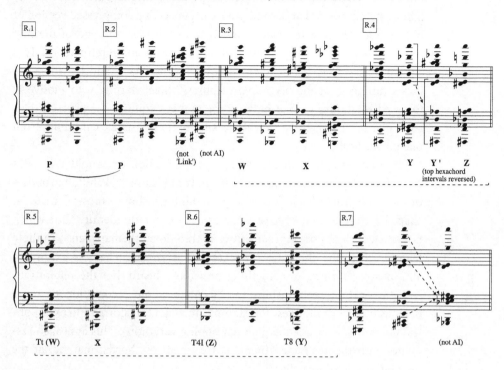

Ex. 4.10 *ASKO Concerto*, trumpet lines in ritornellos 1, 2, and 3

phrase two and three. Furthermore, the phrases string together a number of literal pitch motives. The second phrase begins with a compressed version of phrase one, bringing motives A and B from the start and end of the first phrase together at the beginning of phrase two, as A and B retrograded. This second phrase is then extended, ending with motives C and D, which are picked up again at the beginning of phrase three, starting with motive D followed by motive C. Not only do the motives connect the phrases, their particular arrangement also creates a kind of long-distance continuity from one phrase to the next.

It is interesting to consider these lines in relation to Arnold Whittall's claim for a "late-modern thematicism" in Carter's music. Whittall proposes the idea of *Scheinthemen* as a way of thinking about "musical material shaped into lines that suggest some kind of thematic identity" but which nonetheless eludes structural features of traditional thematicism.[47] In these trumpet lines the thematic "appearance" is strong. There is a kind of allusion of returning to something previously heard, but the reiterations lack the sort of relationships that facilitate sonic recognition of more obvious themes or motives (for example, through transformation by canonical operators, or Schoenbergian developing variation). This approach resonates with the abstracted thematic treatment of chordal material at the opening of each ritornello.

The kind of harmonic/thematic connections *between* ritornellos we have been pointing to so far, can also be found *within* the ritornellos. A closer look at the detailed shaping of harmonic relations between lines and chords in the first ritornello provides a good illustration, particularly as this ritornello sets up some of the principles of motion that inform the large-scale formal trajectory of the piece. After the static reiterations of the opening AI chord, the texture of Rit.1 is rhythmically activated by the successive entry of five melodic lines and one series of low chords, each moving at its own regular pulse rate. The pulse rates of the melodic lines increase as the entries accumulate (5 eighths, 4 eighths, 5 triplet eighths, 4 quintuplet eighths, 2 triplet eighths – see the boxes at the start of each staff in Example 4.11), giving the effect of the music accelerating towards the static chord at the end of the passage.[48] This type of gradual acceleration sets up in microcosm the large-scale motion of the ritornellos across the whole piece, as we shall see below.

---

[47] See Whittall, "The Search for Order: Carter's *Symphonia* and Late-Modern Thematicism," in this volume.
[48] It is interesting to compare this technique with the "polyrhythmic canon" technique in

Carter's *Holiday Overture* that Bernard discusses in "The True Significance of Elliott Carter's Early Music," in this volume.

Ex. 4.11 *ASKO Concerto*, ritornello 1, mm. 7–17

Harmonically, Carter has created a counterpoint of lines that slots together a limited set-class vocabulary into a mosaic of tightly interlaced motives. Pentad 31 – which is so prominent in the opening AI chords of each ritornello – has a similar quasi-thematic role here. As can be seen in the first measure of Example 4.11, the passage begins with a pentad-31 chord sustained in the strings, mimicking the opening chords. As the polyrhythmic lines enter one by one, a new pentad 31 is introduced each time (indicated on the example with dashed lines, and given on the analytical staff below), ordered *also* to unfold one of the AITs and in some cases an ATH (both indicated with solid lines). In the third and fourth lines, the clarinet/violins followed by the trumpet/oboe each begin with a clear melodic statement of pentad 31. The clarinet paces out its regular 5 triplet eighths, while the trumpet enters with a faster quintuplet flurry. Their two pentads share four of their five pitches (indicated by open note-heads on the analytical staff) and the sets are arranged to begin on the same pitch (E4). Additionally, they share inverted interval contours with the same ascending intervals (<–3, +8, +6, –7> and <+6, –1, –2, +8> respectively). The thematic "allusion" between the beginning of these two melodies is strong, the trumpet/oboe a kind of compressed version of the clarinet/violins. The quasi-thematic role of pentad 31 is further emphasized when the following bass clarinet/trombone line enters. Although this line does not literally state a pentad 31, it does trace a march-like ascent through all of the trumpet/oboe's first six pitches two octaves below (filling in F and C on its way), and thus emphasizes the sonority common to the two previous entries. Further quasi-thematic connections can also be found to the clarinet/violins' pcset {1, 3, 4, 9, t}. While this set appears as a melodic line for the first time in mm. 11–13, it is in fact not new to the passage. As shown in staff (i) of Example 4.12, we hear this pcset sustained by brass, piano, and harp as a subset of the second opening chord (mm. 5–6); the set reappears as dyads in the oboe/viola line (mm. 9–10); and as already mentioned, the trumpet/oboe's pentad 31 (m. 13) shares with it four of its five pitches. All these pentad 31s are different enough in their realization to be not heard as a theme but, like the trumpet lines earlier, they create a kind of thematic allusion, as well as making an explicit connection between the sound of chord and line.

With vertical as well as linear emphasis given to pentad 31, it is interesting to consider in more detail the harmonic relationship between the lines and the AI chords which frame them. Staff (ii) in Example 4.12 shows that two of the lines – the clarinet/violins and the trumpet/oboe – also unfold linear aggregates without pitch repetition. The clarinet/violins unfold hex.35 followed by hex.36. The trumpet/oboe actually play an eleven-note line, with pentad 31 followed by hex.32. However, the "missing" pc that creates hex.31 and completes an aggregate, a C, is heard in the bassoon, sustained during the

Ex. 4.12 *ASKO Concerto*, line–chord pitch relations in ritornello 1

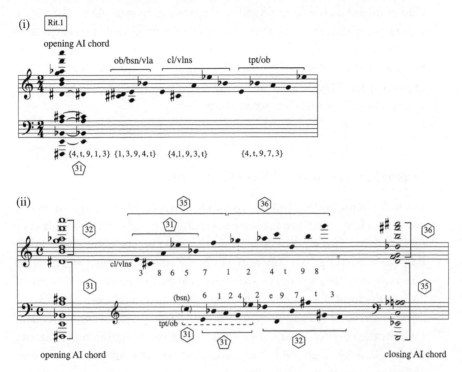

trumpet/oboe's quintuplet flurry. These hexachordal pairs are found as adjacent sets in the opening and the closing AI chord (hex.31/32 and hex.35/36 respectively). Furthermore, the linear aggregates are arranged into a near all-interval ordering and, like the AI chords, do not include compound intervals.[49] While the AI chords present a temporally static yet *spatially* expansive arrangement of intervals and hexachords, the linear aggregates present an expansive *temporal* treatment of the same material within a relatively confined registral space. Even though they are not related by any obvious transformational process, lines and chords are connected by shared features – common hexachordal set types, subset emphasis, and interval diversity.

As we have seen, the opening ritornello chords and the quasi-thematic trumpet lines connect material across the ritornellos while avoiding literal repetition; similarly, chords and lines within ritornellos have elements of relatedness while neither is entirely derived from the other. This way of

---

[49] Despite each line repeating one of its intervals, the sound of the two lines avoids emphasizing any particular interval, just like the AI chords do. On maximal diversity and modifying constraints in Carter's pitch organization see, for example, Capuzzo, "The Complement Union Property in the Music of Elliott Carter," 1–14; also Boland, "The All-Trichord Hexachord," pp. 15–16.

thinking of chord and line as autonomous yet related entities represents a kind of dualistic articulation of musical space and musical time. The widely spaced, static chords are, in a sense, confined to giving voice to an expansive musical space disconnected from a strong sense of temporal unfolding, while the lines carve out a progression through musical time within a limited registral space. This dualism, as we will see next, is fundamental to a second layer of formal organization across the piece.

Formal layers in the *ASKO Concerto*

While the returning tutti sections create the most obvious aspect of the formal design, we also experience the piece as having a strongly directed motion or forward drive. This sense of directed motion was also one of the effects of the Baroque concerto grosso, where typically the ritornello's thematic material was transposed through a large-scale tonal scheme that moved away from and back to the tonic.[50] Using the fundamental distinction between chordal and linear material so clearly presented in the opening ritornello, Carter also achieves the effect of a large-scale trajectory from the beginning to the end of the piece by interleaving two processes, one that organizes the long, unfurling lines of the concertino strand and the other that organizes the much more static chordal textures of the ritornello strand.

In the concertinos, the constantly varied motion and interaction of long melodic lines create the impression of being led through the twists and turns of a series of different musical conversations. The expressive character of each concertino is built around the timbre and register of the different instrument combinations and this plays a particularly significant role in the concertino strand's formal process. With his well-known penchant for exhausting combinatorial possibilities, Carter divides the sixteen-player ASKO ensemble into six separate concertinos in such a way that the registral spaces of high, mid, and low, as well as all their pairings (high/low, high/mid, and low/mid) are covered by one of the concertino sections (see Example 4.13). These three registral spaces are first introduced in concertinos 1 and 2. The first concertino opens with a mid-range trio of oboe, horn, and viola. In the second concertino, this space becomes enclosed by the high/low registral extremes of the duo for clarinet and contrabass. The next three concertinos follow an ascending trajectory, moving from the low register trio of bass clarinet, trombone, and cellos, though the mid/high range of the trumpet and first violin duo, to the sparkling heights of the quintet concertino for piccolo,

---

[50] See, for example, Palisca, *Baroque Music*, p. 148.

Ex. 4.13 Vertical and horizontal pitch space in formal sections of *ASKO Concerto*

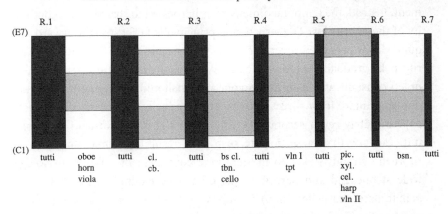

xylophone, celeste, harp, and second violin. This quiet, although rhythmically active and intense, quintet gives way to the solo bassoon "cadenza" which brings the drama back down to earth, both in terms of its mid/low register as well as its humorous character (marked *con umóre* in the score). In effect, the spatial trajectory of the concertino strand is directed towards this dramatic moment of the bassoon's solo entry. The concertino sections have gradually climbed the vertical space, the piccolo reaching its highest note (A♯7) towards the end of its last melodic line (m. 260), and the xylophone stretching up to B7 in its solo melody which ends the section (m. 261). This leaves the registral space of the next concertino with nowhere to move but down, and Carter makes the most of the drama of this moment by contrasting the largest concertino (quintet) playing in the highest register with the smallest (solo) playing in a considerably lower range on a bass instrument. As we shall see, the transition between these two concertinos also represents an important moment in the ritornello strand.

The motion through registral space from one concertino to the next is, of course, not continuous, since the small groups are periodically drawn back into the full ensemble for the ritornello sections. Here, the *fortissimo* AI chords reach from the high down to the low extremes of the ensemble's pitch space, neutralizing the spatial definition found in the concertinos. The registral differentiation between ritornello chords is very slight since the fixed five and a half octave span of each AI chord uses the extreme registers of the high and low instruments.[51] Example 4.14 shows the outer voices of the ritornello chords (compressed by an octave either side for ease of reading).[52]

---

[51] See Capuzzo, "Registral Constraints on All-Interval Rows in Elliott Carter's *Changes*," 80.
[52] It is also interesting to note the symmetrical placement of the outer-voice dyad C7–G♯1. This dyad occurs as outer voices in the first

and last chord of the piece, and also as the only repeated outer-voice dyad in the central ritornello, suggesting a deliberate shaping of chordal registers in the piece.

This wide span leaves room for only relatively small shifts in vertical placement. Instead, the temporal dimension is harnessed to structure the continuity of the ritornellos. The structuring principle is fairly straightforward and
quite easily perceived: over the course of the piece, the duration of each
ritornello gradually becomes shorter. Whereas the concertinos remain more
or less constant, averaging around one and a half minutes, the ritornellos start
out at around forty-three seconds and gradually reduce in duration to
approximately seven seconds for Rit.6, with the final ritornello more of a
tutti cadence than a section as such. The resulting formal shape of the
ritornello strand is akin to the temporal equivalent of a funnel or wedge,
wide at one end and narrow at the other (see Example 4.13). While the
penultimate ritornello (Rit.6) is only very brief, it comes at a significant
point in the musical drama, in-between the quintet concertino and the solo
bassoon cadenza discussed above. This short intervening section functions as
a kind of pivot between concertinos, mirroring their registral shift (see Rit.6 in
Example 4.14). The first chord stretches up to the highest pitch of all the
ritornello sections (E7), descending a semitone in the second chord (E♭7), and
finally dropping an interval 7 (the largest between outer voices) to G♯6 in the
last chord. The low note of this last chord (D1) is also the lowest pitch yet of
an AI chord (with the descent continuing in Rit.7). Thus, the descending
range of the AI chords in Rit.6 supports the shift from the high quintet
concertino to the low solo concertino, and in a sense this moment represents
a *rapprochement* between the formal processes of the two strands.

Following Rit.6, the two formal processes become further intertwined. As
the bassoon cadenza begins, twelve-tone chords continue to regularly punc-
tuate the bassoon melody with brief staccato bursts, as if the chords had been
ejected from the previous ritornello that was too short to contain them and
had now spilt over into the following concertino. For the first half of the
bassoon solo, these chords are evenly spaced every 16 triplet-eighth notes
(mm. 268–75). Halfway through the bassoon solo, the chords thin out to
hexachords and pentads (from m. 276), thickening again a few measures

Ex. 4.14 *ASKO Concerto*, outer voices of ritornello chords (compressed by two octaves
either side)

before Rit.7 (m. 290). From this halfway point in the concertino through the final ritornello to the end of the piece, the pulse stream of the chords gradually speeds up – four attacks spaced at 14 triplet eighths apart, followed by five attacks at 12 triplet eights, four attacks at 7 triplet eighths, two attacks at 9 sixteenth notes, two at 8 sixteenths, two at 7 sixteenths, two at 6 sixteenths, and one attack at 4 sixteenths (the last part of this series is indicated in Example 4.15). The effect is one of forward propulsion, imbuing the vertical dimension with a horizontal impulse. This accelerating motion, as we have already seen, was set up at the very beginning of the piece in the polyrhythmic lines of Rit.1.[53] The accelerating chords are the end result of a gradual process of temporal shrinking in the ritornello strand that has led to a transformation in the function of the tutti chords: the chordal material used to define an entire strand in the piece becomes so truncated it turns into a rhythmic event on the local level. However, the chords are not so much accompanying the solo cadenza line as they are layered on top of it (possibly one of the reasons why the bassoon part was easily extracted as a solo piece later on – see n. 41). It is as if the ritornello and concertino strands are still following their own continuities, only now simultaneously instead of in alternation. That this occurs in the final solo section, where the chord–line dualism is heightened, is of course no coincidence. The formal processes of both strands are directed towards this point and their coming together here further dramatizes their contrast.

After alternating and then overlaying the two strands, Carter's final dramatic gesture of the piece has chord and line each take on characteristics of the other, in a sense merging the two but without losing the chord–line dualism. This happens as the solo bassoon concertino flows seamlessly into the final ritornello (see Example 4.15). The quasi-thematic pentad 31 is central to the merging process. Rather than forming an independent melodic line, the bassoon now draws its pitches A3, B3, D4, E♭4 and G♯4 – comprising the pentad 31 as pcset {9,e,2,3,8} – from the surrounding twelve-tone chords. The bassoon line and TTCs are reproduced on the analytical staff in the example. The bassoon finally merges into the last chords, where the tremolandos of woodwind, brass, and percussion recall the shimmering motion of the earlier bassoon solo. The strings at this point (m. 294) do not participate in the tremolandos but instead hold a widely spread sustained chord till the end of the piece. Like the bassoon line, this chord forms a pentad 31. It is, however, a kind of complement to the bassoon line in that its pcset – {6, t,1,7,0} – has no overlapping pcs with the bassoon's set. These distinct sonic identities of line and chord are, at the same time, presented as fully merged in

---

[53] There does not, however, appear to be any specific connection between speeds at which the lines move at the beginning of the piece and the acceleration rate of these chords.

Ex. **4.15** *ASKO Concerto*, ritornello 7, mm. 291–96

the single ten-note chord of m. 293, where the harp plays the bassoon's pcset and the piano, woodwind, and brass play the strings' pcset. While the bassoon line disappears in the last three measures, the piece does not conclude with the static string chord alone: embedded within the wide chord are the last accelerating staccato attacks (mm. 296–97) in woodwind, brass, and percussion which continue the piece's linear impulse through to its conclusion.

"Emancipated musical discourse"

Form in the *Boston* and *ASKO* concertos arises from Carter's masterful reshaping of the traditional ritornello principle to enable the "kinetic tendencies" of the musical content of each piece to unfold a secondary formal process. In the *ASKO Concerto* the process involves the truncation of time occupied by the ritornello chords which threaten to disappear completely, combined with the ascension of the concertino lines through space towards inaudibility; in the *Boston Concerto* the process involves the transformation of ritornello textures from chordal to linear and back again, while maintaining the shared sonic identity of the "rain" theme. The tensions implicit in these processes create a forward trajectory to each piece that projects across the repetitive ritornello design.

Multi-layered formal designs have long been a hallmark of Carter's music and despite the heralding of a "new clarity" in Carter's late style, the formal designs of these two concertos are no less intricate than some of Carter's most dense middle-period music. What is new in these "concerto grosso" style pieces is the structured formal repetition. However, Carter's handling of the repetitive nature of ritornello form follows his own call, so long ago, for an "emancipated musical discourse" in which traditional forms are not reappropriated but rather reinterpreted in response to the composer's own creative imperatives. Carter's imperatives of a constant growth and non-thematic flow to his music are taken to new heights here in their skillful application to a traditional form that in many respects embodies their opposites.

5 "The matter of human cooperation" in Carter's mature style

John Roeder

Many of the textures of Elliott Carter's music combine two or more simultaneous streams of activity, each distinguished from the others by its repertoire of intervals or chords, tempo, articulation, and contours of pitch and rhythm. This "polyvocalism," as David Schiff aptly calls it,[1] while inspired by Carter's immediate predecessors Ives and Cowell, also draws upon and extends the legacy of the great contrapuntal traditions of the past that he studied thoroughly with Nadia Boulanger. The principles governing those traditions served diverse purposes, on the one hand ensuring the rhythmic and melodic independence of the individual voices, but on the other coordinating them harmonically, through metrical regulation of simultaneity intervals, and motivically, through various imitative techniques such as transposition, inversion, and augmentation. Similarly, one can appreciate Carter's works for the equipoise of independence and interaction they achieve with twentieth-century modernist pitch and rhythmic resources, and one can understand the development of his style as a progressive mastery of contrapuntal process and form.

Accordingly, analyses of his music, like accounts of polyphony, focus on diverse properties. On the one hand, emphasizing the independence of the streams, commentators identify contrasts of interval, rhythm, and expressive character. On the other hand, focusing on integration, they show how, on a large scale, the streams combine to shape the dramatic and expressive trajectories of the music, leading to climaxes and convincing resolutions, and how, more locally, they combine to repeatedly produce distinctive harmonies – all-interval tetrachords (AITs), special twelve-tone chords, all-trichord hexachords (ATHs), and others – according to procedures that Carter cataloged in his *Harmony Book*. For instance, an early polyvocal work, the Second String Quartet, begins with each instrument asserting a distinctive repertoire of intervals, rhythmic and articulative behaviors, and tempo. Despite these contrasts, the streams' pitches combine into some of the important pitch

---

[1] Schiff, *MEC*, p. 26.

structures of the quartet, including AITs,[2] which are shaped by a clearly directed registral process.[3] In the third movement each instrument imitates, with its characteristic intervals and rhythms, the melodic phrases introduced by the viola; then, in the fourth movement, the instruments all accelerate, and take on each other's intervals and rhythm. Most strikingly they together produce several statements of a motive that synthesizes the characteristic tempos, states the two AITs, presents all the ensemble's characteristic intervals vertically or melodically, and exhausts the aggregate.[4]

There is yet another dimension to Carter's counterpoint, however, to which the composer's program notes often allude: the moment-to-moment interaction, contrasting or imitative, of pitch and rhythm among the streams. For example, he describes the Second Quartet as a "four-way conversation ... [in which t]he individuals of this group are related to each other in what might be metaphorically termed three forms of responsiveness: discipleship, companionship, and confrontation."[5] Precedents for such conversations can be heard in the strettos of fugues, or in the motivic interplay in the developmental sections of classical chamber music, but Carter has honed them to a high degree of sophistication and expressivity.

Contrast is the simplest to achieve and to hear, and the composer often presents it in mimesis of familiarly human conflicts. For instance, the first large segment of the Introduction is dominated by Cello's two crescendoing, accelerating, falling series of perfect fourths, which contrast with (among other things) brief, languorous tritones in Viola. After a cadence involving all four instruments, Viola (m. 12) briefly ventures a change of its character by mimicking Cello's gesture with accelerating durations and a strongly directed contour; but it also contradicts Cello by substituting its tritone for the perfect fourth, ascent for descent, and diminuendo for crescendo. Immediately Cello interrupts with a line rising from Viola's lowest to highest pitches by perfect fourths, as if to say "That's my material, and you have to play it with my intervals, not yours!" Viola seems stunned, because it lapses into its longest silence yet; when it re-enters timidly at the next shared cadence, Cello cuts out, as if refusing to associate with such a usurper.

Equally important but less confrontational kinds of responsiveness become apparent to listeners who attend to timing, rhythm, contour, and the sharing

[2] Bernard, "Problems of Pitch Structure in Elliott Carter's First and Second String Quartets"; Harvey, *The Later Music of Elliott Carter.*
[3] Koivisto, "Aspects of Motion in Elliott Carter's Second String Quartet"; Cogan and Pozzi, *Sonic Design: The Nature of Sound and Music*, pp. 59–71.
[4] Schiff, *MEC*, p. 75.
[5] Carter, "String Quartets Nos. 1, 1951, and 2, 1959" (1970), p. 234. See also Schmidt, "On Elliott Carter's String Quartets," in this volume.

of pitches and intervals. In the Introduction, for instance, although each instrument's gesture features a different interval, the gestures exhibit very similar structure. To highlight some important interactions, Example 5.1 lays out the score of mm. 1–10 in a format that rearranges the vertical layout of the parts, and slightly distorts their temporal order. Read from left to right, it shows first that Cello's opening phrase not only establishes its characteristic interval, 5 (the perfect fourth), but does so through a specific sequence of transpositions, down 1 semitone then up 3, that link the series of dyads <{B, E}, {B♭, E♭}, {D♭, G♭}>. (Above Cello's music, these transpositions are shown by labeling arrows that connect nodes containing the dyads.) Violin I's response, although it establishes a different characteristic interval, neverthe-less echoes the transposition-series of Cello, first playing the <−1,3> interval sequence as the pitch series <F4, E4, G4>, then linking the series of minor thirds <{F, A♭}, {E, G}, {G, B♭}>.

The entrances of the remaining two instruments in m. 5 enhance the impression of cooperation by the way that they extend, elaborate, and coor-dinate the pitch and intervallic structures of Cello and Violin I. Violin II's initial dyad provides the only pitch class not yet stated. By itself this may be taken as an effort to be as distinct as possible, or to finish off a process the others began. But its specific pitches also combine with their held dyads in a significant way, detailed in the inset at the top right of the example. Cello's {D♭4, G♭4} has no pitch or intervallic similarity with Violin I's {G4, B♭4}, but the addition of Violin II's {C4, E4} binds them into a hexachord registrally arranged as two 014 trichords, {C4, D♭4, E4} and {G♭4, G4, B♭4}, each manifesting the pitch intervals 1 and 3 that structured Violin I's and Cello's characteristic intervals in mm. 1–4.

The tritone transposition that relates these trichords may be heard to motivate Viola's entrance on a tritone, which creates several other instances of 014 within the now eight-note vertical structure, while maintaining its transpositional symmetry. As shown by the dashed line of the example, Viola's initial B4 can also be heard as joining into Cello's discourse: it is Cello's characteristic interval, 5, over Cello's held {D♭4, G♭4}, just as Cello's first A4 was 5 above {B3, E4}. Indeed Cello's next phrase begins with this very B4, as if accepting Viola's suggestion.

After Violin II plays its mediating dyad, its continuation strikingly affirms the developing consensus. Its next six plucked attacks reproduce the contour of Cello's opening motive, with a slap emphasizing the nadir just as the dynamic climax did in Cello. Also, its characteristic intervals are structured by the same series of intervals <−1,3> that governed the dyad successions in Cello and Violin I. Two of the major thirds it plays, {C, E} and {B, D♯}, may be heard to be extended to augmented triads by the attacks of A♭ and G, respectively. One might expect, therefore, that the last major third in Violin

Ex. 5.1 String Quartet No. 2, mm. 1–10. 1–3-network organization of characteristic intervals, and pitch interactions

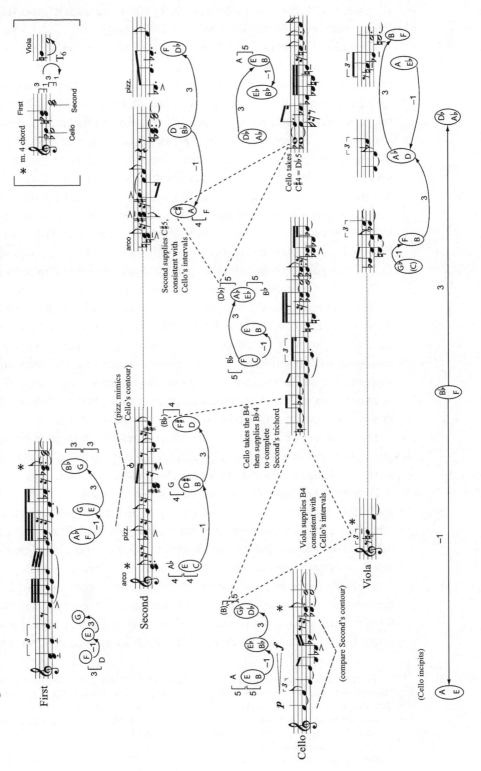

II's phrase, <D4, F♯4>, would be followed by a B♭4. Indeed it is – courtesy of Cello, which seems to be paying forward Viola's favor.

Networks of intervals 1 and 3, supplemented by pitch sharing, also structure the rest of this passage. First, Cello's second phrase states a varied configuration in which both intervals proceed from the same node. Since the first interval 5, {C, F}, has a B♭4 attached above it, the cadential {E♭, A♭} might be heard to imply a D♭5. Just as Viola provided the implied B4 after Cello's first statement, now Violin II provides the implied C♯5, which Cello then takes up to begin its final phrase. (These two pitch events are further associated by the fact that each expands the prevailingly constant register constraints of the passage.) Violin II's next phrase manifests the varied arrangement of −1 and 3. Meanwhile, Viola presents tritones also structured by −1,3; the order is a little vague, but −1 clearly sounds when G♭4 moves to F4, and 3 can be heard in the succession of tritones <B, F> – <D, A♭>. Then Cello's final phrase presents another configuration, this time in the service of a retrograde of its opening five pitches. On the largest scale, the variant −1,3 network can even be heard to connect the three interval 5s that begin Cello's phrases {A, E}, {B♭, F}, and {D♭, A♭}. In other words, each part can be heard as an elaboration, with its characteristic intervals and rhythms, of a clear succession of two intervals.[6] The impression of listening and cooperation suggested by this motivic and transformational interplay explains why the composer says, in the aforementioned program note, that the Introduction presents the instruments' repertoires in a "'companionate' manner."

This concern with detailed, moment-to-moment interactions occupies many of Carter's compositions. Opposition and conflict especially are evident in a series of large works that followed the Second Quartet, including concerti, *A Symphony for Three Orchestras*, and the Third Quartet. Starting in the 1980s, though, Carter began to produce shorter pieces with more transparent textures especially conducive to contrapuntal processes. These are often dedicated to friends, patrons, or other composers, suggesting a renewed focus on companionship. For example, *Enchanted Preludes* for flute and cello (1988) seems to be a portrait of the married couple involved in its commission, and its form can be conceived as a process of a deepening cooperation.[7] Indeed, the composer solicits listeners' attention to musical interactions; for example, his preface to the Fifth String Quartet (1995) states

[6] The detailed reading of Example 5.1 is consistent with Carter's manuscript 1959 "Introduction" to a planned treatise on "musical continuity and rhetoric." This "invite[s] the students' consideration first of the sequential association of single notes in small groups called motives and then in larger grouping[s] of phrases, sentences +

paragraphs." His syllabus guides the student through the composition of short phrases that manifest progressively more complete relationships among the voices. It is quoted in Schmidt, "Emanzipation des musikalischen Diskurses," pp. 216–17.

[7] Roeder, "Autonomy and Dialogue in Elliott Carter's *Enchanted Preludes*."

that "in this score the matter of human cooperation with its many aspects of feeling and thought was a very important consideration." The remainder of this chapter identifies such "cooperation" and shows how it shapes three chamber compositions of the 1980s and '90s: a duet, a solo work, and the Fifth Quartet itself, one of the last putatively conversational works before the advent of Carter's "late late" style.

Some introductory examples

In the flute/clarinet duet *Esprit Rude/Esprit Doux* (1985), composed to celebrate the sixtieth birthday of the eminent composer and conductor Pierre Boulez, the instruments differ in pitch, rhythm, and other respects, as in earlier works. Their interval repertoires are disjoint: Flute plays only 3, 4, 5, 10, and 11 and some of their octave compounds while Clarinet is limited exclusively to 1, 2, and 7 (its two other intervals, 8 and 9, appear later). Each paces its rhythms in its own very slow tempo, and each subdivides its beats in a distinctive way, resulting in a "long-range polyrhythm" in which important beats rarely coincide (these fixed tempos do not correspond simply to the notated shared tempos, which change occasionally).[8]

While this arrangement creates difference, it also manifests balanced coordination. Timbrally, the character-continuities share two types of artic-ulation, the "rough [*rude*]" and "smooth [*doux*]" breathing of the title, and of course they blend well and overlap considerably in range. Each instrument plays one member of each interval class, except the tritone; for example, Flute has small instances of ics 3, 4, and 5, and Clarinet has large instances (intervals 7, 8, and 9) of them. Each can string together its intervals to form melodic instances of the AIT 0137, to which belongs the work's basic motive <Bb, C, A, E>, composed of pitch classes corresponding to letters of the dedicatee's name (Bb = B, C [Ut] = *u*, A [La] = *l*, and E = *e*). Also, the music is shaped to a certain extent by the polyrhythmic scheme. Because each strictly maintains its own tempo, their rhythmic relationship is completely predictable, their respective beats moving through cycles of near-convergence and divergence with respect to each other.[9] Indeed, the piece comprises a complete polyrhythmic cycle beginning with a coincidence of the slow beats on the downbeat of m. 6, and ending when they coincide again, on the downbeat of the last measure. Moments of near convergence are marked by

[8] See also Mead, "Time Management: Rhythm as a Formal Determinant in Certain Works of Elliott Carter," in this volume; and Link, "Long-Range Polyrhythms in Elliott Carter's Recent Music."

[9] Weston, "Inversion, Subversion, and Metaphor," pp. 27–28. Link, "Long-Range Polyrhythms in Elliott Carter's Recent Music," pp. 11–25.

Ex. 5.2a *Esprit Rude/Esprit Doux*, introductory pitch and rhythmic discourse

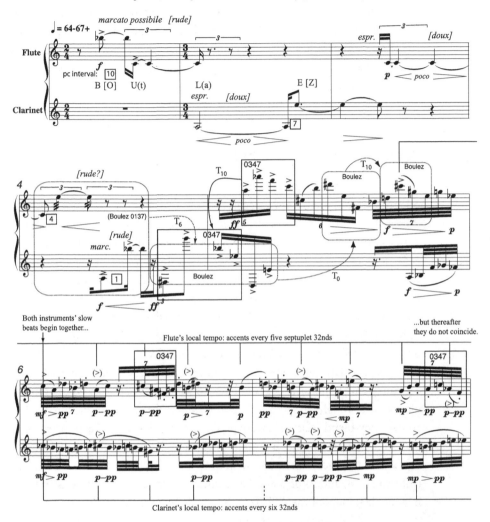

special textures – trills or long slow legato lines in both instruments. All coordinations, then, affect the character and large-scale shape of the music.[10] What makes this piece so entertaining, however, is the variety of ways that this balance is established, tipped, and regained from moment to moment in interactions of contour, pitch, rhythm, and timbre. Examples 5.2a–c, notated at concert pitch, show a few representative excerpts. A close study of these interactions helps explain Carter's specific choices of pitches and rhythms.

[10] Many aspects of this piece are discussed in Truniger, "Elliott Carter: *Esprit rude/esprit doux*." See also Noubel, *LTF*, p. 245. Carter adopted this polyrhythmic technique around the same time that he began to focus on simpler textures; perhaps the continuity and form it provided freed him to concentrate on refining local details.

At the outset, Example 5.2a, Flute and Clarinet alternate *rude* and *doux* melodic dyads, in opposite order. These spell out the motto, <B♭5, C4, A3, E5>, first exactly, and then rearranged into the pitches representing the vowels in "Boulez," C4 and E5, followed by those representing the consonants, A3 and B♭5. Each of the first two dyads manifests a fundamental, invariant aspect of the instrument that plays it – the lowest possible pitch in Flute, and Clarinet's characteristic overblowing interval, the perfect twelfth, in its two characteristic registers. During the second statement of the motive each instrument plays the low pitch that it did the first time, then plays the other instrument's previous high pitch, using the other's initial articulation. Consequently four different intervals are presented – 10, 7, 4, and 1 – each belonging to a different interval class. Thus, although the individuality of each instrument is apparent, the motivic repetition, pitch sharing, timbral alternation, and intervallic variegation imply a close working relationship.

This cooperation unravels near the end of the second statement. After Flute repeats its *doux* C4, it plays Clarinet's high E5 with a *rude* crescendoing flutter tongue. Clarinet finishes the exchange with a *rude* wide interval 1 (plus two octaves), but then, perhaps provoked by Flute's cheekiness, it repeats the 1 (compounding it by another octave) as the incipit of an accelerating series of six *rude*, loud, individually tongued and accented pitches, <F♯3, G6, B♭5, E♭5, D3, E4>. The first three notes could be part of an all-interval tetrachord, but the fourth pc makes a different tetrachord, 0347, with them, so it seems that Clarinet wants to break away from the motto on which it had collaborated with Flute.

Perhaps noticing Clarinet's divergence, Flute enters with a gesture whose first six pitches <A5, A♭6, F6, C6, C♯5, B5> correspond in several ways to Clarinet's: they have the same contour; they continue the acceleration; they present the same series of interval classes, because they are the ordered pc-inversion I_3 of Clarinet's gesture; they use the six notes that Clarinet did not use, thus completing the aggregate; and the first four notes have the same articulation, and form the same unordered tetrachord type, 0347, as the four notes of Clarinet's breakaway gesture. Indeed, as the arrow connecting the solid boxes on Example 5.2a shows, Flute's 0347 can be heard to place Clarinet's 0347 in a transpositional relation that recalls the opening interval 10 of the movement; this minor seventh is prominent in mm. 4–5 between Clarinet's high G6 and Flute's first A5, and between Flute's high A♭6 and Clarinet's B♭5. All these aspects of Flute's response suggest an offer to play along with Clarinet's new ideas, reaffirming the companionate relationship.

At Flute's entrance, Clarinet honks its pitch most out of Flute's range (D3), as if resisting its offer. But Clarinet's final E offers some conciliation, in the sense that it forms, together with the other three non-extreme pitches {F♯, B♭, E♭} of this gesture, a tritone transposition {3,4,6,t} of the Boulez set. (On Example 5.2a, dotted boxes connected with labeled dotted arrows show

transpositionally related instances of this set-type.) Perhaps acknowledging the special functions of the last two Clarinet pitches, Flute slurs together
the two pitches after *its* 0347. Then it continues accelerating through a
series of pcs <3,4,6,t,2,1,8,4,7,3> that complete its own statement of the
aggregate. The first four of these notes (grouped together by a diminuendo)
state exactly the same tritone transposition {3,4,6,t} of the Boulez motto
that Clarinet just stated. The next four of these pcs, {1,2,4,8} (also initiating
a diminuendo), transpose the first four by T_{10}, again stating a form of the
Boulez motto while also recalling the relation of Flute and Clarinet 0347
tetrachords. The last pitches rock between major and minor thirds, the
smallest intervals of its repertoire, which of course dominate 0347, and
which will be the focus of the following measures. When Clarinet re-enters
it first attempts to resume the relation it had with Flute during mm. 1–4: it
begins to imitate Flute's last gesture (the diminuendo) by stating the same
series of interval classes, 1 then 5. It also continues the acceleration,
achieving the thirty-second-note pulse that will dominate its next section.
But strikingly, it refuses to answer Flute's major and minor thirds with
minor and major sixths, playing seconds instead.

This disagreement leads to a new texture starting at the first simultaneous
attack in m. 6. Within a narrow range, F4 to E5, Flute plays all the small
melodic intervals in its repertoire, occasionally forming four-note segments
of the 0347 type on which the instruments just agreed. Clarinet begins in an
even narrower, overlapping range, playing all *its* smallest intervals, 1 and 2.
The instruments contrast in articulation, with Flute featuring light staccato
and Clarinet a smooth legato, but both are *doux*. Rhythmically, as shown by
the bracketing above and below the score, the instruments establish consistent but different tempos through regular accent or group-beginnings, every
fifth septuplet thirty-second in Flute (a tempo of about 90), and every sixth
thirty-second in Clarinet (about MM 85). Despite the tempo independence,
there is a certain amount of local rhythmic interplay. For example on the
downbeat of m. 7, apparently to avoid attacking simultaneously with Flute,
Clarinet withholds an expected accent. It then presents accents every 3 thirty-
seconds, effectively doubling the tempo, but then resumes its 85.33 beat after a
relative loud and high (E5) prompt from Flute.

In just a few measures, then, the piece establishes not only the separate
characters of the instruments, but also a variety of ways that they interact:
pitch sharing, motive formation, imitation in inversion, repetition of transformation, aggregate completion, confinement to distinctive subsets of
respective intervals, register sharing, combined accelerando, beat sharing,
and cueing. It takes many words to describe these interactions, but most are
easy to hear, once the listener focuses on local changes in addition to larger-
scale properties.

Ex. 5.2b *Esprit Rude/Esprit Doux*, reprise and dyadic dialog in mm. 42–47

Measure 42 (Example 5.2b) brings back, for the first time, a return to the exchange of mm. 1–4: Flute and Clarinet alternate *rude* and *doux* dyads, using their characteristic intervals and sharing pitches. Although recognizable as a reprise, the texture is more intense, with louder dynamics, quicker rhythms, and more overlap, and it features not the Boulez motive but the other AIT, 0146. As Clarinet plays the second member of its second dyad, it suddenly switches to a trill. Flute responds with a *fortissimo* attack of another trill, which (as in a previous trill passage) marks a point of near convergence in the long-range polyrhythm. The instruments then alternate trills steadily, Clarinet changing every 7 quintuplet eighths and Flute every 4 triplet quarters. The circles on the Example show how the instruments' dyads combine to make AITs, both 0137s and 0146s. Every trilled dyad belongs to one of these, and most belong to two. Since the changes are staggered, each change seems like a deliberate choice to maintain those two harmonies that have the greatest variety, and most even distribution, of interval classes.

In this context an amusing interplay develops. At first Flute obsessively plays interval 5s, while Clarinet tries out 2 and 8. In m. 45, Clarinet, perhaps observing that its counterpart has played three 5s in a row, doubles one of Flute's pitches, E4, temporarily interrupting the chain of AITs. Now Flute could in fact respond with {E♭, B♭}, keeping its ic 5 while still producing another 0137. But instead it switches to an interval class 1, creating a 0146 AIT instead. Clarinet seems content with the change, as it switches when expected to another 0146-forming dyad. However, this is the fourth ic 2 it has

Ex. 5.2c *Esprit Rude/Esprit Doux*, final harmonic manifestation of the Boulez motive, and polyrhythmic convergence

played, so it now seems to be more obsessive than Flute (it takes one to know one). On Flute's next change, it turns the tables on Clarinet by doubling one of *its* pitches, A4. Clarinet responds by isolating itself, changing to a dyad that is completely below Flute's range and that is also an interval, 6, that does not belong to either instrument's repertoire. Flute nevertheless plays along, transposing its minor third to a high {E♭, G♭} that still forms a 0146 with Clarinet's dyad. Thanks to the "complement union property" of AITs,[11] Flute could have achieved the same goal with any of eight ic 3 dyads, but it selects the one that is a tritone transposition of its previous dyad, perhaps acknowledging the tritone in Clarinet.

Most of the rest of the piece avoids literally restating the Boulez motive, but the conclusion (Example 5.2c) restores it in a repartee that recalls and

[11] Morris, "Pitch Class Complementation and its Generalizations"; Capuzzo, "The Complement Union Property in the Music of Elliott Carter"; Childs, "Structural and Transformational Properties of All-Interval Tetrachords."

transforms the opening measures. In preparation, both instruments play rapid gestures confined to the same narrow register, each emphasizing slightly different pitches (E♭5 in Flute, D5 in Clarinet) and each featuring a characteristic repeated duration (notated as 5 triplet sixteenths in Flute and 7 quintuplet sixteenths in Clarinet). Although they maintain their respective intervallic repertoires, each frequently sounds the interval 6 that both avoided at first. The result is a curious blend of cooperation and tension. In m. 82 both instruments crescendo, as if seeking to break out of an impasse. Clarinet scampers up a whole-tone scale, and as soon as it exceeds the previous upper registral boundary, Flute halts.

The dramatic change in texture leads to two literal statements of the Boulez motive, divided into *doux* and *rude* dyads as in the Introduction. The texture and contents are altered, however, to reflect the new forms of cooperation achieved during the past few minutes of the piece. Flute leads, as in m. 1, but plays the *doux* <A, E> dyad which Clarinet used to respond in m. 2, in the opposite direction (descending rather than ascending). Clarinet answers in m. 83, as in m. 2, but with the *rude* <B♭, C> dyad that Flute played in m. 1, also in the opposite direction. Then Flute plays the *rude* Clarinet dyad of m. 4, and Clarinet plays the *doux* Flute dyad of mm. 3–4; again the directions of the intervals are reversed. These clear recapitulations sound transformed in two significant ways. In contrast to mm. 1–4, where the instruments alternated to produce a single continuous line, they overlap here, producing harmonic intervals as well. As shown in the Example, these verticalities present all six interval classes in the Boulez set, varying among the intervals characteristic of each instrument: Flute's 11, shared 6, Clarinet's 8, Clarinet's 2, Clarinet's 9, and Flute's 5. Also, in contrast to the freer, cooperative acceleration of the Introduction, each instrument now strictly maintains its own established pulse. The instruments now seem to be able to carry on a cooperative discourse while maintaining individuality.

In mm. 85–86 each instrument plays two dyads, one *rude* and one *doux*, continuing the overlapping texture of mm. 83–84. But now they use the other notes of the twelve-tone aggregate. I hear this as suggesting that the latest *doux/rude* exchange can organize the world outside of "Boulez." Rhythmically they are approaching the moment when their respective slow beats will coincide for the first time since m. 6, and so their attacks grow closer together. In m. 87, they have time for a final Boulez set, which they state cooperatively in order, this time both *rude*ly. Up until now, they have always split the set equally, one dyad apiece, but the arrival of the moment of coincidence makes it possible for Clarinet to attack a third note exactly when Flute plays its second one. This is the same E5 that in m. 4 provoked Clarinet to spin off on its own, and Flute gives the same flutter-tongue articulation as it did then, crescendoing challengingly. But Clarinet seems happy at the rhythmic and pitch unison, for it does not play on its next beat, so Flute simply quits its *rude* behavior.

Many other passages in *Esprit Rude/Esprit Doux* are susceptible to close readings of the instruments' interactions, which can be taken to signify conversational and other social processes, as the composer suggests. On first exposure to such accounts, however, such as the reader may have just experienced, the quantity and rapidity of the crossplay may seem overwhelming. Musical streams consist of events much briefer and more abstract than words, and they can associate and diverge more quickly, and in many more dimensions than can a relatively slow and syntactically constrained verbal discourse. One might therefore wonder how well the examples above validate the composer's claim about representing "the matter of human cooperation." But even the simplest social interactions involve rapid and multimodal semioses of emotion and cogitation – in the composer's description, "many aspects of feeling and thought" – such as those documented by studies of nonverbal communication and micro-expressions.[12] In this light, Carter's dense musical flux is not so difficult to grasp, since many of the relationships involve simply the identity or difference of pitch, interval, or contour, and timing with respect to pulse streams, all of which can be readily perceived. In other words, the more complex that social interaction is conceived to be, and the more salient that the musical interactions appear, the more apt the composer's conversational metaphors become. Nevertheless, even such an evocative analogy is limited. The cooperations characteristic of Carter's mature style also have more purely musical functions.

Processes of reconciliation in a solo work

These functions are evident in other music by Carter that is not so explicitly social in conception, when large-scale form and process can be heard to develop out of the specific order and ways in which materials are arranged in relation to each other. As an illustration, consider *Riconoscenza per Goffredo Petrassi*, a brief work for solo violin composed in 1984. Its program notes mention no conflicts or other interpersonal interactions, but merely affirm that the piece celebrates the prominent Italian composer. Nevertheless, the piece clearly alternates three continuities that – at the outset – differ greatly in rhythm, register, loudness, articulation, and interval content.[13] These streams are evident in the annotated excerpts in Example 5.3.

---

[12] Mehrabian, *Nonverbal Communication*; Keltner *et al.*, "Facial Expression of Emotion."

[13] Schiff, *MEC*, p. 139; Noubel, *LTF*, p. 239.

Ex. 5.3a *Riconoscenza per Goffredo Petrassi*, mm. 1–3, the *dolce* stream alternates among 0369s

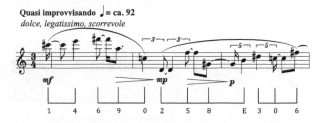

Ex. 5.3b *Riconoscenza*, mm. 10–18, recollection in the *dolce* stream, and 036 combinations in the *dolce* and *marcato* streams

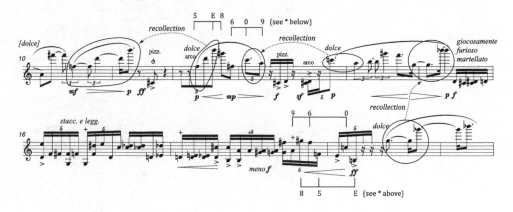

Ex. 5.3c *Riconoscenza*, preliminary contacts among all three streams in mm. 26–38

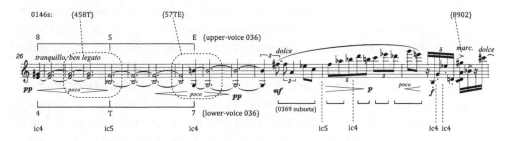

The first of them, marked *dolce*, proceeds as a high legato melody, varying gently in pace, contour, and dynamics (Example 5.3a). It features interval classes 3 and 6 as it shifts every two to four events from a subset of one diminished-seventh tetrachord to a subset of another. Two other contrasting continuities interrupt it in turn. One of them, first entering in m. 11 (Example 5.3b) and thereafter often designated *marcato*, features low, loud, percussive events, including occasional multiple stops and pizzicatos. The third *tranquillo*

Ex. 5.3d *Riconoscenza*, strengthening connection of *dolce* and *tranquillo* streams, mm. 50–67

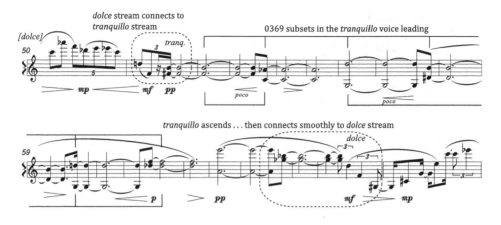

Ex. 5.3e *Riconoscenza*, registral and harmonic contact among all three streams, mm. 76–83

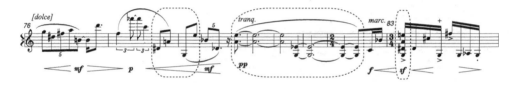

stream, first entering in m. 26 (Example 5.3c), prepared by a long D4, quietly sustains dyads. Along with rhythm, articulation, and dynamics, interval content distinguishes these two continuities: the *tranquillo* dyads belong exclusively to ics 4 and 5, and the *marcato* gestures feature ics 1 and 2 melodically and harmonically, so that the six ics are distributed evenly among the three streams.

One would think that the alternation of these very different kinds of music would produce a discontinuous sensation of cross-cutting, as in Stravinsky's music.[14] Indeed, to Max Noubel, "the successive alternation of characters evolving in the single instrumental part is much more than a simple collage of temporal segments ... It is also a virtual stratification, in which each layer is invested with a singular musical character."[15] However, the *dolce* stream has more rhythmic and melodic continuity than the others, and it has a striking behavior: after each interruption by another stream, it recommences by repeating the last few pitches of its previous appearance. The annotations of mm. 10–18 in Example 5.3b indicate such repetitions. This reaching back to

[14] Cone, "Stravinsky: The Progress of a Method."

[15] Noubel, *LTF*, p. 239 (my translation).

recollect suggests that the *marcato* and *tranquillo* music may be contrasting thoughts within a single predominantly *dolce* persona, rather than completely separate characters, as would be the case in a work for multiple instruments.[16] The suggestion is solidified across the rest of the piece as the streams, despite their differences, gradually connect and share materials, a process that also motivates closure.[17]

The preliminary connections are tenuous. For instance, the first extended *marcato* outburst breaks off, in m. 18, with a mixture of two 036 sets that recall the *dolce* stream's content in m. 12, even as it maintains focus on its characteristic ics 1 and 2, and on the lowest register (Example 5.3b). Similarly, when the *tranquillo* dyad stream first appears in m. 26 (Example 5.3c), its upper and lower voices each unfold a different 036 trichord, alluding abstractly to the diminished-tetrachord successions in the *dolce* stream. More immediately, though, one hears a strong harmonic and rhythmic contrast because the extraordinary duration of each dyad demands focus more on its simultaneities (ics 4 and 5) than on their voice leading, and on the tetrachordal harmony created by their succession. Both such harmonies are 0146s, whose equal distribution of interval classes contrast strongly with four-note-adjacency sets in the other streams. The following *dolce* and *marcato* statements remain distinct from each other and the *tranquillo* music, but offer some more concrete connections, in the form of some surprising melodic ic 4s and 5s, and even an 0146 as the piece's first quadruple stop.

During this passage the three streams also overlap in register, initiating a more concrete sort of connection that is pursued during the subsequent music. So far the *dolce* stream has briefly dipped into first-position pitches, but it has always been high when the lower streams interrupted it. At m. 51, however (Example 5.3d), it is down at F4 when a *tranquillo* dyad enters in the same register. Seemingly in reciprocation, the *tranquillo* stream then ascends to the high *dolce* register, and its following descent leads smoothly to the *dolce*'s retake of <D5, F4>.

---

[16] Such literal recall is not usual in Carter's music up to this point, but the technique takes on enormous formal significance in several of his later pieces. See Link, *Elliott Carter's Late Music*.

[17] Carter has affirmed that the distinct streams represent different facets of a single personality: Q.: It is quite something that you've written so many pieces dedicated to friends and colleagues. How far do the images of, or the ideas about them influence your composition?

EC: I can say that, in almost every case, thinking about the friend has affected the composition. In the case of "Riconoscenza," I remember vividly that Petrassi – like many Italians – was somebody who could talk very seriously about important subjects and suddenly burst into laughter or become terribly angry – then sometimes talk in a very exultant, quiet mood. I wrote "Riconoscenza" so that it has alternations of rather comically angry music, then lofty, slow and quiet sections. (Bons, Interview with Elliott Carter, 16.)

The registral coupling of the *dolce* and *tranquillo* streams during mm. 51–66 accompanies another linkage: the *tranquillo*'s top voice moves among members of a diminished-seventh chord, as does the *dolce* melody. (Harmonically it still emphasizes ics 4 and 5 and 0146 AITs.) Such connections appeared fleetingly, earlier in the piece, but because this passage is the longest *tranquillo* statement so far, it is easier to focus on its voice leading. And now that the connection is made, this feature disappears from the *tranquillo* stream for a while. The linkage also seems to affect the *dolce* stream which, when it resumes in m. 66, makes *its* longest statement. It swells to its greatest intensity in mm. 71–72 then relaxes gradually to the instrument's lowest pitch in mm. 77–78 (Example 5.3e). This nadir combines with the surrounding pitches into a 0146 AIT characteristic of the *tranquillo* stream, and the immediate reiteration of the same pitches as *tranquillo* dyads enhances the unity between those streams.

The *tranquillo* and *dolce* streams now occupy the registral territory of the *marcato* stream, which was absent during their conciliation. In m. 83, the latter plays the other streams' shared pitches as a quadruple stop; as such they are the lowest 0146 that the violin can produce. Then it proceeds into *its* longest and most intense statement, climbing ever higher to culminate in a bravura series of 0146 tetrachords (Example 5.3f). By so doing, however, it reaches into the high register associated with the *dolce* music, and as the tetrachords play out, the *dolce* stream gradually insinuates itself, assumes control, and builds to its own (slowest, highest) climax in m. 98. Its ascent from mm. 92–97 involves its greatest feat of recollection yet, a loose retrograde around the *marcato* climax in m. 95. After it peaks it rapidly falls back down to the lowest register, and the confinement and alternation of all three streams there, in mm. 101–21, creates a stasis that articulates closure for the piece.

Closure is also achieved through the reconciliation of the distinctive interval repertoires of the streams. As shown by boxes on Example 5.3f, in mm. 100–20 all the streams state two distinct all-interval pitch-tetrachords, y = {G3, Db4, A4, C5} and z = {G3, Bb3, F♯4, C5}, in that order. (Together they form a 013467 hexachord, a union of 036s that implicitly underlies many of the piece's earlier passages.) The *tranquillo* stream dawdles a bit before playing z, but as soon as it does, the piece ends with a brief *dolce* phrase that encapsulates them both, signifying perhaps that the dominant persona has assimilated its previously contrasting tendencies.[18] Thus the integration of a single personality acted out

---

[18] Indeed one can hear *another* all-interval tetrachord, labeled x on Example 5.3f, that is also stated in each stream prior to tetrachords y and z. But it is not quite as clear as they are: in the *dolce* stream it does not consist of successive pitches, but rather the first, last, and two highest pitches of a slurred group; and it does not appear in the *dolce* phrase in the final two measures.

Ex. 5.3f *Riconoscenza*, mm. 91–121, integration of all three streams

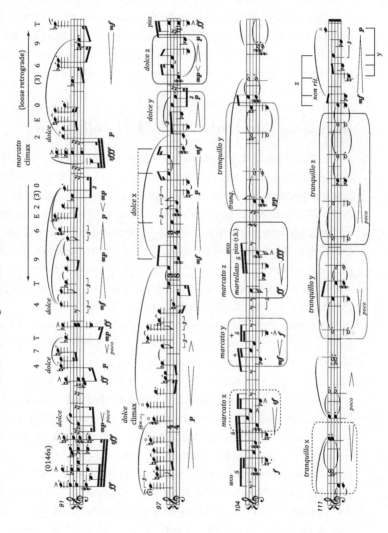

by *Riconoscenza* involves the gradual sharing that progressively deepens from register to interval-class content, and finally to pitch.

In both *Esprit Rude/Esprit Doux* and *Riconoscenza*, then, a conciliation of autonomous musical continuities is achieved through a series of episodes in which dialogue gradually develops and deepens. Since they involve simple pitch and metrical identities, these processes are relatively easy to hear – not as abstract as the hexachordal harmonies and polyrhythmic structures that are often discussed, although certainly contingent upon them. They do not only enact conflict but also, as Carter said about his mature style, they express "the democratic attitude in which each member of a society maintains his or her own identity while cooperating in a common effort."[19]

Increasing cooperation as gradual unification

The Fifth String Quartet, poised on the threshold of Carter's "late late" style, assembles local pitch and rhythmic interactions into a formally determinative process spanning the entire work. Although played without pause, the quartet presents a clear succession of six movements unified internally, and contrasting strongly with each other, by tempo, featured articulation, and associated expressive character. Between them, and in an introduction, the instruments play much more independently. Carter's program notes allude to the process of chamber-music rehearsal, explaining that the "introduction presents the players, one by one, trying out fragments of later passages … at the same time maintaining a dialogue with each other," and that in the interludes "the players discuss in different ways what has been played and what will be played."[20] Indeed it is not difficult to discern allusions to the main movements, especially in their harmonics, pizzicatos, and rapid, light "giocoso" gestures. Contrary to the normal notion of rehearsal, however, there are no literal quotes, suggesting that the materials are manifestations of the instruments' inner characters, not some predetermined course of action. Listeners are further urged by the program note to attend to the "very important" interactions among the parts. Indeed, analysis of several of the intermediary passages shows that their function is more complex than simple rehearsal. The dialogues and cooperations deepen and develop, shaping the interludes into a through-composed process, and unifying the otherwise different musics of the main movements. Moreover, the interactions among the instruments involve pulse to a much greater extent than in earlier works, even

[19] Carter, "Program Note," in *String Quartet No. 4* [score].

[20] Carter, "Composer's Notes," in *String Quartet No. 5* [score].

though (or perhaps because) the composition is not organized by a long-range polyrhythm.[21]

The opening of the quartet (see Example 5.4a) seems solipsistic: Violin I hammers a pair of 0148 quadruple stops; Viola sustains a single timbrally varying pitch; Cello plays a brief swelling 016 trichord spanning the register (C2–B2) where no one else can play; Viola re-enters with a quiet high harmonic; and Violin II snaps a pizzicato on its open lowest string. Not only do these gestures differ in style and timbre, but the instruments never play together, and they share almost no notes. When Viola's harmonic exhausts the twelve-tone aggregate (indicated by a vertical dashed line in the Example) one may wonder if this represents cooperation, or if it is simply a natural consequence of maximal differentiation.

An answer is provided by the following events. After the completion of the aggregate, Violin I replays its pitches, now arpeggiating them expressively in a slow rhythm suggesting three 6/16 measures (indicated by vertical strokes in the bracket above the part), each repeating the time span between its opening chords. (The tempi of the pulses are specified by metronome markings and their prime factorization, consistent with accounts of Carter's tempo relations.[22]) However, it fails to repeat its highest pitch, G5. Violin II supplies a G, but in a surprising articulation and register, thus appearing to complete and cut off Violin I. Cello re-enters tentatively, testing again its low F, then strings together a line with intervallic variety – <F, E♭, A, D>, a 0137 AIT, interlocking with <D, E, B, A♯>, an instance of the other type of AIT, 0146. Although remaining in the low register, its materials echo those of Violin I: a clear pulse (MM 84), a melodic interval (2), a swell to A, and an ending with three quick intervals in the same direction. This last gesture even reaches out of its low register to touch, *leggero*, on Violin I's A♯3, but breaks off immediately after this direct contact. Violin II's second loud pizzicato – 44 quintuplet sixteenths after the first – marks the end of Cello's melody the way it did Violin I's. Already the instruments seem to be taking on roles with respect to each other, even as they stake out different tempi and intervallic repertoires.

Viola's next brief *leggero* line, in m. 10, while also asserting its own durations and intervals, nevertheless mediates between the other instruments. Its pitch-class content includes Cello's 0146 as well as Violin I's 0148, the latter with interval 4s instead of 8s, and its final two pcs complete the aggregate that the others began.[23] As if responding to the mediation,

---

[21] Jenkins, "After the Harvest: Carter's Fifth String Quartet and the Late Late Style."
[22] Lewin, *Generalized Musical Intervals and Transformations*, pp. 61–75. Mead, "On Tempo Relations."

[23] Cello's predilection for AITs can be observed even at the very beginning of the movement, when it adds its <C, B, F> trichord to Viola's D♯. Several recurrences of AITs in mm. 1–13 are pointed out by Bernard, "The String Quartets of Elliott Carter," p. 269.

Ex. 5.4a String Quartet No. 5, Introduction

Violin I initiates a high harmonic, then Cello joins in with the B♭3 that the two instruments have already shared, along with their shared F – the first simultaneity of the piece. They crescendo then cut off at virtually the same moment, the clearest indication so far that they are listening to each other. Perhaps they are anticipating that Violin II will repeat its previous characteristic duration, as they have done, because they cease before it enters, exactly on time. Indeed, Cello subtly invites the violins to share its characteristic harmony. Given Violin I's entrance on B, and the expectation that Violin II will repeat a G, it enters with exactly those notes that will combine with the others' to form a 0146 AIT, {F, G, B♭, B}.

The events of m. 12 support this reading. Cello proposes another double stop combining its already shared B♭3 with a pitch, E3, that is out of reach for the violins but within Viola's range. Viola seems to accept the invitation by answering with its own double stop (including its most recent C5) that combines with Cello to make another 0146. Cello cuts off just after Viola enters, however, perhaps suggesting it prefers associating with the violins. Then Violin II reiterates its pizzicato G3 exactly on time, marking off the Viola–Cello interaction from the earlier ones. Our impression grows that the instruments are taking up harmonic and timekeeping relationships with each other.

The impression is strengthened especially as the following measures introduce new material, but continue the interactions. Violin I breaks into the longest solo yet, stating the entire aggregate save Violin II's G, at a new tempo, MM 64. The beats, articulated by group beginnings and accented events, are indicated in Example 5.4a by the vertical strokes in the bracket above the Violin I part. After four beats at this tempo, it breaks off, but Viola enters exactly on the next expected beat, just before Violin II rearticulates its inexorable slow pulse. Now, surprisingly, Violin II subdivides its glacial pulse into four (MM 32.72), and starts to meander in pitch, happening upon on B♭3 (notated as A♯3), then F4 on its strong beat – the notes shared already by Violin I and Cello. At this moment of arrival its faster pulse dramatically halts, and into the ensuing silence Viola erupts, provoking two quick outbursts in the entire ensemble – a twelve-tone chord, with many pcs shared among the parts, but always fixed in register. Thereafter Violin I plays an even more extended solo, and so begins to establish the *giocoso* texture that will soon be joined by all the instruments to create the first movement.

As the instruments relinquish their independence, however, impressions persist that will guide the hearing of the following interludes. Violin I and Cello seem to be the primary instigators of ideas; Viola and Violin II act in more intermediary or timekeeping roles. Interactions, nonexistent at first, grew from simple pitch sharing and temporal overlap to the coordination of different lines into AITs and aggregates, and to the anticipation or continuation of each other's pulses.

The individual instruments come into focus again as the first main movement concludes, just after its meandering *giocoso* reaches a gentle climax around mm. 59–60. Violin I and Cello return from respectively high and low extremes, each at its own tempo. As the focus shifts to Viola's louder, busy triplets, they accelerate and condense, together now with Violin II, into a narrow registral band. The intensification culminates in loud double stops, grouped by near simultaneity into two AITs (respectively {6T01} in Violin II/Viola and {2478} in Violin I/Cello). The violins and Cello then transmute the chordal pitches into *tranquillo* lines, but Viola continues to strengthen, now playing various quadruple stops at its own tempo (triplet half note). Cello attempts briefly to restore the movement with an expressive line, but Viola's aggressive, regular attacks disrupt and silence the cooperative ensemble playing, forcing a retrenchment to the sparse, tentative texture that is Interlude I. The cooperation of the main movement disintegrates into a sparser texture that is individualistic yet fosters the sorts of discourse that the Introduction exposed.

As the instruments disengage, they revert to alternation, avoiding overlap until just before the next main movement begins. Nevertheless they interact in new ways. Unlike in the Introduction, in which the utterances were so brief that their tempi were scarcely evident, the melodic fragments here are extended enough to suggest faster, entrainable pulse streams, which are even layered to create meter. Examples 5.4b and 5.4c indicate these pulse continuities and their interactions by horizontal brackets connecting the defining events (mm. 64–65 are renotated in the tempo and meter signature of m. 66, rather than of the preceding movement, and without the fading Cello and Violin II; Example 5.4c overlaps with 5.4b by two measures, in order to clarify some of the continuities discussed below). Viola, Cello, and Violin II each take a turn to establish their own tempi, at moments marked in the score by explicit tempo changes. But there is also a tentative rhythmic accommodation, a sustaining of each other's tempi, occasionally even at the expense of one's own. Pulse is immediately palpable in Viola's seven regular chords until the downbeat of m. 67, when first Violin II and then Cello enter to establish their own tempi. These instruments seem to be exchanging ideas the way that Cello and Violin I did in the Introduction; however, they also sustain Viola's pulse, as shown by dotted vertical strokes in the Example, specifically by Violin II's contour- and loudness-accented B♭5, then by Cello's entrance on G4 and dynamic accent on A3, then by accented events in Violin II, notably its final snap pizzicato. Doubled solid vertical strokes show how these quarter-note beats group into a slow quintuple meter.

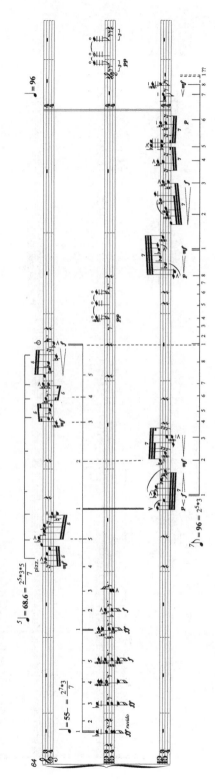

Ex. 5.4b Quartet No. 5, First interlude, mm. 64–73

Ex. 5.4c Quartet No. 5, First interlude, mm. 72–84

Cello's gestures prove to be especially determinative, as they eventually establish a new tempo for the ensemble at m. 72. Once it plays its first accented event, it continues to place accents consistently at MM 96, even across a long silence. In this task it is supported by that snap pizzicato in Violin II, which falls not only on Viola's beat but also on Cello's. This event suggests grouping Cello's beat octuply, as indicated by doubled solid vertical strokes across the MM 96 horizontal bracket. The first loudness peak sustains this regularity when it re-enters (*mf*, m. 70). Yet Viola, after so much support, strikes off on its own. Its first harmonic in m. 69 does not fall on any of the established beats. Neither does its second harmonic, in m. 72; indeed, that moment is especially disruptive because Cello, having just accomplished the global tempo change, breaks off just before it could articulate the octuple downbeat.

Cello essays another pair of double stops in m. 74 (Example 5.4c), as if appealing for support, and this time Violin II answers the call, attacking on Cello's octuple downbeat. Having thus sustained Cello's pulses, however, it proceeds at a different, new tempo. Violin I, long silent, now introduces a new tempo, MM 72, as well. The violins overlap, and seem to be in some harmonic communication, as both focus on 025 trichords produced with their own characteristic intervals (and included in some AITs), but Violin II cedes the spotlight as Violin I crescendos to its peak, which is four of its beats after its entrance. Violin II re-enters on one of its beats, but then changes tempo again. The third of its new beats, which is notated as the moment of next global tempo change, also is a downbeat for the four-beat group in Violin I, and also a beat for Cello! The three instruments seem to be finely synchronized. But then disruption returns, as high, sustained, out-of-time harmonics pass from instrument to instrument. When the last instrument, Violin I, has had its turn, the next main movement, featured sustained chords, begins.

Thus Interlude 1 has introduced a new level of dialogue among the parts. Not only do they overlap, and share pitches and harmonic structures, as in the Introduction, but also each negotiates its own temporal continuity that interacts in various ways with the others'. Yet their coordination is not sufficient to give much shape to the Interlude; it still sounds like a succession of moments, without coherent form.

In the second interlude, however, the instruments interact more coherently to create larger-scale shape. Some aspects of these cooperative processes during its first half are represented schematically in Example 5.4d, in which solid note-heads represent brief solo melodic statements and open note-heads represent sustained pitches that overlap into chords. An alternation of solo melodies and chords creates form. The solo statements grow in presence, with the third introducing a clear pulse. The harmony proceeds as a series of AITs,

Ex. 5.4d Quartet No. 5, Cooperative processes during the Second interlude

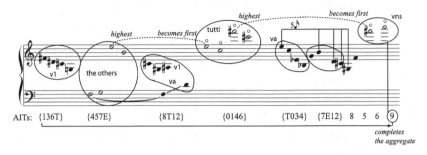

AITs: {136T}   {457E}   {8T12}   {0146}   {T034} {7E12} 8   5   6   ⑨

completes
the aggregate

Ex. 5.4e Quartet No. 5, Third interlude, main harmonies

listed below the Example, that state eleven different tones, and the final pitch of the passage completes the aggregate. The note-groups connect with each other: for instance, the highest pitch of each sustained chord becomes the first pitch of the next.

The subsequent interludes further structure and direct the instruments' materials. As an illustration, Example 5.4e sketches the organization of a striking passage in the third interlude. This is the first sustained passage in the interludes that all four instruments play the same way (in this case pizzicato, as a foreshadowing of the last main movement). Like the passage in the second interlude, its pitch structure is coherent, partitioning the aggregate by instrument into four tetrachords, including three AITs. The last two interludes, IV and V (movements 9 and 11), sound much less fragmentary than the earlier ones, because each is shaped into a clear two-part process. First, one instrument (Cello in IV, and Violin I in V) plays an extended, variegated solo, then the others present a coordinated response that overlaps with a gradual segue into the texture of the following movement.

Retrospectively, then, the interludes seem gradually to develop from discontinuous, tenuously related fragments into large-scale, formally shaped continuities. The tentative engagements in the Introduction gradually strengthen in Interludes 1 and 2. For example, AITs progress from being created opportunistically by single instruments in the Introduction to partitions of the aggregate, coordinated among all four instruments. Pulse continuities, isolated in the Introduction, become more extended and cooperative, with instruments playing each other's beats. Having forged cooperation on the elemental levels of pitch and rhythm, the remainder of the interludes develop textural relations. Each of the last four interludes features an extended solo (5: viola, 7: Violin II, 9: Cello, 11: Violin I), and each successive interlude provides its solo with more support and context. In the end they appear no longer as incidental or tentative but equal in weight and duration to the main movements. Indeed, the main movements are so diverse that the quartet might seem lacking in coherence and continuity without the unifying, directed processes that the interludes construct.

"A very important consideration"

In the sixty years of Carter's music since the Second Quartet, the kinds of pitch and rhythmic dialogues analyzed above seem to be most evident and intense in the decade leading up to the Fifth Quartet. Certainly, scholars' attention to these interactions has explained many details of some of his chamber compositions of this period in addition to those discussed here, for instance, *Enchanted Preludes*,[24] *Scrivo in Vento*,[25] and *Esprit Rude/Esprit Doux II*,[26] suggesting that many other works of his mature style are likewise approachable. But as my analyses of *Riconoscenza* and String Quartet No. 5 have shown, these interactions often go beyond a representation of social cooperation, suggested by the program notes, to shape more purely musical and large-scale aspects of the compositions, just as the combinatorics of a contrapuntal subject shape the form of a fugue. By thus harmonizing the immediate mimetic appeal of program music with the formal exigencies of absolute music, Carter's polyvocalism reconciles two often conflicting tendencies in Western composition.

---

[24] Roeder, "Autonomy and Dialogue in Elliott Carter's *Enchanted Preludes*."
[25] Mailman, "An Imagined Drama of Competitive Opposition in Carter's *Scrivo in Vento*."
[26] Arthur, "Cooperation and Other Unifying Processes in Elliott Carter's *Esprit Rude/Esprit Doux* Trilogy."

Time management: rhythm as a formal determinant
       in certain works of Elliott Carter

Andrew Mead

Elliott Carter has long employed a range of interesting and complex ways of treating time in his music.[1] In the management of multiple tempi, the use of complex polyrhythms and the constant recontextualization of different pulse streams, Carter has found ways to create large-scale musical structures determined in large part by issues of rhythm. Since his music is thoroughly grounded in the practicalities of performance and the constraints of traditional notation, it is possible to specify to a high degree the ways his compositional decisions concerning rhythm can shape both local and large-scale aspects of much of his music from the past half century.[2] In the following, we will investigate a range of Carter's rhythmic practices, from the varied uses and functions of meter in his music to the role of large-scale polyrhythms in determining local and global tempo relations. In the process, we will employ a graphing technique developed from work by Henry Cowell, Karlheinz Stockhausen, and David Lewin to illustrate some of the intricacies of Carter's handling of tempi in his compositions.[3] We will pay particular attention to the ways performance, interpretation, and apprehension can condition our thinking about Carter's compositional use of time.

At the heart of Carter's rhythmic practice is the technique of presenting two or more tempi, simultaneously or in sequence, related by simple ratios. Such an approach is hardly new, but Carter has explored the ramifications of the resulting tempo space far beyond the examples we may find in Brahms, Berlioz, and several other earlier composers.[4] The term, "metrical modulation," has frequently been associated with this process, although it only begins to describe the impact of tempo relations on Carter's music.

Very often relations among tempi are described in terms of metronome marks – absolute speeds related to an arbitrary unit, the minute. This approach, while demonstrably successful and in accord with Carter's usual notational

---

[1] See, for example, Carter, "Music and the Time Screen" (1976), in *CEL*, pp. 262–80.
[2] Some of these issues are addressed in Bernard, "The Evolution of Elliott Carter's Rhythmic Practice."

[3] See Cowell, *New Musical Resources*, as well as Lewin, *Generalized Musical Intervals and Transformations*, and Stockhausen, "... how time passes ...."
[4] See, for example, Epstein, *Shaping Time – Music, the Brain and Performance*.

practice, raises questions of how accurately both listeners and performers can perceive and render specific tempi, and it can draw our attention away from an important aspect of how we take in tempo changes, as simple whole-number ratios that can be comprehended through a wide range of absolute tempi. If we concentrate on the *ratios* as opposed to tempo *rates*, we can much more readily track like changes between different pairs of tempi, and in turn develop an ear for recognizing the replicated experience of a particular ratio in various contexts, no matter what the absolute tempi might be.

For purposes of depicting ratios among tempi, we have a fully formed notational system ready to hand with which we are already familiar: pitch notation, which allows us to track both pitches (frequencies) and intervals (ratios). While it may initially seem counterintuitive to read pitch notation as the indication of tempo, it is appropriate to do so, given that the difference between the two is a matter of perception, rather than structure.[5] Following the implications of this notation, we can point out that the overtone series can represent a given tempo and the tempi of its subdivisions, while the inversion of the overtone series can represent a tempo and the various tempi that arise from grouping its pulses into regular multiples.[6] This is illustrated in Example 6.1. Simple extensions of these ideas allow us to track tempi, whether as beats, subdivisions, or metrical groupings into measures, through the changing temporal flux of a composition.

Example 6.2 is taken from mm. 198–204 in the first movement of Carter's String Quartet No. 1. It is not hard to see from the score that each instrumental entrance is at a new and faster rate, but by graphing the tempi as pitches it is easy to see that each successive entrance is related to the previous entrance in the same way, a ratio of 3:2 by tempo, or its reciprocal, 2:3 by duration. Once all four voices are in, the music unfolds the resulting polyrhythm of 8:12:18:27. Its completion on the downbeat of m. 204 launches the work into a new tempo frame, derived from the rate of the first violin. At the beginning of Example 6.2, the notated tactus is that of the viola's part, shifting to one-half of that of the second violin's part in subsequent measures, but neither of these rates is privileged in the music. This passage occurs at the climax of a broader sweep of changing tempi in the four instruments that occurs after the viola's recapitulation of the cello's opening solo in the middle of the movement. Example 6.3 is a graph of the notated tempi and the various pulse streams within each instrument found in the passage directly preceding the one in Example 6.2. As can be seen from the variety of ratios among tempi in this passage, the subsequent passage in Example 6.2 can be heard as a

---

[5] By which I mean that as one repeatedly doubles the speed of a beat, eventually it will move into the realm of pitch: repeatedly doubling a tempo of 60 bpm will after only a few iterations bring one into the frequency range of a 32-foot reed on the organ.

[6] This point is made in Stockhausen, " . . . how time passes . . . ."

Ex. 6.1 Tempi charted as pitches

This stack represents subdivisions of the bottom tempo by 2, 3, 4, 5, 6, and 7. Note the slight lowering of the top tempo; this represents the difference between the ratios 6/5 and 7/6. Setting G above middle C as 60, the tempi from the bottom up are: 30, 60, 90, 120, 150, 180, 210. Combining ratios is performed by multiplication.

This stack represents successively larger groupings of the top tempo, by 2, 3, 4, 5, 6, and 7. Note the slight raising of the bottom tempo; this represents the difference between the ratios 5/6 and 6/7. Setting G above middle C as 60, the tempi from the top down are: 240, 120, 80, 60, 48, 40, 34+.

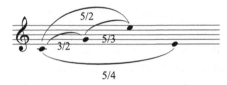

This shows how ratios may be combined through multiplication. Combining the ratios 3/2 times 5/3 yields 5/2, and reducing out the octave, by multiplying by that interval's reciprocal, 1/2, reduces the major tenth (5/2) to a major third (5/4).

clarification and climax of the preceding musical process, in that it effectively creates a sequence of repeated ratios following the earlier variety of ratios.

Another illustration of the analytical usefulness of this graphing technique can be drawn from a consideration of this same work's finale, titled "Variations." As has been noted, this movement is made of several recurring textures, motives, or rhythmic fragments recurring in different combinations, and always at a faster rate. David Schiff identifies seven such "themes," and illustrates their slowest occurrences.[7] Example 6.4 traces one of these motives through its major appearances in the movement, graphed to illustrate both the speed of the motive at its successive occurrences and the tempo of the notated tactus in each instance. Doing so allows us to track with ease the ever more rapid speeds of the successive appearances of the motive, and this approach could be used in a full-blown analysis of the movement to compare the different kinds of changes each identifiable theme goes through in the course of the music.

The preceding examples from String Quartet No. 1 have been largely anecdotal, and are offered primarily as illustrations of the usefulness of our

---

[7] See Schiff, *MEC*, p. 69; Schiff calls the motive in my Example 6.4 "Passacaglia."

Ex. 6.2 Elliott Carter, String Quartet No. 1, mm. 198–205

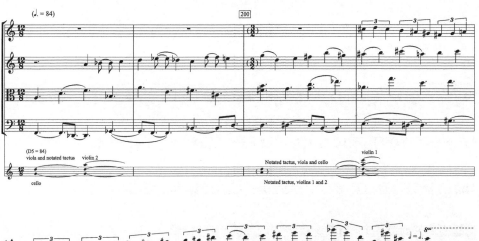

Ex. 6.3 Tempi in Carter's String Quartet No. 1, mm. 180–97

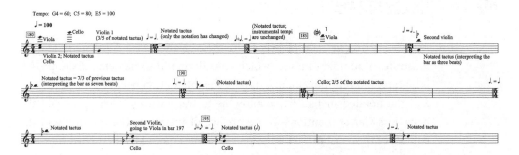

graphing technique. But they do suggest the ways that issues of rhythm and tempo play a significant role in shaping the large-scale formal designs of Carter's music. In what follows, we will trace more specifically some of the ways Carter has used contrasting approaches to meter and tempo to shape how his music unfolds. In each case we will draw an example from a shorter work, and then suggest how some of the ideas we are inspecting manifest themselves over larger time spans.

Ex. 6.4 Recurrences of a motive in the finale of Carter's String Quartet No. 1

A fairly recent pair of pieces for solo piano, *Two Diversions* (1999), illustrates a number of issues worth considering in some detail. Example 6.5 is a graph of both movements, tracing the interaction between pulse streams and the notated meter. These allow us to track with greater specificity the behaviors Carter mentions in the preface of the work: the reframing of the context of the constant stream of pulses in one voice in the first *Diversion*, and the divergent tendencies of the tempi of the two voices in the second.

These movements occasion an opportunity to tease out some of the issues concerning meter in Carter's music. Examples such as those we have considered from the First Quartet can invite us to ignore traditional uses of notated meter as the imposition of a governing framework of variously stressed beats operating across an entire ensemble. In Example 6.2, for instance, the fact that the viola's pulse stream aligns with the initial notated meter does not privilege it aurally, but is the result of the composer's choices in representing his series

Ex. 6.5 Tempi in Elliott Carter's *Two Diversions*

Diversion I

Stemmed notes indicate notated tempi, and note values indicate tactus values
found in the score, to facilitate identification. Ratios are indicated between tempi as an aid.
G4 = 60; C5 = 80

Steady rate of dyads throughout; occasionally doubled.

Diversion II

Upper staff indicates notated tempi, with tactus values as indicated.
Lower staff indicates the principal pulse strings of the
two lines, with certain ornamentation omitted.

of pulse-stream ratios in the score. In this instance, any of the other pulse
streams in the other parts could have been used for the notated meter. And
given a particular notational choice of meter, it is incumbent in most instances for players unfolding pulse streams at other rates to avoid accentuations
implying the primacy of the notated meter.

If this is the case, then what purpose does meter, whether notated or
perceived, serve in Carter's music? As Example 6.2 suggests, and as the second
of the two *Diversions* illustrates as well, notated meter can marshal the interaction of equally important pulse streams that move at different rates, even
when none of the streams in play actually articulates the notated meter. The
limitations of these interactions can be specified clearly, given Carter's use of
traditional notation and his understanding of the limitations of players' abilities
to subdivide time spans, and we shall examine those shortly. But first we shall
consider what is at stake in the first *Diversion*, one in which a single pulse rate,
articulated by dyads, runs steady through the entire piece. One might wonder at
the use of a variety of notated meters and tempi in this piece, given the fixity of
the constant pulse rate, but we can understand this as a desire to surround the

steady pulse with a wide variety of additional musical gestures. Much of this additional music involves shorter phrases, some unfolding brief regular pulse streams of their own, and some showing greater variety. The overall effect is to create a distinction between the steady stream of one voice (represented by C4 in Example 6.5) and the constant changing of the other voice. The changes of meter and tempo work to maximize the variety of notational contexts for the contrasting voices. Once again, though, meter is not being used here in a traditional way, either for the voice with the steady pulse stream, or for the other voice, with its greater variety of gesture. This is not to say that the kinds of regularities in larger groupings of events that can be construed as establishing meter cannot be found in this music, nor that such groupings will not ever align with the notated meter, but dealing with such notational situations can provide players with some of the biggest challenges of playing Carter's work. The dangers lie on either side: one may create inadvertent subtle mis-accentuations based on the contingencies of notating a pulse stream in a contrasting tempo, or conversely miss the opportunity for asserting larger metrical groupings within a pulse stream that might help give greater profile to an unfolding line.

These two brief *Diversions* offer an interesting contrast in attaining rhythmical distinction between two simultaneously occurring musical flows. In the first piece, the contrast is between the regularity of one voice's pulse stream with the variety of different musical gestures that surround it. In the second, contrast may be found between the competing pulse streams, presented in a series of ever-wider ratios. These two pieces provide in miniature an illustration of two strategies Carter has found fruitful to pursue at greater length and complexity in some of his larger works.

The String Quartet No. 3 is a good example of the kind of contrast found in the first *Diversion*, and provides a cautionary note with regard to the use of meter that we have just discussed. As has been detailed elsewhere, in this quartet Carter has divided his ensemble into two duos, each with its own repertoire of movements and ways of acting.[8] For our purposes here, I will only be concerned with the general contrast in rhythmic behavior, although the piece exhibits a wide variety of ways of creating identity and distinction among its constituent ensembles and their musics. Duo II, the second violin and viola, derives its rhythmic process from a constant reshuffling of combinations of regular pulse streams in each instrument. While this creates a great deal of variety of speeds and ratios among speeds, it nevertheless projects great regularity in the nature of its constituent rhythmic elements. In contrast, the music of Duo I, the first violin and cello, entails far greater variety in its

[8] See Schiff, *MEC*, p. 85, as well as Mead, "Pitch Structure in Elliott Carter's String Quartet #3."

rhythms, to a large extent eschewing the kinds of steady pulse streams found in Duo II. Already we can understand the quartet as using the kind of contrast found in the first *Diversion*, only writ large: while Duo II does not contain a single regular pulse stream, nevertheless it represents regularity in contrast to the variety of rhythmic behavior of Duo I. To my ear, these two situations invite a distinction in interpreting the role of the notated meter. I find it useful to ignore the notated meter with regard to the music of Duo II, whose various regular pulse streams establish their own metrical groupings. But in contrast, I find the more irregular rhythmic behavior of Duo I makes even richer sense when heard as unfolding against the traditional emphases of downbeats, upbeats, and subdivisions found in the duo's notated meter.

The lesson we can take away from this is that the relationship between the notated meter and what we may hear in Carter's music can be in flux. To go back to Example 6.2 (from String Quartet No. 1), while it is true that the various pulse streams are independent and only notationally coordinated by the written meter, at the point of their coincidence, the end of the four-part polyrhythm, the ensemble unites within a single metrical frame identical to what is written in the score.

Just as the first *Diversion* offers in miniature certain features of Carter's larger works, so does the second. As we have discussed, this piece derives its contrast from competing steady pulse streams of different rates. Interestingly, in the second *Diversion*, these pulse streams are frequently out of phase with each other, in that there is no point in which an attack of one stream occurs simultaneously with the attack of another. In fact, in those cases where pulse streams are in phase, Carter frequently drops out one voice to avoid simultaneous attacks. This is not to say that they never occur, but they are very rare in the composition.

The idea of unfolding pulse streams simultaneously, and doing so in phase, underlies one of the big developments in Carter's mature rhythmic practice. Many scholars have noted that from *Night Fantasies* (1980) to the *Symphonia* (1993–96) a good number of his compositions have exhibited large-scale polyrhythms that span the entire piece.[9] Frequently these pieces will contain a brief introduction, after which the polyrhythm will open with the simultaneous attack of whatever musical elements are articulating its different pulse streams. The piece will often end with the return of the simultaneity marking the completion of the cycle. There might be a brief coda, although the attainment of the simultaneity might itself be the last event of the piece. These polyrhythms are not always directly apparent in the musical surface, and are often moving at a sufficiently slow rate to make their regularity virtually

[9] See *MEC*, as well as Link "Long-Range Polyrhythms in Elliott Carter's Recent Music." See also Weston, "Inversion, Subversion, and Metaphor," as well as Ravenscroft, "Texture in Elliott Carter's *A Mirror on Which to Dwell*," and Poudrier, "Toward a General Theory of Polymeter."

imperceptible, even when their elements are evident. How can we best understand their purpose in the music?

One way to come to grips with this question is to consider what the constraining factors are in constructing these polyrhythms using traditional notation. What follows is a brief tutorial based on work I have published elsewhere.[10] Two-voiced polyrhythms must be constructed from two numbers that are mutually prime. This is true whether we are dealing with 4 against 5, or with 45 against 56. We will refer to these two numbers, or parts of a polyrhythm, as *limbs*, and their constituent segments as *elements*. Thus, a polyrhythm of 45 against 56 contains two limbs: one of 45 elements, and one of 56; the elements in a limb are segments of equal duration, the sum of which yields the duration of the polyrhythm. In order to determine the metrical frame that can project a polyrhythm, we can work with the formula explained in Example 6.6, in which each limb is expressed as a multiple of some fraction of a time span. The denominators of these fractions indicate subdivisions of these time spans, and the numerators indicate how many of these subdivisions are bundled together to form an element of the limb in question. Thus, for example, a polyrhythm whose limbs are 14 and 15 could be construed as 14 iterations of $\frac{3}{7}$ of a time span against 15 iterations of $\frac{2}{5}$ of the same time span. Such a polyrhythm would complete itself after 6 iterations of the time span, given that $\frac{3}{7} \times 14 = \frac{2}{5} \times 15 = 6$. We shall call such time spans *units* or *time-span units*. By manipulating these fractions in specified ways we can create several basic realizations of the polyrhythm using different multiples of time-span units. We shall call these basic realizations *formats*. Example 6.6 provides an illustration, both as an abstraction and with regards to our sample polyrhythm of 14:15. By fixing the overall duration of the polyrhythm we may determine the related tempi of its various formats' time-span units. Example 6.7 illustrates one possible realization of each of the four formats found in Example 6.6.[11]

As we have noted, each format is based on its own repertoire of fractions parsing its time-span units. At this level of realization, we can shift among formats only at those points where the onsets of their constituent time-span units coincide. It is important to realize that while the number of time-span units in a format may coincide with the number of elements of one or the other limb of the polyrhythm, they only do so when one of the format's constituent fractions is $\frac{1}{1}$. Example 6.8 illustrates how one may shift among formats, presenting two realizations of the polyrhythm 14:15 employing different metrical interpretations at different tempi within a single iteration of the polyrhythm. Obviously, if we were to hear the instances of 14:15 in Examples 6.7

---

[10] See Mead, "On Tempo Relations."
[11] John Link notes that one may derive a complete catalogue of formats by taking the product of the limbs of a polyrhythm and dividing their factors by each limb. (Private correspondence, 2009.)

Ex. 6.6 Constructing polyrhythms

A: Prime factors a, b (for present purposes, A = ab)
X: Prime factors x, y (for present purposes, X = xy)

Formats:

A	X	Fractions		Multiples of time-span units
y/b,	a/x	y/b A = a/x X =		ay
x/b,	a/y	x/b A = a/y X =		ax
x/a,	b/y	x/a A = b/y X =		xb
y/a,	b/x	y/a A = b/x X =		yb

N.B.: You may generate the different fraction pairs by flipping diagonals.

If A or X contains more than one representative of its prime factors, additional time-spans may be derived by multiplying the fraction pairs by ratios of duplicated primes.

Thus, if $X = x^2y^2$, then y^2/b, a/x^2 could be altered by x/y to become xy/b, a/xy, yielding time-span multiple axy.

By fixing the overall length of the polyrhythm we may relate their unit multiplicity by fractions, and thus see the tempo relations of their realizations. For example, ay is derived from ax by multiplying by y/x, so their relative tempi (frequency of unit occurrence) will be related by the same ratio.

Further alterations to fraction pairs may be made by multiplying each side of the equation by a constant. Such constants are equivalent to tempo alterations of their realization. Practicalities are limited by the size of the musical realization of the time span units in question, and thus by their divisibility into practically performable values. Subdividing a time span of a beat into 35 parts is not performable realizable, but subdividing five or seven beats into 35 parts is readily accomplished, to within certain practical limitations of performable tempi.

Sample realization based on 14:15 (14 = 2 × 7; 15 = 3 × 5)

Formats:

	14	15	Fractions	Multiples of time span units
Format A	3/7	2/5	3/7 × 14 = 2/5 × 15 =	6
Format B	5/7	2/3	5/7 × 14 = 2/3 × 15 =	10
Format C	3/2	7/5	3/2 × 14 = 7/5 × 15 =	21
Format D	5/2	7/3	5/2 × 14 = 7/3 × 15 =	35

and 6.8 at the appropriate ratios of tempi, they would be indistinguishable. What is crucial about these different formats is they provide a carefully controlled range of tempi and meters for music surrounding the polyrhythm.

A useful byproduct of thinking of the elements of each limb of a polyrhythm as a fraction of a notated time-span unit is that it allows us to determine from fragments what polyrhythm might be active in a portion of a work, whether or not it is complete, or in or out of phase. Thus, at the outset of the second of Carter's *Two Diversions* we can see that the fraction for the right hand is $\frac{5}{4}$ of a beat, while that of the left hand is $\frac{4}{3}$ of a beat. Combining the two fractions as a ratio, in other words multiplying the first fraction by the reciprocal of the second, we obtain the polyrhythm of 15:16, the narrowest ratio (i.e., closest to 1) found in the work.

Ex. 6.7 Realized formats from Ex. 6.6

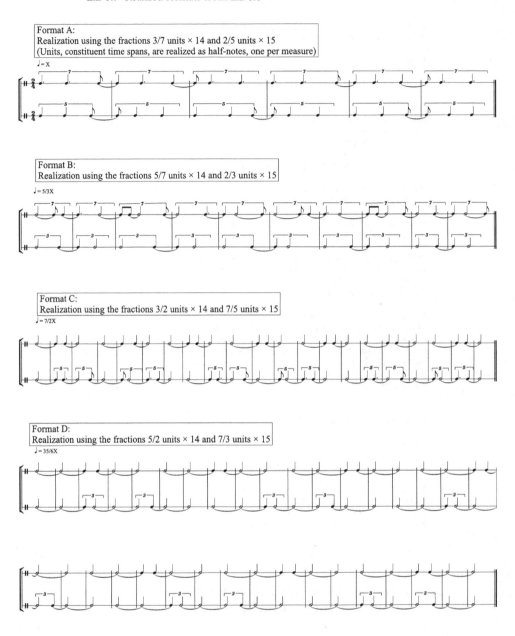

When a polyrhythm is realized over a short duration, we can see that the metric realization can be highly constrained. If the time-span units articulating the limbs are interpreted as beats, then the upper practical performance limits of subdivision will suggest a use of primes no higher than seven, or in combination, probably no higher than nine, twelve, or at slow tempi, fifteen. Thus the fractions we will find applied to time-span units will tend to

Ex. 6.8 Combining formats from Ex. 6.7

> Realization combining Format A (6 units) and Format B (10 units), whose common factor is 2, allowing units to align after every 3 units of A and 5 units of B.
> Similar combinations may occur between pairs of formats whose multiplicity of units share a common factor.

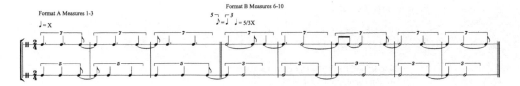

> Realization combining segments of all four formats, shifting among them at points where their respective strings of units coincide. This is one of several possible realizations shifting among formats.

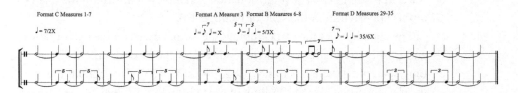

have denominators of 2, 3, 5, 7, and their simpler combinations. Greater flexibility comes into play as we stretch out the overall length of a poly-rhythm's realization. This is because as the distance grows between articulations of each limb's elements, so do the durations of its format's time-span units. So far in our examples we have realized these units as beats or single measures (see Examples 6.7 and 6.8), but as units grow, so they may be realized using multiples of beats, and multiples of measures. This can allow both for greater variety of realization, as well as opportunities for changing formats. Even under these looser conditions, one can see that for practical purposes the divisors of time-span units will tend to be limited to the lower primes, or products thereof. These broader realizations of a polyrhythm can also afford a greater variety of tempi and meters for realization, as the basic number of time-span units in a format may be much more finely divided. By multiplying either side of the basic equations in Example 6.6 by simple ratios, we may alter tempi in ways not immediately suggested by our basic formats.

Let us again consider a short work as an example of some of our ideas about polyrhythms. The first of Carter's two *Esprit Rude/Esprit Doux* is a duet for flute and clarinet about four minutes long, written in 1985 on the occasion of Pierre Boulez's sixtieth birthday. It is based on a polyrhythm of 21:25, which

Ex. 6.9 Deriving polyrhythm in Elliott Carter's *Esprit Rude/Esprit Doux*

Polyrhythm from *Esprit Rude/Esprit Doux* (1984)

$$A = 21 \qquad\qquad X = 25$$
$$3 \times 7 \qquad\qquad 5 \times 5$$

Basic formats from Ex.6.6:

$25 \times 7/5 = 21 \times 5/3 = 35$ time-span units
Used for most of the piece

$25 \times 3/5 = 21 \times 5/7 = 15$ time-span units
Not appearing in the piece

Additional format found at the opening of the piece:

$25 \times 1/1 = 21 \times 25/21 = 25$ time-span units
Derived from the first format by multiplying each side by 5/7

starts in phase after a short introduction. Example 6.9 illustrates the analysis of this polyrhythm in the style of Example 6.6.[12]

The main body of the work employs the format based on the pair of ratios $\frac{7}{5}$ and $\frac{5}{3}$, with 25 iterations of the first, and 21 of the second, unfolded over 35 time-span units (which is to say, $\frac{7}{5} \times 25 = \frac{5}{3} \times 21 = 35$). Throughout the work the clarinet articulates the 25-limb of the polyrhythm while the flute employs the 21-limb. For much of the work, the time-span unit is realized as two measures of $\frac{4}{4}$ at $\downarrow$ = 60–63 beats per minute. Thus the fractional subdivisions indicated by the ratios would be the quintuplet half note and the triplet whole note. The foregoing is illustrated in Example 6.10, which contains a realization of this format employing the specified time-span unit. It contains seventy-one measures, with two measures for each of the time-span units, and a final measure to contain the downbeat marking the end of the polyrhythm, the point at which the two limbs again coincide.

There are several passages in the work, however, that use different tempi and meters, and these allow us to understand some of the constraints of constructing large-scale polyrhythms in traditional musical notation. Some of these changes are trivial. Changes of tempo by a ratio of 3:2 render the triplet subdivision of the basic tempo's half notes as quarter notes in the new tempo; thus each $\frac{3}{4}$ measure at the more rapid tempo represents a half measure of $\frac{4}{4}$ in the basic tempo, and may readily encompass the fractions of the basic time-span unit. This is just as true for that passage that changes the tempo by a ratio of 3:4, in which the resulting measures in $\frac{3}{2}$ are of the same length as the basic $\frac{4}{4}$ measures. Both of these changes are simple renotations of the time-span units of the format, and annotations concerning these passages are found in Example 6.10.

[12] [John Roeder also discusses this polyrhythm in "'The Matter of Human Cooperation' in Carter's Mature Style," in this volume. – eds.]

Ex. 6.10　Metrical realization of polyrhythm in *Esprit Rude/Esprit Doux*

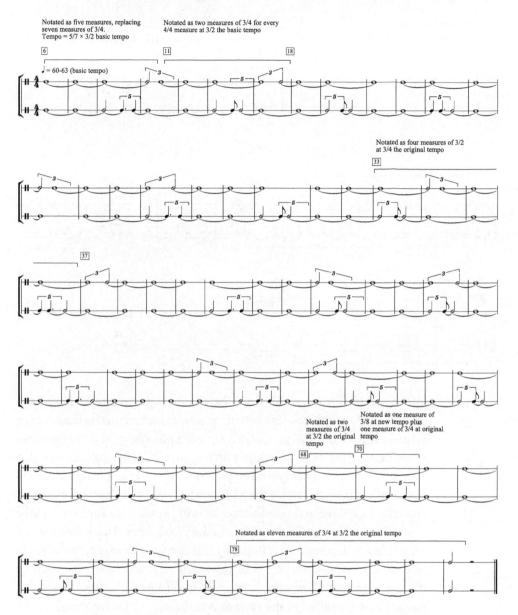

More interesting is the passage that opens the polyrhythm (mm. 6–10), which consists of five measures of $\frac{3}{4}$ at a tempo of 64–67+ beats per minute.[13] We can understand this passage in two ways, both of which can further our understanding of realizing large-scale polyrhythms. Example 6.11 will be useful for the following discussion. One way to think of this passage is in

[13] This passage is discussed in Truniger, "Elliott Carter: *Esprit Rude/Esprit Doux*."

Ex. 6.11 Metrical substitution in the polyrhythm of *Esprit Rude/Esprit Doux*

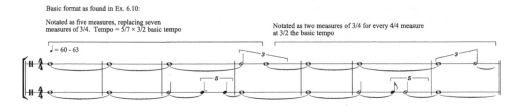

Basic format as found in Ex. 6.10:

Notated as five measures, replacing seven
measures of 3/4. Tempo = 5/7 × 3/2 basic tempo

Notated as two measures of 3/4 for every 4/4 measure
at 3/2 the basic tempo

Realized by substituting two 3/4 measures for each 4/4 measure:

Realized as found in the score:

These five measures replace the seven bracketed measures above.

local terms, that is to say think of these five measures as a replacement of a
given span of several measures within the format with another realization in a
related tempo. Using this perspective, we may understand these five measures
as taking up one-and-three-quarters time-span units of the realization, which
we have realized in Example 6.10 and at the top of Example 6.11 as three-
and-one-half measures of $\frac{4}{4}$ at the basic tempo. More to the point, we can also
construe these three-and-one-half measures in $\frac{4}{4}$ as seven measures of $\frac{3}{4}$ at $\frac{3}{2}$ the
basic tempo, along the lines of what was discussed above. This is found in the
second line of Example 6.11. Realizing this span in this manner is useful in
two ways. First, it is this metrical realization that will follow the opening
passage, and second, writing it out this way helps us to understand this
passage as it is realized in the score as a replacement of seven measures in $\frac{3}{4}$
by the five measures in $\frac{3}{4}$ with a compensatory tempo shift of $\frac{5}{7}$. The third line
of Example 6.11 illustrates this substitution, yielding the actual measures as
they are found in the score. Realizing the substitution this way readily allows
us to see that the correlated subdivision change (from seven measures of $\frac{3}{4}$ to
five measures of $\frac{3}{4}$ at $\frac{5}{7}$ the tempo) would be from quintuplets subdividing the
beats of the faster tempo to septuplets subdividing the beats of the slower
tempo. In other words, seven measures of $\frac{3}{4}$ subdivided by quintuplets can be
replaced by five measures of $\frac{3}{4}$ subdivided by septuplets with no alteration in

the rate of the pulse stream of the subdivisions. Since the resulting number of subdivisions for the entire span is divisible by three, five, and seven, we can see how this will permit any occurrences of elements of either limb of the polyrhythm within the span. Should the span contain no elements of either limb, we would have even greater freedom for substitution in realization.

One of the interesting aspects of this passage is that it not only contains the first attacks of each limb after the initiation, but that one of those attacks occurs on the down beat of the fifth measure of the substituted tempo (m. 10 of the score itself – see Example 6.11, third line). That allows us to consider this passage not merely as a local substitution, but also in terms of a new basic format for the polyrhythm along the lines of Examples 6.6 and 6.9. In this case, the fraction of the 25-limb would be $\frac{1}{1}$, and the fraction of the 21-limb would be $\frac{25}{21}$. 21 would be an impractical divisor if the format's time-span unit was realized as a beat, but considered as a measure or a multiple of measures, a time-span unit may easily encompass such a value, and in this case the basic time-span unit would be four measures of $\frac{3}{4}$, and $\frac{1}{21}$ of the unit would be $\frac{4}{7}$ of the quarter note, or the duration of 4 septuplet thirty-second notes.

The number of time-span units in this format would be 25, which is $\frac{5}{7}$ of the number of time-span units of the format that is used in the body of the work, which in turn is 35. This, of course, is reflected in the tempo relations exhibited as follows: the time-span unit of the principal format used is realized either as two measures of $\frac{4}{4}$, or as four measures of $\frac{3}{4}$ at $\frac{3}{2}$ of the basic tempo. The time-span unit of the format used in the passage at the outset of the piece (which we have discussed above in terms of a local substitution) is realized as four measures of $\frac{3}{4}$. The relationship of tempi thus are as follows: if the tempo of the $\frac{4}{4}$ measures in the body of the work is X, then the tempo of the $\frac{3}{4}$ measures in the alternate realization is $\frac{3}{2}$ X, and thus the tempo of the opening passage, based on the substitution, or the new format, is $\frac{5}{7}$ of $\frac{3}{2}$ of X, yielding a composite change from the opening of the piece to the tempo in the body of the work as $\frac{14}{15}$, or the reciprocal of the relationship between X and the opening. This helps explain the very slight difference in metronome markings between these passages, but also illustrates that the significance of the indicated change is not so much the absolute metronome marking as it is the ratios of the changes of tempo in the course of the work, and thus the recontextualization of the pulse streams in terms of what they might be combined with in various portions of the piece.

It is useful to note that in the above discussion of realizing large-scale polyrhythms we have identified three distinct but related modes of changing the metrical frame. Firstly, in those situations in which the basic time-span units of the underlying format can be realized in multiple measures, we may use substitutions that entail simple ratios with each other such that those places within the time-span unit at which elements of the limbs of the polyrhythm occur may readily be available. Using ratios such as 3:2 or 4:3, one can easily do this, given that these ratios simply indicate the replacement of a tactus with either a triplet or dotted version of itself. Secondly, in portions of a time-span unit or units in which no elements of the limbs occur, such substitutions may be treated with more complex ratios, so long as the replacement passage is of the same duration as that being replaced. In our example above seven measures of three beats subdivided by fives were replaced by five measures with the same number of beats per measure subdivided by sevens. Finally, within the bounds of notational practicality, we may shift from one format that may support the entire polyrhythm to another. In those cases when the time-span unit of the various formats is realized as a beat, we are limited to this last case, and frequently only when the onsets of both formats' time-span units align. This is the case only when the numbers of time-span units used to realize each format share a common multiple. Readers might want to reflect again upon the preceding examples, in which a number of these last issues are illustrated.

Before turning our attention to a larger and more elaborate compositional realization of a large-scale polyrhythm, it is worth taking some time considering how, in addition to providing a systematic context for meter and tempo, the presence of such a polyrhythm can contribute to the large-scale structure of a piece. As David Schiff points out, *Esprit Rude/Esprit Doux* is made of three kinds of music; one that is fast and often *scorrevole*, one that is often marked *giocoso*, and one that is slow and for the most part sustained.[14] The slowest music occurs both at a low dynamic level and a high one. The body of the piece moves through various combinations of these three musics distributed between the two instruments. This is further enriched by two appearances of music played *tremolando*, combining both rapidity and slowness.

The progress of the piece is not simply a list of the various combinations of musics, nor are repetitions of combinations eschewed, but each recurrence is marked by notable changes in the musical characters. The boundaries of these changes are also not firmly or consistently correlated with the elements of the limbs of the polyrhythm, but there are enough intersections of beginnings, high points and ends of the various musics with elements of the polyrhythm to make a lively interaction of these two aspects of the work.[15]

Most interesting is the way that each of the three constituent musics exemplifies the kinds of polyrhythmic structure spanning the piece. Thus, at the outset the two instruments, on top of playing *scorrevole* pulse streams related as 7 to 8, are further working within a larger polyrhythm in which accents on every

---

[14] See Schiff, *MEC*, pp. 139–41.
[15] A more elaborate discussion of these issues may be found in Mead, "Fuzzy Edges: Notes on Musical Interaction in the Music of Elliott Carter."

Ex. 6.12a Local polyrhythms in *Esprit Rude/Esprit Doux* (*scorrevole* music)

fifth note of the flute's septuplets set up an even pulse rate against which the clarinet produces accents on various multiples of three thirty-second notes. This is illustrated in Example 6.12a. The *giocoso* music is also marked by polyrhythms, these occurring within each instrument. Example 6.12b shows two instances of this, one in the flute and the other in the clarinet. As may be seen, each instrumental part is made of the combinations of two distinct pulse streams, although each pulse stream is not complete. The slow music as well is clearly made of polyrhythms unfolding between the two instruments, as illustrated in Example 6.12c. Of particular note is the very end of the piece, in which a coda emerges from a pairing of the *scorrevole* music not dissimilar to that found at the outset of the large polyrhythm, although in a different metrical context. This coda, which produces a variety of musical flow unlike any other passage in the piece, is actually the conclusion of the same 25:21 polyrhythm that underlies the whole piece, only now played twelve times as fast. This is illustrated in Example 6.12d.

We may now turn to a much larger example of polyrhythmic composition, the Oboe Concerto of 1987. What follows is not an analysis of the work so much as an examination of the ways its underlying polyrhythm is realized as a series of different metrical opportunities. The work is played without a break, and the limbs of its large polyrhythm, 63:80, are distributed between the

Ex. 6.12b Local polyrhythms in *Esprit Rude/Esprit Doux* (*giocoso* music)

Ex. 6.12c Local polyrhythms in *Esprit Rude/Esprit Doux* (slow music)

Ex. 6.12d Local polyrhythms in *Esprit Rude/Esprit Doux* (closing music)

soloist and a surrounding coterie, and the orchestra as a whole, respectively.[16] The ensemble is relatively small, consisting of the soloist with the violas and a percussionist playing multiple instruments, and an orchestra made of

[16] This work is extensively analyzed in Link, "Long-Range Polyrhythms in Elliott Carter's Recent Music," pp. 79–89. Schiff indicates the polyrhythm in *MEC*, p. 264.

Ex. 6.13 Large-scale polyrhythm in Elliott Carter's Oboe Concerto

Polyrhythm formats in the Oboe Concerto:

$$A = 63 \qquad\qquad X = 80$$
$$7 \times 9 \qquad\qquad 16 \times 5$$

Carter does not employ all possible formats of this polyrhythm in the Concerto. The following lists several that are employed, starting with that used for the longest span of the work to those derived there from by simple swapping, to those derived through tempo changing fractions.

Primary format:

$$63 \times 10/9 = 80 \times 7/8 = 70$$

Additional formats employed:

By swapping:

$$63 \times 8/9 = 80 \times 7/10 = 56$$

$$63 \times 8/7 = 80 \times 9/10 = 72$$

> N.B.: swapping would also produce a format of 90 units, employing fractions 10/7 and 9/8, but this does not appear in the work.

By multiplying each side by a tempo altering fraction:

$$63 \times 60/63 = 80 \times 3/4 = 60 \quad (6/7 \times 70)$$

$$63 \times 16/21 = 80 \times 3/5 = 48 \quad (2/3 \times 72)$$

$$63 \times 80/63 = 80 \times 1/1 = 80 \quad (8/7 \times 70, \text{ derived as } 3/2 \times 4/7 \times 4/3 \times 80 \text{ in successive moves, read from right to left})$$

$$63 \times 100/63 = 80 \times 5/4 = 100 \quad (5/4 \times 80)$$

four winds, a second percussionist and the rest of the strings. The polyrhythm initiates on the downbeat of m. 2, and is completed on the downbeat of the last measure of the work. The elements of the polyrhythm are quite widely spaced, occurring roughly every fifteen seconds in the orchestra, and every twenty-plus seconds in the solo group. These are beyond the bounds of hearing accurately as equally spaced pulses, and the elements of each limb are articulated in a wide variety of ways, from the highly demarcated to the subtle nudge. Some are points of arrival; some are points of departure. Some are the high points of melodic lines; some are surrounded with musical build-ups and decays. Our point here, however, is not to examine their realizations, but to see how they determine metrical context.

We may analyze the polyrhythm as follows. Example 6.13 illustrates a range of formats derived from 63:80 with their constituent fraction pairs and time-span unit multiples. Not all of these are employed in the composition, but they show the range of possibilities of this polyrhythm. In terms of realization, Carter multiplies the basic time-span unit by 18, which he realizes metrically in a number of ways. At the outset, the time-span unit is realized as six measures in $\frac{3}{4}$, or 18 beats. Carter employs the format based on 70 time-span units at the outset, and sets the tempo at ♩ = 70 bpm, thus providing us with a handy guide through the piece as to which format is being employed.[17] As a rule, the resulting indicated tempo of the tactus will be equivalent to the multiple of time-span units in the format locally in use.

In terms of tempi and format, we can see the piece dividing into two halves, the first comparatively simple, while the second pursues a more elaborate exploration of possibilities before returning to the original format for much of the last two-sevenths of the piece. Interestingly, the second half opens with the format using 72 units, and the change occurs at the only place where this could happen with an alignment of units between 70 and 72. This ratio, 35:36, is the narrowest found in the work.

The first half of the piece is relatively straightforward with regard to the polyrhythm. With one exception, to be discussed shortly, it employs the same format for the entire passage, despite changes in notation. We can understand these changes by taking a closer look at the ways the basic time-span unit is realized. As mentioned, at the outset of the work the time-span unit is presented as 18 beats assembled into six groups of three beats. The soloist's fraction, $\frac{10}{9}$, means that its limb's elements will occur every 20 beats, or every 6 and $\frac{2}{3}$ measures. The orchestra's fraction, $\frac{7}{8}$, determines that its elements occur every $5\frac{1}{4}$ measures. Example 6.14a illustrates the opening of the work, with each ensemble's limb elements indicated by bold-faced numbers. Notationally, the orchestra's fractions are realized as 15 beats plus a dotted-eighth note, but if we reconsider the dotted eighth as the tactus, we could think of this as 21 beats at a tempo $\frac{4}{3}$ of the notated tactus. Doing so does not change the number of measures in a unit of the 70-format, but changes the realization of the unit from 18 beats at 70 bpm to 24 beats at $\frac{4}{3}$ of that tempo, or $93\frac{1}{3}$ bpm. Example 6.14b illustrates this renotation, using the same portion of the polyrhythm found in Example 6.14a.

I am not doing this to return to metronomic notation, but to help explain those passages in the opening of the work in which the tempo changes by $\frac{4}{3}$ (to what Carter notates as 93+ bpm) and the meter changes to $\frac{4}{4}$. Since this notation is easily subdivided by three, we need not shift formats to under-stand these changes, but may contextualize them within the 70-format. The compositional decision to change tempo in this way may result from a desire

[17] This gives us an opportunity to note that Carter does not seem to see his metronome markings as hard and fast, as the setting of the tempo at the outset at 70 bpm, and the use of eighteen beats as the multiplier of the time-span unit would yield a duration of eighteen minutes for the Concerto, slightly more if you add in the first measure. But the performance time in the score is indicated as about twenty minutes, a difference suggesting that it is the relations among tempi, rather than their absolutes, that is of greater interest to the composer. This should come as no surprise, given the current essay.

Ex. 6.14a Elliott Carter's Oboe Concerto, mm. 1–13

Ex. 6.14b Metrical substitution in Ex. 6.14a

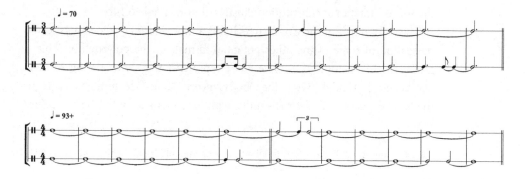

to emphasize the different tacti that are present in the music. A similar case may be made for those changes that alter the original tempo by $\frac{3}{2}$. Here, however, it is necessary to recognize that these changes are coupled with a change of the number of measures used to realize the time-span unit. Both the previous change and this one are comparable to the simple changes by similar fractions found in *Esprit Rude/Esprit Doux*, examined above.

Before considering a more substantive change, we may note still another feature of the realization of the music at the opening, which, though not necessary, nevertheless reflects properties of the underlying polyrhythm. As may be seen in Example 6.14a, the opening music of the solo ensemble employs triplet subdivisions, both at the level of the beat and at the level of the subdivision, while the orchestra employs subdivisions by powers of two. While the orchestra's limb elements entail a subdivision of the beat at the level of the sixteenth note, the solo group's limb elements are articulated at the level of the beat. Nevertheless, Carter has elected to reflect the larger nine and eight subdivisions of the time-span unit all the way down to the fastest notes on the musical surface.[18]

The last portion of the first half of the Oboe Concerto contains the first shift of format, from the 70-format found up to this point to a 60-format. This is accomplished using the last two time-span units of the first half of the 60-format (units 29 and 30), and is effected by the fact that the underlying time-span units of each format are realized as multiples of 18. Thus, the 36 beats of the two units of the 60-format are used to replace 42 beats of the 70-format (two-and-one-third units), in a swap of $\frac{6}{7}$, in which the faster beats are subdivided by 6, and the slower by 7, not unlike the procedure we observed in the opening of *Esprit Rude/Esprit Doux*. The change occurs two-thirds of the way through unit 33 of the 70-format, and replaces its subsequent two units. By working out the position of the polyrhythm in two units of the 60-format, we can easily determine how each limb's elements can be realized. A rhythmic reduction of the passage is found in Example 6.15, with the appropriate units of each format noted. Note that the two-thirds of the 70-format's unit 33 consist of one measure of $\frac{4}{4}$ at 93+ bpm, plus three measures of $\frac{3}{4}$ at 70 bpm, reflecting the sort of notational substitution illustrated in Example 6.14b.

The second half of the Concerto exhibits a more complex and sophisticated navigation of some of the other potential formats of the polyrhythm. This is illustrated in Example 6.16. The chart represents the shifts among formats between m. 210 and m. 320 in the Oboe Concerto. Bold-face numbers represent the basic beats of each format's units, with exceptions as noted. The measure

---

[18] Link, "Long-Range Polyrhythms in Elliott Carter's Recent Music," contains related discussions of the ways Carter elects to use the properties of his polyrhythms to shape the details of his musical surfaces.

Ex. 6.15 Format shift in Elliott Carter's Oboe Concerto, mm. 195–209

The 36 beats of units 29 and 30, 60-format, are equivalent in length to 42 beats of 70-format, or two units plus six beats borrowed from unit 33.

Ex. 6.16 Format shift in Elliott Carter's Oboe Concerto, mm. 210–320

Formats:

100:   **10** | **18** | **18** | **12**

80: 11 units ---|**18** | **18** | **18** | **10 + 8** | (**18**) |

72: **18** | **6**

70: 5 units* ----------------- 20 + 4 | 24 | 24 | 24 | 15 + 4 | 4 units ----------------| (24) | 5+ **25** | **15****+ 12** | etc.

60: 3 units----------|**16 + 2**| **18** |

48: **16** +   **2**| **18** | **18** | **2**

Measures:
    210   217   237   244   267   295   302.5   310   320

* The units within the 70-format are realized with 24 beats, derived from the general multiple of 18 by 4/3. This represents their realization at 93+ as described in the text.

** In this span, the unit is realized at 5/3 the tempo of 70, with the resulting 40 beats realized as 10 measures of 4/4. This span is best read as a local substitution within the 70-format. The 12 beats in the second half of this unit represent a return to 93+.

numbers mark the shift among formats, with the addition of m. 302.5, which indicates the alignment of units in formats 70, 80 and 100. Not all tempo changes are represented here, as some arise from different realizations of a given format. Thus, the second half of the complete 60-format unit is realized as three measures of $\frac{2}{2}$ at 40 bpm, and the units of the 80-format include shifts by 2:3 as well as by doubling. Readers may verify the relations by summing beats within a format and multiplying by the appropriate ratio. Thus, the 24 beats at 72 at the outset are matched by the 16 beats ($\frac{2}{3} \times 24$) at 48, and so forth.

I will forego a detailed explanation of this portion of the work, except to note that the realization of these shifts entails both simple tempo realizations as at the opening of the piece, as well as the use of the kind of substitutions by simple 3:2 ratios and their transformations that we observed earlier in *Esprit Rude/Esprit Doux* as well as in the opening of the present work.

The final portion of the Concerto returns to the format of the opening, with one further excursion to a tempo not heard previously in the work, based on the 56-format. An analysis of the piece would note that these changes align with various significant features of the music, including an accompanied cadenza, an orchestral climax, and the music's quiet coda. Needless to say there is much more that could be said about the Oboe Concerto, but our purpose here is limited to considerations of the large-scale polyrhythm as a compositional constraint.

In addition to two-limbed polyrhythms, Carter has used polyrhythms with multiple limbs to structure some of his compositions.[19] As one may imagine, this increases the limitations on realization within a metrical grid, but it also affords opportunities for mixing a wider variety of musical effects made distinct by their rhythmic behavior. While Carter, in such pieces as the String Quartet No. 4 and *Penthode*, has employed four and even five limbs in his compositions, we will limit our present discussion to two works employing three limbs. As has been the case with our previous examples, we will take a look first at a shorter composition, and then observe the implications of what we have discussed in a work of larger scope.

Esprit Rude/Esprit Doux II, like the earlier work of the same title, was written for a celebration of Pierre Boulez's birthday, in this case his seventieth. It adds a marimba to the duet of flute and clarinet, and rather than being based on a two-limbed polyrhythm, it manifests three separate rhythmic strands. As David Schiff notes, the triple polyrhythm is incomplete, but a closer look reveals that the piece may be read as congruent with a complete two-part polyrhythm of 21:32 in the clarinet and marimba, with an additional limb in the flute. Because of the ratios used, this design would have to be 51 times its current length for completion! As Schiff notes, the polyrhythm's coincidence at the end of the work is displaced by a beat. Because the piece is based on a short excerpt from its underlying polyrhythm, I have elected to represent it by listing the lengths of its elements in terms of fractions of beats. Example 6.17 summarizes these fractions, while Example 6.18 shows a portion of the piece with the elements of the polyrhythm marked.[20]

---

[19] These are discussed in Link, *ibid.*, pp. 49–65.

[20] In *MEC*, p. 149, Schiff identifies a somewhat different set of ratios for the flute and clarinet from those appearing in Example 6.17. This may well be a misprint.

Ex. 6.17 Polyrhythm and ratios in *Esprit Rude/Esprit Doux II*

Ratios of pulse-rates for the three-limbed polyrhythm used in *Esprit Rude/Esprit Doux II*

In the following the notated beat is equivalent to the unit as we have defined it.

Flute: 10 1/5 beats = 51, or (3×17) quintuplet-sixteenth notes = 51/5 units

Clarinet: 13 1/3 beats = 40, or (8×5) triplet-eighth notes = 40/3 units

Marimba: 8 3/4 beats = 35, or (5×7) sixteenth notes = 35/4 units

The clarinet and marimba form a complete polyrhythm of 21:32

21×40/3 = 32×35/4, = 280 units (beats), which is equivalent to 70 4/4 measures. Measure 65 contains six beats, so the polyrhythm is completed at the end of beat 2 of Measure 70.

Ex. 6.18 *Esprit Rude/Esprit Doux II*, mm. 1–11

While the addition of a third limb to the polyrhythm limits the options for metric realization, it is worth asking what sorts of opportunities a three-part polyrhythm can afford. A quick look at the score reveals that each instrument, associated with a single limb of the polyrhythm, is also limited to the subdivision of the notated beat associated with its limb. But further, we can see that in many cases the ways each limb is realized reflect the ways its elements can be

Ex. 6.19 Three-limbed polyrhythm in Elliott Carter's *Triple Duo*

General formula used to construct three-limbed polyrhythms like those in *Triple Duo:*

$$ax \ (yz)/a = by \ (xz)/b = cz \ (xy)/c$$

Number of time-span units = xyz

NB: a, b, c, x, y, and z must be mutually prime to ensure no intersections between pairs of limbs during the polyrhythm.

Values in *Triple Duo:*

Winds: $3 \times 11 \times (13 \times 7)/3$ $33 \times 91/3$ Element length: 30 1/3 units

Piano/perc.: $5 \times 13 \times (11 \times 7)/5$ $65 \times 77/5$ Element length: 15 2/5 units

Strings: $8 \times 7 \times (11 \times 13)/8$ $56 \times 143/8$ Element length: 17 7/8 units

Units: 1001; articulated for the most part as half-notes at quarter = 100 bpm

subdivided by the factors of its constituent multiples determined by the written meter. So, for example, near the opening we hear the flute and the clarinet unfolding long lines of sustained notes, each reflecting its own metrical environment. As may be seen in Example 6.18, the flute subdivides its limb elements by three, while the clarinet similarly subdivides its own limb elements by five. This effectively allows each instrument to establish its own tempo and apparent meter in a comparatively simple fashion, allowing our sense of the music's rhythmic richness to arise from the ways these different strands combine.[21] Like the earlier duo of the same title, *Esprit Rude/Esprit Doux II* uses its underlying rhythmic patterns to shape the combination of different musical rhetorical approaches over the course of the work.

Carter's *Triple Duo* of 1983 is a larger composition that employs a three-limbed polyrhythm unfolding over its span. As is well known, the work is written for flute and clarinet, piano and percussion, and violin and cello, and each duo unfolds one limb of the polyrhythm.[22] Example 6.19 shows the abstract formula that may be used to establish three mutually prime limbs, as well as determine the multiple of time-span units in a given format, and illustrates with a realization of the polyrhythm used in the *Triple Duo*. As may be seen, the large number of time-span units needed for this realization compels their treatment as slow beats in distinction to what we found in the Oboe Concerto, so the question of flexibility of metrical context is greatly limited. In fact, all of the tempo changes in this work arise as different metrical

[21] Link, "Long-Range Polyrhythms in Elliott Carter's Recent Music," discusses the ways Carter's pulse streams engender "apparent meter" in the Oboe Concerto.
[22] David Schiff notes the different multiples and subdivisions associated with each limb, and also remarks on the close relations amongst tempi in the score in *MEC*, p. 121. Both Schiff and Link have noted that Carter does not complete the polyrhythm in the score. See Link, *ibid.*, pp. 111–12; Schiff, "Elliott Carter's Harvest Home."

Ex. 6.20 Tempo changes in Elliott Carter's *Triple Duo*: mm. 43–45, mm. 422–40

interpretations of the single format illustrated, or as the strategic replacement of a span of measures by another that locally can encompass the attacks of elements as needed.

A question that we have repeatedly returned to throughout this study has been just what might be the reasons for the presence of these various large polyrhythms in Carter's music. This is particularly the case here, given how slowly the limbs unfold, but further because for various reasons Carter has not elected to complete the unfolding of the polyrhythm to its convergence, despite employing the rhetorical effect of initiating and concluding the body of the work with the only two ensemble unison attacks in the piece.

It seems to me what is left is three things. First, the stringencies of realizing the polyrhythm greatly limit the kinds of tempo changes that can be made, as well as the locations for those changes in the cases where the tempo is not a simple rewriting of a meter that can project all of the subdivisions readily. Consider Example 6.20. As may be seen, those changes that reflect a rewriting of triplets or dotted notes as the tactus (as in the top system) are simply a recasting of the notation for the format's time-span unit, but those changes that hinge on a rewriting of the quintuplet as a duple or triple subdivision of the new tactus (as in the lower three systems) only do so in those passages where the elements of the other limbs fall on the beginning of a unit. Second, Carter often uses the ends of his limbs' elements to mark changes in musical rhetoric. The large-scale form of the work is a mosaic of different musics, and the polyrhythm forms a frame for assembling different combinations. David Schiff has noted that the last portion of the work acts as a finale, maintaining its own characteristics until the end.[23] We may speculate that Carter's

[23] Schiff, *MEC*, p. 122.

Ex. 6.20 (cont.)

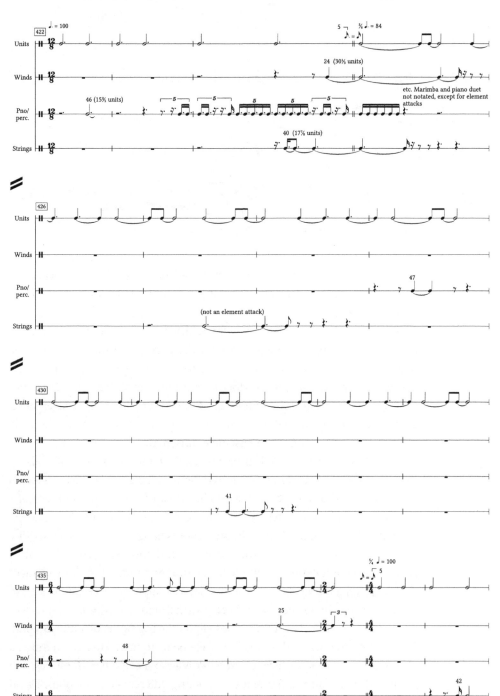

decision to curtail the polyrhythm may have been made in light of the fact that it was no longer needed for delineating rhetorical changes. Third, and perhaps most immediately vivid in the hearing of the work, is the fact that each ensemble maintains its own repertoire of subdivisions for the most part, allowing both the possibilities of hearing different metrical and tempo contexts for each duo, but also the particular ways each duo realizes the implications of the written meter. Thus, the winds persist in triple subdivisions of surface beats, while the piano and percussion unfold quintuplet subdivisions. The strings employ duple subdivisions, but add an additional kind of syncopation at the musical surface by grouping those in threes. As the winds are frequently grouping their own subdivisions by twos, we can see that even from the outset there is a strong favoring of tempi related by 3:2, 4:3, and their reciprocals.

But we should remember a more generalized aspect of Carter's employment of large-scale polyrhythms in his music, demonstrated in part by the variety of ways that these may be realized. By assuming the constraints of doing so, Carter is creating a set of compositional consequences, a set of definable contingencies that can provide for him the variety of interlocked choices composers seek in making music. The wide variety of ways of realizing polyrhythms, from their sets of formats related by specific ratios to the different ways time-span units can be composed out in the musical surface suggests that Carter's rules of play afford him a wonderfully flexible world within which to range.

The preceding has been a very cursory tour of some of Elliott Carter's rhythmic practices, and our illustrations are more a demonstration of tools for analysis rather than analyses themselves. But it should be clear that from a relatively early stage in his development, Carter has considered tempo, meter, and rhythm to be strong forces for shaping compositions, both locally and in the large. In doing so, he has maintained an awareness of the limitations of traditional notation and of musicians' abilities as well, so it behooves us in considering his practices to be aware of those limitations ourselves. By using pitch notation for tempo relations, and by understanding those relations as ratios, we can construct a tempo space through which we may move in ways that can be heard and felt, and we may move beyond any temptation to dismiss Carter's constructions as intellectual conceits. And by investigating the ways Carter employs his larger polyrhythms to shape his musical surfaces, we can begin to sense just how much he has managed to shape time to his expressive ends.

7   "I try to write music that will appeal to an intelligent listener's ear." On Elliott Carter's string quartets

Dörte Schmidt
(Translated by Maria Schoenhammer and John McCaughey)

For Horst Weber, to whom I am indebted for an intensive encounter with American music and for helping me to develop a sensibility for the repercussions of exile.

The instrumental formations of chamber music in the second half of the twentieth century may have become more strongly individualized and emancipated from the norms of its genres, yet the period is by no means as devoid of string quartets as is sometimes assumed.[1] For Elliott Carter among others this genre offers, like scarcely any other, the possibility of linking explorations in musical language with an emphatic sense of artistic ambition; with a critical discourse in relation to a given canon of works; with specific modes of writing (above all, that of motivic-thematic development); with a framework of reflection that is both artistic and theoretical; and with a particular socially institutionalized form of performance. It is precisely those composers critical of tradition for whom the quartet becomes the location for staking out a compositional as well as an aesthetic position, for example Pierre Boulez in *Livre pour Quatuor* (1948/49) or John Cage in *String Quartet in Four Parts* (1949/50). We can do no more than surmise as to whether Carter had heard of these works,[2] but their contemporaneous time-frame at least suggests a context of interest in the principle of the quartet as a genre when, around 1950, he undertook to compose the work that he programmatically titled "String Quartet No. 1," thereby explicitly de-valuing two previously existing

---

I am grateful to the Paul Sacher Foundation Basel and its staff who made it possible once again for me to study the material in its collection and to reproduce hitherto unpublished material. I would also like to thank Antje Müller and Boosey & Hawkes; Anne Shreffler, Felix Meyer, Reinhard Kapp, and especially Marguerite Boland and John Link for their helpful suggestions, and Maria Schoenhammer and John McCaughey for their careful English translations of the text.
[1] Cf. Finscher (ed.), "Streichquartett," esp. col. 1972; also Tilmouth, "String Quartet." For a different view, see Griffiths, "String Quartet." Kummacher discusses Carter's quartets in

Das Streichquartett, pp. 466 ff. Also see Bernard, "The String Quartets of Elliott Carter."
[2] The correspondence between John Cage and Pierre Boulez shows how hard Cage tried to have Boulez's quartet (among other works) performed in New York; thus it is conceivable that this piece was at least "under discussion" in a small circle of people who could facilitate concerts (Carter was among them). Cage's quartet was premiered in August 1950 (before Carter's departure to Tucson) at Black Mountain College (and in March 1951 it could again be heard at Columbia University in New York).

quartets. Only here did the series of "valid" quartets begin, which he sees as concluded with String Quartet No. 5 (1995): "I've written now five, I guess that's all I will write," he replied some years ago to John Tusa, when asked about any new quartet plans – and so far he has abided by his answer.[3]

Composing against the "breakdown of communication"

It is evident that for Carter the string quartet genre was directly linked to his redefining of his aesthetic position in the 1940s. This was probably his reason for rejecting the quartets written in 1935 and 1937 immediately upon his return from Paris and still influenced by the principles of Nadia Boulanger, with whom he studied there from 1932 to 1935. Only one of the quartets – a cycle in three movements – has survived; its neoclassical style and the French performance indications point directly to his study with Boulanger.[4] The 1946 string quartet arrangement of *Elegy* escaped Carter's "ban" possibly because it did not fulfill the requirements of the genre, either in terms of the form or the number of movements.

In a conversation with the composer Heinz Holliger, Carter in hindsight casts his reorientation at the end of the 1940s as a politicized return to his modernist roots.[5] At the beginning of his musical career he was mainly interested in the works of Schoenberg, Berg, and Stravinsky, and became friends with Ives and Varèse. With his growing political awareness he became suspicious of the avant-garde attitude of these musicians – especially while studying with Boulanger. Music (as Carter remembers his concern of that time) was supposed to have something to do with people. The aloofness of the classic(al) avant-garde's "l'art pour l'art" seemed outdated at a time when daily events were of such immediate urgency and when contemporary art could only be conceived as part of a broader technical, social, and political development. Carter decided that neoclassical means provided a more promising way to fulfill that aim. But soon he again had to confront the issue of avant-garde Modernism when it acquired an unexpected timeliness not only because its proponents now lived as exiles in the United States – a circumstance that according to Carter had influenced him profoundly[6] – but also because artistic simplification, or rather popularizing, did not create the

---

[3] Tusa, Interview with Elliott Carter.
[4] See also the discussion, in Meyer and Shreffler, *ECCP*, pp. 36 ff., of Quartet in C, which has survived as a fair copy of the score and probably is the second one, written in 1937.
[5] See Holliger, "Abseits des Mainstreams: Ein Gespräch mit dem amerikanischen

Komponisten Elliott Carter," esp. p. 8. The fate of the English original is currently unknown.
[6] See Carter, "To Be a Composer in America" (1953/94), in *CEL*, esp. p. 204, and "The Time Dimension in Music" (1965), in *CEL*, esp. p. 225.

relationship with the listener he had hoped for – it did not create better listeners. Yet that was the prerequisite if music really was to have something to do with people. If it did not succeed at that, it lost its claim to truth.

Indications of doubt surfaced as early as the late 1930s when Carter introduced the essay "Orchestras and Audiences," a concert review for the journal *Modern Music*, by describing two types of listener. One uses music to stimulate the imagination, to create associations that take him into his own emotional world; he perceives music that tries to tear him away from his egocentric attitude almost as threatening: "he generally rejects any music which jars him out of himself and threatens to afford a new experience, giving way to anger as a protection."[7] Carter describes the other type of listener – with unconcealed sympathy – as objective, though equally enthusiastic. He is open and curious for something new, even if it seems difficult at first; music to him is an invitation to communicate and he accepts the challenge to his perceptual and intellectual abilities. Carter identifies this listener as his ideal and again and again declares him the addressee of his compositional work; his composing revolves around the question of what he must offer in order to trigger that kind of hearing. This is probably the reason why soon after his return from Paris (partly influenced by the political situation) Carter abandoned the idea – which in the 1930s had seemed so attractive – that it was the artistic responsibility of the composer to make the listening experience easy, for example by coming closer to the listener's idea of music. Now Carter deems such ingratiation almost politically suspect. Even in 1984 this is keenly apparent, when, in an interview at Banff Center for the Arts, Carter compared the situation of composers in the early 1980s writing music in line with the dictates of the market to that of populist music under fascist dictatorships. In the same interview he says:

> I find there is what Adorno called a "regression of listening ability," even a loss of the wish to pay attention to music, but only to use it as a background for other activities. It is hard not to feel that this is one of the many types of breakdown of communication we are faced with at a time when focused attention [is] needed more than ever in our democratic and highly complex society.[8]

"Communication" remains the crucial issue in terms of politics as well as aesthetics. By aesthetically repositioning himself Carter tries to develop an alternative relationship with a listener who is to become an active participant in an artistic exchange. He is by no means prepared to make any concessions

[7] Carter, "Orchestras and Audiences: Winter 1938," esp. p. 28.
[8] Johnston *et al.*, "Elliott Carter in Conversation with Robert Johnston, Michael Century, Robert Rosen, and Don Stein (1984)," in Meyer and Shreffler, *ECCP*, p. 253. I thank Anne Shreffler and Felix Meyer for the information about the different versions of this interview.

to the listener's lack of willingness to listen with a critically engaged ear (the reference to Adorno is certainly not coincidental but attests to the significance which the exiled Viennese School had for Carter). This was the background for Carter's often-cited and well-staged escape of 1951, in which he almost programmatically sends the audience "to hell," withdraws to the desert of Arizona, and after a year returns with his new string quartet which is to be his first: a quartet of impressive scale comparable to Arnold Schoenberg's First or Alexander Zemlinsky's Second Quartet (like those predecessors, it is a good forty minutes long). Apparently he wanted to establish a standard, and it is with good reason that the piece is considered the initial impulse for the structurally highly complex way of composing for which Carter later became so well known. This "desert myth" made a prophet of Carter and is a convenient means of trumpeting his return to the "true path" of avant-garde Modernism (as well as for harshly criticizing it).[9]

For Carter this step was not a rejection of his belief in music as a communicative process in which the composer has to take the listener into account, but rather its consequence. In a talk at UCLA in February, 1957 entitled "Sound and Silence in Time," he supported his decisively phenomenological position by introducing a model that comes very close to the active role of the listener in the classic communicative setting of the string quartet ideal: "This establishing a musical pattern and then abandoning it inevitably leaves a kind of echo behind in the mind of the listener, a basis for comparison, an expectation of the future, and as he [or she] listens attentively this psychic silence begins to be alive with the echoes which are shared with the composer and the performer but which never reach the state of physical sound."[10] This constitutes an outright phenomenological counter-position to the structuralist thinking of both European and American serialists. Perception of the audible surface becomes the yard-stick of compositional decision-making, and also for the understanding of a work. It forms the basis of the central focus on the listener.[11]

Around 1970, while he was composing the Third Quartet, Carter again brought his ideal of the listener to the center of the aesthetic discussion. For example, in conversation with Allen Edwards, Carter remarks: "I try to write music that will appeal to an intelligent listener's ear ... It may take many years for the listener to be convinced, but I believe that my training and experience as

---

[9] On the "desert myth," see Eisenlohr, *Komponieren als Entscheidungsprozess*, esp. pp. 166–71, and Shreffler, "Elliott Carter and his America." Richard Taruskin's view that with his First Quartet Carter identified himself "with the romantic, asocial concept of artistry in his priestliest form," reads like an intentional misunderstanding of the desert myth. See Taruskin, "Standoff (II)," p. 281.

[10] Carter, "Sound and Silence in Time," in Meyer and Shreffler, *ECCP*, pp. 133 ff.

[11] Schmidt, "Emanzipation des musikalischen Diskurses," pp. 214–15.

a composer enable me to prejudge a possible future listener. In my opinion, the idea of writing a piece of music that no listener would ever be able to understand or enjoy is utterly incomprehensible."[12] Carter's conviction that music is a form of artistic communication can be traced as a constant through the "style change" of the late 1940s to the present – and what genre could be more fundamental in this respect than the string quartet? Here the listener is a silent, although more active and knowledgeable, participant in an artistic discourse between performers (in a way the listener merely enlarges the circle of knowledgeable participants formed by the performers). This principle, so powerfully captured in Goethe's metaphor of the *Gesprächscharakter* of the quartet, plays a crucial role in Carter's quartets.[13]

Points of departure: American ultra-modernists and the Viennese School in exile

In addition to his allusions to the European Modernism of Arnold Schoenberg, Béla Bartók,[14] and Alban Berg (whose *Lyrische Suite* is suggested in the Scherzo movements of the quartets) – allusions which extend to thematic and motivic formation – Carter, in his First Quartet, also makes audible connections to the music of Charles Ives, Henry Cowell, Conlon Nancarrow, Carl Ruggles, and Ruth Crawford Seeger. Carter cited some of these allusions explicitly in his writings, while others (such as the String Quartet by Ruth Crawford Seeger) appear to be of a more private nature or are directed to the cognoscenti.[15] In the cello solo of the first measures he makes a programmatic allusion to the beginning of Bartók's Sixth Quartet, and a little later (from m. 27 on) the same instrument quotes the main theme of Charles Ives's Violin Sonata.

In contrast to his historical analyses of the early 1950s,[16] in which Carter lists Neo-Classicists prominently among the émigrés, the references in the First Quartet reveal a particular interest in Bartók and the Viennese School, in keeping with Carter's reorientation in the late 1940s.[17] A closer look at the

---

[12] *FW*, p. 77. See also Boretz, "Conversation with Elliott Carter," and Eisenlohr, "Hören und Gesellschaft. Zur Ästhetik Elliott Carters."

[13] See Goethe, letter to Zelter, November 9, 1829, in Hecker (ed.), *Briefwechsel zwischen Goethe und Zelter*, vol. 3, p. 233.

[14] Bartók, whose Fourth Quartet is alluded to in Carter's First Quartet, is among the models that played a role in Carter's neoclassical phase as well: the finale of the Quartet in C bears a strong resemblance to the beginning of the finale of Bartók's Fifth Quartet; cf. Meyer and Shreffler, *ECCP*, p. 37.

[15] See also Shreffler, "Elliott Carter and his America," and the notes on the First Quartet in Meyer and Shreffler, *ECCP*, p. 101. See also Rao, "Ruth Crawford's Imprint on Contemporary Composition."

[16] See for example the mention of Hindemith and Milhaud in Carter, "To Be a Composer in America."

[17] His collaboration with Eduard Steuermann in the New York Section of the International

references invoking European Modernism reveals not merely the use of an abstract aesthetic canon, but also a reaction to the presence of émigrés repeatedly cited by Carter as an important influence. All of the "European" allusions audible in the First Quartet can be related to the public presence of the émigrés in American musical life of the post-war years, even to the work of certain string quartet ensembles (which also implies a particular way of thinking about quartet performance). To a certain extent, Carter's phenomenological stance attaches itself to these impressions. For example, from the 1930s on the work of the Kolisch Quartet (or rather the Pro Arte Quartet which the exiled members of the Kolisch took over) was crucial in making Bartók's quartets known. In December 1948 the newly founded Juilliard Quartet began with the first cycle of performances of all the Bartók quartets with Eugene Lehner, former member of the Kolisch Quartet, as musical adviser. Along with Bartók and Schoenberg, Berg's *Lyrische Suite* also plays an important role in the repertoire of the Juilliard Quartet; Raphael Hillyer remembers this as the first piece they worked on.[18] Carter may have heard them premiere this piece in New York.[19] Shortly before he went to Arizona, a recording of the *Lyrische Suite* with the Pro Arte Quartet was released on Dial Records.[20] Schoenberg's first Quartet, Op. 7, also belongs in this context. In addition to its remarkable length, it shares with Carter's Quartet a contrapuntal approach, as well as the integration of the four traditional movements of a string quartet into a formal continuum. In 1944 it had been at the core of Kolisch's chamber-music class "Democratic Principles of Ensemble Playing" at Black Mountain College, where that year, on the occasion of Arnold Schoenberg's seventieth birthday, a Summer Music Institute had been created and immediately garnered national attention. In the *New York Times* Roger Sessions called it "one of the most vital signs of what must and can be achieved for music in the United States."[21] In their books on Schoenberg published in the United States in the late 1940s, Dika Newlin and René

Society for Contemporary Music most likely played a role. In 1943 Carter was among the founders of the "Forum Group for Young Composers," that was part of the ISCM; see "A Good Citizen of Contemporary Music: Carter's Involvement with Musical Institutions," in Meyer and Shreffler, *ECCP*, esp. pp. 9 ff.

[18] In 1946 Robert Mann tried to get Lehner as violinist for the Juilliard Quartet. Although he declined, he was willing to assist with the Quartet at rehearsals. See Stein, "Playing in Time for Schoenberg," p. 62. See also Botstein, "Gespräch mit Raphael Hillyer" (for the Bartók quartets, see pp. 157 ff.).

[19] The work was on the Juilliard Quartet's debut concert program at Town Hall, New York, in December 1947. See Olmstead, *Juilliard: A History*, p. 158.
[20] The work was recorded together with Schoenberg's Third String Quartet in the WOR Studios in New York on January 24, 1950 and was released on Dial Records, 4. The recording is available on the CD edition *In Honor of Rudolf Kolisch* (Music & Arts, CD-1056, 2003).
[21] Sessions, "Report on Black Mountain." Kolisch's class is not mentioned specifically. Nevertheless one may assume that by way of the summer-class students it was talked about in New York.

Leibowitz extensively discuss the formal concept of Schoenberg's First Quartet among others. For Newlin, an interest in compositional principles clearly relates to a political mission, and she encourages the younger generation of American composers to take on the task of continuing this tradition that had been driven out of Europe.[22] Carter was probably aware of this aspect of the topic. As if to translate Newlin's message into composition, the composer now produces a quartet that follows up the aesthetic emancipation from Europe – the stance of the ultra modernists of the 1920s and '30s – with a kind of enactment of solidarity with the exiled European avant-garde. The consequences of this act, both compositionally and for performance practice, were to lay the foundation for Carter's future work.

The voices of the First Quartet with their themes and motives address this context in a manner that is still quotational. Carter allows the music itself to make its point. His textural and formal aims consist above all in attaining coherence in this multi-voiced space. If one reads Carter's forewords to the scores of the subsequent quartets from the perspective outlined here – in which he highlights the importance of discursive models – his retreat from motivic-thematic shapes comes to be seen as a consequence of connecting closely with the practical performance experience of quartet playing. In his cover notes to the recording of the first two quartets by the Composers Quartet, Carter speaks (regarding String Quartet No. 2) of "behavior patterns" from whose interactions, combinations, and oppositions a musical discourse emerges, held up as an abstract form, as against the "more nearly literal recurrence of ideas" in the First Quartet. It is now all about following the actions and behaviors of the participants, leading to the most varied activities and types of movement, and beyond this a play with the basic situation of the quartet: players and instrumental voices as coextensive, and thus the behavioral patterns of instruments heard as a dramatization of those between players. The systematic study of the performance situation of the quartet is a basic idea that can be traced all the way to the fifth and final quartet.

Programmatically, this line connects Carter to a model that was central for him and present in the concert life of the post-war period: the formal dramaturgy of the Second Quartet is inspired by Charles Ives's Second String Quartet. Composed as early as the 1910s, it was premiered only in

---

[22] Newlin, *Bruckner, Mahler, Schoenberg*, p. 277: "those traditions will never again be able to find firm root in their native soil. Therefore it is in our country, if anywhere, that they must live and grow, nurtured by younger generations. If the facts and ideas set forth here have made it clear that the cultivation and preservation of these traditions is, indeed, worthwhile for American musicians, they will have conveyed their most important message."

1946 by a student ensemble of the Juilliard School[23] and in the same year was recorded by the Walden Quartet. It was released only in 1954. Ives explicitly named the first two movements of his three-movement work after forms of dialogue: "Discussions" and "Arguments" – and apparently these titles were so remarkable, that Olin Downes singled them out in his *New York Times* review of the performance of 1946.[24] In the late 1950s Carter makes them the point of departure for the form of his Second Quartet, in which two types of interaction can be traced through the nine formal units lasting only about twenty minutes in total: egalitarian cooperation and dominance or confrontation.[25] This is borne out by a system of referential meters constituting the form, which should be considered the outcome of a critical examination of and engagement with Schoenberg's formal ideas.[26]

In the Third Quartet (1971), by dividing the four voices into two duos (violin/cello; violin/viola), Carter not only breaks with the idea of the equality and independence of the four participants that had carried the Second Quartet; he also uses this new dramatic concept to confront the virtual space of the self-contained movement that he had developed in the Second Quartet – secured by referential meters that gave it form – with the physical space of the performance. In the earlier quartets, duets were also possible, but only intermittently, in ever-changing combinations, and always within the framework of the superimposed "time screen." Now the two duos interact as fixed groups. This should also be reflected in the seating arrangement: the two pairs are placed far enough apart that they can be heard as independent sound sources, while remaining close enough to each other that they can still be perceived together.[27] In the end, the listener creates the connection. Each duo has its own characteristic tempi and intervals as well as its independent

---

[23] The concert took place on May 11, 1946 in the Macmillan Theatre at Columbia University as part of the Annual Festival of American Music.

[24] Downes, "Ives Music Played at Columbia Fete." The review notes that "the Quartet" was performed, but mentions the titles of the first two movements only. The following performers are mentioned: Robert Koff (1st violin), Walter Levin (2nd violin), Rena Robbins (viola) and Alla Goldberg (violoncello). Later Koff and Robert Mann founded the Juilliard Quartet and Levin founded the LaSalle Quartet whose repertoire is also significant in this context. I am grateful to Felix Meyer for bringing the review to my attention. The role this piece played in creating solidarity between American Ultramodernism and the exiled Vienna school in

the early post-war period is apparent from the fact that, along with Schoenberg's String Trio, Op. 45 (1946) and Wallingford Riegger's Second String Quartet (1948), it was performed by the Walden Quartet in 1949 in Darmstadt in a concert put forth as a special event by the American military government; see the report in Borio and Danuser (eds.), *Im Zenit der Moderne*, vol. 3, p. 537.

[25] See Schmidt, "Emanzipation des musikalischen Diskurses."

[26] See Schmidt, "Formbildende Tendenzen der Musikalischen Zeit." By referential meters I mean the notated meter, used to coordinate the parts in the score. This is distinct from the real meter of the individual voices.

[27] See Carter, "Performance Notes," in *String Quartet No. 3* [score].

Fig. 7.1 Elliott Carter explains his Third Quartet, Juilliard School, late 1970s; Collection Elliott Carter, Paul Sacher Foundation

formal processes including its own movement plan. In a draft for a talk of September 1974, Carter likened the idea of the quartet to the rather static idea of a brick wall (see Figure 7.1):

> The third quartet deals with the matter of agreement + disagreement in a simultaneous way ... Within each duo the two players are for the most part in agreement and further the expression of mood + ideas of each other but more or less drastically oppose the music of the other duo ... To organize this quickly shifting music with its large variety of perspectives the general plan of two courses of bricks in a brick wall in which the break between one brick and the next in the upper course comes in the middle of the bricks in the lower was thought of, so that each brick in the upper course overlaps 2 halves of different bricks in the lower.[28]

Carter actively confronts this combinatorial concept with a notion of the composer's responsibility to give shape to multi-layered, continuous, and dramaturgically conceived formal processes. In this he draws on his experience with the synchronization of separate musical worlds in such works as the Double Concerto. The layers of the duos each follow their own "time screen," coordinated in a pulse scheme over long stretches, yet with different reference pulses (for example immediately at the beginning: $\frac{6}{4}$, $\quarternote = 105$, $\frac{12}{8}$, $\dottedquarternote = 70$). At the formal seams where tempo modulations are called for, this situation sometimes creates complex superimpositions, such as at the beginning in

[28] Carter, "3rd String Quartet BBC Talk," pp. 6–7.

mm. 9–29. In the above-quoted draft for a talk Carter discusses the practical consequences of this situation for the performance:

> Since throughout the work Duo I + Duo II never play at the same speed although with few exceptions their measure lines do coincide – the matter of keeping together which always sounds like keeping apart requires great concentration on the part of the players. To ease this problem the American Composers Quartet that is playing the work in this program derived what is called a click-track which records metronomic beats on a stereophonic tape – one channel of which is heard only by the players of one Duo through a small ear-phone and the other track only by the other Duo. This click-track was first made according to the metronomic indications of the score and then was adjusted to meet the various expressive needs felt by the players and the composer. And after much rehearsal now the tape is not followed mechanically but acts as a guide to keep the players in the right relation to each other. This relieves the tension of playing complex rhythmic passages and allows the performers to concentrate more completely on the musical expression which, I think you will agree with me, they do most successfully.[29]

Carter's ideal is an expressive freedom that is always aware of its relation to the exact tempo; the technical support serves this very freedom (it is certainly no coincidence that the treatment of tempo described is closely related to Schoenberg's idea).[30] It is open to discussion whether the ambition of some quartets to perform this piece without a click-track is actually confining because in the end the problem of coordination commands too much of their attention. At least in this composition, the practical dimension of performance is plainly visible.

In the Fourth Quartet (1986), Carter returned to the classic four-movement cycle with impetus toward the finale. (However, the movements are joined without breaks. The combination of multi-movement and through-composed form, which had played such an important role for the Schoenberg circle, remains the model – sometimes called double-function form.) Structurally, the individualization of the voices is pushed the farthest, with the four instruments essentially operating in four independent time layers and their partial or complete coincidence producing the formal units of the piece.[31] Regardless of its polyrhythmic design, the piece is probably structurally the simplest among the quartets – in this respect it is a sort of counterpart to the Third Quartet. In his introduction to the score, Carter politicized his dramatic interest and explicitly made a connection between the structural idea and a model society:

> A preoccupation with giving each member of the performing group its own musical identity characterizes my Quartet No. 4, mirroring the democratic attitude in which

---

[29] *Ibid.* pp. 11–13.
[30] See for example Stein, "Playing in Time for Schoenberg."

[31] See also Link, "Long-Range Polyrhythms in Elliott Carter's Recent Music," pp. 49–56.

each member of a society maintains his or her own identity while cooperating in a common effort – a concept that has dominated all my recent work. In this Quartet, more than my other scores, a spirit of cooperation prevails.[32]

This sounds almost like a utopian image with a connection to the ideas of the violinist and quartet leader Rudolf Kolisch, who in 1944 wrote in notes to "Democratic Principles of Ensemble Playing": "Ensemble playing is not only a *musical* but also a *social* activity. As such it reproduces in the microcosm of musical performance all the sociological and psychological problems of collective work."[33]

Carter's interest in the conditions of this particular way of making music also shape the scenario of the Fifth Quartet (1995), in which he uses the rehearsal process – understood as an embodiment of cooperative action – as the guiding dramatic principle:

> One of the fascinations of attending rehearsals of chamber music, when excellent players try out fragments of what they later will play in the ensemble, then play it, and then stop abruptly to discuss how to improve it, is that this pattern is so similar to our inner experience of forming, ordering, focusing, and bringing to fruition, and then dismissing our feelings and ideas. These patterns of human behavior form the basis of the fifth string quartet.[34]

The image of the rehearsal situation also brings to mind that the material is already available and does not need to be created in the process of conversation – this could reflect the impression of some listeners as well as of performers that, as in a retrospective reflection, they encountered in this piece typical gestures from the first four quartets – almost as if Carter wanted to revisit the principle of *conclusio* which concluded the Second Quartet, but now, at the end of his series of quartets, as a conclusion to the genre and a summing up of his contributions.[35]

Structural thought and compositional work

The central premise under which Carter undertakes the task of ascertaining a structural basis for the musical discourse – resolved in the quartets in an exemplary manner – contrasts with serial thinking in that it does not adopt the postulate of an analogy with language derived from the field of generative grammar: according to Carter, in a conversation with Benjamin Boretz, this

[32] Carter, "Program Note," in *String Quartet No. 4* [score].
[33] Rudolf Kolisch, "Democratic Principles of Ensemble Playing," notes for a seminar at Black Mountain College, Summer 1944, Kolisch Collection, Houghton Library, Harvard University, Cambridge, 5 pages, quote on p. 1 (emphasis in the original).
[34] Carter, "Note from the Composer," in *String Quartet No. 5* [score].
[35] See the commentary on this work in Meyer and Shreffler, *ECCP*, p. 294.

analogy takes language to be a "matter-of-fact communication," and assumes an agreement about vocabulary, grammar, and syntax that precedes speaking. But these circumstances do not apply to music.[36] The structural consequences which Carter draws from this criticism resemble statements of French post-structuralist linguistics and philosophy born of a skepticism towards established systems of propositions. The task, as Michel Foucault remarked, "consists of not – of no longer – treating discourses as groups of signs ... but as practices that systematically form the objects of which they speak."[37]

The complexity of Carter's compositions, pointed out again and again, is based on a pitch space conceived as an area of action. Thus traditional constitutive notions of the quartet, usually based on motives and themes in the traditional sense, are on trial. Carter developed both form and musical shapes from the attributes of the participating voices as they move through time, thereby giving a special importance to the temporal layer. Borrowing from one of Schoenberg's phrases on harmony, one could speak of "structural functions of musical time," manifesting themselves not so much in distinctive durations but rather in formally effective tempo relationships.[38] At the level of creating basic materials, general syntactic criteria of traditional thematic creation no longer apply. Instead one perceives a method informed by Kolisch's idea of a connection between "tempo and character" that employs particular behavior patterns that are shaped by motives in the broadest sense.[39] Carter's concept of time as a process has consequences for his composing at the rhythmic level that are related to what René Leibowitz outlined for the Schoenberg school: "Such a carefully balanced superposition of different rhythms creates an extremely rich polyphonic rhythm. In this sense, the term polyrhythm seems to me out of place, for one of the conditions *sine qua non* of polyphonic richness and variety is that the rhythm must display the same qualities which are inherent in the other elements of such musical discourse."[40] Near the end of both the First and Second Quartets Carter pursued this concept even in the internal structural level by creating motivic materials from the superposition of rhythmic layers which, in the scores printed in 1955 and 1961, he indicated specifically in a cue staff.[41]

[36] Boretz, "Conversation with Elliott Carter," 4.
[37] Foucault, *The Archaeology of Knowledge*, p. 54.
[38] On this parallel, see Schmidt, "Formbildende Tendenzen der musikalischen Zeit." Also see Mead, "Time Management: Rhythm as a Formal Determinant in Certain Works of Elliott Carter," in this volume.
[39] Kolisch gave his famous talk on "Tempo und Charakter in Beethovens Musik" in German in December 1942 in New York and published it the following year first in English.

David Schiff has pointed out the likely influence of Kolisch's ideas of thinking of tempo in structural terms; see *MEC*, p. 41, and Meyer and Shreffler, *ECCP*, p. 92.
[40] Leibowitz, *Schoenberg and his School*, p. 276. See also Kapp, "Shades of the Double's Original."
[41] In the First Quartet, see the last movement, mm. 209–12, 237, and 241. In the Second Quartet, see mm. 458–59 and 463 including the upbeat.

In the First Quartet thinking in metric layers is still directly connected to thinking in terms of themes.[42] A page of sketches entitled "Themes. Improvisation of Cello" is a good illustration of how Carter thinks about individual instruments or rather voices: several themes have been given metronome markings and Roman numerals relate them to "movements."[43] And in a note on the *Allegro scorrevole* music, Carter considers the connection between tempo and character as it affects the large-scale formal sections: "allegro fragments. alternating with quiet ideas of diff. tempo of fragments."[44] Such sketches can be interpreted as harbingers of the dramatic plan for the overall development that Carter made for the Second Quartet, where he further developed his "thematic" thought.[45] In the sketches for the Fourth Quartet similar considerations repeatedly appear in the context of meter and tempo. Figure 7.2 presents such a page of sketches (undated) with the self-explanatory title "systems of confrontation" that tries out the relationships between the instruments. The notes at the bottom across the page refer to the main tempo at the beginning of the *presto* movement (MM 94.5) and connect to the network of tempi that underlies the piece (see Figure 7.3).

In spite of the complex and formally effective treatment of the tempo layering, the sketches for the First Quartet contain no formal plans, and among those for the Second Quartet, there is only the above-mentioned dramatic remark. Probably because the dramaturgy of the Third Quartet works through the possible combinations of the individual sections of the two duos, there are no sketches on the large-scale organization of tempi nor are there any overarching dramatic outlines. In the Fourth Quartet, Carter seems to need both again in order to connect the space of the four instruments' independent tempo layers with a formal process. Only for this quartet does Carter outline the temporal plan, on a "polyrhythmic graph" consisting of several pages taped together with the various layers color coded. Apparently the chart was tacked to the wall as a composition aid as suggested by holes left by thumb tacks.[46] Coloring can be found in the numerous sketches concerned with the planning of internal tempo and harmonic structures, which in this quartet came before the concrete formulation of the composition. The formal organization has as its complement a system of referential tempi that integrates the individual tempo layers into a kind of

[42] All 538 pages of sketches on the First Quartet are accessible at the Library of Congress website: memory.loc.gov/diglib/ihas/loc.natlib.ihas.200155638/pageturner.html
[43] *Ibid.*, p. 21.
[44] See *ibid.*, p. 205.

[45] See Schmidt, "Emanzipation des musikalischen Diskurses," pp. 227 ff., ill. of the sketch on p. 228.
[46] Link ("Long-Range Polyrhythms in Elliott Carter's Recent Music," p. 97) has a diagram with the coincidence points of the four tempo levels that carry the form. A similar graph for *Esprit Rude Esprit Doux* (1985) is reproduced in Meyer and Shreffler, *ECCP*, p. 260.

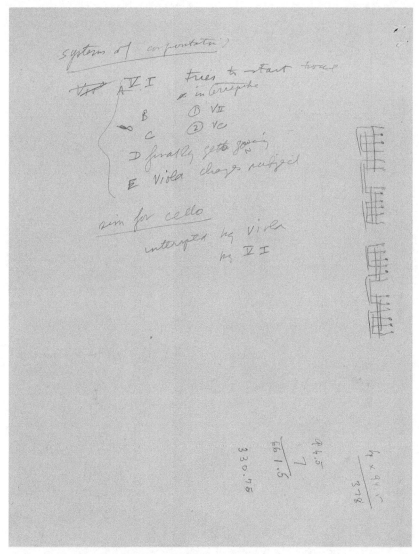

Fig. 7.2 Page of sketches for the Fourth Quartet; Collection Elliott Carter, Paul Sacher Foundation

tempo network,[47] something that does not exist in this form in any of the other quartets. The sketch allows one to see at a glance how to move from one tempo to another (see Figure 7.3).

In the Fifth Quartet, Carter uses the structural advantages of polyrhythmic form as well,[48] but he ties them to a continuous pulse (MM 96), which in

[47] See also Benadon's comments on "tempo networks," in "Towards a Theory of Tempo Modulation," esp. pp. 565 ff. It remains to be investigated how closely MM 63 and MM 84 in Carter's Fourth Quartet resemble Benadon's "tonic tempo."

[48] Carter sketched various sections in the previously used form of the "polyrhythmic graph," as shown on a sketch from February

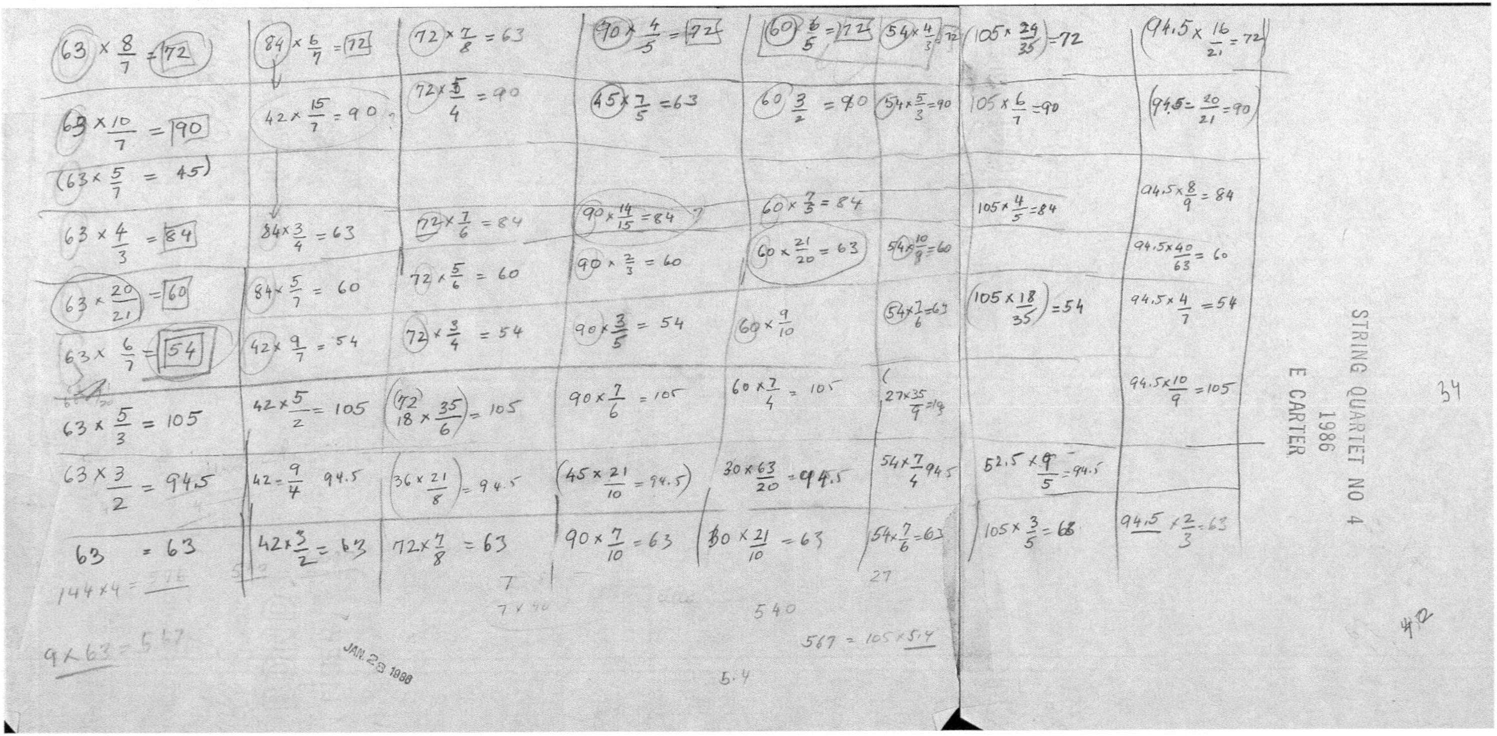

Fig. 7.3 Page of sketches for the Fourth Quartet; Collection Elliott Carter, Paul Sacher Foundation

several places becomes the referential tempo and thereby acquires metric and thus also *gestalt*-like qualities.[49] In a parallel dramatic process this tempo is assigned to the instruments – with the first violin clearly in a leading metric role[50] – and to a repertoire of fragmentary gestures usually associated with character descriptions reminiscent of the previous quartets and representing in condensed form the *gestalt*-like quality of the relation between tempo and character.

The formation of compositional material also yields interesting information about harmonic aspects of the quartets. The sketches for the First Quartet reveal the starting points. In retrospective remarks on this quartet from around 1960, Carter himself repeatedly directs attention to his use of the all-interval tetrachord [0146].[51] He does so especially in "Shop Talk by an American Composer," in which he illustrates the "'key' four-note chord," as he calls it, and refers to the much-discussed postcard to Michael Steinberg which contains the harmonic scheme of the Second Quartet built of two all-interval tetrachords and the remark that the First Quartet only uses one of them.[52] Thus the pitch structure of the Second Quartet was explained with respect to those two set classes and has been understood as a further development, derived from the First Quartet.[53]

Among the source material for the First Quartet are two undated sketches on the pitches Carter used to build his harmonic space. On both pages there are also notes on the tetrachords in question: one of them has a system of permutations on a twelve-tone row which Carter divides into two-, three-, four- and six-tone segments, combining their original and retrograde forms and finally interlacing row segments, the way Schoenberg and Berg also did.[54] In the lower portion of the page Carter examines the possibilities of four-note chords which complement each other to form the total chromatic and which are derived from a permutation of the three-note groups. Here is a mechanism derived from a twelve-tone row, which resembles the one fundamental

---

3/4, 1995. Also see Aylward, "Metric Synchronization and Long-Range Polyrhythms in Elliott Carter's Fifth String Quartet."
[49] At the beginning of the "Giocoso," m. 25 (pulse in Vla); in interlude I, mm. 72–77 (pulse in Vln I and Vc); in Interlude II, mm. 124–27 (pulse in Vla); and very prominently from the end of interlude IV, mm. 242–50 (pulse in Vln I, Vla, Vc), throughout the entire Adagio sereno (MM 48) and the subsequent Interlude V (MM again 96), mm. 251–308 (pulse in the Tutti).
[50] See the review of form, pulse, and tempo in Kim, "Stylistic Analysis of Elliott Carter's String Quartet No. 5," pp. 109–11. However,

the *gestalt*-like character of the tempi is not discussed.
[51] See CEL, pp. 214–24.
[52] See for example Schmidt "Emanzipation des musikalischen Diskurses," pp. 222 and 238 (with an illustration).
[53] Bernard, "Problems of Pitch Structure in Elliott Carter's First and Second String Quartets." Compare Koivisto, "Aspects of Motion in Elliott Carter's Second String Quartet," 19–52, and Roeder, "'The Matter of Human Cooperation' in Carter's Mature Style," in this volume.
[54] See Carter, sketches for the First String Quartet, Library of Congress website (see n. 42), p. 219.

to the works from the Second Quartet onward – except that instead of combining the two possible all-interval tetrachords Carter uses two transpositions of the same one combined with a symmetrical tetrachord that completes the total chromatic: A = [0146], B = [0146], C = [0347] with the interval structure: minor third, minor second, minor third (see Example 7.1).[55]

The second page of sketches shows how Carter continues to work with these segmentations: it has a list of seven hexachords notated in specific registral placements and derived by adding a fixed interval to changing tetrachords.[56] From these hexachords Carter derives three-note subsets – with two of the total possible three-note groups missing in each instance. In the space below, the composer notes the same all-interval tetrachord labeled A in the sketch of the rows (see Example 7.1), now dissected into the various intervals it contains. A first glance at this material reveals that Carter's starting point for systematic thinking about pitch was apparently twelve-tone rows and related permutations, as we know them from Schoenberg or Berg. At the same time, while working on the First Quartet, he went beyond serial thought by trying out chord structures that seem to anticipate the thought process that led to the *Harmony Book*.[57]

Thus the function of the all-interval tetrachord [0146], which Carter in retrospect singled out in the context of the First Quartet, was not a structural one in the sense of a "nexus-set," but rather an initial impulse for sketching out the analytic harmonic organization which in subsequent quartets was to play an increasingly elaborate role. Another indication that Carter may have been thinking along these lines is the fact that for the Second and Third Quartets he retroactively produced extensive analytical "sketches" designed to communicate these aspects of harmonic organization to third parties. For the Second Quartet, Carter differentiates systematically between, on the one hand, the "general harmonic scheme" and the two all-interval tetrachords, supplemented by symmetrical tetrachords,[58] and on the other, the

[55] See the harmonic plan for the Double Concerto which Carter published in "The Orchestral Composer's Point of View," p. 246, and my remarks on the analytical sketch "general harmonic scheme of Quartet II + Double Concerto" in Schmidt, "Emanzipation des musikalischen Diskurses," p. 223.
[56] Carter, sketches for the First Quartet, Library of Congress website (see n. 42), p. 17. This sketch is discussed in Stephen Soderberg, "At the Edge of Creation: Elliott Carter's Sketches in the Library of Congress," in this volume.
[57] The similarity is shown by the comparison: *HB*, synthesis: 2+4, i4, p. 109,

and p. 352. The hexachords for the First Quartet have been formed from the major third G–B, to which a tetrachord is added each time: two of tetrachord 3 (a semitone apart, resulting in two of hexachord 39); two of tetrachord 1 (a semitone apart, resulting in two of hexachord 41); two of tetrachord 7 (one an inversion of the other, resulting in two of hexachord 35); and a tetrachord 5 (resulting in hexachord 21). The points of departure are chords on G, and derived from them chords on E and B.
[58] Transcript in Schmidt, "Emanzipation des musikalischen Diskurses," p. 223.

Fig. 7.4 Analytical diagram for the Third Quartet; Collection Elliott Carter, Paul Sacher Foundation

aforementioned postcard to Michael Steinberg. The latter, by adding tempo layers, gives this mechanism its rhythmic form in two voices, which in the last movements of the Quartet plays an important role, thereby implicitly raising the issue of motivic development (interestingly Carter calls the all-interval

Ex. 7.1 Transcription of a sketch for the First Quartet

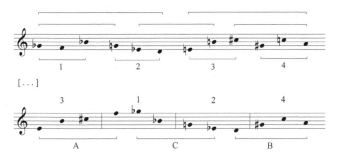

chord "motive" A and B).[59] Thus after his systematic work for the First Quartet, Carter returns in the Second Quartet mainly to the chordal scheme derived from manipulations of the twelve-tone row.

For the Third Quartet, Carter returned to the other aspect of harmonic organization: chord synthesis and analysis and the related fixed-register chords. This coincided with the compilation on his *Harmony Book* during the 1960s. Again, we find analytical notes addressed to third parties: three such pages are in the collection of the Paul Sacher Foundation in Basel and reproductions of slightly modified versions of two of them appear in David Schiff's book, indicating that Carter notated this at least twice with minor differences (not relevant in terms of content). The idea of taking an all-interval twelve-tone chord in a fixed register as a starting point and then deriving from it intervals fixed in register, as well as its contiguous three-note subsets, is reminiscent of sketches from the First Quartet. In these outlines of the harmonic system for the Third Quartet, the distribution of the intervals plays a fundamental role in determining the form, in contrast to the Second Quartet, in which the characteristics of the intervals are assigned to the instruments and become part of their "behavior patterns." A page entitled "Fixed Pitch- (Rhyme-Scheme)"[60] shows that ten pitch intervals of the main chord are each assigned to one of the ten formal sections of the two duos (the eleventh interval, the major second, occurs in all formal sections). There is also a page that lists three- and four-note groups akin to the sketches for the First Quartet but now using the numbering scheme of the *Harmony Book*: a repertoire made up of notes assigned to each duo as well as chords which both duos share. In an as yet unpublished analytical sketch (Figure 7.4), Carter notates the interval reserves of the two duos and their shared "combination chords" in a formal outline with measure numbers, like a skeleton of the pitch organization which carries through this formal process. Thereby Carter creates a consistent harmonic space that provides both a concrete architecture of

[59] See Schmidt, "Emanzipation des musikalischen Diskurses," p. 238.

[60] See Schiff, *MEC*, p. 80.

pitch as well as an interconnected abstract system of intervals and chord classes.

A look at the sketches of the Third Quartet gives us an idea of how Carter worked with this harmonic space: in a small music notebook there are notes on various four-note groups, some of which are marked in colored pencil for further use (the colors indicate the repertoire to which a collection belongs). Apparently Carter examined not only the duos but also the individual instruments moving in the duo space. Numerous analytical annotations in the sketches – probably added later – on various formal components refer to these preliminary studies and are apparently meant to assess the positioning of a passage in the space thus created (for example, by marking collections in a particular color so as to indicate more clearly to which repertoires they belong, or with measure numbers to indicate their place in the overall score).

In the Third Quartet, Carter develops the systematic aspects of the harmony that he laid out in the sketches for the First Quartet and examined in the Second Quartet on a very limited scale with regard to the possibilities of the all-interval tetrachords. Both the later analytical comments and, after 1960, his simultaneous work on the *Harmony Book* reveal that he had both compositional and theoretical purposes in mind. Carter explicitly places the latter in the context of a contemporary debate on the consequences of twelve-tone thought as indicated not only by the explicit reference to the work of Stefan Bauer-Mengelberg and Melvin Ferentz "On Eleven-Interval Twelve-Tone Rows," which he cites on the "Fixed-Pitch-(Rhyme-Scheme)" sketch as the source for the all-interval chord used in the Third Quartet.[61] The development of his own classification system with its own numbering can be attributed to internal efficiency but also has to be seen as a statement, especially when it is so clearly meant to be a public communication: apparently Carter does not want his harmonic organization to be described in terms of set theory informed by serial thought. It is probably no coincidence that Carter so distinctly marked his chord system in the analyses for the Third Quartet, the score to which was published in the same year that Allen Forte published *The Structure of Atonal Music*.[62] Carter does not react with a "counter theory," but with a genre that traditionally merges theory and composition into one: the string quartet. Having already critically examined earlier models, he now arrives with his Third Quartet at a point of critical engagement with contemporary alternatives. Maybe this is why for the two subsequent quartets – at least as it seems now – there was no longer the need to project analysis toward the outside, and instead there is a kind of internal review of the genre.

---

[61] Bauer-Mengelberg and Ferentz, "On Eleven-Interval Twelve-Tone Rows." See the illustration in Schiff, *MEC*, p. 80.

[62] Forte, *The Structure of Atonal Music*. See also Link, "The Combinatorial Art of Elliott Carter's *Harmony Book*," pp. 19–21.

Since the 1990s Carter has enjoyed his most productive period of all as a composer. In 1998 he even dared to step onto the opera stage, which around 1970 he had used metaphorically in order to insert into a great tradition his structural interests in creating parallel courses of simultaneous musical processes. And at that very point he ceased devoting himself to his perhaps most successful genre, the string quartet, which itself had manifested these dramatic structural interests in such an emphatic way. The reasons for this will most likely be found by looking at Carter's distinct handling of genres. In this area as well, the redefinition of his aesthetic standpoint around 1950 can be seen as a reorientation that is revealed by his focus on a few fundamental genres. First there was a wide range of choral works, music for the stage, songs, chamber, and orchestral music; then in the late 1940s the focus was narrowed to chamber-music works, in particular quartet settings in the *Eight Etudes and a Fantasy* for woodwind quartet and the *Eight Pieces for Four Timpani*, culminating in the First String Quartet. Up to the time of the Third Quartet, Carter seems to be preoccupied with systematically examining the possibilities of a few genres under clearly defined premises.

With the Third Quartet the period of narrow focus on specific genres comes to an end. This shift is reflected in Carter's writings. In his liner notes on the First and Second Quartets for the recording by the Composers Quartet in 1970, Carter reflects on modern European and American positions against the background of his own reorientation of the late 1940s. But in the mid-1970s (that is, after having completed the Third Quartet) he began in his own writings to place the complexity of the quartets into a larger historical frame and thus into the great tradition of the European history of music. In the above-quoted introductory talk on the Third Quartet for the BBC he goes back to the polytextual motet of the late Middle Ages, arguing that the "multiplicity of ideas" in the Third Quartet "is, of course, nothing new since renaissance polyphony in both church and secular works such as madrigals often combines several ideas of different character together – indeed in the very earliest examples of western polyphony different vocal parts [have] quite contrasting texts – sometimes even in different languages."[63] He goes on to cite the Bach cantatas and operas by Mozart, Verdi, and Mussorgsky as important precedents.

One could see Carter's approach to genre as complementary to that of Beethoven, whose retrospective absolutism produced an aesthetic hierarchy that placed the string quartet at the pinnacle of chamber music. It was this hierarchy that made the string quartet a locus of aesthetic self-discovery.[64] Whereas Beethoven, having systematically gone through all possible genres,

[63] Carter, "3rd String Quartet BBC Talk," p. 3.   [64] See Schmidt, "Kammermusik mit Bläsern und der Umbau des Gattungssystems."

through tactical reduction aimed at the communicative basic constellations of symphony, quartet, and piano sonata and – at the end of his life as an artist – drew the essential consequences there, so Carter, at the end of the 1940s, in an emphatically charged understanding of the genre, connects with the quartet and, after a fundamental clarification of compositional thought, he again widens his view. Whereas in the Fourth and Fifth Quartets, under the specific conditions of the genre, he systematically brings this self-discovery to an end (that is, to the reflective review of the Fifth Quartet), in his later music he begins to experiment – in a wider range of genres and in the most varied situations – with the possibilities of musical language that he had already developed. He proceeds in the same way with the idea of the quartet. He does not abandon it completely but brings it in contact with new situations. If one wants to find out how the idea of quartet composition continues in Carter's music, one needs to look at works like the Piano Quintet (1997), a work in one movement in which the piano plays opposite the string quartet – four individuals forming an entity; at the Oboe Quartet (2001), which does not present the oboe as an idiosyncratic sound source but instead, based on a modified version of the idea of the duo of the Third String Quartet, tests its ability to come together with the three string instruments in an emphatic chamber music context; and at the Clarinet Quintet (2007), which connects with the formal ideas of the quartet compositions via its five closely connected movements that are played without pause, and that in a way presents an alternative to the piano quintet. It contrasts the string quartet with a melodic instrument that has the potential to project multiple voices, while the piano as a harmonic instrument has, not the same, but equally important possibilities on that level. Carter writes in the program note to the Clarinet Quintet: "Having written a Clarinet Concerto and five string quartets work on this was particularly attractive."[65] We can assume that he will continue to find attractive such potential for making productive connections between his experiences with the various genres.

[65] Carter, "Composer's Notes," in *Clarinet Quintet* [score].

8   Composition with intervals: melodic invention in Elliott Carter's recent concertos

Stephen Heinemann

> Composing, for me, is putting into an order a certain number of sounds
> according to certain interval-relationships ... What survives every change of
> system is melody.   Igor Stravinsky[1]

Many analytical studies of Elliott Carter's music have appropriately dealt with his innovative rhythmic practice or his nascent use of harmonic materials that anticipated or paralleled contemporary developments in pitch-class set theory. Carter himself has observed, "My music is based above all on harmony. The fundamental element is my harmonic choices."[2] But melody is unquestionably essential to Carter's artistry. While he embraced athematicism as enthusiastically as any other modernist, he nevertheless found that the melodic line was conceptually appropriate to his musical goals, and he has used melody, often in quite expansive forms, to represent the instrumental characters, and by extension the scenarios of conflict, that permeate his compositions.[3]

This study will examine linear composition within complete and incomplete spatial sets, as a consequence of permutable pitch sets, and as essentially improvised musical material that is freed of restrictions beyond interval content. Aspects of asymmetry, counterpoint, and rhythmic organization will also be considered. Four of Carter's recent solo concertos provide the material for this study: the Oboe Concerto, commissioned by Paul Sacher for Heinz Holliger, completed in 1987 and premiered in 1988 (the only one of the four concertos to employ a concertino, here a small group consisting of four or five violas and percussion); the Violin Concerto, co-commissioned by Ole Böhn and the San Francisco Symphony, completed in 1990 and premiered that year with Böhn as soloist; the Clarinet Concerto, commissioned by Pierre

[1] Stravinsky, *Poetics of Music*, pp. 37, 39.
[2] Szersnovicz, "Le Temps restitué," quoted in Link, *ECGR*, No. 603.
[3] In his notes for a recording of the 1961 Double Concerto, Carter observed, "the musical ideas are not themes or melodies but rather groupings of sound materials out of which textures, linear patterns, and figurations are invented." A traditional idea of "melody" as something constructed from motives and subjected to repetition and variation does not apply to this study; the term refers to any musical line in which the temporal progression/succession of pitches in (usually various) rhythms is perceived as a connected event, often by dint of being performed by a single instrument, possibly unified by means other than repetition and variation.

Boulez for Alain Damiens and the Ensemble Intercontemporain, completed just before Carter's eighty-eighth birthday in December 1996 and premiered in Paris the following month; and the Flute Concerto, co-commissioned by the Jerusalem International Chamber Music Festival, the Berlin Philharmonic, and the Boston Symphony Orchestra, completed in 2008 and premiered that year in Jerusalem with Emanuel Pahud as soloist.[4] Unlike other concertos composed during this time span,[5] each of these works features a solo monophonic instrument of great technical agility, and all share an approach to melodic invention based on a limited availability of intervals.

A brief discourse on the various meanings of *interval* is therefore appropriate. Post-tonal theorists have formalized four types of intervals, usually measured in semitones: the ordered pitch interval (opi), the distance from one pitch up or down to another; the unordered pitch interval (upi) between two pitches, with distinctions of direction (and, therefore, the order of the pitches) erased; the ordered pitch-class interval (opci), the distance from one pitch class to another, where the second is the next higher representative in pitch space (or to the right in modular space) relative to the first; and the unordered pitch-class interval (upci), also called interval class, the smallest possible distance between two pitch classes. For example, given pitches D5 and F3 (in that order as applicable): their opi is -21; their upi is 21; their opci is 3; and their upci is 3. The variety of interval types can lead, if benignly, to imprecision of expression: for instance, what is often described as an "all-interval row" (as opposed to spatial set) is specifically an all-ordered-pitch-class-interval row that is not regarded as losing its "all-intervalness" if its constituent elements (i.e., pitch classes) are realized in pitch space in a disposition that duplicates or omits unordered pitch intervals; similarly, an "all-interval tetrachord" is specifically an all-interval-class tetrachord.

Carter's interval technique

With the Second String Quartet in 1959, Carter began to develop a compositional technique, simultaneously simple and ingenious, in which certain intervals are assigned to instruments and serve in various ways as a basis

[4] Daniel Barenboim conducted the premiere of the Flute Concerto; his wife, Elena Bashkirova, is its dedicatee.

[5] Carter also wrote solo concertos for cello (2000) and horn (2006), as well as the de facto piano concertos *Dialogues* (2003) and *Interventions* (2007). The cello and horn concertos do not employ the interval technique described herein, perhaps because the technique may require more dexterity than is usually associated with those solo instruments. *Interventions*, on the other hand, frequently treats the piano as a monophonic instrument and does employ interval technique (using an interval repertoire of upic 2,3,6,7,8,E).

Ex. 8.1 Interval technique: unordered pitch-interval classes for Oboe Concerto soloist

for melodic invention. I will refer to this practice as *interval technique*. The four standardized interval types are insufficient to account for interval technique, which is based primarily on the treatment of intervals related by inversion as non-equivalent. What is operative in Carter's technique is not specific intervals between pitches, nor intervals between pitch classes, but equivalence classes of intervals between pitches – essentially, unordered pitch intervals with octave equivalence. This fifth interval type is the *unordered pitch-interval class*, abbreviated *upic*, and is formalized as follows:[6]

For any two pitches x and y, upic (x,y) = |y-x| (mod 12)

In this definition, compound intervals are expressly equivalent to their simple intervallic correspondents,[7] so that upi 7, 19, 31, 43, etc., are all members of upic 7. For example, while the upi between pitches D5 and F3 is 21 and the opci and upci are 3, the upic between them is 9.[8]

Carter applies interval technique in the four concertos discussed here by assigning an *interval repertoire* of unordered pitch-interval classes to each of the solo instruments: oboe, upic 2,3,6,7,8,E; violin, upic 1,3,7,8,T; clarinet, upic 1,2,4,7,9; flute, upic 1,4,6,7,9,T. Only one representative of each unordered pitch-class interval is included, and the tritone is excluded from the violin and clarinet interval repertoires. A summary of the oboe's melodic possibilities is shown in Example 8.1. The oboe (and each of the other solo instruments considered here) is assigned upic 7, and as such can move, for example, from C up to G or from C down to F. However, it will be denied its inversion upic 5, so it cannot move from C down to G or from C up to F. The oboe and flute, having access to the tritone, can move, for example, from C up or down to F♯. Once a new pitch has been reached, the interval repertoire is applied to it. Given a heterogeneous interval repertoire, any pitch is potentially no more than two notes removed from any other.

[6] The vertical lines signify absolute value, not cardinality.

[7] In the Second String Quartet, Carter distinguishes between compound intervals and their simple equivalents, assigning upi 16 to the first violin and upi 4 to the second, upi 6 to the viola and upi 18 to the cello, but he abandoned this practice in later works.

[8] Interval types are calculated as follows, where for pitch C4 = 0 and for pc C = 0 (thus,

in this example, D5 = 14, F3 = −7, D = 2, and F = 5):

opi = y-x = −7−14 = −21
upi = |y-x| = |−7−14| = 21
opci = y-x (mod 12) = 5−2 = 3
upci = lesser of opci(x,y) and opci(y,x)
      = 5−2 = 3
upic = |y-x| (mod 12) = |−7−14| (mod 12)
     = 21 (mod 12) = 9

Ex. 8.2 Flute Concerto, solo part, mm. 225–31

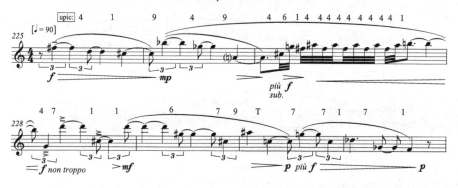

A brief, representative sample from the Flute Concerto is shown in Example 8.2. The upic of each successive pair of notes is shown above the melodic line; compound intervals appear only in m. 228. The composer takes great care in introducing pitch classes in octaves other than that initially established, so that, for instance, the F♯5 of the opening is absent for slightly more than three measures until the appearance of G♭4, while four of the pitch classes that are stated more than once, 01TE, appear only in a single octave. Pitch classes 3 and 4 do not appear at all, and pc 5 arrives only at the end of the phrase. The entire interval repertoire is employed, but with varying emphasis, so that upic 4 is prominent in the first half but absent from the second, while upic 7 and T occur only at the end, the latter a single time. Interval technique permits the tremolo in m. 227, a favored device for animating a dyad. This phrase is an example of *interval-based melodic practice* – that is, melody independent of a spatial set – that encompasses the majority of the lines in these works.

Example 8.3 illustrates a passage of interval-based melodic practice that is a particularly clear example of the *scorrevole* character of the Clarinet Concerto's fourth movement; this passage culminates the movement and is one of the clearest nods to jazz in Carter's works. His sketches reveal that the bracketed measures (214–20) were added after the composition of the others, resulting in one of the most visceral passages in all the concertos, a set of relatively conjunct lines (employing only upi 1, 2, 4) that evokes, for this writer, the improvisational style of Eric Dolphy.[9] The lines dovetail across the brief rests except for an intervallic anomaly in m. 219 and a large leap in m. 220.

[9] The resemblance of Dolphy's improvisation to aspects of Carter's composition, albeit in the realm of polyrhythm, is a significant subtext of Folio, "An Analysis of Polyrhythm in Selected Improvised Jazz Solos," pp. 123–32.

Ex. 8.3 Clarinet Concerto, solo part, mm. 214–26

When Carter applies his interval technique, every note represents a possibility for moving to another based on the unordered pitch-interval classes that are assigned. The limited availability of these upics would appear to limit the availability of pitch classes: the simplest melodic decision – does the line next move up or down? – eliminates half (or more) of the pitch classes from consideration. This presupposes, however, that such decisions are necessarily made on a note-by-note basis, which is a tenuous claim to make even in compositional environments that emphasize ordered sets but is especially incongruent with the flexibility of Carter's technique, as will be discussed presently.

Interval repertoires and their source chords

In three of the concertos considered here, the intervals that are assigned both to the solo instruments and to their accompanying ensembles are derived from two kinds of sources – the all-interval dodecachord and the inversionally symmetrical dodecachord. A dodecachord that provides the interval

Ex. 8.4 Retrograde-inversional invariance (RI); parallel-inversional invariance (QI)

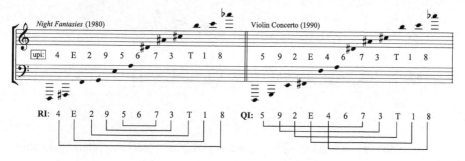

repertoire for a work is therefore referred to here as a *source chord*.[10] Carter remarked in 1990:

> Very often, in recent years, I have started my pieces by deciding that I would take a certain chord and use that as a basis of a composition. And then I fool around, turn it around and discover what its elements are … but then I really don't know what the next step is. I mean, if somebody asked me to write a piece, I might say, "Well, I'll see if I can use that chord in this piece." Then there's a whole other series of decisions which have to do with what kind of piece it will be … One decision piles on the other, and then I begin to see what in a chord would contribute to this effect.[11]

There are 1,928 distinct forms of all-interval dodecachords. Eighty-eight of these have a structure resembling that of the first chord in Example 8.4. Each interval is reflected by its inversion, so that interval 4 at the bottom of the chord is mirrored by interval 8 at the top. The intervallic reflection is shown with brackets below the chord. This structure is formally called "retrograde-inversional invariance," or RI invariance.[12] Carter's *Night Fantasies* uses all eighty-eight forms of these RI-invariant chords; the first chord in Example 8.4 is the chord Carter labeled as Number 86. John Link observes that Carter's attraction to RI chords was stimulated by "his own practice (in the Double Concerto and Piano Concerto, for example) of using large chords, spread out

---

[10] This term could be expressed accurately but wordily as "interval source chord." Schiff calls such a chord a "twelve-tone tonic chord" (*MEC*, p. 48). Schiff uses the term "source chord" in a different context in the first edition of *MEC*.

[11] Bernard, "An Interview with Elliott Carter," 205. The first ellipsis is in the original.

[12] The all-interval row from Alban Berg's Lyric Suite, represented in pc notation as 5409728136TE and forming the opci string E89T7652341, is perhaps the best-known example of this type of structure, and motivated the famous Bauer-Mengelberg and Ferentz 1965 study ("On Eleven-Interval

Twelve-Tone Rows") that would so influence Carter. Further work on this topic was contributed by Morris and Starr, "The Structure of All-Interval Series," 366. Also see Slonimsky, *Thesaurus of Scales and Melodic Patterns*, pp. iii, 175, 243. Luigi Nono subsequently employed an all-interval row in *Il canto sospeso*, a work that Carter recalled "had impressed me so much on hearing it … that I wanted to understand its musical content in detail" (Bernard, "An Interview with Elliott Carter," 206). The history of all-interval rows is discussed in detail in Bernard, "Chord, Collection and Set in Twentieth-Century Theory."

Ex. 8.5 Oboe Concerto: QI-invariant source chord

over the entire registral space of a composition, to serve as referential sonorities."[13] Example 8.4's second chord, a source chord from the Violin Concerto, is a variation on RI-invariance. This structure inverts the lower hexachord of the *Night Fantasies* chord, thus reversing the order of intervals. Inversionally related intervals now appear in a parallel structure rather than a mirror structure, which is again shown with brackets. This parallel-inversional invariance is called QI invariance.[14]

In QI- and RI-invariant structures, the tritone occupies the middle position within the string of eleven intervals, and the total range, as in every all-interval dodecachord, is sixty-six semitones. Carter's first use of the QI structure was in his 1984 duet *Esprit Rude/Esprit Doux*, and he has continued to use such structures, further expanding his vocabulary with his introduction of the "Link" chords.[15] In Example 8.5, the QI-invariant source chord for the Oboe Concerto is shown. The oboe takes its intervals from the upper hexachord of the source chord, plus the center tritone. The orchestra employs the other intervals and shares the tritone.

In Example 8.6, the three source chords for the Violin Concerto are illustrated. These chords bisect into three different hexachordal set classes, but the lower half of each source chord contains the same unordered pitch intervals as the lower halves of the others, and the upper halves also match each other's intervals. Intervals are given to the violin from the upper hexachord of the source chords, the orchestra employs the complementary intervals from the lower hexachord, and both lack the tritone.

[13] Link, "The Combinatorial Art of Elliott Carter's *Harmony Book*," p. 15. Capuzzo, "Registral Constraints on All-Interval Rows in Elliott Carter's *Changes*," 79, quotes Carter as expressing "a desire to have chords that are spread over a large range and use all twelve notes."

[14] The QI label first appears in Morris and Starr, "The Structure of All-Interval Series," 370. Inverting one hexachord of an RI-invariant chord to produce a QI-invariant chord (or vice versa) is not a general property of these structures. Koivisto, "Syntactical Space and Registral Spacing in Elliott Carter's *Remembrance*," 160, lists the nine hexachordal set classes from which QI-invariant chords can be constructed.

[15] See *HB*, p. 358, for a description and list of "Link" chords. [An updated version may be found at http://www.johnlinkmusic.com/ linkchords.html. –Eds.]

Ex. 8.6 Violin Concerto: QI-invariant source chords

Ex. 8.7 Clarinet Concerto: inversionally symmetrical source chord; upic 7 in source chord

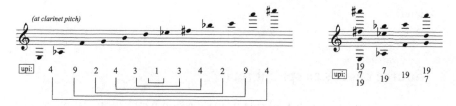

In Example 8.7, the source chord for the Clarinet Concerto – called the "Clarinet chord" in Carter's sketches[16] – is transposed for B♭ clarinet for comparison to the part in the score (his sketches and draft scores are written at concert pitch, but he transposes his final versions). This source chord is not QI-invariant, but picks up where the Violin Concerto will be shown to leave off: the chord is an inversionally symmetrical dodecachord that spans forty-five semitones and contains only unordered pitch intervals 1, 2, 3, 4, and 9 between consecutive pitches. This source chord is realigned on the right of the example, which demonstrates the veiled prominence of upic 7 in both simple and compound forms – the latter consistently represented as upi 19, with both forms combining to link the lowest and highest pitches. My assertion regarding the prominence of upic 7 is supported by an examination of the upic content of the "Clarinet chord." The sixty-six intervals of any dodeca-chord can be summarized in a *dodecachordal upic vector*, a five-position integer string that directly provides the number of occurrences of upic 1 through 5. Quantities of upic 7 through 11 are deduced as the mod 12 complements of upic 5 through 1 respectively; unlisted as redundant is upic 6, since there will always be six tritones. Accordingly, the upic vector of the "Clarinet chord" is <66784>, indicating eight occurrences of upic 7. Carter thus completes the clarinet's interval repertoire (upic 1,2,4,7,9) by substitut-ing upic 7 for upic 3, ensuring that all unordered pitch-class intervals except

---

[16] This chord is shown in Heinemann, "The American Premiere of Elliott Carter's Clarinet Concerto," and was later verified in Carter's   sketches as described in Heinemann, "Melodic Practice in Elliott Carter's Clarinet Concerto."

the tritone are represented once.[17] Unordered pitch interval 19 is especially prominent within the concerto and may refer to the solo instrument's unique acoustical property of overblowing at that interval. Unlike in the Oboe and Violin Concertos, all the pitches of the source chord are within the soloist's range, if barely so – the highest pitch, a written C♯7, appears only twice in the piece.

Finally, the Flute Concerto features two prominent inversionally symmetrical dodecachords, one that occurs near the beginning and the other near the end, but the flute's interval repertoire cannot be teased out of them in the manner of the "Clarinet chord," and their examination will be reserved for later.

Source chords as spatial sets

Source chords play a crucial role in the development of interval repertoires and other aspects of compositional design, but they are not abstractions relegated to background status. Their structures play a unifying harmonic role and, pertinently to this study, may serve as a means for organizing certain melodic passages. The significance of spatial sets, or fixed-register pcsets, in Carter's music has been noted often.[18] The three spatial hexachords at the beginning of Example 8.8, each of which is the upper half of a transposed and/ or inverted source chord, are transcribed from a Violin Concerto sketch, dated September 8, 1989, showing connections by two common tones, E5 and C6. Carter labels these spatial sets as 5–37, 13–6, and 20–21. In each of these hyphenates, the first number refers to hexachords as labeled in Carter's *Harmony Book* and the second number refers specifically to the spacings shown here; this second number does not appear in *Harmony Book*, but is consistently associated with these spacings in Carter's Violin Concerto sketches. Although Carter made several revisions of this passage to reshape the rhythm, he preserved the hexachordal structure of the initial sketch with little alteration in the final score. Transcriptions of two of these sketches are represented on the remaining staves of Example 8.8. Hexachords 5–37 and 13–6 appear, arpeggiated, as a melody in the first draft of the short score. On the staff below this melody, Carter wrote an additional E5 and A4, apparently

[17] The prominence of upic 7 and the derivation of the interval repertoire are seen in Carter's sketch, dated June 7, 1996, in which the "Clarinet chord," numerous subsets of pitches in combination with upic 7-related dyads, and a list of potentially available intervals appear. It is not evident from this sketch whether the design of the chord preceded or resulted from the choice of upic for the interval repertoire.

[18] The seminal study of these sets is Bernard, "Spatial Sets in Recent Music of Elliott Carter." Koivisto, "Syntactical Space and Registral Spacing in Elliott Carter's *Remembrance*," deals extensively with spatial sets within QI invariance.

Ex. 8.8 Violin Concerto: spatial hexachords and melodic realizations

to emphasize E as a common tone between the chords and A as a member of Chord 13–6 – an appropriate emphasis, since the A is skipped over in the arpeggiation from the G♯4. In the second draft of the short score, the additional E5 and A4 from the first draft are inserted into the figure, the rhythm is altered, and the end of the phrase is shortened. In the first draft of the final score (not shown here), a slur from D♯5 to E5 and dynamic markings are added, including a diminuendo to the phrase's zenith, D♭7. In the final score (mm. 360–61), only the dynamics are changed, now featuring a crescendo to the D♭7 so that the high point of the dynamics coincides with the high point of the contour. One might expect that such arpeggiations and their variations would be common, given the significance of the spatial set to works such as "Anaphora" from *A Mirror on Which to Dwell,* but the passage in Example 8.8, plus three other passages not shown here, are the only places in the solo violin part with complete hexachordal spatial sets that are unquestionably traceable to the source chords; as such, they constitute approximately one per cent of the violin part.

Spatial sets play a much larger role in Carter's Oboe Concerto. An early sketch (dated July 26, 1986) had some of the basics of its opening in place, including low chords and timpani rolls that would in fact begin the finished work, although specifics of pitch, meter, and timpani rhythm would change. The entrance of the solo instrument was in its lowest register, characterized immediately by speed and technical difficulty, and the source chord was not to be found. These aspects changed greatly in the opening of the finished piece, shown in orchestral reduction in Example 8.9. In the first measures of the score, the orchestra plays the lower half of the source chord at pitch. The

Ex. 8.9 Oboe Concerto, mm. 1–9

oboe enters at m. 4, playing the upper half of the source chord (shown in Example 8.5) descending from the top A6 to the bottom D4; the entire source chord is thus literally present. The character of the oboe part could not be more different from the early sketch. The oboe maintains its source chord's pitches until the end of the multiphonic that begins in m. 8.

Spatial sets are even more crucial in the Clarinet Concerto. This concerto's seven short movements are defined in part by instrumental groups – successively piano/harp/marimba, unpitched percussion, muted brass, woodwinds, strings, unmuted brass, and finally the full ensemble. Carter composed the work in such a way that the soloist has the option of playing each movement in close proximity to each accompanying group, leaving time to relocate to a different part of the orchestra. The assignment of one set of intervals to the soloist and an opposing set to the orchestra, a technique common to the other works considered here, is eschewed in this concerto: the clarinet interval repertoire is also the orchestral interval repertoire, although the latter is treated somewhat more freely due to voice-leading/harmonic considerations. As befits its capacity as the prototypical doubling instrument, the clarinet solo agreeably mimics the quality of each of the instrumental groups in turn, but it abandons this chameleonic portrayal in the final movement where it moves to the fore – literally – and asserts a more characteristic opposition. The beginning of the solo part is played against an orchestral backdrop of the source

Ex. 8.10 Clarinet Concerto, solo part, mm. 30–44

chord. After the brief opening flourish that recalls the opening of the Violin Concerto, the clarinet's notes are all from the source chord, and all but the highest and lowest pitches of the chord are present, thus forming an inversionally symmetrical decachord. Given the large range of the source chord, such instances of incomplete spatial sets are not unexpected, and they recur with some frequency in the solo part (including mm. 222–26, shown in Example 8.3). Example 8.10 shows the end of the first movement, where the source chord's upic 7 is motivic: the three upi 7s and the five upi 19s shown in Example 8.7 are all rendered as melodic intervals, several of these appearing twice. With the addition of E3 and C♯7, the source chord is now complete. The spatial set is bracketed in the example.

While the two prominent dodecachords of the Flute Concerto do not have the compositional import of interval repertoire-generating source chords, they are nonetheless structurally significant, effectively bookending the work harmonically. The opening of the Flute Concerto, featuring one of these dodecachords, is shown in reduced form in Example 8.11. After an initial orchestral blast of a [0146] chord, the flute plays a rapid nineteen-note figure that uses upic 1,4,7,T; upic 4 and 7 are prominent, upic 1 appears at the beginning, middle (approximately), and end of the figure, while upic T is saved for the penultimate dyad. The first eight pitches are inverted at T_9I to become the next eight. The complete figure is echoed in the strings, whose pitches enter at roughly the same time as they are played by the flute, although the non-flute upic 3 is prominent, even including a [036] attack. The resultant third-heavy dodecachord (its upic vector is <56984>) has the opi structure 44331313344, inversionally symmetrical around an E5/F5 axis. This is followed by another [0146] chord, now *piano*, that holds two common tones

Ex. 8.11 Flute Concerto, mm. 1–5

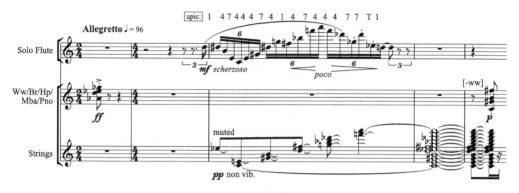

with the first; both [0146] chords are pitch subsets of the dodecachord. The flute's intervals 9 and 6 will not debut until the eighth measure (not shown), and Carter strangely subverts them in the sixth measure by introducing an interval not part of its "legal" repertoire: the figure A4–B♭4–C♯5 produces upic 3. Such anomalies are much more common in this work than in the others, with roughly two dozen in all, six of them in the first eighteen measures alone (the first tritone is followed immediately by upic 8), as if the flute were in the process of learning its own language.[19]

Intervallically permutable pitch sets

One interesting consequence of Carter's interval technique is its effect on pitch sets. In these concertos, unlike in some pieces ("Anaphora," for one),[20] spatial-set pitches can immediately precede or succeed others only if they are related by assigned intervals. A result of this technique may be called the *intervallically permutable pitch set* – a pitch set that may occur in some orderings but not in others according to a given interval repertoire.[21] Shown in Example 8.12 are the twenty-four permutations of four pitches from the Clarinet Concerto source chord which form a [0146] tetrachord; these permutations are shown in pairs of sets where the second of each pair is the retrograde of the first. (If a permutation is permissible, its retrograde will

---

[19] The score originally showed the A–B♭–C♯ figure as A–B–C♯, and this, with its two anomalous appearances of upic 2, was played at the premiere. The "correction" of B to B♭ eliminates those particular anomalies but introduces upic 3.

[20] Weston, "Inversion, Subversion, and Metaphor," pp. 59–88, explores pitch structures in "Anaphora" in great detail.

[21] Generally speaking, ordered pitch or pitch-class sets can be regarded as *syntactically permutable*, in that they may be reordered according to the properties inherent in the compositional design. For example, the property of combinatoriality is often employed to reorder hexachordal pitch-class sets in a twelve-tone environment.

Ex. 8.12 Intervallically permutable pitch set (pitches drawn from Clarinet Concerto source chord)

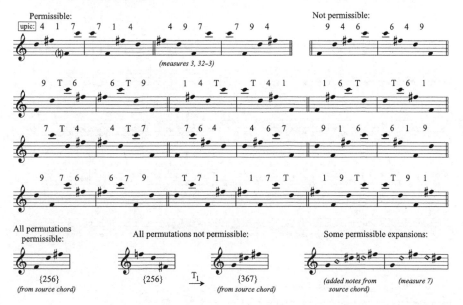

be as well.) Four of these twenty-four sets have permissible orderings when filtered through the clarinet interval repertoire; the third set shown appears early in the piece (m. 3) to open the soloist's statement of the source chord and again in mm. 32–33 (see Example 8.10). The intervallically permutable set is a function of pitch, not pitch class, as the trichordal subset at the bottom of Example 8.12 demonstrates. Depending entirely on pitch-space disposition, the same pitch-class set may be permissible in all orderings, not permissible in all orderings, or some mix of the two. The final sets in this example illustrate a process referred to herein as *expansion* whereby pitches (here taken from the source chord) are inserted between notes of an existing pitch set. The final pitch set here appears in the Clarinet Concerto in m. 7. This expansion process is significant with respect to the potentialities of compositional technique, as it gives the composer great flexibility in manipulating and elaborating pitch structures. Taking this perhaps to an extreme, a composer conceivably could begin with a pair of notes and, through expansion, insert a note between them, then insert notes within the resultant pairs, and so on, constructing a phrase, section, or composition with the original notes at the beginning and end.

Example 8.13a, a transcription of a sketch from the Oboe Concerto, shows Carter addressing the technique of the intervallically permutable pitch set. In a variety of pitch sets he calls "homophones," orderings are presented that alternate between being permissible first for the orchestral interval repertoire of upic 1,4,5,6,9,T, then for the oboe interval repertoire of upic 2,3,6,7,8,E. (In

Ex. 8.13 Oboe Concerto: (a) transcription of sketch dated Jan. 23, 1987 (interval numbers added by author); (b) score excerpt, mm. 28–34; (c) score excerpt, mm. 36–45

the original sketch, orchestral sets are circled in red pencil, oboe sets in green; in this transcription, interval labels are added in order to clarify the stratification.) Seventeen pairs of sets comprising twelve different set classes are considered. The fourth pair of sets is realized in the finished composition as

shown in Example 8.13b: the oboe set appears first, and both sets are transposed up thirteen semitones.[22] More complex intervallically permutable pitch
sets occur a few measures later and are shown in Example 8.13c. The
orchestra repeats the oboe's pitch sets, but the order of pitches is filtered
each time through its distinct interval repertoire.[23] Additionally, the arc of the
second oboe set (mm. 41–43) is nearly mirrored by the ensuing orchestral set.
These set pairs exemplify an elegant means of conveying a strong unity within
a passage without sacrificing the identities of the soloist and the orchestra as
expressed through their interval repertoires.

Disrupted symmetries

Carter remarked in 1990:

> I doubt if I ever do the sort of thing that Schönberg does, for instance, in *Moses und
> Aron*, in which you go up the chord one way, and come down the other. There are
> very literally symmetrical passages in Schönberg … and I, on the whole, find that my
> temperament forces me to avoid that as much as possible … I try always to destroy
> the sense of symmetry. It seems to be a natural inclination on my part. I think the real
> reason is that I have a sense of music always progressing, and symmetry seems to
> prevent or block that progression.[24]

The soloist's final flurry in the Flute Concerto provides an illustration of the
disruption of melodic symmetry (see Example 8.14). It consists of twelve
notes that complete an aggregate, leaving the concerto's second prominent
dodecachord in its wake. The accompaniment this time is built with only flute
intervals, and the flute uses only its upic 1,4,7,9. The inversionally symmetrical dodecachord's opi structure is 41422522414, and the last six notes of the
flute line are a retrograde inversion of the first six, a relatively unusual
instance of symmetry in Carter's music. Using the retrograde inversion,
however, results in an interesting disrupted symmetry: while the succession
of intervals is symmetrical around the interval 9, the gesture itself is not
symmetrical as such since the notes continue to ascend (or "progress") rather
than make a literally symmetrical up-one-way-down-the-other gesture. The
symmetry is realized around an F5/G♭5 axis; this axis is thus a half-step
higher, and the dodecachord a whole-step smaller, than at the beginning of
the work (Example 8.11), creating a progression from the first dodecachord to

---

[22] According to Carter, "The actual notion of
'absolute pitch' is not significant in my pieces.
The pitches are chosen registrally as a matter
of instrumental practicality" (*FW*, p. 110).
[23] The violin's C5 is a doubling of another
part and is incidental to this passage; the

technique of returning to D4 here resembles
the return to C4 in the third oboe set in
Example 8.13a.
[24] Bernard, "An Interview with Elliott
Carter," 203.

Ex. 8.14 Flute Concerto, mm. 295–97

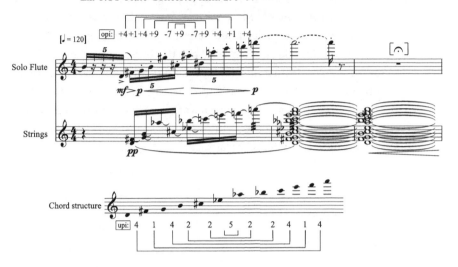

the second. While the strings hold the chord to the end (another three-plus measures beyond those shown here), the piano, vibraphone, and harp offer a few subsets of the chord, and the winds crescendo with the strings to the end on another subset (D4, G4, B4, C♯5, D♯5, G♯5) that is, unsurprisingly, an all-trichord hexachord. This is the sole concerto considered here in which the soloist does not play at the end.

The disruption of symmetry manifests itself twice in Example 8.15, from the conclusion of the Violin Concerto at the final intersection of its long-range polyrhythm. The first disruption of symmetry is through spacing. The orchestra has a chord at the point labeled Chord 1 in Example 8.15. In Example 8.16, Chord 1 is shown first; the low tied notes are held over by the strings and form one of the source hexachords. However, the remainder of the chord does not follow the source chord's QI-invariant pattern, but rather creates an asymmetrical twelve-note chord that uses the violin's intervals 10 and 8 circled in Example 8.16. Here, the "integrity" of the orchestra's interval repertoire is sacrificed in favor of the twelve-note sonority, even though the interval repertoire is readily available, as shown in the three hypothetical substitutes following the actual chord. The RI and QI forms naturally employ orchestra and violin intervals simultaneously, while the inversionally symmetrical form uses only the orchestra intervals.

The second manifestation of disrupted symmetry is by means of incompleteness. In Example 8.15, Chord 1 is followed by the brief cadenza-like passage in the solo violin.[25] The circled common tones at the end lead into a

---

[25] In this example, the last chord of the $\frac{7}{4}$ measure is elaborated in the staff above it; the original presents it as a footnote to the score and the solo part. The elaboration was added

Ex. 8.15 Violin Concerto, mm. 619–26

Ex. 8.16 Violin Concerto: final chords; hypothetical final chords

five-note set, an incomplete version of spatial set 13–6 (as shown in Example 8.8). Echoed in the high strings, as indicated here, this spatial set becomes the upper half of Chord 2, the final chord of the concerto.[26] In Chord 2, the violin's five notes are reflected below, forming an inversionally symmetrical

after the world premiere in San Francisco, prior to the London premiere and recording session.

[26] Porter, "Fancy's Rainbows, Wit's Momentary Fires," 96, describes this as "one of Carter's 'vanishing like a puff of smoke' endings."

decachord using only intervals associated with the violin; interval 3 occupies the center position here but is not a literal part of the violin's pentachordal spatial set. In opposition to Chord 1, here the "integrity" of the dodecachord is sacrificed in favor of the interval content. This assertion is supportable only if there are plausible alternatives – that is, if it is possible to construct not only an inversionally symmetrical ten-note sonority *without* upi 3 but also an inversionally symmetrical twelve-note sonority *with* upi 3. These two constructions are shown in Example 8.16 as hypothetical final chords following Chord 2.

The idea of substituting an inversionally symmetrical sonority for an all-interval construction extends to the source chord of the Clarinet Concerto. Carter could have followed a stratification plan similar to that of the other concertos, making the same intervals available to the soloist (upic 1,2,4,7,9) while assigning their inversions to the orchestra. Consider the following opi constructions: T583E619472 and TE835679412. These RI-invariant dodecachords are also "Link" chords in which five proximate intervals form an all-trichord hexachord (respectively, E6194 and 56794), which is one of the fundamental harmonic constructions in this concerto as well as in many of Carter's other works.[27] But the sharing of materials by soloist and orchestra is essential to the characteristic mimicry of the Clarinet Concerto; as such, the original inversionally symmetrical source chord is representative of the dramatic goals of the composition in a way that an RI-invariant chord, with its concomitant intervallic stratification, cannot be.

Counterpoint

So far, melodic invention has been considered only in terms of its single-line realization. Counterpoint, in certain ways, is even more broadly vital – not just in its traditional musical sense as the art of combining melodies or in the extended musical sense of polyrhythm, but in its rhetorical sense as the evocation of opposition. Counterpoint is the central metaphor of Carter's music. It is more than a matter of texture or technique; the dialectics of his compositions depend upon an expanded vision of counterpoint. This vision is particularly integral to a concerto, a genre traditionally associated with conflict.

---

[27] These "Link" chords are two of four that have an RI-invariant structure; no "Link" chord is QI-invariant.

Ex. 8.17 Flute Concerto, duet, mm. 103–10

Example 8.17 contains an excerpt of an extended passage of melodic counterpoint from the Flute Concerto, a passage unique among these concertos in that the solo instrument is counterpointed by the tutti's own representative of that instrument. The lines move at moderate speed in a complete absence of rhythmic variation, the solo flute employing its upic 1,4,6,7,9,T and the orchestral flute its upic 2,3,5,6,8,E. The two instruments occupy similar pitch spaces; when the soloist rests, the orchestral flute moves up to take its place registrally. The lines meet at unisons with some frequency (more so in the twenty measures preceding this excerpt) and cross occasionally. The counterpoint is characteristically non-imitative. The tessitura rises gradually toward its conclusion in four measures of tremolos (the only time the instrumental lines appear to be conscious of each other) beginning and ending with [0146] statements. Particularly in its lack of rhythmic contrast within or between parts, the passage is highly unusual for Carter, and is especially instructive in terms of the differentiation afforded by the separate interval repertoires: the orchestral flute, separated not only by its relatively distant placement on the stage but also by its musical materials, is a distorted echo of the soloist.

Another approach to counterpoint grows out of an elaborate sketch, dated August 10, 1986, from the Oboe Concerto. Labeled by Carter as "oboe counterpoint," it contains two lines that diverge, then converge, and then cross. Relative durations are shown, with longer notes for the upper line and shorter notes for the lower, but specifics of rhythm do not appear. The sketch would become the cadenza-like passage shown in Example 8.18. This is exaggerated compound melody, a duet for the oboe with itself, accompanied only by light percussion hits that articulate the

Ex. 8.18 Oboe Concerto, solo part, mm. 362–77, with analytical markings

orchestra's portion of the long-range polyrhythm. The oboe's interval repertoire is preserved from one note to the next within the oboe solo taken as a whole, within the "upper-voice" melody in mm. 362–70, and within the "lower-voice" melody in the same measures. Dynamics, attack, and duration differentiate the oboe's two lines. These differences are easily apparent even when the lines converge and cross at m. 368. Here, for the first time, upic 4, which is not in the oboe repertoire, occurs between the lines, so to speak, and the polyphonic effect is thereby enhanced. This upic-4 voice-crossing strategy is one aspect of the original sketch that survives in the finished score. The polyphony is completely distinctive even when the two parts are on a unison D5 at m. 370.[28]

[28] Carter's manuscript of this passage, from the two preceding measures through the first six notes of m. 371, is beautifully reproduced in Meyer and Shreffler, *ECCP*, p. 272. A voice-crossing passage similar to this one is analyzed in Capuzzo, "Registral Constraints on All-Interval Rows in Elliott Carter's *Changes*," 87–92.

Rhythm and performance issues

Although a detailed examination of rhythm in Carter's melodic invention is beyond the scope of this study, a glance here and below points to a significant aspect of Carter's melodic practice. At m. 371 of the Oboe Concerto, the orchestra returns, and the character of the counterpoint takes a new, rhythmically defined, turn. As indicated in Example 8.18, the oboe oscillates between C4 and A♭4 at a constant speed. Other notes are added to the mix, and a second, slower oscillation between D♯4 and D5 gradually asserts itself; this latter figure eventually predominates and is the agent of the metric modulation at m. 374. Particularly notable is Carter's solution when the rhythms of the oscillations intersect, at the point marked "N.B." in m. 372: the D♯4/D5 oscillation prevails, but, rather than simply displace the G♯4 by a note, Carter moves it over *two* notes – the oboe's interval repertoire does not permit D♯4 and G♯4 to appear consecutively. The rhythmic regularity of the individual lines in this example contrasts with the necessary complexity of their notation within a notated metronomic speed that is different from either of the perceived speeds. The metronomic speed here (and through much of Carter's oeuvre) functions as a common denominator between two (or more) perceived speeds.

The performer's task of decoding Carter's notation can be daunting. A simplification of the notation that accurately represents its rhythmic content benefited clarinetist John Bruce Yeh in his preparation of the solo part for the April 1998 American premiere of the Clarinet Concerto with the Chicago Symphony Orchestra conducted by Pierre Boulez. A month earlier, Oliver Knussen, who had led the London premiere that January, was conducting in Chicago and prepared for Yeh a rhythmic simplification of the final movement, part of which is shown in Example 8.19 where the original notation (a) is aligned with Knussen's renotation (b). This is further clarified in (c) by rebarring the passage to expose the underlying meter. (Indications of phrasing and dynamics have been omitted here.) The rhythms are revealed to be imaginative but relatively uncomplicated. Beginning at m. 436 and continuing to the end of the piece (m. 447), the solo part, as in most of Example 8.10, employs only the pitches of the concerto's source chord.

The first melodic line examined here, from the Flute Concerto (see Example 8.2), has a similarly syncopated appearance but is fairly regular on its own terms: the first five notes are equal in duration, each lasting four triplet eighth notes, or MM 67.5 against the notated MM 90. As the line develops, the durations vary but continue to employ the triplet eighth as the least common denominator. As with Example 8.19, a rhythmic simplification of this passage would be quite feasible and potentially helpful to the soloist for preparation, if

Ex. 8.19 Clarinet Concerto: (a) solo part, mm. 434–38; (b) Oliver Knussen's renotation; (c) author's rebarring of (b)

not for performance.[29] The composer's projection of convincing yet straight-forward rhythms at different speeds simultaneously is, like interval technique, testament to Carter's inventiveness and craftsmanship.

The vast majority of Carter's melodic lines are composed according to interval-based melodic practice. Melodies are freed from the spatial con-fines of the source chord but interval technique still obtains. Carter's interval-based melodic practice yields many of his most virtuosic lines – scales and near-scales, trills, and tremolos – but all without recourse to traditional thematic practice, since the interval repertoire provides ample unification. Reference to source chords is indirect as only the intervals remain intact but the intervals are sufficient: a melodic line abstracted from any of these concertos can easily be identified as belonging to that concerto and that one only – a significant accomplishment. In these works, the source chord's literal presence varies greatly from one piece to another, and pitches are not drawn freely from the chord, being selected instead through interval technique. The source chord always gives way to the interval technique; the interval technique never gives way to the source chord. For Carter, pitches are characteristically the agents of intervals. There may be no more fundamental entity in music than the pitch, but there is no more fundamental *relationship* in music than the interval – and Carter's music is about relationships, not entities, which is why counter-point is the central metaphor of his music.

For each of these concertos, to varying degrees, Carter composed the solo line first, entrusting the generation of a convincing harmonic environment to the intervallic components of the source chord and their interaction with the principal melody. Certainly, any attempt at explanation beyond the "how"

[29] Yeh used Knussen's renotation for preparation but Carter's original notation for performance, since the latter is constructed to reflect the conductor's beat (Heinemann, "The American Premiere of Elliott Carter's Clarinet Concerto," 36).

and into the "why" of melodic construction remains elusive. But it is apparent that, for the composer, the most salient characteristic of interval technique is its utility in the spontaneous creation of melody – and this spontaneity, which is not only portrayed in the music but is integral to the compositional process, is the force that moves the music forward.

PART III

Sketch studies

9   Left by the wayside: Elliott Carter's unfinished Sonatina for Oboe and Harpsichord

Felix Meyer
(Translated by J. Bradford Robinson)

It is a well-known fact that Elliott Carter composed far more music in his early years than his "official" catalogue of works suggests. For one thing, several of his surviving early works were never released for publication; among these are the theater scores for Sophocles's *Philoctetes* (1931) and Plautus's *Mostellaria* (1936), both located today at the Paul Sacher Foundation.[1] For another, he withdrew a number of works by either partially or totally destroying them. Carter himself put this fact on record when David Schiff, then preparing his study *The Music of Elliott Carter*, showed him a list of works published in Claire Reis's compendium *Composers in America* (1938) and containing, among other things, a symphony (1937), a concerto for English horn and orchestra (1937), a flute sonata (1934), two string quartets (1935 and 1937), and a one-act comic opera entitled *Tom and Lily* (1934).[2] All these works were marked "destroyed" when Reis's catalogue was reprinted in Schiff's book.[3] There is now some evidence that Carter did not distance himself from these compositions quite as radically or as early as Schiff implied with his statement that "[i]n the late '30s Carter destroyed nearly all his student efforts."[4] At least one of the two string quartets (probably the one of 1937) most likely survived in the *String Quartet in C* preserved at the Paul Sacher Foundation.[5] Moreover, a revised later version of Reis's list, published in 1947 in the second edition of *Composers in America*, reveals that Carter still acknowledged at least the flute sonata and the two string quartets as late as the 1940s.[6] Still, these observations do not alter the basic fact that no trace remains of most of the works on Reis's list. We must therefore continue to assume that Carter's body of early works is heavily reduced and grants only a partial glimpse into his musical influences and artistic evolution during the first decade of his career. Further, we should probably redouble our efforts to find other extant sources for Carter's early music. After all, the possibility cannot be precluded that one or another of his rejected works of the 1930s will eventually resurface. This applies in particular to those pieces that

---

[1] See the list of "Juvenilia and Unpublished Works in Manuscript" in Link, *ECGR*, pp. 16–20.
[2] "Elliott C. Carter," in Reis, *Composers in America* (1st edn, 1938), p. 57.
[3] Schiff, *MEC* (1st edn, 1983), p. 72.
[4] *Ibid.*, p. 71.
[5] Meyer and Shreffler, *ECCP*, pp. 36–37.
[6] Reis, *Composers in America* (rev. and enlarged edn, 1947), pp. 60–62, esp. 62.

managed to reach performance and may have been copied out for this purpose. One such conceivable case is the flute sonata, which was premiered at Harvard University's Paine Hall on May 25, 1932[7] and thus must have originated in 1931 or 1932 (at least in its first version) rather than 1934, as stated by Reis. Another case might be the musical "portrait" of the writer and social activist Muriel Draper, which, though absent in Reis's or any other list, was presented at New York's Hotel St. Regis on April 10, 1938 during a "High-Low Concert" organized by Vladimir Dukelsky (aka Vernon Duke).[8]

Less well known is the fact that even in the 1940s and '50s Carter worked on several compositions that never entered his definitive canon. Unlike the above-mentioned works of the 1930s, however, these pieces were left unfinished, i.e., Carter put them aside largely at the sketch stage, either because he was dissatisfied with what he had written or because another project intervened.[9] And unlike the rejected early works, he carefully preserved the manuscripts for these projects – a token not only of his growing esteem and self-confidence but also of the fact that he now pursued a more rigorous and systematic approach to composition, using his sketches increasingly to work out fundamental problems of harmony and rhythm that retained their relevance beyond the specific context of any particular work. Among these unfinished projects are a Piano Trio begun in the late 1940s, an orchestral work inspired by a commission from the League of Composers in 1952 (it is called "Symphony No. 2" in the sketches), and a Sonata for Two Pianos on which he worked in the winter of 1956–57.[10] Another is the Sonatina for Oboe and Harpsichord, which was sketched out as early as 1947 and has been neglected until just recently. This three-movement composition is especially interesting if only because it progressed further than most of the other unfinished works. Indeed, its first movement exists in a more or less complete draft that was given its world premiere by Heinz Holliger (oboe) and Peter Solomon (harpsichord) in Basel on December 5, 2008 during a concert in celebration of the composer's one-hundredth birthday.[11] But the Sonatina also merits special attention because it gives us a more precise understanding of that decisive period of change during which Carter parted ways with the

---

[7] The author is grateful to John Link for drawing his attention to the announcement of this concert in the *Harvard Crimson* (May 25, 1932).

[8] This concert series, as curious as it was short lived, is discussed in Duke, *Passport to Paris*, pp. 364–67.

[9] One exception is the substantial vocal duet *The Difference* for soprano, baritone, and piano (1944), a finished setting of a poem by Mark Van Doren.

[10] The Sonata for Two Pianos is discussed in Meyer and Shreffler, *ECCP*, pp. 122–23.

[11] This concert tribute, entitled "Carter 100+," was organized by the Swiss Chamber Soloists in conjunction with the Paul Sacher Foundation and took place in the Great Auditorium of the Basel Academy of Music. Besides the Sonatina, the program also included Carter's Sonata for Flute, Oboe, Cello, and Harpsichord, *Figment IV*, the *Eight Etudes and a Fantasy*, and the Oboe Quartet, as well as works by Johann Sebastian Bach.

neoclassical premises of his earlier music and sought a more "rational" approach to the musical material. Finally, a knowledge of this piece furthers our understanding of two well-known compositions from Carter's accepted canon, for it draws on the Woodwind Quintet of 1948 for its material and presages the Sonata for Flute, Oboe, Cello, and Harpsichord by being written for the harpsichordist Sylvia Marlowe.

As the sketches and drafts for the Sonatina are undated, we must turn to other sources to deduce the details of its genesis. Particularly important in this connection is a letter of summer 1946 in which the work is mentioned. At that time Carter was vacationing with his wife and three-year-old son on the estate of Sidney Lanier's grandson in Eliot, Maine, where he was reworking his early *Adagio* for cello and piano into the *Elegy* for string quartet, preparatory to its performance by the Lanier Quartet. Writing from Eliot in early August, he sent the following message to his pianist friend John Kirkpatrick: "This summer is more than usually busy with me. I am writing a ballet for Lincoln Kirstein about Ariadne's thread & the labyrinth as well as a harpsi-chord & oboe sonatina for Sylvia Marlow[e], a piece for the Harvard Glee Club, & a cello sonata for Bernard Greenhouse, who is an unusually fine cellist."[12] To be sure, this statement should not be taken to mean that he was already busy elaborating these four works (the ballet *The Minotaur*, the Sonatina, *Emblems*, and the Sonata for Violoncello and Piano); it probably means only that he was involved with their general conceptual framework and had at best committed to paper a few preparatory sketches. The passage should thus be read less as a progress report than as a declaration of intention, perhaps with the purpose of showing that other performers were evincing greater interest in his music than the addressee. (Kirkpatrick had previously distanced himself from Carter's Piano Sonata, which he called "awfully intellectualized."[13]) This scenario is supported by Carter's present recollec-tion of a rainy and unproductive summer in which he produced practically nothing apart from the *Elegy* for string quartet.[14] It is also reinforced by the known long gestations of the ballet score (summer 1946 to March 13, 1947), the choral piece (autumn 1946 to September 1947), and the Cello Sonata (summer to December 11, 1948). But what about the Sonatina? In the absence of any written references, special importance attaches to Carter's oral

[12] Letter of August 4 or 5, 1946 from Elliott Carter to John Kirkpatrick; John Kirkpatrick Papers, Irving S. Gilmore Music Library, Yale University.

[13] See Kirkpatrick's letter of January 1946 to Elliott Carter, *ibid*. This interpretation is reinforced by the fact that Carter's mention of the four works in his letter of August 1946 is preceded by the remark that the Sonata would most likely be performed by Webster Aiken.

[14] Elliott Carter, memories of the years 1946 and 1947, videotape (March 19, 2009); Elliott Carter Collection, Paul Sacher Foundation. The author wishes to express his sincere thanks to Elliott Carter for answering the questions sent to him, and Virgil Blackwell for videotaping his response.

reminiscences. These unquestionably imply, since they refer to his stay in the village of Èze on the Côte d'Azur in southern France,[15] that the Sonatina arose in summer 1947, and thus at the same time that he was busy finishing the already advanced score of the choral work, *Emblems*.

The curious circumstances surrounding Carter's visit to France in summer 1947 deserve mention, not least because he recalls that they were partly responsible for the Sonatina's being left unfinished.[16] The fact that he, along with his wife and son, settled specifically in Èze-Village in summer 1947, after a brief stopover in London, was the result of an unexpected offer. The composer Samuel Barlow owned a spacious, château-like twelfth-century home in Èze, which he placed at the Carters' disposal after the tenant originally foreseen, Secretary of the Navy James V. Forrestal (later Secretary of Defense in the Truman administration), canceled on short notice.[17] It was here, in the so-called Maison des Riquiers, perched on a steep slope overlooking the Mediterranean, that the Carters tried to settle down comfortably in July and August 1947. But in the absence of servants, it proved difficult to run a household in the somewhat dilapidated building, which had served as headquarters of the Nazi occupiers during the war. Moreover, as inhabitants of a "tourist attraction," the Carters were regularly monopolized by visitors, especially friends from England to whom they had mentioned their holiday abode. The hoped-for peace and quiet failed to materialize, and Carter, burdened with duties as host and *châtelain*, could not pursue his projects with the requisite concentration, although an old and out-of-tune Steinway grand was available for his use. It was only after returning to the United States, in his newly acquired summer home in Dorset, Vermont, that he recovered his concentration. But rather than finishing the Sonatina he had drafted in Èze, he completed his Allen Tate setting *Emblems*, probably under the pressure of his obligations toward G. Wallace Woodworth, the director of the Harvard Glee Club and the one who commissioned the work.[18]

In the case of the Sonatina, Carter was under no such obligation, for it had never been formally commissioned, nor was it subject to a deadline. Instead, the work's point of departure was his casual promise to write something for the New York harpsichordist Sylvia Marlowe (1908–81), whom he had met a

[15] *Ibid.*

[16] *Ibid.* Regarding Carter's stay on the Côte d'Azur in summer 1947, see also Meyer and Shreffler, *ECCP*, pp. 84–85, and his letter of June 7, 2007 to James Levine (photocopy in the Elliott Carter Collection, Paul Sacher Foundation).

[17] Carter mentions that Forrestal committed suicide a short while earlier (*ibid.*). In fact, however, Forrestal, exhausted and suffering from depression, did not pass away until

May 1949, a few weeks after resigning his position.

[18] It is impossible to ascertain whether Carter worked on *Emblems* as well as the Sonatina in Èze. However, at least the first section of the choral piece, and perhaps more than that, had definitely taken shape before Carter's stay in France (see G. Wallace Woodworth's letter of June 19, 1947 to Elliott Carter, Elliott Carter Collection, Paul Sacher Foundation). The entire work was completed in September 1947.

short while earlier. In the late 1920s Marlowe, after studying piano and organ, had sought further training from Nadia Boulanger in Paris. There, like Carter at a later date, she became aware of the great pioneer of modern harpsichord playing, Wanda Landowska, whose concerts left such a deep impression on her that she taught herself to play the instrument and decided, in the late 1930s, to devote her career entirely to the harpsichord. Her performance of both volumes of the *Well-Tempered Clavier*, given in two recitals at New York's Town Hall in May 1939, was probably the first complete presentation of that work in America on an historical instrument.[19] But Marlowe did more than play an important role in the revival of the "old" harpsichord repertoire in America. In an effort to generate broad-based acceptance for her instrument, she was also fond of playing jazz and dance music, and even appeared for a while in a nightclub (called the Rainbow Room in Rockefeller Center) with a mixed program of classical and popular music. So unusual were these activities that they left a mark on literary history in the mystery novel *Blue Harpsichord* by Francis Steegmuller (aka David Keith).[20] Not least of all, she attempted to establish the harpsichord in contemporary music by asking composers with whom she was befriended to write new works for her. In this respect she followed the example of Landowska, who had been the driving force behind such well-known compositions as Manuel de Falla's Harpsichord Concerto (1923–26) and Francis Poulenc's *Concert champêtre* (1926). In this way Marlowe spawned a large and mainly American repertoire of music for or with harpsichord which, over the years, drew contributions from Vittorio Rieti, Arthur Berger, Harold Shapero, Henry Brant, Virgil Thomson, Alan Hovhaness, Ben Weber, Henry Cowell, and of course Carter. All the same, after abandoning the abortive Sonatina, it was not until the Sonata for Flute, Oboe, Cello, and Harpsichord of 1952 that Carter was able to satisfy Marlowe's request.

In 1946, when Marlowe asked Carter to compose a piece for her, he could not have known that this unconventional performer would champion contemporary music enduringly for decades on end. For at that time she had just begun her patronage activities, singling out as her first composer the Italo-American Vittorio Rieti, whose *Partita* for flute, oboe, string quartet (or orchestra), and obbligato harpsichord she performed with Julius Baker (flute), Mitchell Miller (oboe), and the Kroll String Quartet at a concert sponsored by the League of Composers in New York's Times Hall on March 13, 1946. We can only speculate whether it was in the context of this concert that Marlowe approached Carter with a request to write another new

---

[19] See "Sylvia Marlowe" in Palmer, *Harpsichord in America: A Twentieth-Century Revival*, pp. 110–17, esp. 110.

[20] Steegmuller, *Blue Harpsichord*.

work, or whether they even first met on that occasion. What is clear, however, is that Carter attended the concert (he belonged to the League's advisory board and was friends with Rieti) and that he found the performances good enough to seriously entertain the idea of writing a piece for Marlowe no later than summer 1946, as we know from his above-mentioned letter to John Kirkpatrick. And we may assume that it must have been all the easier for him to agree to Marlowe's request as he had long followed the emergence of a new harpsichord repertoire and was well aware of the instrument's compositional potential. After all, Marlowe's more prominent colleague Ralph Kirkpatrick, a friend of Carter's since their days at Harvard, was likewise interested in contemporary music and had given a concert in the Carnegie Chamber Music Hall as early as November 20, 1939 with new works for and with harpsichord by, among others, Ernst Levy, Otto Luening, Robert Oboussier, and Florent Schmitt. (Carter attended the concert and devoted a section of his survey-review of New York's music scene to it.[21]) Moreover, his teacher Walter Piston had written a Sonatina for violin and harpsichord for Kirkpatrick in 1945 – a work that Carter encountered at its premiere (on November 30, 1945) and discussed in an article on Piston which he wrote in spring 1946 for *Modern Music*.[22] This work may even have influenced Carter's decision to compose a duo sonatina, with the choice of oboe (instead of violin) made natural by the fact that he himself had studied the oboe in his youth. (Apparently he had no particular oboist in mind when he took on the project.[23])

As already mentioned, the sources suggest that Carter originally envisioned a piece consisting of three movements, one moderately fast, another slow, and a fast finale. Of these three movements, however, only the first survives in more or less complete and fully elaborated form, not only in a large folder of sketches but in a continuous draft. The second movement, in contrast, exists only in a fragmentary draft and a smaller number of sketches, while the finale merely survives in a few jottings in a separate sketchbook and on several loose leaves of sketches. (The latter are located in the New York Public Library, whereas all other documents form part of the Elliott Carter Collection at the Paul Sacher Foundation.) In short, the density of the source material decreases from movement to movement and fairly accurately mirrors the music's degree of completion. This suggests that Carter originally prepared preliminary sketches for all three movements and then applied himself to their detailed elaboration, of which, however, only the first movement was to reach provisional completion.

---

[21] Carter, "American Music in the New York Scene" (1940), in *CEL*, esp. p. 52.

[22] Carter, "Walter Piston" (1946).
[23] Carter, memories of the years 1946 and 1947, videotape (see n. 14).

A cursory glance at the nine-page draft of this 228-measure first movement[24] may convey the impression of an elegant *divertissement* in a neoclassical vein. This association is evoked not only by its organic flow of ideas, undergirded by a continuous eighth-note pulse, and by its themes, now jazzily syncopated, now soaringly melodious, but also by its largely linear texture. Indeed, precisely this linear quality gives the movement the character of a three-part invention for large stretches at a time – and connects it far more closely with a work such as Piston's Sonatina than, say, Florent Schmitt's Trio for Harpsichord, Flute, and Clarinet, whose "heavy chords and soggy sonorities" Carter took issue with in the above-mentioned review.[25] (See Figure 9.1.)

Nevertheless, as with Carter's other works from this period, initial appearances prove deceptive, for behind the seemingly conventional façade are forces at work that point far beyond the realm of Neoclassicism. This is evident in the very opening of the movement, which we shall now examine more closely with an eye to two features. First, it very clearly reveals Carter's tendency to emphasize the specific characters of his instruments and to make them manifest in a markedly stratified compositional fabric. Thus, the main theme is deliberately laid out in two overlapping layers: a long harpsichord line in pulsating eighth notes, highlighting the instrument's "mechanical" character (notwithstanding the slightly unrealistic expression mark *molto legato*), and a gentle, melodious oboe melody that enters on the weak second beat of m. 3 and proceeds in a more supple rhythm. To a certain extent this already prefigures the antithesis that will appear more distinctly in the opening movement of the Sonata for Cello and Piano (1948), with its combination of a relentlessly ticking pulse in the piano and an expressive, flexible cantilena in the cello.[26] Unlike the Cello Sonata, however, the antithesis in the Sonatina resides not in contrasting conceptions of tempo, but in the juxtaposition of rhythmic evenness and rhythmic symmetry: if the harpsichord part follows an "open-ended" principle of continuous development, the oboe melody in mm. 3–7 forms a rhythmic palindrome, i.e., it is laid out in mirror-symmetry as a series of increasingly short and then increasingly long durations (6+2+1+2+2+1+1+1+1+1+2+2+1+2+7 eighth notes), with the

---

[24] The following discussion of the first movement relates mainly to this manuscript, which is accompanied by fifty pages of sketches and fragmentary drafts. The manuscript is incomplete only in the sense that the dynamics and articulation marks are merely hinted at for large stretches at a time. On the other hand, it must be considered non-definitive, primarily because of Carter's several subsequent annotations regarding possible transpositions and cuts. Beginning in m. 84 the measure numbers were reduced by 1, for Carter evidently counted m. 82 twice as it extended over the line

break. The five-measure units of his numbering system were thereby shifted by 1, beginning in m. "90" (= m. 89).

[25] Carter, "American Music in the New York Scene" (1940), in *CEL*, p. 52.

[26] Carter himself later interpreted this antithesis as a conflation of the rhythmic legacies he inherited respectively from Stravinsky and Schoenberg; see his comments to this effect in Holliger, "Abseits des Mainstreams: Ein Gespräch mit dem amerikanischen Komponisten Elliott Carter," 4–9, esp. 5.

Fig. 9.1 Sonatina for Oboe and Harpsichord, draft of movement 1, p. [1] (mm. 1–24); Elliott Carter Collection, Paul Sacher Foundation, Basel

symmetry broken only by a slight lengthening of the final note. But the two parts also contrast in their syntactic subdivisions: as the phrase marks clearly reveal, the longer harpsichord line (up to the penultimate eighth note in m. 7) obscures the $\frac{4}{4}$ meter with four phrases of 9, 9, 9, and 27 (=3 × 9) eighth notes each, whereas the shorter oboe melody, which enters later and ends earlier (on beat 1 of m. 7), consists of two phrases of thirteen and nineteen eighth notes each, likewise not aligned with the notated meter. Finally, the two lines stand out by being in contrary motion, with the harpsichord line first rising and then descending (complemented from m. 4 on by a second voice in the left hand), whereas the oboe part does just the opposite. The contrary motion exactly converges in one passage – namely, at the turning point on the final eighth note of m. 4, where the harpsichord changes direction on its peak pitch (Ab5) and the oboe does the same on its lowest pitch (C4). Otherwise it merely governs the general melodic flow rather than the progress from one note to the next. In other words, it is not carried out with contrapuntal rigor, and thus reinforces the impression of two voices apparently unfolding independently of each other.

Nonetheless, a close relation pertains between the pitch structure of the harpsichord part and that of the oboe part, for Carter derived the pitch structure of both parts from a single twelve-tone row. This row, with its final two dyads Ab–Db and Bb–Eb, has a striking potential for generating quasi-tonal cadential formulae. It lies in more or less plain view in the oboe melody, where there is an interpolated A4 after note 6 and an extra F5 at the end (see Example 9.1).

In contrast, the introductory harpsichord melody is based on a transposed inversion of this row. Admittedly it is only at the opening that this can be easily discerned, for the accumulated interpolation of tones already heard, and finally the rearrangement of tones in the last segment of the row, lead the melody increasingly farther away from its starting point (see Example 9.2).

Here it is striking that Carter replaces the fourth note (B) with a Bb and does not use it until m. 4. Consequently, the harpsichord's twenty-note ascent

Ex. 9.1 Sonatina for Oboe and Harpsichord, movement 1, mm. 3–7 (oboe) and twelve-tone row

Ex. 9.2 Sonatina for Oboe and Harpsichord, movement 1, mm. 1–3 (harpsichord) and inversion of twelve-tone row

before the entrance of the oboe contains only eleven pitch classes. This modification serves a dual purpose. First, it imparts special significance to the entrance of the oboe, which enters precisely on the omitted pitch B, thereby completing the total chromatic. Second, it situates the harpsichord's head-motive in the realm of G minor, whose relative key, B♭ major, later proves to be the tonal center of movement – and of the Sonatina as a whole.

That the two opening instrumental lines are anchored in a twelve-tone row – which, as shown by the annotated Figures 9.2 and 9.3, is also set down in the sketches – comes as a surprise. True, Carter is known to have come into contact with Schoenberg's earliest twelve-tone compositions in the 1920s; and even later he paid close attention not only to Schoenberg's music but to that of Berg and Webern. But there is nothing in his earlier compositions to suggest that he worked with twelve-tone constellations – a fact thoroughly in keeping with his relatively rare and guarded early comments on the music of the Viennese School[27] and his belated study of the literature on twelve-tone music in the latter half of the 1950s.[28] Should Jonathan Bernard's claim that "Carter … reached his maturity in the early 1950s in a state of fundamental mistrust of the Viennese influence"[29] perhaps be revised in view of the Sonatina? Not necessarily: hints of row-based techniques on which Carter could take his bearings can be found in several composers working in his immediate surroundings but outside the Viennese School's direct sphere of influence. One example is Walter Piston, who combined free voices with themes constructed on the basis of a twelve-tone row in the third movement of his *Partita* for violin, viola, and organ (1944). (Carter, in his article on Piston, not only mentioned this point in the text but expressly referred to it in an annotated musical example.[30]) Most of all, the relation to the row remains entirely subliminal as the piece progresses, except in the partly exact, partly modified restatements of the main theme, whose two components (the oboe and harpsichord parts) almost always appear in combination and occasionally in inversion.[31] The subliminal effect results from the fact that later themes are derived by fragmenting and further developing motives from the thematic material stated at the opening. This principle of

[27] A certain skepticism can be sensed even in his expressly positive statements. One of his concert reviews, for example, ends in a commentary on Anton Webern's String Quartet, Op. 28, with the ambivalent words: "A transparency and sensitiveness to sonority distinguish it from other twelve-tone works; they make it absorbing if puzzling listening." (See Carter, "Coolidge Crusade; WPA; New York Season" [1939], in *CEL*, p. 40.)

[28] See Bernard, "The Legacy of the Second Viennese School," esp. 364–65; and Meyer and Shreffler, *ECCP*, p. 140.

[29] Bernard, "The Legacy of the Second Viennese School," p. 364.

[30] Carter, "Walter Piston" (1946), in *CEL*, pp. 173–74.

[31] Admittedly an exact combined restatement of both the oboe melody and the harpsichord line occurs only in mm. 151 ff., and an exact combined inversion of the two elements is set aside for the end of the movement (mm. 220 ff.).

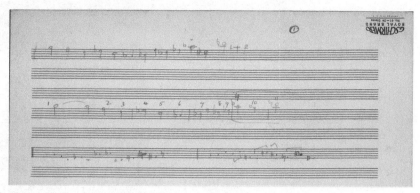

Fig. 9.2 Sonatina for Oboe and Harpsichord, sketches for movement 1 (top third of a page from the folder "unidentified sketches"); Elliott Carter Collection, Paul Sacher Foundation, Basel

The bottom two-thirds of this sheet of sketches, reproduced here in excerpt, are devoted to other projected works, including an otherwise unknown Septet. It is one of two sheets on which Carter set down various forms of the twelve-tone row. (The other one contains the row in retrograde and retrograde inversion, surrounded by sketches of the theme's continuation and symmetrical rhythmic structure.) The top line reveals a preliminary form of the oboe melody (beginning on G5) with a roughed-out rhythm in double note values; in the middle is a version of the same melody with a slightly more precise rhythm, marked with numbers; and at the bottom is the twelve-tone row and its inversion. The sketches of the row at the bottom indicate that the tenth note originally read A♭ and was only later altered to A. But precisely this A♭ appears at the corresponding position in the two alternative versions of the theme, without being altered later. This implies that the row was not firmly defined from the outset as an abstract, "pre-compositional" determinant, but assumed shape along with the theme.

thematic-motivic development is plain to see in the continuation of the main theme (see Figure 9.1). The two oboe phrases in mm. 7–9 and 10–14, with their cadential formulae, unmistakably proceed from the leaps of a fourth in mm. 6–7 (m. 9: D5–G5; mm. 13–14: E♭5–A♭5) and pass this motive on to the crisply syncopated second theme (m. 16: A♭5–E♭5; mm. 17–18: B♭4–E♭5, D5–G5). In this way the movement's thematic structure evolves in a highly organic fashion in accordance with the principle of "developing variation," with sharply etched entities such as the above-mentioned second theme, or a melodious gesture based on a descending scale (mm. 67 ff.), forming nothing more than temporary way-stations in a constant process of development and transformation.

In sum, the twelve-tone row did not serve Carter as an omnipresent axiom so much as a backbone for the main theme, which was then freely manipulated (and which itself departs from the row). Nevertheless, the very fact of this dodecaphonic link, as well as the rhythmic palindrome in the oboe theme, point to an awareness on Carter's part that the basic principles of his musical language, rooted in traditional thematic and tonal precepts, were not entirely

Fig. 9.3 Sonatina for Oboe and Harpsichord, sketches for movement 1 (top half of a page from the folder "Sonatina"); Elliott Carter Collection, Paul Sacher Foundation, Basel

This sketch of the piece's opening suggests that Carter, when designing the pitch structure of the introductory ascent in the harpsichord, originally drew more closely on its underlying twelve-tone row. To be sure, the head-motive already contains, as in all the other sketches, a B♭ instead of the "row-conform" B, and the interpolated repeated notes after D (note 5 in the row) and F♯ (note 6) are already established. But the second half of m. 2 and the beginning of m. 3 present, as befits their position in the row, the pitch pairs B♭–F and A♭–E♭, separated by other interpolated pitches (unless the first pitch in m. 3 is actually a B♭). The changes notated above and below lead further away from the row, and the lower half of the page (not shown here) presents a new draft that precisely matches the final version up to the entrance of the oboe.

viable. Indeed, there is something unstable about the first movement of the Sonatina, where the principle of "developing variation" is united with a very extended and volatile type of tonality. Only rarely, as in the above-mentioned second theme or the melodious gesture based on a descending scale (mm. 67 ff.), do the melodic ideas immediately subjected to the overriding process of development congeal into sharply etched themes; and only rarely do clearly defined points of tonal relation emerge over several measures at a time, even though the movement as a whole reveals a certain gravitational attraction to the main tonality of B♭ and the secondary tonality of B.[32] (One visible sign of this associative rather than preset key scheme [at least at the local level] is the

---

[32] This same tonal polarity is at work in other pieces from this period in Carter's career, for example the Piano Sonata and *Emblems*. In the Sonatina, the main tonality of B♭ is already hinted at in the B♭-major/minor chord at the end of the main theme (m. 7) and strikingly reinforced by the B♭-major chord of the final measures – the only sustained major triad in the entire movement (mm. 226–28). In contrast, the secondary tonality, B, comes to the fore especially clearly at the end of the first

fact that Carter, after completing the draft, added transposition instructions such as "1/2 tone higher" in several passages.) Finally, because of this thematic and tonal instability, the three main sections of the movement (mm. 1–107, 108–50 and 151–228) ultimately resist classification in terms of sonata-allegro form. Although the third section is unquestionably conceived as an abridged and modified recapitulation, the second section, which extends rather than intensifies the process of thematic-motivic development found in the first section, cannot be viewed entirely as a development. Only a bare outline of the fractured traditional formal pattern can be descried, overlaid with elements of free fantasy.

Viewed in this light, it comes as no surprise to find that Carter was on the lookout for new principles of tonal and rhythmic organization that would allow him to build larger musical structures without relying on traditional formal models. However, the new approaches he tried out in the Sonatina – the connection with a twelve-tone row and the "geometric" rhythmic design – did not prove to be harbingers of the future. Finding them too restrictive and mechanical, Carter limited himself to applying them to isolated effect. It was not until the Sonata for Violoncello and Piano (1948) and the String Quartet No. 1 (1950–51) that he took the decisive step toward a technical redefinition of his musical language, and revealingly he decided in favor of two more flexible procedures better suited to meet his specific need for expression: metrical modulation (in the Cello Sonata) and the melodic and harmonic anchoring of the texture in selected reference intervals or reference chords (in the String Quartet).[33]

Regarding the Sonatina's slow second movement, which survives in an incomplete three-page draft and a thirteen-page folder of loose-leaf sketches, a few comments must suffice. As can be seen from the fragmentary sixty-five-measure draft, it opens with a richly ornate descending oboe solo which, after reaching its lowest point (A♯3) and surging upwards in m. 15, is followed by an antiphonal interplay between the two instruments. This opening is reproduced in Figure 9.4, which also demonstrates, as in the first movement, that Carter subsequently considered making a few alterations (note in particular his comment "salta" in the final staff, referring to a prospective "leap" over mm. 25–27). Then, beginning in m. 28 (i.e., on page 2 of the draft), the dialogue between oboe and harpsichord seems to intensify, as far as we can tell from the increasingly sketchy notation. Thereafter, only two hastily written separate sheets of sketches shed light on how the movement was meant to proceed. They suggest that Carter envisioned a return to the antiphonal texture and the material of mm. 15 ff. and

formal section (mm. 103–07), with its thinned compositional fabric – namely, at the point where the solo harpsichord strikes the octave figure B5–B4–B5 several times.

[33] See also Schiff, *MEC*, pp. 54–72 and 106–11, and Bernard, "The Evolution of Elliott Carter's Rhythmic Practice," esp. 167–74.

Fig. 9.4 Sonatina for Oboe and Harpsichord, draft of movement 2, p. [1] (mm. 1–28); Elliott Carter Collection, Paul Sacher Foundation, Basel

wanted an oboe solo at the end. In other words, the movement was meant to unfold in a symmetrical arch. It was also clearly meant to function as the work's expressive center, for, compared to the light-footed, rhythmically propulsive outside movements, it is dominated by an intense cantabile impetus richly garnished with rapid figuration.

Finally the third movement, preserved only in a few sketches, merits attention particularly for its relation to the final movement of the Woodwind Quintet, composed in 1948. This connection is already evident in the earliest sketches for the Sonatina's finale, located in a sketchbook preserved at the Paul Sacher Foundation and later marked "Sketches of Woodwind Quintet" in Carter's hand. The inside dust cover contains, beneath the headings "Sonatina for harpsichord" and "[Sonatina for] oboe," preliminary thoughts on the movement's formal design and material (see Figure 9.5a). On the opposite page, headed "Oboe Sonatina" and "Finale," we find a sketch of the opening of the oboe part (see Figure 9.5b). The formal outline set down on the first page is presented twice, once as a series of digits, and again as a series of digits and letters, revealing that Carter was intent on interweaving a symmetrical form and a rondo-like design. (The series of digits beginning with 123451 and ending with 154321 relates to shorter formal units, whereas the series of letters ABCD is used to identify longer composite units, each beginning with formal member 1 and thus functioning in the manner of a refrain.) The column in the lower right-hand

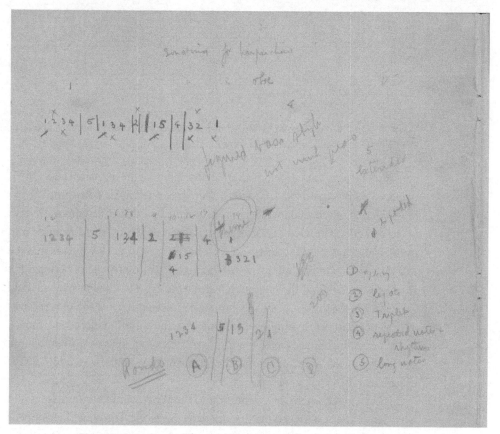

Fig. 9.5a Sonatina for Oboe and Harpsichord, sketches for movement 3, inside dust cover of sketchbook; Elliott Carter Collection, Paul Sacher Foundation, Basel

Fig. 9.5b Sonatina for Oboe and Harpsichord, sketches for movement 3 in sketchbook, p. [1]; Elliott Carter Collection, Paul Sacher Foundation, Basel

corner of the page then provides a verbal decryption of the numeric codes: "1 [=] opening," "2 [=] legato," "3 [=] triplets," "4 [=] repeated notes + rhythms," "5 [=] long notes." Each formal member is thus assigned particular features of rhythm or articulation. The way that Carter envisaged converting these features into music is illustrated by the sketch of the oboe part on page 2, which is marked with the corresponding numbers. All the same, two discrepancies between the verbal description and the oboe sketch strike the eye. First, the passage marked "3" in m. 2 of the third staff initially proceeds in sixteenth notes and only receives its designated triplet rhythm in an addendum in the bottom staff. Second, the "5" in the penultimate measure of the fifth staff refers to a long-note interpolation still to be inserted. This implies that the formal design and the sketch took shape in parallel rather than consecutively.

It is easy to see where the connection to the Woodwind Quintet resides and why Carter later reassigned the document to this work. The oboe sketch opens with the same theme that underlies the final movement of the Quintet – likewise a rondo. (It appears in mm. 8–11 of the Quintet in the same key, B♭

Ex. 9.3 Woodwind Quintet, movement 3, mm. 67–75, clarinet and oboe

major, and is assigned to the oboe, as befits its origins.) Not only that, the continuation of the Sonatina sketch ultimately found its way into the later work as well. This can be seen in mm. 67ff. of the Quintet finale (see Example 9.3), where the return of the rondo theme (in the clarinet) adopts verbatim not only the head of the Sonatina theme but also a good part of the four measures that follow (alternating in clarinet and oboe).

These "trace elements" from the Sonatina's finale in the second movement of the Woodwind Quintet are the remains of an overhaul process that can no longer be reconstructed in detail. It is clear, however, that before abandoning the Sonatina project, Carter elaborated the oboe sketch described above in two further sketches for oboe and harpsichord: a twelve-measure fragment located on the verso of the sketch shown in Figure 9.2, and a two-page handwritten version of the first fifty measures (up to and including the projected passage in "long notes"), which already differs noticeably from the sketch reproduced in Figure 9.5b, and which is preserved today in the folder of Quintet sketches located in the Library of Congress.[34] And it is equally clear that, when he embarked on the final movement of the Quintet in 1948, the composer proceeded seamlessly from the sketches for the Sonatina's finale. This, too, is suggested by isolated sheets of sketches preserved in the Library of Congress, on which the melodic line taken and elaborated from the Sonatina sketchbook, though still written on a single staff, is already broken down into several instruments by verbal annotations. True, in his further work on the Quintet's finale Carter steadily moved further away from this point of departure. But even in its final form the movement still bears

[34] The author wishes to thank Stephen Guy Soderberg of the Library of Congress for   graciously allowing him to examine this bulky folder containing some 120 pages of sketches.

unmistakable traces of its origins, as can be seen not only in its main theme, its tonality of B♭ major, and its rondo form, but also in the prominent role the oboe plays whenever the main theme appears *in extenso*, i.e., at the beginning of the "primary" refrains in mm. 88 ff., 67 ff., and 173 ff. (but not in the "secondary" refrains introduced solely by the theme's head-motive, i.e., mm. 146 ff. and 186 ff.).

Why Carter left the Sonatina unfinished is a matter of guesswork. It is safe to assume, however, that his reasons for abandoning it had little to do with either his unfavorable working conditions in summer 1947 or with practical considerations – such as, for example, the limited performance prospects of a piece for this combination of instruments. Carter more probably came to the conclusion that the draft of the first movement, and whatever was meant to emerge from the sketches for the second and third, could not be forged into a convincing whole; in particular, he may have felt there was a discrepancy between the advanced harmonic language of the opening movement and the more conventional, traditionally notated B♭-major tonality of the finale. And as far as the specific elaboration of this first movement is concerned, it seems that Carter became aware that the new approaches he tried out in it imparted the desired "systematic" backing to a tonal language then in the process of dissolution, but threatened to stifle his artistic imagination. Unlike his sketches for the finale, which could be "salvaged" in the backward-looking Woodwind Quintet, this draft probably seemed to him obsolete, at least by the time he came to compose the Cello Sonata, which made the decisive advance toward a new principle of rhythmic organization tailored entirely to meet his needs, and which also brought about an initial, albeit still tentative, rapprochement with a new harmonic language.

As quickly as Carter lost interest in the Sonatina, and as skeptically as he still regards it today (after reading through the first movement he declared "There is too much Hindemith in it"[35] and granted permission for only one performance, namely, at the Basel birthday concert mentioned earlier), the surviving materials are none the less valuable as historical documents. For one thing, they demonstrate that his post-war realignment was by no means straightforward and teleological, but proceeded in a slow, empirical process of trial and error. For another, they expand our knowledge of the preliminary history of two published works. Being intended for Sylvia Marlowe, the Sonatina is the predecessor of the Sonata for Flute, Oboe, Violoncello, and Harpsichord of 1952, the composition with which Carter, six years after Marlowe's original request, finally placed at her disposal a work based on a fundamentally new conception and on advanced compositional premises.

[35] Carter, memories of the years 1946 and 1947, videotape (see n. 14).

(Marlowe apparently had some difficulty coming to terms with this work and presumably would have felt happier with the Sonatina, had Carter managed to complete it.[36]) But most of all, the piece stands in a direct relation to the Woodwind Quintet, as the sketches for its third movement prove to be the genetic origin of the Quintet's finale. In all likelihood, subliminal cross-relations of this sort occur more frequently in Carter's oeuvre than has previously been assumed. With this in mind, it is worth seeking broad-based support from the sources, and devoting no less attention to abandoned projects and fragments than to finished compositions, when studying Carter's complex artistic evolution.

[36] This assumption arises from Carter's statement in an untitled program note to the recording of *Night Fantasies* and Piano Sonata (1969): "The performances on this record are remarkable, especially in view of some I have had to suffer through in the past." Text most recently reprinted as "Two Sonatas, 1948 and 1952" (1969), in *CEL*, quote on p. 231.

10 At the edge of creation: Elliott Carter's sketches in the Library of Congress

Stephen Soderberg

> ... any given moment ... is a bridge from a previous one to a succeeding one
> and contains both the elements of unexpectedness as well as intelligible relation
> to the past and anticipation of the future, not always fulfilled in the way
> anticipated.   Elliott Carter[1]

The Library of Congress holds over 17,000 pages of musical sketches and holograph scores by Elliott Carter. Sketches account for the bulk of the material and cover nearly all the works Carter produced between 1932 and 1971.[2] With the kind permission of Elliott Carter, much of this material has now been digitized and made available by the Library of Congress on the internet. Progressing from work to work, we discover throughout these sketches a detailed account of Carter's personal solutions to the critical, practical, and theoretical problems confronting nearly all Anglo-American and European composers during this period. While the total number of items in this collection (hereafter abbreviated EC-LC) is impressive enough, the number of sheets of sketches for each major work indicates a hidden story line: Piano Sonata (1945–46) – 115; Cello Sonata (1948) – 211; String Quartet No. 1 (1951) – 275; Variations for Orchestra (1955) – 780; Double Concerto (1961) – 1,979; Piano Concerto (1965) – 3,761.[3] The increase in the number of sketches that occurs throughout this twenty-five year period parallels a significant transition in Carter's compositional approach and musical style. As Carter gradually moves away from the neoclassical style of his early compositions, there is an emergence in the sketches of new materials that would become significant in the creation of his mature works. The survey that follows traces connections between pieces and compositional ideas that reach across the chronological boundaries of Carter's compositions and leave their mark in sometimes unexpected places. While the number of sketches

[1] Carter, "Time Lecture" (1965/94), in *CEL*, p. 318.
[2] The rest of Carter's material (after 1971 and some items before that date) is available at the Paul Sacher Foundation in Basel, Switzerland.
[3] Over the past fifty years, discrepancies have arisen in the method of counting manuscript material. The original counts given here are in sheets, with each sheet consisting of two pages. The final Library of Congress count will be given in pages to coincide with digitization which counts one image per page. When counted as pages rather than sheets, the numbers in this progression are effectively doubled.

explodes with the Double Concerto, we will be concerned mainly with the sketches dating from the period between the mid 1930s and the late 1950s that lead up to that explosion.

" . . . intelligible relation to the past . . . "

We begin by exploring sketches that reveal connections between some of Carter's neoclassical compositions in the 1930s and early 1940s. As David Schiff has noted, the third movement of Carter's Symphony No. 1 of 1942 "pursues the conventions of American populism."[4] This is especially true of the signature "fiddle tune" in the opening four and a half measures of this movement. However, this was not the first appearance of this particular tune in Carter's music. Before it made its way into the Symphony, Carter used it in the original 1936 piano version of his ballet *Pocahontas*. The fiddle music was removed from the final 1939 version of the ballet.[5] This might lead us to assume that we now have the full story of the fiddle music: that it was written for *Pocahontas* in 1936, was later deleted from the 1939 version, and then reappeared in the Symphony No. 1. But, buried in the EC-LC sketches, we discover this same theme in a third, earlier work, which was the progenitor of the two now familiar works. The sketches indicate that the fiddle music was originally conceived as a stand-alone work for violin and piano.

There are many pages containing various versions of the fiddle music as it was reworked for the Symphony finale, but one double sheet of manuscript has a pencil notation in Carter's hand that says unequivocally that this material was originally a "violin piece" written in 1935/36, "used in first version of *Pocahontas*; used as last mvmt of Sym 1." This notation is at the bottom of an incomplete violin-piano score containing the fiddle music in a setting that cannot be matched very well beyond the first four measures to either the Symphony or *Pocahontas*. After Carter's note was discovered on the incomplete score, the complete piece was located just a few pages away.[6] The beginning of this unpublished and unperformed "violin piece" is given in Example 10.1. It should be noted that, while ostensibly complete, this piece was never released or approved for performance by Carter, and the work as discovered in the sketches should not be considered a performing score.[7]

[4] Schiff, *MEC*, p. 276.
[5] Schiff, *MEC*, pp. 225–26. The piano score for the 1936 version can be found in the *Pocahontas* folder in EC-LC.
[6] The incomplete score can be found at http://lcweb2.loc.gov/diglib/ihas/loc.natlib.ihas.200181910/enlarge.html?

page=31&size=1024&from=pageturner. The 107-measure score can be seen on five pages beginning at http://lcweb2.loc.gov/diglib/ihas/loc.natlib.ihas.200181910/enlarge.html?page=47&section=&size=1024.
[7] Conversation between Soderberg and Carter, August 2009.

Ex. 10.1 Opening of unpublished "Violin Piece" written in 1935–36

The "fiddle music" example demonstrates a situation that is doubtless quite common with many composers. Over a dozen years, a single, well-defined idea found its way into three very different works – the "Violin Piece" (1935/36), *Pocahontas* (1936), and the Symphony No. 1 (1942). Carter's 1946 Piano Sonata illustrates this "regenerative idea" in a different way. The Piano Sonata sketches in EC-LC contain two documents that appear to date the beginnings of the Sonata's composition. The first is a manuscript Carter labels at the bottom: "Sketch for fugue in Piano Sonata written in 1938–9?" If Carter's proposed date is accurate, this sketch places the idea for the fugue at least seven years prior to its ultimate appearance in the Sonata. The subject is identical to that of the final version appearing at the *Allegro giusto* in the second movement, but subsequent entrances and episodes are very different. There is a note at the top of the page: "subject too long?" – a question that Carter evidently did not return to. The second document is the verso of this early fugue sketch, which contains six fugue subjects in various stages of completion. At the top of the verso is: "Six preludes and fugues for piano." None of these is recognizable as having been worked into any subsequent music, but Carter was obviously entertaining the idea of writing a set of fugues at this time.

These two documents remind us that at this time ("1938–9?") Carter was just a few years past his intense counterpoint studies with Nadia Boulanger (1932–35). Could it be that this fugue material was conceived at an even earlier time, during Carter's contact with Boulanger? Looking through the counterpoint exercises of those years, we indeed find two items directly related to the Piano Sonata – but they are not at all what we might expect. EC-LC contains 105 sheets of exercises that Carter wrote under Boulanger's tutelage. One of the exercises *is* a fugue, but not one that bears any relation to the Piano Sonata's fugue. These exercises are all meticulously copied out in ink. Clearly they were special to Carter on several levels: as a personal achievement, as a record of the interest Boulanger took in him (he identifies places in the exercises where Boulanger had made written notes and suggestions), and, quite likely, as a record and reminder of his introduction to much older musical ideas that were to become important in his own development. With a couple of exceptions, there are few other significant stray marks in these exercises beyond Boulanger's. However, it is in the exceptions where the connections to the Piano Sonata are found.

Among the counterpoint exercises are two sheets with pencil sketches resembling the fugue subject of the Piano Sonata on their versos. Certainly these were written after the exercises were reviewed – but exactly *when* is impossible to determine. Since both of these sketches are written on the versos of exercises, they could not have migrated from another box of sketches. To date, no other fragments of this material are known to have been found anywhere outside of the counterpoint exercises and the Piano Sonata sketches proper. It is certainly possible Carter wrote new material on the versos of these exercises after leaving Paris, but it is also possible that these scribbles were done earlier, during the time he was studying with Boulanger. An indication that his counterpoint studies may have found their way into the Sonata's fugue is in a letter from Carter to Frank Scheffer dated February 20, 1993 (copies in the Library of Congress and the Sacher Foundation). The letter is mostly a brief description of his more complex counterpoint exercises under Boulanger's guidance. He ends the letter: "Later, I learned of the remarkable rhythmic methods of the composers like Ciconia, Matheus de Perusio – those in between Machaut and Du Fay. Nadia B[oulanger] often showed this music to us, and it was certainly very influential on my musical thinking." It is well known that the medieval isorhythmic technique worked its way into the Carter Piano Sonata in a fugue episode containing a pentatonic "melodic row" as the color with the rhythmic pattern of the fugue subject used as the talea.[8]

---

[8] See the verso of the original Carter analytical notes for the Piano Sonata in EC-LC.

Ex. 10.2 Inversion of the Piano Sonata's fugue subject

If these two sketches discovered with the counterpoint exercises were indeed made during Carter's studies with Boulanger, then the first of them would indicate that Carter's first ideas for the Piano Sonata's fugue came several years earlier than the 1938–39 time-frame noted above. Adding to the mystery, this sketch is not of the now-familiar subject itself, but of its *inversion* (see Example 10.2). And this raises a much more intriguing question than that of simply dating the beginnings of the Piano Sonata's composition. Was this really the original form in which the subject came to Carter? Or did he have the "real" subject already in his head, and he wrote out its inversion just to see how, or if, it would work? The second of the two sketches found with the counterpoint exercises provides another interesting link (again, not necessarily to Boulanger, but possibly to the time-frame of Carter's studies with her). It pushes the origin of another key element of the Piano Sonata back in time – not the fugue, but a characteristic "jazzy" figure from the first movement. Example 10.3a shows the right-hand line in a piano sketch found on the verso of a four-part counterpoint exercise (*c*. 1935?). For comparison, Example 10.3b shows the top line of mm. 36–39 from the first movement as they appear in the Piano Sonata score completed in 1946. In Carter's own post-compositional analytical notes (on a single sheet located in the Piano Sonata sketch material in EC-LC), he refers to the jazzy eighth–sixteenth–eighth-note "theme," which first appears in the score at m. 36, as derived from the "basic figure of [Movement] I," the arpeggiated sixteenths that first appear in m. 3 (see Example 10.3c). But the discovery of the sketch in Example 10.3a suggests that there may have been an "historical derivation" that was in the reverse order from the "contextual derivation" as it occurs within the composer's final version. And again, as with the fugue subject, we are drawn back to Paris in the mid 1930s where the seeds may have been sown that were to grow into the Piano Sonata a decade later.

The 1946 Piano Sonata is unquestionably one of the landmark piano works of the twentieth century. Most accounts point to this Sonata as the close of Carter's early period, but it certainly is not an abrupt close, or a definitive close at all. Several authors have pointed out how many compositional techniques and stylistic elements from Carter's early period were developed

Ex. 10.3a Early version of a first-movement theme for the Piano Sonata from verso of a counterpoint exercise (*c.* 1935?)

Ex. 10.3b Piano Sonata (1946), mm. 36–39, melodic line

Ex. 10.3c "Theme derived" as represented in Carter's analytical notes (1946–47?) for the Piano Sonata

further and brought forward into his later works.[9] Still it is important to remember that an artist's creative trajectory is not simply an unrelievedly gradual, and hence predictable, process. The path, at times, can take unexpected turns and improbable shifts which, unless they are pure coincidence, can still be understood as rational steps when viewed in hindsight. In the case we will now turn to, hindsight is provided by examining Carter sketches most of which do not "fit" the context in which they are found.

"… anticipation of the future …"

We now turn to a string of related ideas that, perhaps unexpectedly, make their first appearance in Carter's early sketches. These ideas – scraps of ideas at first – appear initially centered on ways to complete the aggregate. Emerging in the sketches as if *ex nihilo*, they often bear little or no apparent relationship to surrounding material. Considered by themselves or in relation to the sketches where they are found, they seem each time to return to nothing. However, these sketches indicate that beginning in the mid 1940s Carter was starting to think about two compositional ideas that he would

[9] For example, David Schiff notes "Stylistically, *The Minotaur*, like the Sonata, seems to be a dead end; but it indicates that Carter constructed his breakthrough style of 1948–55 out of a fusion of American and European elements" (*MEC*, p. 20); and Charles Rosen discusses the "long line" in the Piano Sonata as an important aspect carrying into Carter's mature music (in "Elliott Carter: The Sustained Line"). See also Bernard "The True Significance of Elliott Carter's Early Music," in this volume.

Ex. 10.4 Row found with sketches for the *Holiday Overture*

gradually develop over the next six decades, and with them would create some of the most original and challenging music of our time. The first idea, metric modulation, has been commented on extensively by the composer and others. Source material for metric (or tempo) modulation in the EC-LC sketches begins with the 1948 Cello Sonata on the verso of a sheet of stationery from the Stafford Hotel in Baltimore.[10] On the back of the stationery is a chart laying out the metric modulations for the entire Sonata, arguably making it the first "time screen." Starting from the Stafford stationery, the development of this idea can be followed in the EC-LC sketches through the first three string quartets, as well as the Variations for Orchestra, the Double Concerto, the Piano Concerto, and the Concerto for Orchestra. The second idea, which we will concentrate on here, concerns some of Carter's early ideas about aggregate formation and the organization of harmonic material that eventually resulted in the *Harmony Book*. As Joseph Straus has noted, "Although Carter has never identified himself as a twelve-tone composer, all of his music can be described as the thorough and systematic exploration of the aggregate of twelve pitch classes, especially its division into smaller collections and the combination of smaller collections to create larger ones."[11] Although there may be hints found earlier and in other places, the clearest indication of Carter's early aggregate explorations is a fragment found in the sketches for a 1944 work celebrating the liberation of Paris. Among the sketches for the *Holiday Overture* there is a complete two-piano reduction (thirteen pages, undated). At the bottom of the last page of that score, among some scribbled four-part chord progressions that were evidently being tried out, there is a line that has no apparent melodic connection to the *Holiday Overture*, but may have some connection to the piece's chord progressions. Carter overtly labels this line a "row" (see Example 10.4). This is the first known example to date of a twelve-tone row found in the EC-LC sketches. But the nature of the row's trichord content and the way Carter has bracketed trichords and

[10] See the first two images of the digitized Cello Sonata sketches at http://lcweb2.loc. gov/diglib/ihas/loc.natlib.ihas.200155639/ full.html. From 1946 to 1948 Carter commuted from New York to Baltimore

to teach composition at Peabody Conservatory.

[11] Straus, "A Revisionist History of Twelve-Tone Serialism in American Music," 377. See also Straus, *Twelve-Tone Music in America*.

Ex. 10.5 Row found with sketches for the Piano Sonata

Ex. 10.6 Row found with sketches for *The Minotaur*

tetrachords, and then begun to test the content as chords below the row, imply that he was more interested here in unusual harmonic progressions than fully ordered twelve-tone rows. This row expresses an unconventional way of getting from an F-minor triad to a G-minor triad – and, in the process, completing the aggregate without repeating any notes.

Returning to the Piano Sonata sketches once more, we find another instance of a row: a single line at the bottom of a page where Carter is again working on the fugue. This is a row that begins with the head of the fugue subject (labeled [O] by Carter in Example 10.5) but soon goes in another direction to complete the aggregate. Note, however, that Carter has arranged the completion such that the head of the fugue *almost* appears in the retrograde – the first three notes transposed up a tritone, the second two up a perfect fourth, even though all five notes of the fugue head could have been transposed by a tritone (the brackets are Carter's). It would appear that Carter was looking for a way to break the symmetry that a simple transposition would create, and yet remain within the possibilities of a twelve-tone row. Again, there is no indication that this or any other twelve-tone row made it into the Sonata.

The next example is from the sketches for the 1947 ballet *The Minotaur*. There are indications that Carter intended to use a row at least as a bass line reflecting the drama unfolding on stage. There are three attempts at writing a row here. Between these attempts Carter has written "Establish mystery – frightened maids – violent Pasiphaë" and "moving bass, shadowy – theme of suspense." The third version of the row, for which he wrote out the three canonic forms, R, I, and RI, is shown as Example 10.6. This is another tonally

Ex. 10.7 Carter's analysis of the trichord content of the hexachord [013468] Forte 6-Z24

"harmonic" row, the original form going from an F-minor triad to a D-major triad. The rising fifths of the first hexachord of row O also recall the head of the "Seikilos Song," an important underlying element of the ballet, pointed out by David Schiff.[12] But still no ordered row has been discovered in the final version.

In the sketches for the Woodwind Quintet of 1948, no serial row has been noted, but there is an interesting page containing lists of major, minor, diminished, and augmented triads.[13] At the top of the page Carter has written, "Chromatic progressions or progressions having no common key." Many of the triads are crossed out – perhaps because these are too tonally suggestive or too "close" to a reference triad. Here we are nearing a more methodical listing of harmonies and a lasting break with the idea that trichords and larger chord formations are "naturally" based on stacks of thirds. It will come as no real surprise that this break happens during the composition of the First String Quartet (1951), the work offering the most radical change in Carter's musical language up to that time. The earliest-known example of Carter's identification of chords by a self-devised numbering system is a sketch with numbered trichords and stamped "Carter Str Quartet No.1 – 51."[14] Example 10.7 reproduces one system on the manuscript page that gives us Carter's numbering of trichords in an analysis of the hexachord written on the left (6-Z24 [013468]). Since Carter did not assume inversional equivalence, his first complete list of trichords numbered nineteen, not twelve.[15] This leads to the interesting question of what number he initially assigned to each trichord and why. Were numbers assigned purely on the basis of compositional considerations? Was it more or less random? Or was there a third possibility?

[12] Schiff, *MEC*, pp. 231–32.
[13] http://lcweb2.loc.gov/diglib/ihas/loc.natlib. ihas.200181916/enlarge.html? page=41&section=&size=640
[14] This sketch was discovered by John Link in 2007 among the sketches for Carter's Third Quartet. The entire page can be viewed at http://lcweb2.loc.gov/diglib/ihas/loc.natlib. ihas.200155638/pageturner.html? page=17&section=&size=640. Carter has

often stamped each page of his sketches with his name, the title of the work, and the year of completion.
[15] See Link, "Carter's Harmonic Context." Link also notes that at the bottom of the page this sketch contains the earliest-known record of Carter's recognition of the all-interval tetrachord (0146). Dörte Schmidt also discusses this sketch in "On Elliott Carter's String Quartets", in this volume.

Table 10.1 Carter's early numbering of trichords (derived from sketch Example 10.7)

Carter's No.	Prime form	n (Span)	Partitions of n (Interval string)
1	012	2	1–1
2	013	3	1–2
3	023		2–1
	(013′)		
4	014	4	1–3
5	024		2–2
6	034		3–1
	(014′)		
7	015	5	1–4
8	025		2–3
9	035		3–2
	(025′)		
10	045		4–1
	(015′)		
11	016	6	1–5
12	026		2–4
13	036		3–3
14	046		4–2
	(026′)		
15	056		5–1
	(016′)		
16	027	7	2–5
17	037		3–4
18	047		4–3
	(037′)		
19	048	8	4–4

Examining Carter's ordering, it becomes apparent that the trichords are ordered first according to interval span (column 3 in Table 10.1) and second according to the lexicographic order of their interval strings in prime form (column 4).[16] Interestingly, this taxonomic approach to ordering also provides a simple combinatorial formula for generating all transposition-equivalent classes for all set cardinalities, although rotationally equivalent interval strings need to be omitted, as Carter clearly does with interval spans n=7 and n=8. For example, interval string 1–7 is a rotational equivalent

[16] "Lexicographic order" is also known as "dictionary order" and here refers to the ascending ordering of, firstly, the first elements in the interval string, secondly, the second elements, and so on. Interval strings are given here in a format that accords with the way Carter gives them in *HB*. For example, the string for the triad E–G–B is given as 3–4 (E to G is three chromatic steps, G to B is 4).

interval string 4–1, and therefore does not appear.[17] Carter's ordering is a clear indication that he had focused on a fairly intuitive mathematical idea that could make possible the extensive hand calculations necessary to eventually generate the complete chord list that is the foundation for the *Harmony Book*. This places the first steps toward the *Harmony Book* some time in the early 1950s during the composition of the First String Quartet. This is not to say that Carter at this time had the idea of generating a list of all possible chords in the twelve-tone universe (let alone felt any compositional need to do so); but this example does indicate that he had the procedural seed that would let him do just that as he began expanding the systematic organization of his harmonic palette.

As a composer Carter was undoubtedly dissatisfied with this initial ordering since, among other things, it splits up inversionally related trichords and mixes symmetrical with asymmetrical chords. So, as evidenced by the final order found in the *Harmony Book*, over the next several years he made some changes to this three-note chord list. First, he included inversional equivalence, reducing the number of trichords to the familiar twelve. Second, he placed the five symmetrical trichords together in the order 4–4, 3–3, 2–2, 1–1, 2–5, followed by the asymmetrical trichords in the order 3–4, 1–5, 2–4, 1–4, 2–3, 1–3, 1–2.[18] This reverses the order of interval spans from largest span to smallest in each of the symmetrical and asymmetrical groups, while still maintaining the basic generating idea from his original combinatoric procedure.[19]

The "Proto-Harmony Book"

In 2007, what we will now refer to as the "Proto-Harmony Book" (PHB) was discovered among the sketches for the Third String Quartet. This document is the first known instance of Carter having worked out – and numbered – all the set classes from tetrachords through hexachords (the trichords are missing here). In content and arrangement, the PHB is strikingly similar to the basic set-class lists in the *Harmony Book*. It is stamped "Quartet No. Three – E

---

[17] This is known as the "Necklace Problem," first solved by mathematician John Howard Redfield in 1927 but more often associated with a 1937 proof by George Pòlya. The first list of all the chords in the twelve-tone universe with no duplicates was published in 1917 by the American composer Ernst Lecher Bacon. For further discussion and citations, see Bernard, "Chord, Collection and Set in Twentieth-Century Theory"; Link, "The Combinatorial Art of Elliott Carter's *Harmony Book*"; and Nolan "Combinatorial Space in Nineteenth- and Early Twentieth-Century Music Theory." See also Hook, "Why Are There 29 Tetrachords?"

[18] See also Link, "The Combinatorial Art of Elliott Carter's *Harmony Book*," pp. 7–8.

[19] The one exception is 2–5 which is placed after 1–1 as the last symmetrical trichord. Interestingly, ic 1 and ic 5 are the only ics that can generate the chromatic scale, so they belong together in that important musical sense.

Ex. 10.8 The first tetrachord entry in the "Proto-Harmony Book" showing three transpositions of [0123] completing the aggregate

Carter – 1971" at the bottom of the first page. This stamp, plus the content of the PHB, clearly indicate that it "belongs" with the sketches for the Third Quartet and suggests it was created in 1970–71. But the presence of another date stamp implies a more complicated story. Three pages of the PHB (Parts 1 and 3 below) are also stamped "Nov 21 1965." So at least three of the six pages making up the PHB were probably assembled during or just prior to 1965 (the year the Piano Concerto was completed), making them available throughout the composition of the Concerto for Orchestra and the Third String Quartet. But the PHB does more than help to date the history of the creation of the *Harmony Book*. Since all the four-, five-, and six-note chords are numbered, and since this numbering is different from that used in the *Harmony Book*, the PHB can be helpful in deciphering Carter's chord references in previous sketches, not only for the works in the period 1965–71, but possibly sketches created back as far as those for the Double Concerto. And finally, the generation and arrangement of chords in the PHB sheds more light on the material we have examined above beginning with the sketch of trichords found with the *Holiday Overture*: the page in the PHB that lists tetrachords gives further evidence of Carter's continuing investigation of ways to complete the aggregate, and chord numberings throughout the PHB are further evidence of Carter's penchant for generating chord lists by writing out interval strings, as we noted in the trichord list above.

There are several layers of organization to the PHB. The pages are divided by chord cardinality, and each cardinality is arranged according to specific criteria. The first page – for reference we will call this Part 1 – contains the twenty-nine four-note chords. It is dated "Nov 21 1965" at the top of the page and stamped "Quartet No. Three – E Carter – 1971" at the bottom. Part 1 is further divided into three sections in a characteristic way that we find maintained in the *Harmony Book*. The first section contains all the four-note chords that, by simple transposition, can combine with themselves to create the aggregate. Thus the first three tetrachords in Example 10.8 are all members of set class [0123] and together partition the aggregate. This aggregate-completion technique explains the presence, both here and in the *Harmony Book*, of the early appearance of the asymmetrical tetrachord [0136] which appears out of place in the midst of all the symmetrical chords at the head of the list. The next asymmetrical chord does not appear until number 16 (number 17 in the *Harmony Book*). The second section of Part 1 also consists of triples of four-note chords that partition the aggregate. Here, two of the four-note chords are related by transposition, but the third is a different type entirely. The third section lists all four-note triples that make up the aggregate such that two are related by inversion and the third is, again, a different type. This three-section system is carried over into the way the four-note chords are listed in the *Harmony Book*, with the exception that Carter corrects a mistake he made in the PHB: at first he took the interval string 2–4–4 to be asymmetrical when, in fact, it represents a symmetry; in the PHB it appears in the third section, but he moved it up to the second in the *Harmony Book*.

The next three pages are undated, but their somewhat awkward stapling-in between Parts 1 and 3 suggest they were added after Parts 1 and 3 were already in use. The first two pages – Part 2a – contain all thirty-eight five-note chords with their seven-note complements. The following single page – Part 2b – contains the thirty-eight five-note chords (without their complements), but in a different order and numbering from that in Part 2a. It is quite likely that Part 2b came before 2a, since 2b contains errors (duplication of two set classes and omission of two others) that are corrected in 2a. But even more interesting is how Carter lists the pentachords in the earlier 2b, all of which begin on E, the bottom line of the treble staff. Chord no. 1 is the chromatic pentachord, with the interval string 1–1–1–1 and span 4. The next chords are all ordered according to increasing interval spans from interval 5 to interval 9. This ordering follows the same principle we encountered above in Carter's initial ordering of the trichords. However, it differs from what later appears in the *Harmony Book*, where the five-note chords, like all the other chords, are ordered into symmetrical and asymmetrical groups.

The last two pages – Part 3 – contain all fifty six-note chords. Both pages are stamped "Nov 21 1965" at the top. Part 3 is itself divided into three sections: (1) "residue repeats," (2) "residue inverts," (3) "residue-different." "Residue" clearly is Carter's word here for a set-theoretic complement,[20] and "different" indicates that there is no transpositional or inversional relationship. So "residue-different" indicates pairs of chords that are "z-related" (in Allen Forte's terminology). (3) is further divided into asymmetrical and symmetrical pairs of hexachords with respect to inversion, in effect creating four distinct sections to Part 3. There are at least two distinct numberings running through the fifty six-note chords. One of these numberings follows the sectional divisions just described and will find its way into the hexachord categories in Chapter I of the *Harmony Book*.[21] The other numbering system orders the hexachords according to their increasing interval span, similar to

---

[20] To this day "residue" is apparently Carter's preferred term for set-theoretic complement (see, for example, Carter, *HB*, p. 29).

[21] See the editors' preface to Chapter I, in Carter, *HB*, p. 3.

what we have already seen in Carter's early ordering of the trichords and of the five-note chords.

We began this survey by noting a few early ideas that could be traced back to the time during or soon after Carter's studies with Nadia Boulanger – a time when Carter was attempting to find his personal voice as a composer while working within the prevailing neoclassical milieu of the 1930s and '40s. The sketches strongly suggest that his working within the status quo (as in the "fiddle tune") and stretching it (as in the Piano Sonata) developed into attempts to move away from that mostly tonal model. At first these attempts were tentative and retained tonality's fingerprints. Such was the case with the aggregate completions (as "harmonic rows") found with the sketches for the *Holiday Overture* and *The Minotaur*; the fleeting idea of turning the head of the Piano Sonata's fugue subject into a twelve-tone row; and the listing of "chromatic progressions" of tonal trichord pairs found in the sketches for the Woodwind Quintet.

Arriving at the trichord analysis of hexachords in the sketches for the seminal First String Quartet, we note that tonality was not so much thrown out at this point as overwhelmed – tonal triads were joined by non-tonal trichords as equals to form Carter's first list of all possible three-note set classes. His characteristic numbering indicates that Carter had the simple key available that could be used to generate a complete set-class list. In the PHB, both the tetrachord and pentachord lists are arranged in groups of chords that partition the aggregate. The hexachords also appear as complement ("residue") pairs – again as ways to complete the aggregate and an indication that, consciously or not, Carter was heading toward the encyclopedic *Harmony Book*. Strategies for completing the aggregate are, after all, no more than partitions of the twelve-tone chromatic. It is a short step from this concept to partitioning the *sub*-sets of the total chromatic or, using Carter's terminology, "analyzing" and "synthesizing" the pitch-class sets in the twelve-tone universe. It is here – with the PHB's complete chart of sonorities in hand, the complex relationships among those sonorities within reach, and the initial contributions to what will prove to be a startlingly original collection of works – that this survey leaves Elliott Carter. He is standing at the edge of creation – anticipating a future "not always fulfilled in the way anticipated."

PART IV

Music and text

11   *Three Illusions* ... and maybe a fourth: a hermeneutic approach to Carter's recent music

Max Noubel
(Translated by Jean-Luc Demizieux and Evan Rothstein)

> ... for nothing comes to us except falsified and altered by our senses.
>
> Michel de Montaigne[1]

The *Three Illusions* (2002–04)[2] mark Carter's return to the orchestral trip-tych, a genre he employed twice previously, first with the *Three Occasions* (1986–89) and then with *Symphonia: Sum Fluxae Pretium Spei* (1993–96).[3] The *Three Occasions* resulted from three independent commissions which at first were not intended to form a coherent ensemble, even though this solution seems logical a posteriori. By contrast, *Symphonia* was, according to Carter, conceived from the start as a large orchestral triptych, initially suggested by conductor Oliver Knussen. Although each piece of these two sets may be presented separately, performance in the form of a triptych is of much greater interest. Taken as a whole, *Symphonia* appears as a work with excep-tional coherence, ranking it among the monuments of the late twentieth-century symphonic repertoire. Concerning the *Three Occasions*, David Schiff has noted that the three movements "together form a sixteen-minute long symphonic suite equal in length, and emotional depth to the two orchestral sets of Ives."[4] Like the *Three Occasions*, the *Three Illusions* were composed separately; nothing thus prevents a conductor from programming only one of the movements. Each piece played separately, although it would not fail to excite the enthusiasm of the public, would nevertheless risk sounding like a brilliant showpiece and leave a rather superficial impression. As with the other triptychs, we contend that the music acquires greater significance and reveals its true depth only through a performance of the complete grouping of three pieces.

---

[1] Montaigne, *Complete Essays*, p. 454.
[2] The movements of *Three Illusions* are *Micomicón* (2002), *Fons Juventatis* (2004), and *More's Utopia* (2004). First complete performance, Symphony Hall, Boston, Massachusetts, Boston Symphony Orchestra, James Levine, cond., October 6, 2005; *Micomicón* was first performed at the same venue on January 15, 2004.

[3] The movements of *Three Occasions* are *A Celebration of some 100 × 150 Notes* (1986), *Remembrance* (1988), and *Anniversary* (1989); those of *Symphonia* are *Partita* (1993), *Adagio tenebroso* (1994), and *Allegro scorrevole* (1996).
[4] Schiff, *MEC*, p. 311.

None of the movements of *Three Illusions* lasts longer than three minutes; although this is about the same length as the first of the *Three Occasions, A Celebration of Some 100 × 150 Notes* (1986), such dimensions have been reserved more frequently for the solo or small ensemble pieces which Carter has composed in recent years in ever greater abundance. In spite of their modest size and relatively light density of material, the triptych is far from being of minor importance among the composer's recent production. On the contrary, it represents a high point of the art of concise musical discourse, allying efficiency and subtlety of musical dramaturgy. Carter masterfully "juggles" a carefully restricted vocabulary, which he controls fully and which is sufficient to give full rein to his overflowing musical imagination.

To make sense of the *Three Illusions*, it is necessary to embrace its sometimes-aphoristic content and its elliptical or even allusive nature. It is also important to take into account the "earnest detachment" with which Carter now deals with composition. The harmonic and rhythmic systems, as well as the elements of instrumental dramaturgy employed here, are not new.[5] This attitude connects him with certain Baroque composers' ability to draw on materials and musical ideas already exploited in order to create something new without yielding to facility or renouncing any of their deeper artistic aspirations. Is Bach himself not a good example of this? Finally, although the musical universe of this *Ultima Pratica* – however subtle and varied – is roughly the same as that which preceded it, one recognizes that it is the prism through which Carter reveals this universe that changes – in the minutest details – our perception of it. This deforming, or rather reforming, prism is part of the composer's ongoing challenge to the order of his own musical world. In the case of the *Three Illusions*, it is as though Carter constantly mixes up the cards of his single pack, displaying a range of combinations always surprising despite the remarkable economy of means. To someone familiar with Carter's music, then, each piece of this triptych appears as a unique listening experience because it is paradoxically both familiar and disconcerting.

It would be misleading, however, to regard these miniatures as the work of a magician's sleight of hand, however ingenious. Their emotional strength and substance are rooted in more than half a century of compositional experience and result from a conception of worlds recomposed not as closed spaces like sonic *Utopiae* or "Nowhere Islands" but as open, or rather permeable, spaces. Of course each work is an end in itself but it is also connected to the rest of Carter's artistic production through streams of

---

[5] Though this article is not devoted to the study of the technical details of Carter's harmonic language, it is worth pointing out that, as in some other works belonging to the *Ultima Practica*, each of the *Three Illusions* is built on registrally ordered all-interval twelve-tone rows.

resonance, like those that connect the works of all great artists. Viewing a painting of the *Nympheas* by Claude Monet, Paul Ricœur said that the work of art is not an "object of perception" but a "future of perception" in the sense that its closed space refers far beyond its own boundaries. In the case of Carter's music, it seems appropriate to say that a "porosity" integral to his compositions allows those streams which carry persistent traces of past experiences to filter through the new prism, so that these experiences find a new singularity. In other words, if Carter only very rarely refers to himself through self-citations or direct allusions to his previous works, as in the manner of Charles Ives, his music feeds on the same *affetti*, the same types of behavior, the same range of relations reworked with boundless inventiveness. It seems no exaggeration to say that, to some extent, Carter's works "speak" to one another from a distance. A diagonal approach to Carter's production, which takes into account the filtered return of past experience throughout his oeuvre and which goes beyond considerations of genres or periods, might prove fruitful and reveal unexpected perspectives. This approach should rely on a cross-analysis of major morphological, relational, or behavioral archetypes, thus shedding light on these musical "intertextual references." But an overly systematic catalogue of such gestures would probably be fruitless. The contribution of such a study to the knowledge of Carter's musical thinking is of interest only if envisaged within a hermeneutic framework that goes beyond mere static observation and remains permeable to a global dynamic interpretation.[6] Only under this condition can *networks of meaning* be brought to light.

If we accept Paul Ricœur's contention that as soon as there is meaning there is interpretation and that every work ends up escaping its creator, we necessarily need to accept the subjective dimension of interpretive analysis. Michel Butor said that he did not speak of Baudelaire, but that Baudelaire spoke of him. In the case of Carter, this would seem to reflect the composer's own convictions; in spite of all the extra-musical comparisons he has provided in order to explain his music, he believes such explanations or references to be unnecessary for an understanding or appreciation of the music itself. In fact, he has always denied imbuing his works with programmatic intent, in the spirit of a tone poem or explicit narrative, even if he has often spoken of "auditory scenarios" to describe the complex plays of relations that unfold in and determine the shape of his works. The anthropomorphic dimension of the instrumental behaviors and of their play of relations, which is so present in his comments, is, to him, no more than a way of describing metaphorically what is first of all a play of sonic forces. In this

[6] See also Esclapez, "Pour une herméneutique de l'analyse," pp. 73–83.

sense Elliott Carter has always regarded himself as the heir to ideas of Igor Stravinsky, who stated that music expresses nothing but itself.[7] However, the way Carter speaks about his music, even considered with appropriate distance, is itself an interpretive analysis of his own work, a subjective speech that we must not entirely reject. If ultimately there is something transgressive in interpreting what should not be interpreted, there is, however, no betrayal, since on the one hand Carter himself makes such interpretation and, on the other hand, interpretation like Carter's is careful not to lose contact with the score and the reality of the performance, and remains rooted in them. The hermeneutic approach cannot be a series of mere meanderings. It should be guided by a precisely defined question which develops in concentric circles *from* the work and only *for* it. Having assumed this interpretive freedom and defined its limits, we shall attempt to subject the *Three Illusions* to this type of approach. Without neglecting an examination of the harmonic and rhythmic language employed, we shall also appeal to the interpretation of the extra-musical sources that inspired this work.

An artist of broad culture, Carter has often drawn his inspiration from literary works.[8] In the case of the earlier triptychs, we can cite the epigram from John Donne's verses that accompanies *Anniversary* (1989), the third piece of the *Three Occasions*; and the seventeenth-century English poet Richard Crashaw's Latin poem "Bulla," which accompanies *Symphonia*.[9] The pieces that make up the triptych *Three Illusions* explicitly refer to a very old legend and to two important canonical works of sixteenth-century literature: the *Fountain of Youth* myth (II. *Fons Juventatis*); *Don Quixote* (1505–15), Cervantes's masterpiece (I. *Micomicón*); and *Utopia* (1516), the most renowned work by English humanist Sir Thomas More (III. *More's Utopia*). It is worth pointing out that Carter places the slow movement at the end and begins with the two more dynamic movements, each nevertheless very different in character. Thus he breaks with the usual fast–slow–fast structure he adhered to in the previous two orchestral triptychs. Of the three movements, *Fons Juventatis* is seemingly the lightest, with the most appealing sonority, and for this reason can be immediately appreciated by the audience. It is not used, however, to conclude the cycle brilliantly as might have been expected; it is instead set halfway through the triptych and thus holds the place Carter dedicated in previous triptychs to lamentation and dark meditation. In fact, *Remembrance* (1988), composed in the memory of Paul Fromm, takes the form of a funeral oration, while *Adagio tenebroso* (1994) is "an obsessive twenty-minute brooding on a single, darkly ominous

[7] Stravinsky, *Chronicle of My Life*, 1936 edn, p. 91.

[8] On text–music relations in Carter's music, see Bernard, "Poem as Non-Verbal Text."

[9] For more details, see Schiff, *MEC*, pp. 316–17.

soundscape, as if the bubble were hovering over a war-torn wasteland."[10] Familiarity with the great subtlety of Carter's thinking would indicate that this choice for the order of movements in *Three Illusions* goes far beyond the simple fact of refusing once again to respect convention. We shall attempt to show that this change has a meaning and symbolism that go much deeper.

Micomicón

Carter had originally intended to use the title *Gallematius* for this piece, choosing to replace it with *Micomicón* quite a bit later on, this latter title having been selected initially for the guitar piece *Changes* (1983).[11] This change of title is obviously a warning against searching for a direct translation of the literary narrative into the musical discourse. Nevertheless, the final choice confirms the composer's long-standing interest in the Spanish author's work, and argues for a comparative approach to their creative thought. By referring to this famous episode from Cervantes's *Don Quixote* for the first piece of the triptych, Carter joins the long list of composers attracted by the character of the ingenious hidalgo, who wavers between madness and wisdom, and his numerous vivid adventures.[12] The title of Carter's *Micomicón* refers to the passage in which the priest and the barber of Don Quixote's village devise a scheme in order to take the knight-errant home. Young and beautiful Dorothea pretends to be the princess heiress to the great kingdom of Micomicón in Africa. She talks the old hidalgo into promising to kill a giant in order to free her from his grip so that she can return to her village. With the help of the false Princess Micomicona, the priest hopes to keep Don Quixote under his own control. This story is in Part 4, Book I and unfolds in a discontinuous way, beginning in Chapter 29 and ending at Chapter 37. It is discontinuous because within these chapters the Micomicón story is interrupted and gives way to other lengthy narratives, as is common in Cervantes's novel. Thus, in the course of these successive chapters the reader must follow first the account of Dorothea's true story, then a conversation between Don Quixote and Sancho Panza, and finally, the long and dense tragic story of a jealous husband, all fragmented and interspersed throughout several chapters. These narratives are then interrupted at Chapter 35 by the frightful battle

[10] Northcott, "Affirmations of a Modern Master," p. 11.

[11] Carter used the title *Gallematius* at the top of his final draft score. Only later did he cross out *Gallematius* from the draft and replace it with *Micomicón*. *Micomicón* was Carter's preferred title for his guitar piece *Changes* until David Starobin raised some concerns about it. Their correspondence about the title is at the Paul Sacher Foundation with the *Changes* manuscripts. (The author wishes to thank the editors M. Boland and J. Link for bringing this information to his attention.)

[12] We shall content ourselves with mentioning, among many works, Richard Strauss's tone poem *Don Quixote*, Op. 35 (1897) and Maurice Ravel's three melodies *Don Quichotte à Dulcinée* (1932).

between Don Quixote and the wineskins. This short passage, in which the "Knight of the sorrowful countenance" dreams that he is fighting against the giant who threatens Princess Micomicona, finally brings us back to the main story. This procedure of formal organization, which consists of inserting unexpected events or totally unrelated stories into the main discourse, reminds us of the Carterian principle of "broken continuities" that is found in many of his works, including the triptych *Three Illusions*.

Before we focus in more detail on the music of *Micomicón*, it may be useful to point out some of the other common points of contact between the Spanish writer's work and that of the American composer. Beyond quite remarkable formal connections between the two works, it is interesting to note their common inclination for plurality of events and diversity of character types. Furthermore, the characters in Cervantes's novel are inclined to disguise themselves, which corresponds quite well in Carter's music to the changes in behavior, and sometimes in identity, undergone by the instruments. In Cervantes's novel, as in Carter's work, we find a perspective on time that is multi-layered, involving a constant altering of the narrative time and the duration of events as well as the rhythm with which events unfold. There is a kind of equivalence between the sequences of poetic meditation, of conversation, and of grotesque combat in the novel and the types of passages in *Micomicón*: those that are almost static and made up of slowly moving harmonies, those made of fast exchanges between the instruments and those featuring the "sonic cataclysms" that may occur in Carter's music. It is also worth underlining that both the writer and the composer play remarkably well with contrasts: adventures and misadventures, dream and reality in Cervantes; order and disorder, suspended time and action time in Carter. The art of conversation is another particularly interesting point of contact. Conversation is at the center of Cervantes's work and takes place most often between Don Quixote and Sancho Panza. It involves various levels of language: popular, refined, poetic, or trivial. A parallel may be drawn with Carter, whose interest in everything relating to dialectic is well known; it will suffice to mention his love of Plato's dialogues. The characters/instruments, most notably since the String Quartet No. 4 (1986), maintain conversations or engage in commentary between themselves, even if Carter, in contrast to Charles Ives in his String Quartet No. 2 (1907–13), does not give any extramusical signification to these "comments." Beyond the formal use of dialogue, conversation in Cervantes's work implies a subtle play on language. This play appears in the proper nouns and testifies to the will to avoid fixing a single meaning or truth to words. For example, the noun "Micomicón" is the doubling of the Spanish word "mico" ("monkey"), with its connotation of mockery and trickery. The princess, then, is doubly deceitful. It is of little importance to know whether Carter has or has not taken this humor into account; what is interesting to note is a similar state of mind of both writer and composer, for whom the language is a means of teasing not only the protagonists of their literary or musical works but also their readers or listeners. Finally, another common element connects Carter with Cervantes, one derived from previous considerations but far from the least important: the art of developing parallel universes, each with its own specific style and independent existence, which William James calls "sub-universes" and which Alfred Schütz has remarkably developed in relation to *Don Quixote*. Schütz propounds the thesis "that Cervantes' novel deals systematically with the very problem of multiple realities stated by William James, and that the various phases of Don Quixote's adventures are carefully elaborated variations of the main theme, viz. how to experience reality."[13] While this constant play between reality and illusion cannot be transposed as such to Carter's music, it does correspond to his use of specific sonic worlds deployed both successively and simultaneously. Their constant evolutions are like so many illusions, incessantly calling into question our very perception of these sonic worlds, obliging us constantly to reinterpret them.

We shall now turn to the music itself. Throughout almost the entire duration of *Micomicón*, two layers of different tempi move in parallel with each other. One layer is rather lively and characterized by a succession of varied events. This heterogeneity relates closely to the multiplicity of situations presented in Cervantes's novel. Moreover, this layer is rooted in a certain "reality," even if, as we shall see, it is constantly distorted. This layer can be seen as close to Sancho Panza's world. The other layer is slow and more homogeneous, despite the major changes it undergoes throughout the work; this layer seems to correspond to Don Quixote's often meditative universe. Toward the end, a brief and violent orchestral surge destroys these two parallel worlds before giving way to a short moment of suspended time, abolishing all action. The three successive main parts of this piece are followed by a brief coda. As always with Carter, this very simple structure is marked by a very subtle internal organization.

The first part, *Allegro* $\quarternote = 120$ (mm. 1–31) introduces the most lively layer, relying almost exclusively on winds. After a violent cymbal roll, there is a brief duet between Trumpet 1 and Trombone 1. This fanfare of sorts is characterized by strongly accented repeated notes (which form the pentachord 5–10 {65320}), each part articulating a different pulse. This is followed by brief interventions by the brass, which state fragments of a continuous melodic line evolving with each entry. These melodic fragments are like comments forming a freely developing conversation between protagonists. To measure the

---

[13] Schütz, "Don Quixote and the Problem of Reality," p. 136.

diversity of these interjections, one may note, for example, the contrast between the trumpet solo (mm. 7–8), with its tempestuous and premptory phrase ending with the descending minor ninth interval A4–G♯3, and the dark, expansive phrase played by Horn 2, Horn 4, and the tuba (mm. 9–11). In both cases, the use of the same transposition of hexachord 6-Z17 {987521} plays the role of "reconciling factor." This conversation ends in the middle of the first part (m. 15) with a *fortissimo* chord and gives way to an unexpected comment, a sort of chirruping played by the flutes and the xylophone in the extreme upper register. A new and completely different section begins at m. 19. A series of chords on various transpositions of hexachord 6-Z17 are hammered out more or less regularly. A new and important change occurs at m. 24, where the instruments play in unison an *expressivo* melody consisting of large, disjunct intervals moving within a wide range, from G♯3 to G6. Here the woodwinds speak with a single voice. Their statement thus takes the form of a monologue in contrasting response to the dialogue initially distributed among the members of the brass. This first part ends with a section (mm. 28–31) that brings back the hammered chords followed by the insistent repetition of the note C♯4 in the horns. This repeated note is situated at m. 30, that is, in a symmetrical position in relation to the call of repeated notes in the Trumpet 1 and Trombone 1 at the beginning of this section. The axis of symmetry is situated on the *fortissimo* chord at m. 15, that is, when the succession of brief heterogeneous sections begins.

The slow sound-world that develops in parallel is not heard until the conversation between the brass has begun. It is entirely allotted to the strings, with very soft dynamics. The harmonic fields unfold on either side of an arch-shaped melodic line. This melody progresses unperturbed at a regular speed of MM 48. Starting from G5 (m. 5), it rises to reach its peak on C7 (m. 13) and stabilizes on this note, which is repeated three times (mm. 13–17). The second C7 is situated halfway through the first section (mm. 15–16). Then the melody descends in an irregularly undulating line from G♯6 to A♮4. In the rising part of the arch (mm. 5–12) a stable harmony can be heard that consists of a twelve-note chord, the notes of which are distributed between D1 and G♯6. The notes are organized around the central tritone E4–A♮4, which separates hexachords 6-Z36 {65432E} and 6-Z3 {789T01}. The harmony heard below the three C7s (mm. 13–17) is built up from two inversionally related twelve-tone chords, the notes of which spread between F♯1 and C7 (see Example 11.1). Each of these two chords contain the same intervals, but they are distributed symmetrically on either side of an axis around D4–E4, so that the interval in the lowest position on the first hexachord is to be found again in the very high-pitched register on the second hexachord. It is worth pointing out that this symmetrical chord occurs at the axis of structural symmetry of the first section.

Ex. 11.1 *Micomicón*: harmonic symmetry in mm. 13–17

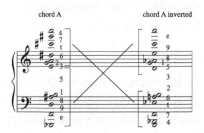

The second half of this section (mm. 17–32) is not as stable harmonically, which may be explained by the variety of events occurring in the other temporal layer. We can also notice compressions and dilations of the harmonic span, which gives rise to the "breathing" of the texture that accompanies the undulations of the line. Thus, the twelve-note chord of mm. 17–18 spreads between F♯1 and C7, whereas the twelve-note chord of mm. 24–27 occupies only a range contained between F3 and C♯6. The last chord of this passage, in m. 32, is even further compressed since the hexachord 6-Z17 {23469T} is contained between D♯3 and A♯4. In spite of the strong independence of the two layers, there exists a mutual responsiveness between the two temporal worlds that is reinforced later on, as we shall see below.

The second part, *Meno mosso* ♩ = 72 (mm. 33–66), is marked by a shift in roles. The slow layer, which develops continuously, has become almost exclusively the sphere of the winds, while the lively layer is now the preserve of the strings and other instruments. This layer begins with a brief transitory section (mm. 33–35) in which the strings present a nervous, tempestuous music characterized by *forte, marcato* sixteenth notes that descend toward the low register. This gesture, as short as it is unexpected, may be interpreted as the reverse image of the flutes' chirruping in the first part. It may also be taken as an anticipation of the fast stream of the strings (mm. 67–73) that appears along with the orchestral surge at the end of the piece. Then a surprising moment of musical "enchantment" occurs (mm. 36–48): a delicate sonic quivering is produced by the combination of the crystal-clear timbres of the piano, harp, xylophone, and violins that play very softly in the upper register. A piano solo ending with an undulating melodic line in the lower register puts an end to this particularly seductive passage, which could be seen to evoke the charm with which the princess maintains Don Quixote under her spell.

The following section gives rise to a climate of concern marked by the attack of low strings (mm. 54–58) that signals the entrance of the timpani. Here again these simple pulses, which contribute to the increasing dramatization of the passage, are particularly interesting if taken as reminiscences of the hammered chords in the first part. The timpani's interventions, at first sporadic, turn into a violently energetic, virtuoso solo (mm. 62–64). As a kind of "intertexual reference," it seems as if the extraordinary timpani part accompanying the entrance of the trombone in the finale of the Variations for Orchestra (1954–55) has here filtered through the prism. This particularly tense and dramatic passage makes sense only if it is considered in the context of the sonic environment provided by the winds, which participate in the increasing power of the timpani through a generalized crescendo. This episode could correspond, in Cervantes's book, to Don Quixote's fight against the wineskins. Interpreted more generally, however, it can be seen as the manifestation of the inevitable misadventure that always follows any adventure in this novel.

During the whole of this second part, the slower second sonic layer undergoes several mutations. It appears firstly in the woodwinds and traces a melodic line which moves at a speed of MM 54. During the moment of "enchantment," this sonic material shifts primarily to the brass (mm. 36–44). The texture is restricted to the lower register. The *pianissimo* dynamics and the use of mutes give an impression of distance, which contributes to making the melodic line less perceptible. The sonic "enchantment" having disappeared, the woodwinds come again to the fore. The harmony then expands registrally and the melody becomes more clearly perceptible again. Then overlapping entries of the brass and woodwinds alternate in order to create *chiaroscuro* effects. Even the strings make a one-off contribution (mm. 53–54) and the melody, which has again come into focus, then moves from one instrument to the other. Independent as this sonic universe is, it nonetheless enjoys a degree of "porosity" which allows traces of past experiences to filter in from the other universe. In fact, between the measures 52 and 55, which bring the four horns to the fore, Horn 1 constructs a broad melodic phrase on heptachord 7-Z18 {123469T}, with each note "harmonized" by a different transposition of tetrachords 4-Z15 or 4-Z29. This phrase recalls the intervention of Horn 2, Horn 4, and the tuba during the brass conversation in the first part of the movement. One might argue that these two phrases do not really have the same melodic outlines or even the same registers, that the first one is simply a line while the other is intimately tied to the three other horns by way of the harmonic "weight" they lend to it. Yet all the complexity and richness of the interpretation of Carter's music lie in this play of resemblance between often fleeting components; they affect the listener by leaving a trace in the memory and by giving a glimpse or perhaps only a feeling of the presence of several streams of meaning. While the dynamic progression of the timpani solo develops on one level, on the other the winds become more and more prominent. The melodic line, which stands out in the upper register and which is strengthened by homorhythmic writing (mm. 55–64), takes the shape of an arch. Starting from A♯3, it reaches its peak on G♯6 (m. 60) and then descends more jerkily until the end of this second part.

The third part (m. 67 to the end), which is shorter, is characterized by a faster tempo in both layers. The first violins play an ascending melodic line marked *cantando* that rises up to C♯7 in the upper register at the regular speed of MM 160 and then descends quickly. A counter-melody in *marcato* sixteenth notes played by the second violins and the violas (the anticipation of which has already been observed at mm. 33–35) accompanies the melodic ascent. After the melodic descent, it continues its rapid sonic flow in the violins. The slow temporal world is mainly assigned to the woodwinds. They move quite irregularly at the speed of MM 72 before they settle into longer durations. Then the brass are combined with the woodwinds to initiate a section of strong polyrhythmic agitation that leads to the piece's climax. The music reaches its full power in the following two measures, which are built up on two twelve-note chords. The first one consists of attacked chords in triplets played by the winds, while the strings, supported by the piano, harp, and vibraphone, sustain the notes of the chord. The twelve-note tutti chord sounds violently at m. 75, then fragments into the woodwinds, brass, and strings, and finally quickly dies away. A delicate sonic veil played *pianissimo* by the divided strings creates a brief moment of great serenity. This brief coda is built up of a twelve-note chord. The notes of this chord gradually die away until all that remains is a sonority reduced to four notes which make up tetrachord 4-Z15 {TE24}. As if to mark the passage of time, this static moment is speckled with a few sonic "particles" on the notes foreign to the chord (percussion 2, piano). This kind of "sonic apnea" concludes the first piece of the triptych.

Fons Juventatis

Elliott Carter has said little about the version of the *Fountain of Youth* legend that inspired him: "According to a myth that recurs in medieval French literature, Jupiter fell for the nymph Juventas (youth) and turned her into a fountain, whose waters rejuvenate all who bathe in it."[14] Carter may or may not have thought of it in relation to the piece, but when Cervantes's and More's works were being written at the beginning of the sixteenth century, the *Fountain of Youth* was indeed an object of quest. In fact, it was while searching for it that the Spanish explorer, Juan Ponce de Leon, discovered Florida in 1513. This digression allows us to note that the utopian search for an absolute or an illusion implies traveling or movement, be it real or produced by the imagination. Don Quixote is a *caballero andante*, a knight-errant, Raphael Hythloday, a navigator.[15] However,

[14] Carter, "Programme Note," in *Three Illusions for Orchestra*.
[15] In Thomas More's book, the fictional character Raphael Hythloday is a traveler-philosopher. His long description of the perfect society on the island of Utopia, which he claims to have discovered during his travels, makes up the major part of the work.

in order not to stray too far from our subject, we shall accept the common interpretation of the *Fountain of Youth* as a symbol of life, purification, rejuvenation, and – supreme illusion – immortality. In fact, the Carterian *Ultima Pratica* seems to be a metaphoric plunge into the regenerative waters. Has this not been a particularly fertile creative period for Carter, astounding all commentators with the extraordinary freshness of its compositions and spontaneity of invention? Although these qualities have always been present in Carter's music, they have never seemed so natural or accessible, if one is to judge from the way these works instantly communicate with audiences. There is often a quality of youthful mischief in these pieces. The textures, which have become ever clearer since the end of the 1970s (a time when Carter returned to vocal music), now reach a degree of both transparency and lightness which would have been difficult to imagine at the time when a massive orchestral piece like Piano Concerto (1964–65) was being composed. A taste for sonic "hedonism," hitherto restrained, is also characteristic of this later period, and in *Fons Juventatis* this contributes to the impression of the piece as a seemingly inexhaustible fountain of life. The central piece of the triptych appears as a "distraction" that may give the illusion of escaping the ineluctable end. However, the link between this and the final piece, *More's Utopia*, thwarts this illusion. As Montaigne stated, "nothing fixes a thing so intensely in the memory as the wish to forget it." If we accept the idea that there is a philosophical dimension to Carter's music, then it would be tempting to say that there is wise resignation in trying to stop the yearning for this joyful fountain by opposing it, as we will see in closer detail below, with a sound image of death. Montaigne also did say that "philosophizing is learning to die."

Let us listen to what the music of *Fons Juventatis* is telling us. The events occurring in this piece are framed by two gestures of the same nature that sound like two large anacruses (m. 1 and m. 64) and answer each other symmetrically. Accompanied by an ascending *glissando* in the harp, both gestures are a kind of sonic quivering played in the upper register by the woodwinds and strings in sixteenth-note sextuplets on a twelve-note chord. Each of these "upbeats" is associated with a tutti chord which assumes the role of a "downbeat," but in both cases this chord does not immediately follow the anacrusis but, rather, is placed at a certain distance. The brief, violent tutti chord at m. 8 answers the initial anacrusis. By closing these first eight opening measures on themselves, this first "downbeat" seems to foreshadow the inescapable drying up of the sonic source that, as has already been seen, is inscribed in the very organization of the triptych. Were *Fons Juventatis* not followed by *More's Utopia*, this punctuation might simply appear to be a means of interrupting the sonic flow, contradicting the instrumental dramaturgy in order to better reveal its vitality. This kind of procedure is frequent in Carter's music: witness the seventeen chords repeated at a constant speed at the end of *Night Fantasies* (1980), which struggle in vain to contain the successive, unrelenting musical events, or the violent chords at the beginning (mm. 6–28) of the Cello Concerto (2001) which fail to interrupt the melodic line of the solo cello. In both of these examples, as in many others, it is life itself in all of its insolent liberty which emerges victorious and is magnified by these sonic barrages. After the first "downbeat" of *Fons Juventatis*, the vital stream will, of course, continue. However, the sounding of the second "downbeat" will, in retrospect, modify the meaning of the first one. This second "downbeat" appears not at the end of the piece (which instead will end with the second anacrusis) but just beyond the final double bar, at the beginning of *More's Utopia*. There it takes the form of a sonic outburst, announcing the arrival on this musical island in the middle of nowhere, where life seems to have ceased or been suspended, petrified within sustained chords. The first "downbeat" chord in m. 8 thus has a prophetic role: it sets the music under the sign of fate, of the inexorability of death. While life seems to resist this brief interruption, we understand after hearing the "fateful downbeat" which marks the beginning of *More's Utopia* that eternal youth was only an illusion, and that our mortality was only momentarily suspended. In the eight opening measures, snatches of solos (clarinet, bass clarinet, flutes 1 and 2) and a *tremolo* are played successively by the woodwinds, horns, and strings in the middle register within a relatively restricted range. This vibration of sonic matter can be taken as a metamorphosis of the initial quivering. It is significant that these components are preceded by a sustained C5 (flutes 1 and 2, mm. 2–3); placed immediately after the initial upbeat, this sustained note suspends the music for a moment, creating here again a kind of apnea. Such a suspension is to be found again in a symmetrical position at the very end of the piece, that is, after the last breath on the notes D2 and F3 (harp, mm. 65–66).

The central body of the piece witnesses the introduction of a new and intensely expressive sound-world in which the strings evolve in principally five-voice contrapuntal writing. However, before the contrapuntal framework settles in and unfolds freely, it is suddenly interrupted by two episodes of very different character. The first episode (mm. 12–20) is none other than a proliferation of snatches of solos which had already appeared in the introduction, here played in sixteenth-note sextuplets by the woodwinds. It is worth noting that this passage moves forward through a kind of mutation of various states. First it presents rapid melodic cells that move from one group of instruments to another, covering a range from F♯2 to A♯6. Then, with the entrance of trumpets 1 and 2 (m. 17), the registers become narrower, as does the overall range which, from then on, is confined between F♮4 and C♯6. The fragments then progress more rapidly, transforming the music into a sonic flow which, scarcely begun, is already abruptly interrupted. This episode is another example of the ephemeral infiltration of traces of past experiences through the prism of a new musical project. In effect, these fragmented interventions by the instruments are no less than one of the many variants of the ongoing "Carterian discussion": this sonic flow is related to the numerous rapid *scorrevole* passages which infiltrate works such as String Quartet No. 1 (1950–51) and are especially prevalent in *Allegro scorrevole* (1996), the final piece of the triptych *Symphonia*. The second episode is divided into two sections which are also very distinct. The first section presents an agitated, unstable music, played entirely pizzicato by the strings (mm. 29–33), recalling some passages in the *Boston Concerto* (2002). In addition to the pizzicato, there are some scattered sonic remnants from the adjoining parts. The second section takes the form of a long tremolo played mainly by the winds (mm. 34–36) and also marking the return of an element already found in the introduction. The tremolos will reappear in a tutti at the end of the piece (mm. 61–64) where they will be directly linked to the last measure of the long contrapuntal layer of the strings. They thus precede the large final "anacrusis" (m. 64). These two episodes, which interrupt for some time the unfolding of the contrapuntal structure, are unexpected, one might even say dramatically inappropriate, interludes. In fact, they impose quite suddenly a climate of lightness in contrast with the expressive intensity introduced by the strings. But above all their presence gives a specific rhythmic dimension to the beginning of this central part of *Fons Juventatis*. This results from the conjunction of all aspects of opposition, whether timbral, registral, dynamic, or through different types of connection, that is, by continuous transformation or by contrast. This global interpretation of the Carterian rhythm (which precludes neither the discrete action of the polyrhythmic architectures nor the subtle relations between the tempi that hold throughout the work at all levels) is related to that employed by Boucourechliev when speaking about Beethoven: "The notion of rhythm must be extended to all the parameters involved, especially if one approaches music as a system of differences. And this to the extent that the slightest change in harmony, pitch, duration, intensity, timbre, register, attack or mass leaves a mark, a crease in the musical time."[16]

Let us now listen to the contrapuntal structure in the strings. Its first short intervention (mm. 8–12) is in itself an interpretation on the local scale of the central part's overall structure, since its continuity is interrupted twice and allows a few scattered remnants from the "interludes" to filter in. Each contrapuntal line has its own rhythm, but it is only the main voice, played by the violas followed by the violins, that moves steadily forward at the speed

---

[16] Boucourechliev, *Essai sur Beethoven*, pp. 46–47.

of MM 122.66. When the contrapuntal structure reappears (mm. 21–25) the melody played by the violins remains in the foreground. Its ambitus unfolds toward the upper register (the arrival on the highest note G♯6 is underlined by a more harmonic texture), while the constant tempo MM 122.66 is maintained. The large central contrapuntal development, which begins in mm. 37–60, is characterized by increasingly expressive intensity, driven by the principal melody which moves from one group of instruments to another. The principal melody begins with the first violins at the regular tempo of MM 184, passing then to the cellos (m. 39), where the rhythmic values stretch into more expansive phrases. When the viola takes up the melody, the numerous *marcato* sixteenth-note groups create a nervous character. Here the rhythmic irregularity of the principal melody is highlighted by contrast with the first violin line, which moves at the regular speed of MM 55.2. The cello takes over the melody (m. 50) and imposes its *cantando* style. After a general deceleration due to a lengthening of durations, the entire framework suddenly accelerates before dissolving into a broad tremolo. With its extraordinary lyricism, this contrapuntal structure contrasts with the lightness found at the beginning of the piece and makes this *Fountain of Youth* stand for the very opposite of a carefree moment. Placed at the core of the triptych, the vital flow that runs so intensely takes on an evident symbolic value. It is the painful awareness of the ephemeral character of life, of its ineluctable end that lightness had – in vain – attempted to hide.

As in many of Carter's works, the end of *Fons Juventatis* is eluded. The anacrusis which concludes the piece leaves the music in suspense, as if it would be virtually prolonged into the succeeding silence. But the "fateful downbeat" which opens the last movement of the triptych definitively removes all illusion or hope of eternal life. The effect is all the more striking because of the artificial separation of the "upbeat" and "downbeat" gestures created by the break between the two pieces. This manner of delaying an event recalls the break between the first two main parts of the String Quartet No. 1 (1951) which interrupts the "Allegro scorrevole." While the return to the real tempo in the Quartet actually underlines the vitality of the musical flow and affirms its unalterability, the break between the last two pieces in the triptych only accentuates the inevitability of death.

More's Utopia

The choice of Sir Thomas More's *Utopia* testifies to the aversion Carter has always had to all forms of totalitarianism, whatever its nature – political, religious, or even artistic. This "completely happy society with no central government, which followed draconian laws that governed almost all human activities"[17] indeed comes under the totalitarian order. Carter has not failed to notice the shortcomings of utopias, probably because he has always been aware that many of them have become the sad reality of our society. At the same time, if indeed Carter has taken an interest here in this very first communist illusion, it is only insofar as it metaphorically represents the opposite of his musical world and of the relationships he establishes between the instruments. There is no need to launch into an exhaustive analysis of *Utopia* to notice all the food for musical thought it provides; it will suffice to evoke some essential principles on which the utopian republic rests. Happiness may be envisioned only through collective action. The individual cannot indulge in solitary contemplation, even if there would appear to be the freedom to do so; the social contract exerts a diffuse pressure on the individual which constrains him to renounce contemplation in order not to live on the fringe of the community. If freedom of worship or of expression exists, it remains so limited that the individual cannot exercise it; it is the same for freedom of movement. If Carter's music is action, it is a response to the need for change, constant evolution, and freedom of movement. Whether enacted individually or collectively, this action always escapes that which would confine it within a constraining frame. Anything that falls into the category of strict repetition or which paralyzes individual initiatives is most often carefully avoided or limited. Carter's thinking constantly involves a continual give and take not only between order and disorder but also between those two states that are both contradictory and indispensable at the same time, namely action and contemplation. Each time one of these two states is imposed too strictly or for too long, instrumental particularities are emancipated and tend to the opposite.

Before we turn to the music, it would be useful to introduce an important piece of information concerning Sir Thomas More's work. Book II, in which Raphael Hythloday describes the utopian society, cannot be appreciated with the appropriate critical distance without having read Book I.[18] This first book takes the form of a complex, seemingly heterogeneous set of contradictory reflections that are interrupted, taken up, and sometimes abandoned before the end. The free-ranging discussions, inspired as much by theater as by Plato's dialogues, enable the careful reader to keep ideological excesses at bay and to better perceive the utopian world presented in Book II. In the same way, the first two pieces of the triptych are, with their differences in terms of musical content, a means of preparing the listener for the strange musical

---

[17] Carter, "Programme Note," in *Three Illusions for Orchestra*.

[18] The English humanist's critical distance appears in Raphael's family name. In effect,

Hythloday means "twaddle teller" in ancient Greek.

insularity of *More's Utopia*, in which individual expressions, multiple transformations, or "enchantments" have been banished.

More's *Utopia*'s music begins with a large sonic outburst (mm. 1–2) which
establishes an ominous climate right from the start. Its construction of three
chords piling up on one another so as to form a tutti, *fortissimo* twelve-note
chord sums up by itself most of the piece's organization. Much of the music
will in fact consist of successions of held chords forming large, slowly changing harmonies. As in the other two pieces, the harmonic fields are all built of
registrally ordered all-interval twelve-tone rows. Following the initial outburst, the percussion alone dominates for several measures, joined progressively by pitched instruments. It is as if a sound-world were in the process of
being born. A new harmonic field establishes itself as the percussion's sonorities die away (mm. 7–16). This opening section recalls the Double Concerto's
Introduction (1961), where the music gradually emerges from a chaos of
percussion. A quite similar situation can also be found at the beginning of the
opera *What Next?* (1997–98), in which, after the terrible shock of the accident
(symbolized by the percussion), the characters regain consciousness and one
after the other start singing a few words.[19] Unlike the situation in these works,
however, no individual instrument is allowed to blossom in *More's Utopia*.
Everything freezes into chords. A snatch of English horn alone manages to
stand out (m. 14). The instruments seem to be petrified in chords that are
organized like bricks, as if to form a moving sonic wall. The sonorities do not
attempt to blend together or to produce subtle mixtures of color, but most of
the time play on contrasting effects of register, dynamics, or timbres.
Expressivity is forbidden and the sonorities are cold and devoid of the
vibrations and quivering that gave *Fons Juventatis* all its liveliness. Around
the middle of the piece (mm. 25–28) an unexpected change occurs. A melodic
line can be heard, at first in the strings, which are then doubled by the
woodwinds. The writing is homophonic and the texture confined mainly to
the upper register. The melodic outline takes on the shape of an inverted arch.
Starting from A6, it slowly descends to B3 (MM 26.66) and then rises more
quickly to B6 (MM 48). Just like the anacrusis gesture at the end of *Fons
Juventatis*, the momentum gathered by this melodic rise is stopped by a new
chord which serves as a "downbeat" and re-establishes a more static music.
The latter, however, does not last long. The strength of the chords suddenly
grows and triggers a short, violent moment of agitation which leads to a tutti
chord (mm. 35–37). A stream of meaning from *Adagio tenebroso* seems to
have filtered into the music. In fact, around the end of *Symphonia*'s central

---

[19] On the connection between the Double
Concerto and *What Next?*, see Schiff,
"Keeping up with Carter," 4, and Schmidt,
"*What Next?* oder: Ein Portrait des Künstlers
als grand old man."

piece, a sonic cataclysm also occurs (mm. 271–89). In both works these "catastrophes" make us fully aware, in retrospect, of all that occurred before. The sonic surge of *Adagio tenebroso* allows one to grasp fully the slow progression of the music, while at the same time it appears as a kind of extreme, exacerbated concentration of the expressive intensity of the work as a whole. *More's Utopia*'s brief and brutal violence reveals a bleak world in which everything occurs with immutable monotony and regularity. This regularity is provided by a polyrhythmic framework that relies on three main pulses: MM 5 (mainly for the background), MM 5.33 (mainly for the chords which highlight the brass), and MM 6.42 (mainly for the strings in the upper register). As in the utopian society, the freedom of action is perfectly framed and controlled. Thus, the inverted-arch-shaped melodic line that might have appeared as an attempt at emancipation is in fact perfectly contained between two MM 6.42 pulses. Stability comes back at the end of *More's Utopia*. The instruments once again freeze into held chords which, this time, are played very softly. For a moment, time remains suspended on a *pianissimo* chord played by the strings as a short apnea recalling those heard in *Fons Juventatis*. But before the music catches its breath, a brief and ultimate *fortissimo* chord puts an end to all forms of life. This last "downbeat," which arrives with the force of a falling guillotine blade, symbolizes the shattering of all hopes and no doubt alludes to Sir Thomas More's tragic death, as he was beheaded under Henry VIII.

Three Illusions is an essential work for understanding the magnificent blossoming of Carter's *Ultima Pratica*. I have tried to demonstrate that these three miniatures contain the quintessence of Carterian thought. As in other works of this period, but with an incredible economy of means, these pieces act like filters, allowing threads of meaning from previous works to flow in and be heard in a new way. A hermeneutic approach, referring to literary sources which were important to the composer, illuminates this new hearing as long as it remains strongly rooted in the musical "reality" of the work, its coherence, and its structural originality. It is only in this way that *Three Illusions* assumes its metaphysical dimension, and can be heard as a meditation on life and death.

12 Layers of meaning: expression and design in Carter's songs

Brenda Ravenscroft

Elliott Carter's status as one of the leading musical interpreters of contemporary American poetry is unchallenged. His literary inspiration includes many of the major American poets of the twentieth century, figures such as Robert Lowell (1917–77), Hart Crane (1899–1932), John Ashbery (b. 1927), and William Carlos Williams (1883–1963). While Carter's vocal writing includes an opera and a few pieces for *a cappella* chorus,[1] he has focused his compositional interests on song cycles in which a solo voice is paired with a variety of instruments: with piano, for example in his 1994 cycle *Of Challenge and of Love*; with orchestra, as in *Of Rewaking*, his 2002 song cycle; or with chamber ensemble, for instance *In the Distances of Sleep*, composed in 2006. Most remarkably, he has not yet expressed all he has to say through the voice: in his centennial year, 2008, he added two new vocal works to his repertoire, *Poems of Louis Zukofsky* (1904–78) for clarinet and soprano, and *On Conversing with Paradise* for baritone and chamber orchestra on texts by Ezra Pound (1885–1972).

Carter's approach to text setting places the poem at the center, with the goal of the creative process to produce a work in which the meaning of the words is distilled into music. David Schiff describes it as follows:

> Carter sets a text to music in much the same way that Balanchine weds music to dance – both artists seek out material that will challenge and stimulate their own imaginations; they extend their own languages to encompass the creations of others. In Carter's settings there is no mannered, reductive rendering of the text; there are no interludes or parentheses indicating, in the tired romantic tradition, how the composer *feels* about the poems. Instead there is absolute artistic sympathy which clarifies the text for the listener.[2]

Finding the right text, one that will both inspire his imagination and allow itself to be expressed through his musical language, has not always been easy

---

[1] Early works for *a cappella* chorus include *Heart Not So Heavy as Mine* (1938), *Musicians Wrestle Everywhere* (1945), and *Harvest Home* (1937 rev. 1997). In 2007, Carter completed a vocal sextet, *Mad Regales*, setting three poems by Ashbery. In his notes for the sextet he explains that his realization of "how skillful modern choruses are ..." inspired him to return to *a cappella* choral writing. (Carter, "Composer's Notes," in *Mad Regales*.)

[2] Schiff, *MEC*, 1st edn., p. 281.

for Carter, despite his strong literary background. After focusing his early compositional efforts on vocal writing, Carter took a long hiatus from the medium for a period that lasted almost thirty years, from 1947 to 1975. When asked in 1971 about how he felt about "dealing musically with a literary text" he admitted that he found it "difficult to find a text that I would like to set to music," and went on to explain that he lacked "the time or the patience" to focus on song writing.[3] A few years later Carter did return to text setting when he received a commission from Speculum Musicae to compose a song cycle in honor of the United States Bicentennial and on the recommendation of Robert Lowell, with whom he shared a close friendship, he selected the poetry of his contemporary Elizabeth Bishop (1911–79).[4] The composition of *A Mirror on Which to Dwell*, six songs for soprano and chamber orchestra, initiated a renewed focus on song writing that continues to this day.[5]

Since Carter's interpretation of a poem lies at the core of his musical setting, it is important to understand how he selects poetry for his compositions. His attraction to a particular poet is based in part on his identification with some element or theme in the poetry that parallels a current compositional interest of his, allowing him to reflect this quality in his music.[6] Many of the poems he has chosen to set musically have undercurrents of meaning that appeal to his well-developed appreciation of irony, wit, and contradiction, allowing him to explore multiple perspectives in the music. Writing of Bishop's poetry, he notes, "I was very much in sympathy with their point of view, for there is almost always a secondary layer of meaning ... that gives a special ambiance, often contradictory, to what the words say."[7] Similarly, the "constant shifting qualities" of Lowell's poetry led him to choose it for *In Sleep, In Thunder*, while Ashbery's poetry appealed to him because of the "sardonic humor that implies a deeper undertone."[8] By exploring the technical means by which Carter expresses these layers of meaning in his songs,

---

[3] *FW*, p. 106.

[4] Schiff recounts this fact in *MEC*, p. 170. Other friendships with poets have also been artistically productive for Carter. Kramer discusses how the relationship between Carter and Ashbery influenced the composition of *Syringa* in "Song as Insight."

[5] Griffiths claims that Carter's return to vocal music also exerted an influence on his subsequent non-vocal writing. Observing that Carter's instrumental works composed after the early 1980s have a vocal quality, both in terms of their smaller scale and in their attention to lyrical linearity, he also notes that Carter started to focus his concertos on "singing instruments" such as the clarinet, oboe, and horn. See Griffiths, "'It's Full Choir of Echoes'," p. 26.

[6] After selecting a poet, Carter's creative process is to take a larger number of poems than he will ultimately need, and to explore their expressive and compositional possibilities, often working through preliminary musical settings before settling on a limited group of texts for the final work. For the *Mirror* cycle he initially selected thirteen of Bishop's poems before whittling it down to six, and there are sketches for several poems that did not survive the final cut for *In Sleep, In Thunder*.

[7] Carter, Untitled program note to the recording of *A Symphony of Three Orchestras* and *A Mirror on Which to Dwell*.

[8] Carter's comments about Lowell's poetry are included in "Program Note," in *In Sleep, In Thunder*; he describes his attraction to

we can gain insight into his compositional practices and into the process by which he "clarifies the text."

In the case of Bishop, the layers of meaning Carter mentions in his comments resonated with his contrapuntal approach to texture, whereby layers of independent lines, each with their own organizational characteristics, unfold simultaneously, and he was attracted to the expressive possibilities presented by the distinct personae depicted in her poems. His setting of "Sandpiper," the third song in the *Mirror* cycle, presents a clear example of this approach. The opening of the song establishes two linear continuities whose behaviors contrast in rhythm, pitch, and articulation, setting up the narrative framework in which the song unfolds. The oboe depicts the bird of the title running on the beach through fast (MM 525) staccato notes, while the swelling and subsiding sustained gestures in the strings and piano represent the ocean waves. The soprano, while conveying the meaning of the poem through her words, also interacts with these instrumental continuities in such a way that the voice loses its musical independence, alternatively adopting the rhythmic characteristics, interval repertoire, and articulation of the oboe when the poem focuses on the sandpiper, and emulating the contrasting rhythmic and intervallic features of the strings/piano when the poet's attention turns to the waves.[9]

The combination of structural and musically descriptive elements in "Sandpiper" exemplifies Carter's complex approach to setting texts musically, which is both deeply abstract and, at times, profoundly illustrative. Although his music is not usually thought of as representative in the sense of conventional text painting, contrary to Schiff's assertion that there is no "reductive rendering of the text," Carter frequently uses the musical surface to illustrate aspects of the text, as he does in "Sandpiper." Most often, however, his interpretation of the poem is not only reflected in surface features but also permeates the deep structure of the song, a technique Gavin Thomas refers to as "structural pictorialism."[10]

In "O Breath," for example, the last song in the *Mirror* cycle, Carter combines a compellingly descriptive musical surface with a complex underlying rhythmic scheme.[11] Characterizing the poem as being about "breathing,"

Ashbery's poetry in "Composer's Notes," in *Mad Regales.*

[9] Weston, in "Inversion, Subversion, and Metaphor," also identifies three "strands" in the song – oboe, strings/piano, and voice. His analysis focuses primarily on aspects of pitch organization. Carter's use of rhythm to shape the structure of the song "Sandpiper" and to guide his setting of the text are explored in depth in Ravenscroft, "Setting the Pace: The Role of Speeds in Elliott Carter's *A Mirror on Which to Dwell.*"

[10] Thomas, "Crashing Through the Picturesque," 286.

[11] The analytical ideas presented here are published in an expanded form in Ravenscroft, "The Anatomy of a Song." David Harvey devotes a short section of his book *The Later Music of Elliott Carter* to analysis of "O Breath," elaborating particularly on

Carter's musical setting presents two representative musical continuities: the instrumental ensemble, which proceeds with calm sustained chords that delicately swell and fade to suggest the breathing pattern of the sleeper in the poem, and the soprano, the voice of the poet, whose anxious melismatic fragments form an aural contrast.[12] Drawing on his considerable control of technical aspects in order to evoke the sleeper's steady breathing patterns as expressively as possible, Carter groups the sustained notes into intermittent gestures with characteristic pitch, registral density, and dynamic contour profiles that suggest the slow inhalation and exhalation of a sleeper (Example 12.1). However, in the same way that the sleeper has powerful yet unfathomable feelings "moving invisibly" under the distinct breaths perceptible on the surface of her skin, the music has a hidden rhythmic scheme that underlies the musical surface of sustained contour gestures. Three slow-moving pulses, projected concurrently by the instrumental ensemble, control the rhythmic organization of the entire song. Typically of Carter's music of this period, these large-scale pulses have complicated relationships to the notated meter of $\frac{12}{8}$, although they are close to each other in terms of actual speed. In Example 12.1 each staff presents one of the three pulses, measured as the distance between successive attacks, regardless of the note duration.[13] In the lowest staff the pulse is comprised of an attack every 43rd sixteenth note, articulating the speed MM 8.37, the middle staff presents a pulse with an attack every 37th dotted-quintuplet sixteenth (MM 8.11), and in the upper staff the pulse comprises attacks separated by 65 triplet-sixteenth notes (MM 8.31). Although the pulses do not start (or finish) together, the relative metric placements of their attacks and the durations for which the pitches are sustained are coordinated so that notes in the three pulses coalesce into the audible "breathing" gestures.

In addition to organizing rhythm and representing the forces beneath the sleeper's skin, Carter uses the pulses to symbolize the underlying ambiguities in the text. Although the speaker reaches a sense of reconciliation and resignation at the end of the poem, her words suggest an undercurrent of doubt that she and her lover can ever be equal partners. Symbolically, the

Carter's establishment of temporary pitch foci in both voice and instruments (pp. 65–70). Weston's analysis of "O Breath" examines the contrasting pitch, registral, and rhythmic characteristics of the song's two strands, as well as suggesting ways in which synthesis between them is achieved ("Inversion, Subversion and Metaphor," pp. 192–235).

[12] Carter's statement about "O Breath" was made during an interview in 1983: "There was a poem about breathing, for instance. I made an accompaniment which sounded like one kind of breathing, a very slow rhythm that faded in and out, and juxtaposed against it a rather hysterical kind of breathing for the singer." (Rosen, "An Interview with Elliott Carter," p. 40.)

[13] The range specified in the overall tempo indication, ♩ = 56–60, has been interpreted as 60 for the purposes of this analysis. Instrumentation is indicated next to notes, with + signs used to indicate where a new instrument enters with a pitch that doubles an already sounding pitch.

Ex. 12.1 *A Mirror on Which to Dwell*, "O Breath", mm. 1–6

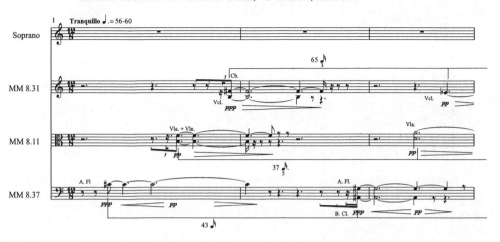

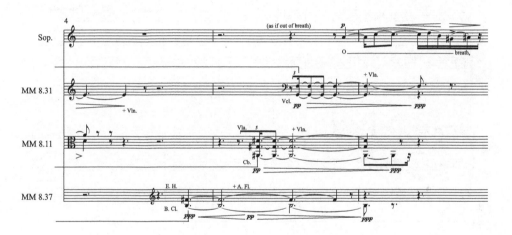

pulses converge on each other towards the end of the song – the quintuplet pulse even "overtakes" the sixteenth pulse – but they never articulate a simultaneous attack. Like the speaker and her sleeping lover, the pulses are able to become very close to each other, but can never meet. This technique – that is, the use of structural features to signify his layered reading of a poem – is arguably the most characteristic aspect of Carter's approach to text setting, and is exemplified in his setting of the opening of "In Genesis," the last song in *In Sleep, In Thunder*.[14]

The "constant shifting qualities" Carter identifies in Lowell's verse render "In Genesis" full of contradictions: God is both powerful and impotent, Eden

[14] In "Listening to the Music Itself," Sallmen provides a detailed analysis of the song, focusing primarily on pitch relationships.

Ex. 12.2 *In Sleep, In Thunder,* "In Genesis", mm. 1–8

is a place of both beauty and dreariness,[15] and the sinister act of patricide is celebrated with a suburban "cookout." Correspondingly, Carter establishes a framework that initially seems to represent the stability and perfection of a God with a scheme of the world, and then undermines it by introducing structural anomalies that disrupt the order.

Example 12.2 shows how two pulses with consistent rhythmic, pitch, and timbral attributes control the musical material in the opening of the song: one, comprising an attack every 16th eighth note (MM 11.25) is articulated by perfect-fifth dyads in the brass instruments; the other, presenting an attack

[15] Literary critic Guy Rotella elaborates on the profound effect Lowell's spiritual crisis had on his poetry, describing it as a "dual capacity for worship and desecration." See Rotella, *Castings*, pp. 46–49.

every 7th dotted-eighth note (MM 17.14), features the pitch A♭3 in the strings (often doubled by winds). Unlike the God of Lowell's poem, everything Carter does is by "design or intention," and attacks that do not conform to the two pulses are carefully placed. The first significant example occurs when the voice enters with its opening single-word sentence, "Blank." The accented attack in the tenor is carefully placed 8 eighth notes after the last pulse attack in the brass, bisecting the pulse and momentarily doubling the speed. In contrast, the belabored figure of God appears to enter randomly in m. 7, out of step with the overall rhythmic design and conforming to neither of the two pulses. Furthermore, Carter seems to be playing with our conventional notions of intervallic stability; the accented tritone B3–F3 ("with whom"), while symmetrically framing A♭3 ("God"), works against the relatively stable perfect fifths, the prominence of the "devil's interval" suggesting all is not well in the heavenly kingdom. (The phrase closes symmetrically with the tritone F3–B3 followed by G♯3.)

To further capture the contradictory quality of Lowell's poetry musically, Carter frequently sets up symmetrical or ordered pitch structures, and then deliberately subverts them. So, while the symmetrical rhythmic placement of the first tenor note, F♯3, is paralleled by its placement as the axis of symmetry in the pitch range of the vocal phrase (E♭3–A3), the choice of F♯ as the opening pitch is surprising since the other three vocal phrases all start with A♭3, or an enharmonic version thereof, and the centrality of A♭3 can easily be observed in both the voice and strings. Interestingly, all of Carter's early sketches for the song *do* set the first word "Blank" to A♭3, making the avoidance of this pitch in the final version of the song an intentional choice on Carter's part to destabilize the "natural" order.[16] A parallel example can be seen in the opening piano flourish in m. 1,[17] where the pitches would be symmetrically arranged around the axis A♭3, were it not that the opening E6 is one octave too high. Once more the implicit balanced design is undermined. A few measures later, Carter blurs the established norms in another slightly off-kilter moment: in m. 6 the string/wind pulse presents an attack in the expected position, but draws from the "wrong" pitch repertoire, articulating an A1/E2 perfect-fifth dyad instead of the expected A♭3. The "correct" pitch occurs, accented, one beat later, this time ambiguously accompanied by D♭3, a perfect fifth below. These intentional structural irregularities stand in contrast to the stability and order suggested by the large-scale pitch and

---

[16] I viewed Carter's sketches for *In Sleep, In Thunder* and *Of Challenge and of Love* at the Paul Sacher Foundation in Basel, Switzerland, in December 2004, with kind permission of the administration.

[17] The second piano gesture, m. 6, introduces a "Link chord" that becomes a central feature of the song's harmonic language; in this case the chord embeds the ATH not once but twice.

rhythmic schemes, allowing Carter to express the layer of irony implicit in Lowell's poem.

Having introduced the main features of Carter's approach to text setting using examples from songs from the mid-1970s and early 1980s, the remainder of this chapter is devoted to detailed analysis of two songs from Carter's mature period. "End of a Chapter" is the fifth song of his 1994 song cycle *Of Challenge and of Love*, for soprano and piano, and "Metamorphosis" is taken from *In the Distances of Sleep*, composed in 2006 for mezzo soprano and ensemble. Each analytical discussion starts where Carter does, with the words. After exploring the context, form, and meaning of the text, I examine Carter's reading of the poem, and elucidate the technical means by which he achieves his expressive goal of creating a musical analogy of the text.

Of Challenge and of Love: "End of a Chapter"

The last song in Carter's *Challenge* cycle, which sets texts by the American poet John Hollander, is appropriately titled "End of a Chapter." Writing in the program note for the score, Carter explains that he was "fascinated" by Hollander's poetry for many years, and notes that for the cycle he selected poems that shared "an undercurrent of irony and deep anxiety."[18] Given the brevity of the text for "End of a Chapter," which takes the form of a single prose sentence, and the simplicity of emotional tone and language, these qualities are, on first reading, difficult to discern: " . . . But when true Beauty does finally come crashing at us through / the stretched paper of the picturesque, we can wonder how we / had for so long been able to remain distracted from its absence" (ellipsis in original).

Hollander's carefully drawn distinction between the superficially picturesque and the truly beautiful suggests an aesthetic judgment, where beauty, with its associated, relatively abstract qualities of formal harmony, symmetry, and integrity of design, is valued more highly than the representational accuracy of the picturesque. Implied in this distinction is the notion that the truly beautiful is more sophisticated, more rare (it "finally" becomes apparent) and more vital (once we have become aware of its presence, we "wonder" how we could possibly have overlooked its absence "for so long"), while the picturesque is omnipresent, acting as a brittle ("paper") barrier to our recognition of beauty.

A closer reading of the poem starts to reveal some of the embedded complexities, not only formally, but also thematically. The text is composed

---

[18] Carter, "Program Note," in *Of Challenge and of Love* [score].

as a two-part complex sentence, with a dependent clause set up by the sub-
ordinating conjunction "when," followed by an independent clause. However,
the opening ellipsis implies there is missing text that precedes the sentence –
perhaps a fuller discussion about aesthetics – and the co-coordinating conjunction "But" refines this implication, suggesting that some earlier argument is
being refuted by the opinion presented in the poem. The opening of the poem
thus, retrospectively, introduces an element of underlying anxiety by suggesting
that the speaker's emphatic distinction is not an aesthetic perspective shared
by all. As we shall see later, Carter's sensitivity to this undercurrent is reflected
in his setting.

Formally, Carter's setting reflects the syntactic structure of the poem. In
addition to opening with an eight-measure piano prelude and closing with a
three-measure piano postlude, Carter inserts a six-measure piano interlude
between the two clauses of the sentence that comprises the poem, thereby
dividing the song into two parts.[19] Like the text, Carter's setting, at least on the
surface, appears to be focused primarily on clarity and simplicity, possibly
because these are qualities with which "true beauty" are associated. Certainly,
the simplicity of Hollander's words in "End of a Chapter" parallels the
directness and lucidity of Carter's musical style of the 1990s. The complexity
and density of earlier works, such as the songs in *In Sleep, In Thunder*, have
been replaced in this period by a kind of "lightness," where his familiar
musical language is presented in a condensed, almost transparent form.[20]
This is not to suggest that Carter's pitch and rhythmic vocabulary is less
sophisticated than in his works from the 1970s and '80s but rather that the
distinguishing features of his language are presented with little adornment,
the elegance of their structural design clearly revealed to the listener through
the absence of the density that characterizes his earlier works.

Compared to the songs from the *Mirror* and *Sleep* cycles, the texture of
"End of a Chapter" is greatly reduced, not only because it is scored for the
piano instead of an instrumental ensemble, but also because the piano
accompaniment is sparse to the point of starkness. The rhythmic design is
also a model of refinement, the song being organized around a polyrhythm of
two pulses in the ratio 32:27, with few non-pulse attacks clouding the
structural framework. The lower piano part presents an attack every 16th
triplet-eighth note, articulating a speed of MM 27, although initially attacks

---

[19] Since the "End of a Chapter" is only fifty
measures long, this means that one-third of
the song excludes the voice; this is an
unusually high proportion for Carter, in
whose songs purely instrumental passages are
rare.

[20] After referencing Carter's quotation of Italo
Calvino's words in the composer's program
note for *Con Leggerezza Pensosa* (1990) – the
title means "with thoughtful lightness" –
Schiff discusses the "idea of lightness" in
Carter's oboe and violin concertos in *MEC*,
pp. 29–30.

occur more frequently by being placed on even subdivisions of sixteen, such as every 4th triplet-eighth note. The second pulse, articulated by the upper piano part until the voice takes over when it enters in m. 9, comprises an attack every 9th eighth note, presenting a similarly slow speed of MM 32. The two pulses start together on the downbeat of m. 2 and proceed, almost continuously, through to the last measure, where they articulate their final attack – simultaneously.[21] The notational simplicity and the coordination of the pulses to start and finish together are characteristic of Carter's later musical style, as is his execution of a musical witticism near the end of the song. Having been entirely consistent until this point, the pulse presenting an attack every 9 eighth notes misses the expected vocal attack on the downbeat of m. 47. The absence of this attack is emphasized by the supportive silence in the piano and the pun is made explicit by the next words in the voice, "absence," which are sung accented. According to Arnold Whittall, in his 1997 review of Carter's music from the 1990s, "'play' is a privileged image for Carter and it is fundamental to the remarkably positive, optimistic tone that pervades his later compositions."[22]

The pitch repertoire in "End of a Chapter" is similarly constrained, allowing Carter to display his favored pitch structures of the mid-1990s with great clarity. As is his practice in several other songs, Carter features referential pitches: F♯4/G♭4 and G♯4/A♭4 occur prominently throughout the piece in both voice and piano, most notably in the introduction, where the piano right hand is limited almost exclusively to *tenuto* statements of G♭4 and A♭4, and in the setting of the "paper of the picturesque" (discussed later).[23] Starting in m. 35, pc 6 is articulated for the first time as G♭1 and this change seems to liberate the pc from its register; in the last measures of the song, mm. 46–50, it occurs repeatedly in the piano as F♯2/G♭2. The overall pitch content is likewise restricted in these three passages, with fixed pitch schemes controlling the registral placement of pcs. The piano introduction is particularly dramatic in this regard since, starting in m. 2, all twelve pcs are fixed in register until the

---

[21] In an early sketch for the piece, dated September 24, 1994, Carter outlines its rhythmic framework, indicating only the meter, barlines, and metrical positions of the attacks comprising the two pulses, suggesting that the rhythmic skeleton was in place before being fleshed out with pitch (sketches for *Of Challenge and of Love*, Paul Sacher Foundation).
[22] Whittall, "Summer's Long Shadows," 14.
[23] Other songs in which one or two pitches play a referential role include "Under the Dome," the second song in the *Challenge* cycle, which features a stable C5/E5 dyad in

both voice and piano, "Argument" (*Mirror* cycle), where G♯4 is repeatedly associated with "days" and B4 with "distance," and "Insomnia" (*Mirror*), in which the referential pitch C♯7/D♭7 occurs at structurally significant moments. The prominence of A♭3 in the opening of "In Genesis" was discussed earlier. I discuss referential pitches in the songs from the *Mirror* cycle in my dissertation "Texture in *A Mirror on Which to Dwell*." See also Harvey, *The Later Music of Elliott Carter*; Weston, "Inversion, Subversion, and Metaphor"; and Sallmen, "Listening to the Music Itself."

Ex. 12.3 *Of Challenge and of Love*, "End of a Chapter," opening piano chord and mm. 9–17

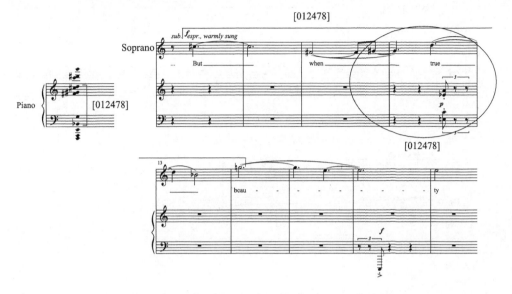

voice enters in m. 9 and initiates the introduction of new pitches. The static pitch environment of the opening, which covers a narrow registral span of nineteen semitones, allows the listener's attention to be drawn to the emerging cross-pulse and creates a sense of growing tension or anticipation, which is relieved by the singer's entry at the end of m. 9.

Carter's use of twelve-tone chords is restricted to a solitary significant articulation of an all-interval "Link" chord by the piano in the first measure of "End of a Chapter." The generous registral spacing of the chord, covering an extraordinarily wide range of sixty-six semitones, stands in marked contrast to the constrained range of the twelve fixed notes that follow it. Having introduced the all-trichord hexachord (ATH) [012478] indirectly through this chord, Carter proceeds to use the ATH as his primary means of organizing the pitch content of the song.[24] As can be seen in Example 12.3, the connection between the opening piano chord and the ATH is made explicit when the voice enters in m. 9 and articulates the *same* ATH, albeit with two pitch classes {7t} assigned to different registers. Although the piano is largely silent for this opening vocal phrase, its only notes, presented as a tetrachord in m. 12, form another example of the ATH when combined with the two vocal notes in the same measure, pcs 8 and 2.

---

[24] The focus on the ATH is consistent with Carter's approach to harmony in the 1990s. See Carter, *HB*, p. ix.

Ex. 12.4 *Of Challenge and of Love,* "End of a Chapter," mm. 33–39

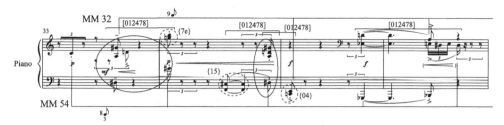

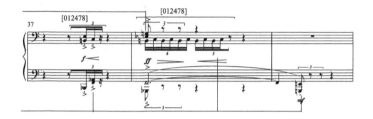

While almost every pitch in the song can be accounted for as a member of an ATH, the piano interlude from mm. 33–39 (see Example 12.4) is of special interest not only because of the clarity and intensity of its presentation of the ATH, but also because it exemplifies the sophistication of design associated with the notion of "beauty." Specifically, in this passage Carter explores the hexachord's "complement union property," in which the ATH always results from the combination of a member of the subset set-class [0167] with any [04] set-class member, provided there is no pitch-class duplication between the tetrachord and the dyad.[25] Carter introduces set-class [0167] in mm. 33–34 in the form of a piano chord {2389} (circled on the score) and subsequently proceeds to articulate three of the four possible [04] set-class members that will combine with {2389} to produce the ATH (circled with broken lines). Pitch-class set {7e} occurs in m. 34, followed by pcset {15} in the same measure, and pcset {04} occurs on the downbeat of m. 35. The fourth possibility, pcset {6t}, is omitted. Carter uses texture and rhythm to distinguish the successive presentations of the ATH, separating each statement from the next by rests, while at the same time creating continuity between consecutive chords by holding at least two pitches in common between them. D♯3/E♭3 and D4 are held invariant between the statements in mm. 34–35 and mm. 35–36, B♭1 and

[25] Morris introduced the concept of the complement union property in "Pitch Class Complementation and its Generalizations." In general, this property refers to two set-classes X and Y, for which the union of any X-class set and any disjoint Y-class set will always produce set-class Z. See also Capuzzo, "The Complement Union Property in the Music of Elliott Carter," and Roeder, "A Transformational Space for Elliott Carter's Recent Complement-Union Music."

E3 occur in statements of the ATH in both mm. 35–36 and m. 37, and F2, B2, and C3 are held in common between m. 37 and m. 38.[26]

This passage, in which the triplet-eighth-note pulse is temporarily doubled in speed from MM 27 to MM 54, also demonstrates the technical means by which Carter makes the cross-pulse explicit: pulse attacks are emphasized through a variety of means; stress accents, dynamic accents, pitch accents, and accents created by contrasting articulation.

Carter's appreciation of Hollander's distinction between beauty and the picturesque finds its musical form in his settings of these passages. Example 12.3 shows how the words "true beauty" soar above the almost silent piano accompaniment, expanding the fixed pitch-registral framework significantly for the first time, and set *subito forte* with the expressive indication "warmly sung." The rubato rhythms and use of melisma create a lyricism to the line that parallels the structural elegance discussed earlier and the near-solo voice suggests a kind of "truth," unadorned and without artifice. After the violent "crashing" from which "beauty" emerges, set *fortissimo* at the registral extremes of the song (the voice articulates its highest pitch A5), Carter's depiction of the "stretch'd paper of the picturesque" is contrastingly minimal, characterized by repetition. The voice, doling the words out syllabically to a repeating F♯4–G♯4 two-note motive, is set against sparse staccato interjections in the piano. The piano articulates only four pitches in this five-measure passage (C4–E4–F4–B4), the piano's tetrachord combining with the singer's two notes to create a single extended ("stretch'd") version of the ATH.[27] In contrast to the expansive range associated earlier with the words "beauty," the registral span of this passage is less than one octave, its meager resources suggesting the aesthetic impoverishment of the "picturesque."

Although I have discussed ways in which Carter seems to reinforce Hollander's high-minded distinction between beauty and the picturesque, his setting also suggests a sensitivity to the ambiguities in the text and a recognition of Hollander's underlying anxiety about the aesthetic issues on which the poem is focused. The overall economy of musical material, implying that beauty is to be found in simplicity, does not reconcile well with the extreme pitch limitations placed on the depiction of the picturesque, where the restrictions give rise to inelegant repetition. Furthermore, while the fixed pulse grid in which the song unfolds could be interpreted as representative of the formal harmony associated with beauty, its metaphoric significance – the music is corralled – undermines the lyrical freedom that Carter emphasizes

[26] The original score appears to have an error in the right-hand piano part of m. 38, beat 2, where the triplet beat ends with a sixteenth-note rest. The rest has been corrected to a triplet-eighth-note rest in Example 12.4.

[27] The pitch content of this passage also "repeats" earlier materials, being a subset of the opening pitch-registral scheme (the first six notes of m. 2).

when the speaker sings of beauty. And what is the meaning of the three-measure piano coda that ends the song? Articulating various combinations of only six pitches (which form an ATH) in dull, accented attacks that converge towards the final simultaneous pulse attack, the passage seems designed either to reinforce the "absence" of beauty, or to suggest, ironically, the triumph of the mundane.[28]

"Metamorphosis" from *In the Distances of Sleep*

In 2006, at the age of eighty-nine, Carter published another collection of song settings of American poems, *In the Distances of Sleep*.[29] His decision to set texts by the twentieth-century poet Wallace Stevens, a poet whom he had admired since the early 1930s, indicated that he had overcome the text-setting obstacles that had previously caused him to avoid them. Early in his career Carter had found Stevens's poems "challenging to set to music because of their quick changes of character, use of irony and employment of unusual words."[30] However, as has been discussed earlier, qualities such as irony, which invites multiple perspectives of interpretation, are ones to which Carter has been actively attracted in his more mature period. His setting of the poem "Metamorphosis" as the second song of the cycle allows us to examine the technical means by which Carter responds to and conveys the undertones embedded in Stevens's text.

On the surface, "Metamorphosis" is an autumnal poem, filled with images of the wind, night, and decay, with the themes of age and autumn conveying a dark view of the world.[31]

Formally, the poem is divided into 4 four-line stanzas. The first two stanzas are clear structural units, each ending with a statement of a month, first

---

[28] Schiff characterizes the passage as "insensitive" and suggests it serves as a reminder to the listener "not to take the words too seriously" (*MEC*, p. 168).

[29] In 1998–99, between the composition of *Of Challenge and of Love* (1994) and *In the Distances of Sleep* (2006), Carter produced another song cycle, *Tempo e Tempi*, which sets the poetry of the Italian writers Eugenio Montale (1896–1981), Salvatore Quasimodo (1901–68), and Giuseppe Ungaretti (1888–1970). The libretto of his 1998 opera, *What Next?*, is written by the Welsh music critic and scholar Paul Griffiths (b. 1947). In 2002, Carter returned once again to American texts, choosing the poetry of William Carlos Williams for his song cycle *Of Rewaking*. A subsequent short solo piece for soprano, *La*

Musique, written in 2007 to commemorate the 150th anniversary of the publication of Baudelaire's *Les Fleurs du Mal*, is a setting of a poem from that collection.

[30] [unattributed], "New Carter Song Cycle: European Premiere in London." Schiff, who studied with Carter in the 1970s, recalls that his teacher felt Stevens's poems were unsuitable for text-setting because "they lacked the requisite drama and the presence of a clear 'persona'" (*MEC*, p. 166).

[31] Lensing discusses the predominance of "poems of autumn" in Stevens's oeuvre, explaining how these poems of "departure, dislocation, and an enveloping destitution" reflect aspects of Stevens's own life in "Stevens' Seasonal Cycles," p. 120.

Ex. 12.5 "Metamorphosis" by Wallace Stevens

Yillow, yillow, yillow,
Old worm, my pretty quirk,
How the wind spells out
Sep – tem – ber . . . .

Summer is in bones.
Cock-robin's at Caracas.
Make o, make o, make o,
Oto – otu – bre.

And the rude leaves fall.
The rain falls. The sky
Falls and lies with the worms.
The street lamps

Are those that have been hanged,
Dangling in an illogical
To and to and fro
Fro Niz – nil - imbo.

"September" and then a hybrid version of October, "Oto-otu-bre," in which the Spanish for October, *octubre*, is combined with the Italian *ottobre*. However, the syntactic structure is slightly at odds with the stanzaic division in the second half of the poem. In the third stanza the repetition of "falls" connects each successive sentence in the first three lines, culminating with the collapse of the sky, which "Falls and lies with the worms." The stanza ends by introducing a new image ("street lamps") in a run-on line that disconnects it from the previous three lines and links it with the fourth stanza, driving the poem forward to its conclusion. The poem thus divides more broadly into a bipartite structure, with the clearest break occurring after the word "Oto-otu-bre," between the second and third stanzas, and subsidiary breaks occurring at the end of the first stanza and after the third line of the third stanza. While Stevens does not use any other formal devices such as end-line rhyming, his use of repetition creates sonic connections towards the end of each of the two main textual divisions. The last "o" of "make o" at the end of the third line of the second stanza ("make o" itself being a repeated phrase) is echoed at the start of the fourth line by the "O" of "Oto-otu-bre"; similarly "fro" both concludes the phrase "to and fro" at the end of the third line of the fourth stanza and is the opening syllable of the final line of the poem.

The poem describes one phase of the seasonal cycle, the progression from autumn (September, then October) to a desolate winter. The first half of the poem sets the scene: the leaves are "yillow," the word "yellow" as withered as the leaves themselves, summer is dead and decayed, and the robin has migrated to Venezuela. In the second part of the poem the inexorable progression intensifies and the poem is enlivened by the active descriptions of the process – the descent of the leaves, rain and the sky – until, finally, the grotesque "falling" of the street lamps, "hanged" and "dangling" like corpses, completes the metamorphosis into the frozen "nil" of winter.

Despite the dark and disquieting images presented in the poem, Stevens's wordplay and near-nonsense sounds suggest a witty undercurrent that undermines the poem's serious tone.[32] Opening with the transformed version of the color yellow, "yillow," the robin's cheerful chirping, "make o, make o, make o," contrasts with the wind's moaning lament, and leads us to the comically fabricated month, "Oto-otu-bre." The poem concludes with pure invention, "Fro Niz-nil-imbo," suggesting in turn the words frozen, nil and limbo (and, perhaps, November). There is little doubt the humorous undertone would have appealed to Carter, a speculation supported by the surface features of his musical setting in which there is a notable absence of heaviness. The expressive indication *Leggierissimo*, the prevalence of staccato articulation, the very soft dynamic levels, and the high registral placements of the instruments – two flutes, alto flute in G, marimba, and strings (with cello and bass playing harmonics) – all conspire to create the droll undertone of the song. Because the instruments play high in their high registers, the lowest pitches and darkest tone often fall to the mezzo soprano; this unusual arrangement is reminiscent of "Insomnia" (*Mirror* cycle), where the placement of the soprano below the accompanying piccolo, marimba, violin, and viola helps to suggest the inverted world described by the singer.

Carter's setting parallels the formal structure of the poem, with the most significant musical changes occurring halfway through the song, between the second and third stanzas, and the final musical unit incorporating the fourth, run-on line of the third stanza with the fourth stanza. Just as the first two stanzas describe the landscape in which the events of the second half of the poem unfold, Carter uses the first half of the song to depict the autumnal scene musically and to establish the structural features of the song. Most notably, the first part of the song is dominated by sounds suggesting the wind that heralds the transformation from autumn into winter. In the setting of the first stanza, fast rhythmic figurations in the wind instruments, each with its own individual speed, present sinuous chromatic passages that usually span only a third, helping to depict the swirling winds of the opening, while sustained harmonics in the cello and bass, slowly mutating through semitonal shifts, add a high whine of lament to the overall texture. The voice, while set

---

[32] Lensing goes further, suggesting that "Metamorphosis" "seems in almost every line to be nudging us in the ribs and making jokes." See *Wallace Stevens and the Seasons*, p. 111.

Table 12.1 *In the Distances of Sleep,* "Metamorphosis"

Instrument	Figuration	Speed	Ratio
Flute 1	sextuplet-sixteenth notes	MM 648	6
Flute 2	quintuplet-sixteenth notes	MM 540	5
Alto flute in G	sixteenth notes	MM 432	4
Mezzo soprano	triplet-eighth notes	MM 324	3

apart from the winds and strings through its slightly higher dynamic levels (*p* rather than *pp*), distinctive timbre, and pitch attributes (discussed below), also participates in the overall rhythmic scheme. Although the voice's attack density is considerably less than those of the wind instruments, its rhythmic profile is also based on a consistent underlying subdivision or speed relative to the overall tempo of ♩ = 108. (Both the vocal speed and the overall tempo remain constant throughout the song.) Linear characters in the opening are thus defined primarily by the speed of the rhythmic figuration, as presented in Table 12.1. The marimba does not participate in the descriptive scene-setting, but proceeds with isolated chords and dyads.

The division of the texture into distinct linear entities, each with specific rhythmic and pitch attributes, recalls the kind of complex layering Carter used in earlier works such as the songs in the *Mirror* cycle. In "Metamorphosis" the three wind instruments cohere into a multi-strata layer; the strings, while distinct from the winds in rhythmic behavior, share their chromatic pitch structure and serve the same musical function; and the voice, although connected to the winds through its underlying rhythmic structure, is independent in function and associated more closely with the marimba through pitch.

Against the largely chromatic backdrop of the opening, pitch organization in the voice and marimba is focused on Carter's favorite chords from his later period, the ATH, and two of its subsets, the all-interval tetrachords (AITs) [0146] and [0137]. As in the other songs in the cycle, these chords act as referential harmonies without controlling the pitch material exclusively. Example 12.6, which reproduces the first fifteen measures of the marimba and voice, shows that in addition to the repeated use of the ATH and the two AITs Carter creates harmonic unity by linking unrelated materials through common trichordal and dyadic subsets, particularly interval class (ic) 5, which is usually articulated as a perfect fourth (P4). The first vocal phrase in m. 3, which features an opening P4 interval as part of the non-ATH set class [012467], is strongly connected to the second phrase in mm. 4–5 by holding five pitch classes in common, four of which occur in the same register (E4–B♭4–D5–F5), as well as through the spatial layout of the ATH in mm. 4–5, which emphasizes ic5 through the perfect-fifth intervals that

Ex. 12.6 "Metamorphosis," mm. 1–15

open and close the vocal phrase and the isolated P4 in the marimba. The rising P4 of "spells out" in the voice of m. 7 is answered by the falling P4 of mm. 8–9, which is unconnected to either the ATH or the AITs and echoed in the marimba's dyadic articulation of the ATH in m. 9.[33] Other trichordal gestures in mm. 13–14 – [025], [016], [026] – connect the marimba's non-ATH material to the ATH through their common subset structure.[34]

Although the pitch and rhythmic behaviors of the voice and marimba remain consistent for the first half of the song, changes occur in the pitch organization of the wind instruments at the start of the second stanza, identifying this moment as a subsidiary structural break and helping to depict the progression from September to October. Instead of chromatic passages, the fast figurations in the wind instruments expand to take the form of intermittent gestures featuring wide intervallic leaps, suggesting musically a more forceful wind blowing the season forward.

---

[33] There are many other instances of P4 dyads being emphasized through the spatial organization of the marimba's notes, for example in mm. 11–12.

[34] In "'Linking' and 'Morphing'," Boland focuses on the techniques by which Carter connects non-ATH harmonic material to the referential ATHs.

Ex. 12.7 "Metamorphosis," mm. 1–15, pitch interdependence

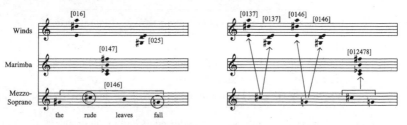

In the second half of the song significant changes in the overall texture and variations in the rhythmic and pitch organization parallel the changes that occur in the second part of the poem. Transformations in the established behaviors of the instruments reflect, in a general sense, the process of metamorphosis portrayed in the poem but, paradoxically, as the poet's attention turns to more direct descriptions of the autumnal events using active verbs – falling, lying, dangling – Carter assigns a more abstract role to the ensemble. Rather than continuing to set the scene musically by depicting the windy turmoil of autumn, the ensemble now conveys the composer's understanding of the underlying mood or tone of the poem. Two passages are particularly instructive in this regard and each elucidates the technical means by which Carter realizes his expressive intentions.

The start of the third stanza presents a striking contrast to the earlier, more active section. Sustained pitches replace the high-density rhythmic activity in the winds, and the strings are silent except for a brief mournful passage as "the sky falls." In the last phrase, "and lies with the worms," the voice is accompanied only by isolated attacks in the marimba with two brief interjections on a high-pitched metal pipe. The expansiveness of the setting enhances a sense of suspended motion: while the durations of the first two stanzas are seven and six measures respectively, the first three lines of the third stanza unfold over ten measures. The stillness and sparseness of the setting, perhaps presaging the frozen immobility of winter, conveys a tone of sadness and loss.

The textural cooperation and absence of rhythmic differentiation in this passage is matched by a new interdependence between instruments in terms of pitch structure. Example 12.7 reproduces the pitch content of an especially economical segment. The system to the left shows that while the voice presents a complete statement of the AIT [0146], the other instruments articulate incomplete versions of AITs and the AHT: trichords [016] and [025] in the winds and tetrachord [0147] in the marimba. As is characteristic of Carter's late practice, all three chords are "completed," some in multiple ways, when combined with the two most prominent pitches in the vocal line,

Table 12.2 "Metamorphosis," pulse streams

Instrument	Duration between attacks	Pulse speed
Flute 1	5 sixteenth notes	MM 86.4
Marimba	7 sixteenth notes	MM 61.7*
Flute 2	9 sixteenth notes	MM 48
Alto flute in G	11 sixteenth notes	MM 39.3

*The marimba's pulse was foreshadowed earlier; in the setting of the phrase "Falls and lies with the worms" successive attacks are separated by 7 sixteenth notes.

pcs 1 and 7.[35] The system to the right in Example 12.7 shows how grouping pc 1 with the both the first and second wind trichords yields statements of AIT [0137], while the addition of pc 7 to each trichord creates different versions of the [0146] AIT. Similarly, grouping pcs 1 and 7 with the marimba tetrachord gives rise to a full statement of the ATH.

A second passage – the last five measures of the song – exemplifies Carter's appreciation of underlying irony in Stevens's text and shows him drawing on new rhythmic resources for his setting of the final phrase of the poem. As the poem describes the inevitable decline into the frozen stasis of winter, the music, rather than sustaining the elegiac tone suggested earlier, reverses its energy and starts to come to life. The phrase "Fro Niz-nil-imbo" is set to accented *forte* attacks in the voice and is accompanied by similarly accented attacks in the winds and marimba.[36] Moreover, the music literally pulses with vitality; each instrument presents a different pulse, as can be seen in Table 12.2, with the pulses coordinated to finish with a simultaneous *fortissimo* attack on the downbeat of the final measure.

The coalescing of these emerging pulses helps to drive the song to a climactic end, as well as to emphasize the tone of defiance that Carter seems to read into the poem, an interpretation possibly drawn from the use of a nonsense final word at the moment of culminating darkness. The song thus ends with angry resistance rather than resignation and fatalistic acceptance of the ultimate decline into winter, invoking Dylan Thomas's challenge to the inevitability of death, "do not go gentle into that good night."

In an interview published in 1990, Carter described his approach to setting texts: "I wanted to explore the way one could suggest things that were in the poem, emphasize certain details, evoke its general ambiance – but also to

[35] Their prominence results from their positions as the highest and lowest pitches of the phrase.

[36] The cello and bass resume their sustained harmonics in the fourth stanza, recalling the opening of the song and implying the cyclical nature of the seasons.

make counter-suggestions against its contents, and so forth."[37] Two decades later, his approach remains unchanged and his late songs are rich with detail and nuance. If anything, as we have seen in the analyses above, his appreciation of the layers of meaning in the texts he sets – the ambiguities and paradoxes embedded in the words – has deepened and his expressive range has intensified while the technical means by which he achieves his expressive goals have become more economical.

Elliott Carter recently completed a new song cycle, *What are Years*, on poems by Marianne Moore (1887–1972) scored for soprano and ensemble. The cycle was premiered at summer festivals in 2010. The last line of the title poem "What are Years" offers not only a classic example of the kind of contradiction to which Carter is drawn in the poems he chooses but also a poignant allusion to the limits of the aging composer's own life and to the enduring nature of the remarkable music he has given us: "This is mortality, / this is eternity."

[37] Bernard, "An Interview with Elliott Carter," 187.

13   Text, music, and irony in *What Next?*

Guy Capuzzo

Introduction

Carter's opera *What Next?* (1997–98; Paul Griffiths, libretto) abounds with irony. Nowhere is this clearer than in the character of Kid, the sole child among the six characters. At first blush, Kid, a twelve-year-old boy, may appear to play only a minor role in the opera. Kid stands in no clearly defined relation to any of the five adults – indeed, none of them knows who Kid is.[1] His singing role is minimal, confined to a few short phrases and a four-measure soletto toward the end of the work. Further, Kid remains silent at several crucial junctures, including episode 2, "Everyone makes a statement," and episodes 32–35, in which the adults attempt to cooperate in hopes of being rescued from the opera-opening accident.

The irony behind this is that Kid *does* play an important role in *What Next?*.[2] Although he is unknown to the other characters, rarely sings, and is silent at crucial junctures, the music associated with him adds layers of irony to the opera. This chapter studies the role of Kid to explore how Carter and Griffiths impart dramatic significance to a terse, anonymous character, thus clarifying the interaction of text and music in *What Next?*. I shall use a repeating all-interval tetrachord, $X = \{C4, D4, F\sharp4, B4\}$, as a point of departure for the study of text–music relations in episodes 10–14, in which the other characters all attempt to interact with Kid on stage. The focus on X throws light on several key aspects of the opera: the role of irony, which Carter himself emphasizes; the emotional distance between the five adults and Kid; and how each adult deals with the aftermath of the accident. The relationship between X, Kid, the English horn, and the adults assumes a number of musically suggestive guises.

---

[1] In his libretto for *What Next?*, Griffiths provides a brief description of the opera's general situation in the voice of each adult character. Mama's statement reads in part, "I don't know who Kid is." In episode 22, Rose, referring to Mama, asks Kid, "That woman – is she your mother?"

[2] In the present study, I am most interested in the following aspects of irony, as defined by the *Oxford English Dictionary*: "A condition of affairs or events of a character opposite to what was, or might naturally be, expected; a contradictory outcome of events as if in mockery of the promise and fitness of things."

Most published work on *What Next?* addresses the opera's formal design and general features, and is not analytic in nature.[3] An exception is Anne Shreffler's "Instrumental Dramaturgy as Humane Comedy: *What Next?* by Elliott Carter and Paul Griffiths." Shreffler's commentary on the vocal music of mm. 454–60 demonstrates her claim that *What Next?* "permits the creation of musical irony to an extent that would not be possible in an instrumental work."[4] The present chapter builds on Shreffler's article and the research cited in note 3, offering close readings of several extended passages in *What Next?*. In contrast to Shreffler's analyses, which address vocal music only, I shall devote particular attention to the interaction of singing with instrumental music. More broadly, the present chapter forms a point of contact with recent studies of text–music relations in Carter's music, as well as irony in twentieth-century opera.[5]

Preliminary information about *What Next?*

Examples 13.1 to 13.3 serve to orient the reader to the basic dramatic, formal, and pitch features of *What Next?*. Because the writings cited above cover much of this information, I shall present the material in synoptic form. The reader is urged to consult the aforementioned sources for further insights into the opera.

I begin with descriptions of *What Next?* by Griffiths and Carter. Griffiths describes the opera's general situation as follows:

> There has been an accident. Of the six "victims," all quite unhurt as far as we can see, the five adults have *different views* of how they are related and how they have come to be in the same place at the same time [emphasis added].[6]

I have italicized the words "different views" because they highlight an essential feature of both Griffiths's libretto and Carter's music, one that dates back to String Quartet No. 2, if not earlier: what David Schiff calls "polyvocality."[7] Carter's liner notes, reproduced here in their entirety, nicely complement Griffiths's remark:

---

[3] Schmidt, "*What Next?* oder: Ein Portrait des Künstlers als grand old man"; Noubel, *LTF*, pp. 246–57; Schiff, "Keeping Up with Carter"; Griffiths, "Before *What Next?*"; Meyer and Shreffler, *ECCP*, pp. 302–09; Whittall, "A Play of Pure Forces."

[4] Shreffler, "Instrumental Dramaturgy," p. 160.

[5] Recent studies of text–music relations in Carter's music include Ravenscroft, "Finding the Time"; Sallmen, "Listening to the Music Itself"; Griffiths, "Its Full Choir of Echoes"; and Ravenscroft's and van Dyck-Hemming's contributions to the present volume. On irony in twentieth-century opera, see Rupprecht, *Britten's Musical Language*, pp. 209–15.

[6] Griffiths, libretto for *What Next?*.

[7] Schiff, *MEC*, pp. 25–27.

Ex. 13.1 *Dramatis personae* (Griffiths); relations among characters

Dramatis personae (Griffiths)

ROSE	A bride and a performer, late twenties (soprano)
MAMA	A mother and much else, late forties (soprano)
STELLA	An astronomer, indeterminate (contralto)
ZEN	A supposed seer and not much else, late forties or older (tenor)
HARRY OR LARRY	A bridegroom and a clown, early twenties (baritone)
KID	A boy, twelve (boy alto)

Relations among characters

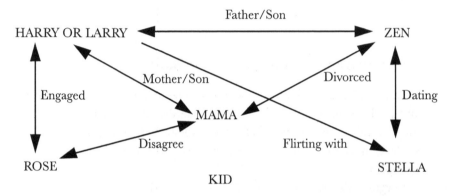

Ex. 13.2 Form

1	2	3	4	5	6	7	8	9
Sextet	Quintet	Quartet	Solo	Duet Apart	Trio Apart	Solo	Duet Apart	Solo Plus Soletti

10	11	12	13	14	15	16	17	18	19
Solo	Solo	Solo	Solo	Solo	Solo	Trio	Duet Apart	Quintet	Mute (Interlude)

20	21	22	23	24	25	26	27	28
Quartet	Quartet	Soletti And Solo	Solo	Duet Apart	Solo	Quintet	Duet Apart	Soletto Plus Solo

29	30	31	32	33	34	35	36	37	38
Soletto Plus Solo	Duet Together-Apart	Sextet	Solo	Trio	Solo	Duet Together	Soletto	Quintet	Solettto

Titles of episodes 10–14:

10: "Mama tries to explain"
11: "Zen tries not to explain"
12: "Rose tries to explain"
13: "Harry or Larry does not try to explain"
14: "Stella cannot explain"

Ex. 13.3 All-interval tetrachords and their combinations in *What Next?*

[0146]+[0146]	[01236789]
	[02345679]
	[01345689]
[0137]+[0137]	[01236789]
	[02345679]
	[01345689]
[0146]+[0137]	[0134679T]
	[01234569]
	[0134578T]
	[0124678T]*

*[0146] ⊂ [012478] ⊂ [0124678T]
*[0137] ⊂ [012478] ⊂ [0124678T]

> When I decided to accept a commission for an opera from the Berlin Staatsoper conducted by my friend, Daniel Barenboim, I wanted to present a contemporary subject of wide concern. Seeing Jacques Tati's movie *Trafic*, I realized that an automobile accident (or some other accident) could be such a subject. I discussed a possible libretto with Paul Griffiths and how to treat the subject somewhat *ironically* and *humanly*. He invented quite sharply defined different characters so necessary for a work that has its only real event happen as the curtain rises [emphasis added].[8]

I have italicized the words "ironically" and "humanly" to draw attention to two additional long-standing aspects of Carter's music: irony and a preoccupation with human interaction.[9] Example 13.1 reproduces Griffiths's presentation of the *dramatis personae*[10] and offers my interpretation of the main relations among the opera's characters in the form of a network.[11] Mama's placement at the center of the network reflects her close connection to three of the five remaining characters – Mama is Harry or Larry's mother, Zen's former wife, and Rose's future mother-in-law. By contrast, Kid's placement at the bottom of the network, combined with the absence of arrows pointing to or issuing from him, graphically represents his isolation. While there are many sensible paths to navigate through the network, I shall provide one possibility: Mama and Zen are divorced; Zen is Harry or Larry's father and is dating Stella;[12] Harry or Larry is Mama's son and Rose's fiancé but he flirts with Stella; Rose and Mama do not get along. The double-headed arrows in

[8] Carter, liner notes for *What Next?*.
[9] Carter's brief article "Mozart's Human Touch" elaborates on Carter's interest in human interaction; see also Shreffler, "Instrumental Dramaturgy as Humane Comedy," pp. 148 ff. Several of Carter's vocal works contain program notes in which he emphasizes the role of irony, including "Quatrains from Harp Lake" from *Of Challenge and Of Love*. Irony plays a role in Carter's conception of his instrumental music as well; he describes the Duo for Violin and Piano as "a series of ironic interactions" (Schiff, *MEC*, p. 120).
[10] Griffiths, libretto for *What Next?*.
[11] Example 13.1 is modeled on a similar network in Buchler, "Dramatic Oppositions."
[12] In Griffiths's libretto for *What Next?*, Mama states, "Stella is presumably [Zen's] current girlfriend."

the network indicate reciprocal relations; the single-headed arrow issuing from Harry or Larry and pointing to Stella indicates that Harry or Larry's romantic overtures to Stella go unrequited. For instance, in episode 3, Harry or Larry kisses Stella and says "There you go, honey," to which Stella responds, "Who?," with the stage direction "outraged." Later, in episode 37, Harry or Larry says, "I love you, Stella," to which Stella responds, "Piss off." One reason for Harry or Larry's romantic interest in Stella may be Rose's pregnancy; Harry or Larry is likely the father of Rose's child and, in keeping with his character, is dodging the responsibilities of fatherhood by turning to Stella. Two lines support the idea that Harry or Larry is the father of Rose's child: "Don't call me Daddy" (Harry or Larry, episode 3), and an exchange in episode 37: "Rose is pregnant" (Stella), "Rose, is that true?" (Mama), "You know your son" (Rose), "What does that mean?" (Harry or Larry), "Means what it says" (Rose), "Pregnant" (Stella).

Example 13.2 situates episodes 10–14 within the context of the opera's complete formal design. Prompted by Kid's line "A big Mac" at the close of episode 9, the adults direct their attention to Kid during episodes 10–14, which form the longest stretch of consecutive solos in the opera. While episode 15 is also a solo, its text distinguishes it from the prior solos, as does its title, "Mama looks back." By contrast, episodes 10–14 share similar titles (which appear in the libretto but not the score): "Mama tries to explain," "Zen tries not to explain," "Rose tries to explain," "Harry or Larry does not try to explain," and "Stella cannot explain." For this reason, I shall refer to episodes 10–14 as the "explanation episodes." We shall see that the qualifiers "tries to," "tries not to," "does not try to," and "cannot" provide significant clues to each character's personality. During the explanation episodes, each adult walks over to Kid (as per the stage directions), addresses him directly, waits for a reply, and is answered not by Kid's singing voice, but instead by the English horn in a brief orchestral interlude.

Turning to the larger formal plan of the opera, the thirty-eight episodes ostensibly form a symmetrical nineteen plus nineteen design due in large part to the orchestral interlude at episode nineteen. Typical of Carter, however, the apparent symmetry of the opera's formal design accords neither with the duration of the episodes nor with the distribution of the opera's dramatic and rhetorical weight. For this reason, I do not regard the form of *What Next?* as symmetrical.[13]

The pitch language of *What Next?* is largely based on the set classes in Example 13.3. The use of all-interval tetrachords, the all-trichord hexachord,

---

[13] On the form of *What Next?*, see Schiff, "Keeping Up with Carter," 4; Schmidt, "*What Next?* oder: Ein Portrait des Künstlers als grand old man," pp. 168–71; and Shreffler, "Instrumental Dramaturgy as Humane Comedy," p. 156.

and combinations of all-interval tetrachords into octachords is common in Carter's music.[14] The notation "[0146]+[0146]" indicates that a pitch-class set (pcset) from set class [0146], combined with a second, non-overlapping pcset from [0146], yields a pcset from [01236789], [02345679], or [01345689]. The second row works similarly, substituting [0137] for [0146]. The third row's notation "[0146] + [0137]" indicates that a pcset from [0146], combined with a non-overlapping pcset from [0137], yields a pcset from a different group of octachords, namely [0134679T], [01234569], [0134578T], or [0124678T]. The asterisk to the right of [0124678T] indicates that this octachord is the only one present that includes Carter's signature all-trichord hexachord [012478] as a subset. It thus admits of the two possibilities shown at the bottom of the example, each indicated with an asterisk. First, as indicated by the symbol ⊂, a pcset from [0146] can act as a subset of [012478]. Then, a pcset from [012478] can act as a subset of [0124678T]. Second, a pcset from [0137] can perform the same function as [0146]. Carter exploits this property of [0124678T] throughout *What Next?*, distinguishing [0124678T] from the other octa-chords in the example.[15] Two closing points about Example 13.3 are in order. First, the relative anonymity of integer notation should not mask the fact that several of these octachords are well known: [0134679T], the ubiquitous "octatonic collection," is equivalent to Messiaen's second mode of limited transposition; [01236789] is equivalent to Messiaen's fourth mode of limited transposition; and [0124678T] is equivalent to Messiaen's sixth mode of limited transposition.[16] Second, the set classes in Example 13.3 work in tandem with, not independently of, the pitch-interval assignments of each character's vocal line: Zen favors "small" intervals such as 1, 2, 3, 4, and 5; Rose favors "large consonant" intervals such as 7 and 10 in addition to Zen's 4; Stella favors "large dissonant" intervals such as 6 and 11; Harry or Larry favors small intervals and the large 8; Mama draws freely from all intervals; and Kid's singing role in the opera is minimal, such that no distinctive interval profile emerges for him.[17] However, I shall demonstrate that Kid's melodies rely heavily on X and its transformations.

[14] Carter, *HB*, pp. 31–32; Schiff, *MEC*, p. 241.
[15] Jenkins, "After the Harvest: Carter's Fifth String Quartet and the Late Late Style," analyzes passages from Carter's quartet that involve [0146], [0137], [012478], and [0124678T].
[16] Messiaen, *Technique de mon langage musical*.
[17] Whittall, "'A Play of Pure Forces'?," 9, and Shreffler, "Instrumental Dramaturgy as Humane Comedy," pp. 159–60, discuss each character's interval repertoire. Roeder, "Voice Leading as Transformation," pp. 54–57, develops the idea of small, medium, and large categories to analyze interval assignments in Carter's music. See also Heinemann, "Composition with Intervals: Melodic Invention in Elliott Carter's Recent Concertos," in the present volume.

First pass

I shall make two passes through the explanation episodes. The first pass is an overview, where I focus on X = {C4, D4, F♯4, B4}, its transformations, and its function as a formal "frame."[18] X first appears in episode 10, where the adults take turns explaining the accident to Kid. Griffiths describes Kid as a "foil" to the adults: "Kid is too young to be playing games, so he's a kind of foil."[19] As stated earlier, none of the adults knows Kid, and Kid does not sing during these episodes. Instead, X gives voice to Kid, who comes to represent the objective reality of the accident. As such, the silent child stands in contrast to the singing adults. Two features of X draw attention to it: the fixed pitches (not just fixed pcs) {C4, D4, F♯4, B4}, and the fact that the English horn typically performs X. In all, X grants Kid a musical presence that adds a layer of irony to the explanation episodes.

Example 13.4a presents the first pass, showing X and its transformations in a block-chord reduction. Round note-heads indicate the fixed interval class (ic) 6 {C4, F♯4}, while triangular note-heads indicate the changing ic 3s. Transformations of X involve holding the ic 6 {C, F♯} and transposing the ic 3 {B, D} to any ic 3 that does not overlap with {C, F♯}. Because {C, F♯} holds from chord to chord, X_n indicates the T_n transposition of the ic 3 only. For instance, T_9 maps the ic 3 {B, D} in X onto {G♯, B} in X_9. I shall refer to T_n transpositions of X as the "X_n tetrachords."[20] While pcs C and F♯ always appear as the pitches C4 and F♯4 in Example 13.4a, transformations of X in later examples retain pcs C and F♯ but do not always retain the pitches C4 and F♯4. Carter's realization of the four bracketed chords at the end of Example 13.4a appears in Example 13.4b.

Two aspects of Example 13.4a are significant. First, the transformations of X at the beginnings of episodes 12 and 14, with their new ic 3s, forecast the highly subjective (even skewed) explanations of the accident to be given in those episodes by Rose and Stella, respectively. This is not to say that Rose and Stella are less grounded in reality than Mama, Zen, and Harry or Larry. But the divergence of X_n tetrachords in Rose's and Stella's explanation episodes corresponds with Griffiths's episode titles: "Rose tries to explain" (but perhaps cannot), and "Stella cannot explain." As explanations diverge from reality,

[18] The notion of framing in connection with Carter's music is original with Schiff, *MEC*, 1st edn, p. 153, and Lochhead, "On the 'Framing' Music of Elliott Carter's First String Quartet." See also Cone, *Musical Form and Musical Performance*, pp. 14 ff.

[19] Mayer, Interview with Paul Griffiths.

[20] In the present chapter, transpositions of sets other than X_n tetrachords (and Y_n tetrachords, discussed below) work in the normal manner, with *every pc* transposed by n. Capuzzo, "The Complement Union Property in the Music of Elliott Carter," and Childs, "Structural and Transformational Properties of All-Interval Tetrachords," present other contextual transformations for all-interval tetrachords.

Ex. 13.4a First pass: X and its transformations in episodes 10–14

Round noteheads: Fixed ic 6 {C, F#}
Triangular noteheads: Changing ic 3s
X_n: T_n transposition of the ic 3 only

Ex. 13.4b Carter's realization of the bracketed chords in Ex. 13.4a

the X_n tetrachords diverge from {C4, D4, F♯4, B4}. Second, through their placements at the beginnings and endings of episodes, the tetrachords in Example 13.4a perform a framing function, as a frame surrounds a picture, but allowing for interplay between the chords and the music they surround. The "framing chords" provide an ironic commentary on the singing that occurs within them – no matter what an adult sings, X or an X_n tetrachord gets the first word, last word, or both. This is one sense in which Kid, represented by X and the X_n tetrachords, acts as a foil to the adults as per Griffiths.

The non-overlapping pairings of ic 6 and ic 3 in Example 13.4a suggest the compositional space in Example 13.5.[21] The central node of the space

---

[21] The space is a subset of one in Morris,
"Compositional Spaces," 345.

Ex. 13.5 Compositional space suggested by Ex. 13.4a

Box = present in Example 13.4a

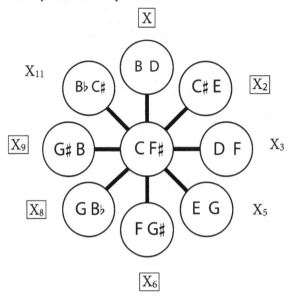

houses the fixed ic 6, while the outer nodes house every possible non-overlapping ic 3. The union of the central node with any outer node is a pcset from [0146] or [0137]; the union of all the outer nodes is a pcset from [0134679T]. The space embeds two subspaces. Each subspace consists of a clockwise T_3 cycle formed by every other outer node (or a counterclockwise T_9 cycle formed by every other outer node). The first subspace contains X, X_3, X_6, and X_9. The second subspace contains X_2, X_5, X_8, and X_{11}. Alternately, each subspace may be viewed as two pairs of T_6-related outer nodes. For instance, the first subspace contains X and X_6, which relate by T_6, as well as X_3 and X_9, which also relate by T_6. Similarly, the second subspace contains X_2 and X_8, as well as X_5 and X_{11}. Viewing the Example 13.5 space as the union of two subspaces, each generated by T_3/T_9 and T_6, points to the origin of the T_3, T_6, and T_9 transformations that attain significance in the score and my analyses.[22] While the framing chords in Example 13.4a do not use every tetrachord in the space, episodes 10–14 do. The space thus represents a compendium of harmonic possibilities that Carter draws on.

---

[22] The present chapter thus exhibits the influence of Lewin's analysis of Debussy's *Feux d'Artifice*, in which particular transpositions and inversions attain substantial analytic significance. See Lewin, *Musical Form and Transformation*, pp. 97–159 (particularly pp. 106 and 109–12).

Ex. 13.6 "Mama tries to explain"

Second pass

The second pass through episodes 10–14 offers detailed analytic sketches that rely on two guiding principles: (1) Transformations of X attain dramatic significance; (2) The space in Example 13.5 interacts with text–music relations. Two features are new to the second pass: X obtains a partner Y; and Z, the union of X and Y, gains prominence. I shall also offer general observations regarding text–music relations specific to each episode. The sketches are selective and illustrative rather than exhaustive; they provide one lens through which to observe Carter's treatment of text and music in the episodes. In this regard, the second pass is akin to writings that focus on one feature of a composition, such as motivic activity, rather than aspire to an overarching analytic account.[23]

Example 13.6 reproduces the voice part from the end of episode 10, "Mama tries to explain." As before, round note-heads indicate the fixed dyad {C, F♯}, while triangular note-heads indicate the changing ic 3s. The excerpt is an attempt by Mama to sing X = {C4, D4, F♯4, B4}. The shifting ic 3s that set "Yes, something strange has happened to us" portray her inability to explain the accident to Kid. Carter's setting of "We're not going to let that bother us,

---

[23] Schachter, "Motive and Text in Four Schubert Songs" is exemplary in this regard.

Ex. 13.7 Framing function of Z

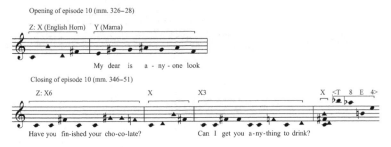

are we?" replaces the fixed ic 6 {C, F♯} with {E♭, A}. This suggests a second, more serious failure on Mama's part to maintain contact with reality: we expect the ic 3 to change, but not the fixed ic 6. With "Have you finished your chocolate?" and "Can I get you anything to drink?," Mama comes closer to X by restoring {C4, F♯4}. The statements of X that follow these last two efforts by Mama to comfort Kid create an ironic effect by interrupting her and flaunting the {B, D} ic 3 that she seeks to sing. While Kid does not respond to the questions Mama directs at him, X and the English horn give voice to Kid by "answering" Mama's questions.

The episode closes with T_6, T_3, and T_9 transformations from X_6 to X to X_3 to X, answered by a new all-interval tetrachord, $\langle T8E4 \rangle$. Taken together, X_6, X, X_3, and $\langle T8E4 \rangle$ create a pcset from [0124678T] that figures prominently in the explanation episodes. I shall label this octachord Z; it contains pcs {024568TE}. Example 13.7 reveals that Z appears not only at the close of episode 10, but at the opening as well. The episode opens with X in the English horn, C4–B4–D4–F♯4. This statement of X shares three pitches with Kid's phrase "A big Mac" at the close of episode 9 (D4–B4–F♯4), strengthening the association of X, Kid, and the English horn. Mama then sings the remaining pcs of Z in the following measure, which I shall label as Y = {458T}. The union of X and Y is Z. The episode closes with the succession X_6–X–X_3–X–$\langle T8E4 \rangle$. The union of these pcsets is also Z. By appearing at the opening and closing of the episode, and by pairing X with Y, Z shares in the framing function of X.

Example 13.8 situates Examples 13.6 and 13.7 in a broader context. The top staff reproduces Mama's vocal line from Example 13.6, omitting repeated notes. The grand staff provides the instrumental accompaniment in block-chord reduction. Each measure shows the relative rhythmic position of its pitches. Parentheses on the grand staff (mm. 340 and 342) indicate notes that do not appear in the instrumental accompaniment but are "borrowed" from Mama's vocal line to form an all-trichord hexachord (labeled "ATH") or all-interval tetrachord (labeled "AIT"); prominent set classes in *What Next?* (see Example 13.3) often result from a combination of instrumental and vocal

Ex. 13.8 Vocal line from Ex. 13.6 with instrumental accompaniment

pitches. Asterisks indicate embellishing material, to be defined presently. Three features emerge from the example. First, while the majority of Mama's pitches appear in the accompaniment, the vocal line exhibits a high degree of autonomy in its near-exclusive use of X_n tetrachords. Second, the accompaniment initially presents pcsets from [012478], and then presents eight-note combinations of [0146] and [0137] (labeled "8" for octachord); I consider other material to be embellishing.[24] Third, at the end of the first system, the T_9 transformation associated with the X_n tetrachords extends to a pair of octachords as well. In its balance of autonomy and dependence (Mama's vocal line exhibits its own structural logic based on the Example 13.5 space although nearly all of Mama's pitches also appear in the orchestra), the interaction of vocal line with instrumental accompaniment is representative of all the explanation episodes.[25]

---

[24] Carter has confirmed the notion of "primary" and "embellishing" material in his music: "I don't follow everything strictly from beginning to end. *Most* of the time. But I find that there are certain things that I need for me, for my ear, for the way I like things to sound, and these passages get into that just because – there are a hundred different pieces, and they don't necessarily follow the logic of the harmonic structure. I mean, it's like that in the Double Concerto – I always feel it started there. The idea in the First String Quartet that there was a dominating harmony, but that there were many little wanderings from it, but mainly it was insisted upon." (Capuzzo, Interview with Elliott Carter.)

[25] On autonomy in Carter's music, see Roeder, "Autonomy and Dialogue in Elliott Carter's *Enchanted Preludes*."

Ex. 13.9 "Zen tries not to explain"

Z, which framed episode 10, also figures prominently in episode 11, "Zen tries not to explain." Example 13.9 provides a block-chord reduction. The shared Z represents the common ground between Mama and Zen – they were once married. It also yields a certain amount of irony: while Zen harbors no lingering romantic feelings for Mama, she longs for him to remarry her. The following exchange occurs in episode 27: "If it were possible for you to really love me" (Mama, stage direction "warmly"), "If oysters were open to persuasion" (Zen, stage direction "amusedly"), "If I could call you husband and think I spoke the truth" (Mama), "If Saturn's rings would take a collect call" (Zen), "If there were to be another wedding we could share" (Mama), "If time would stop and turn again and listen" (Zen). However, despite the shared Z, there are significant differences between Mama's and Zen's explanation episodes. For one, whereas Mama sings all-interval tetrachords, Zen sings the all-trichord hexachord C4–D4–E4–C$\sharp$4–(F4)–E4–G4–G$\sharp$4; an asterisk indicates an added F4 on the example. Further, Zen's music presents Z not as the union of X and Y, but as the union of X_9 and Y_9, placing T_9 in a new context. Y_n transpositions work identically to X_n transpositions. Y_9 retains the ic 6 from Y, {4T}, while transposing the ic 3 by T_9, from {58} in Y to {25} in Y_9. The prominence of X_9 looks to the following episode by Rose, which opens with X_9 and its literal complement. However, while the shared X_9 may suggest a personal connection between Zen and Rose, no such connection exists beyond their shared interval 4. The network in Example 13.1 bears this out; no arrows connect Zen and Rose.

Rose's use of personal pronouns in episode 12 highlights her attempt to "try to explain." She begins by addressing Kid ("Would *you* like an autograph? A photograph?"), acknowledges their common situation ("Just while *we're* waiting"), then redirects the monologue to her alone ("Something to help *you* to remember the time when *you* saw *me*?"). As befits her

Ex. 13.10 "Rose tries to explain"

self-involvement,[26] her music has little in common with the other explanation episodes. Example 13.10 indicates that Rose sings several all-interval tetrachords, an all-trichord hexachord (bracketed below the staff), and T_3 of Z (bracketed above the staff).[27] It is telling, however, that only one of these pcsets duplicates one from the other explanation episodes: Rose's all-interval tetrachord D5–D5–G4–D5–E4–G$\sharp$4 ("... we're waiting? Something to ...") contains the same pcs as the third tetrachord in the penultimate measure of Zen's episode. However, because Rose and Zen barely interact in the opera, I do not assign significance to this shared pcset. Rose's accompaniment music, chiefly all-trichord hexachords played by the piano (Carter states that "Rose is a lieder singer and so is often accompanied by the piano"), also does not form strong connections with the other explanation episodes.[28] Rose's music thus illustrates the episode's title and conveys irony: she tries to join the other characters in their efforts to explain the accident to Kid, succeeds to a certain degree by replicating the other characters' set classes, but in all but one instance falls short of duplicating the pc content of the other characters' music. This is a classic Carter trait: missed connections despite good-faith efforts.

One feature of the music preceding Rose's entrance is significant from the perspectives of Carter's pitch language as well as text–music relations. In the opening measure, the English horn projects X_9, which performs two functions. First, with regard to pitch language, X_9 forms an aggregate with the preceding octachord, as stated earlier. It is perhaps for this reason that X_9

[26] In Griffiths's libretto, Rose's description reads in part, "the important thing is that I was on my way back after a performance. It's not at all unusual for me to be surrounded by wellwishers. It's relatively immaterial to me who these people are."

[27] Because Z is highly symmetrical, T_3 of Z is equivalent to T_9 of Z, or T_1I of Z, or T_7I of Z. For this reason, I do not ascribe significance to this instance of T_3.

[28] Carter's statement appears in Meyer and Shreffler, *ECCP*, p. 307.

Ex. 13.11 "Harry or Larry does not try to explain"

precedes X; aggregates tend to articulate formal boundaries in *What Next?*.[29] Second, with regard to text–music relations, the T_3 move from X_9 to X creates a reference to Mama's vocal music. "Have you finished your chocolate?" sets X_6, while "Can I get you anything to drink?" sets X_3. T_9, the *inverse* of Rose's T_3, maps X_6 onto X_3. What emerges is a musical depiction of Rose's dislike of Mama: Rose describes Mama as "rather confused" (episode 22) and an "angry queen" to Rose's "princess" (episode 25). Whereas Mama sings T_9-related tetrachords, Rose's music begins with T_3-related tetrachords. In a subtle form of rebellion, Rose's T_3 undercuts and undoes Mama's T_9 – a musical representation of Rose thumbing her nose at Mama.[30]

Example 13.11 shows that Harry or Larry's episode opens with Z, formed by the union of X and Y. On the one hand, the presence of Z suggests his familial relations to Mama and Zen, whose episodes also begin with Z. One link to Mama's episode in particular is the prominent use of X_n tetrachords. Specifically, the repeated use of X_2 mirrors the repetitive words that Harry or Larry sings.[31] On the other hand, the staccato, *marcato*, *fortissimo*, low-register stabs of this instance of Y contrast with the sustained *pianissimo*

[29] Examples include episode 1, "Star Starts," mm. 1–45 and episode 19, "The Singing Stage," discussed in Example 13.13. On the interaction of aggregates, texture, and form in Carter's music, see Capuzzo, "Registral Constraints on All-Interval Rows in Elliott Carter's *Changes*," and "Variety Within Unity."

[30] Gollin, "Multi-Aggregate Cycles," 169, develops the idea of one operatic character "undoing" another's transposition T_n via its inverse T_{12-n}.

[31] Whittall, "A Play of Pure Forces," 10, notes that Carter at times "match[es] verbal repetitions with musical repetitions" in the opera.

voicing of X to set Harry or Larry apart, signaling his reluctant cooperation with the other adults and his relative indifference to Kid (dynamics only apply to mm. 372–74).

Harry or Larry is irreverent, carefree about the other adults, and occasionally insulting to them. For example, in episode 29, Harry or Larry asks, "Is she [Mama] crazy or am I? Is he [Zen] really such a jerk? How did that stargazer [Stella] get here?" The accompaniment expresses his irreverence by fusing X_n tetrachords that until now have been kept apart, suggesting a "breaking of the rules." For instance, in m. 375, X and X_9 sound together in a single, five-note attack. Similarly, in m. 378, X_2 appears with an additional pc 8 "borrowed" from X_9 or X_6 (neither instance is the result of a block-chord reduction). These chords create a musical representation of Harry or Larry spitting in the face of reality, and relate well to the madcap quality of his music.

In the final explanation episode, Stella "cannot explain." After an initial attempt to describe the accident to Kid ("I must have been taking you with me. We were driving to the observatory and the others were perhaps …"), Stella aborts the attempt and retreats to the world of astronomy ("All we can look at are probabilities. The world now seems to be made of rainbow … We reach out a hand to touch it and find ourselves waving in empty space"). By episode 23, Stella is further removed from rational thought: "But now I fear the stars and planets are painted on my eyes, their orbits and occultations take place within my brain, their spheres and ellipses are made out of thought."[32] Two features of the music emphasize her growing distance from reality. First, as her episode proceeds, the music bears less and less resemblance to the music of the other explanation episodes. As shown in Example 13.12, the episode opens with X_8 and X, followed by their T_6 transpositions, X_2 and X_6. Later, Stella sings two of these tetrachords, repeating X_6 at "observatory" and X_8 at "All we can look." However, the surrounding music does not employ the X_n tetrachords. Second, as Stella's mind grows denser with confusion, the texture of her accompanying music grows denser as well, from tetrachords on the top system of the example to pentachords and hexachords on the lower systems. The pentachords and hexachords result from the union of two X_n tetrachords attacked simultaneously. For example, X_2 and X_5 sound together in m. 405, while X_2, X_5, and pc 8 sound together in mm. 409 and 413. This recalls a similar technique in Harry or Larry's episode. However, where simultaneous X_n tetrachords signal irreverence for Harry or Larry, they signal confusion for Stella. The absorption of all-interval tetrachords into all-trichord hexachords in Stella's music presages the same

[32] In Griffiths's libretto, Stella's description reads in part: "[P]erhaps I'm suffering from some temporary mental disturbance."

Ex. 13.12 "Stella cannot explain"

technique at the opening of episode 19, where X sounds for the final time in the opera.

Stella's final point of contact with X is telling. In the phrase, "We reach out a hand to touch it and find ourselves waving in empty space," the highest pitches of the phrase, C5 and F♯5, set the words "to touch" (mm. 419–20). As Stella "reaches out a hand to touch it" – "it" being "the world" in the libretto, and reality by extension – the fixed ic 6 dyad is present, but the {B, D} ic 3 needed to complete X is absent, portraying her inability to maintain contact with reality. Instead, {G, B♭} appears, forming X₈.

Conclusion

The detailed analyses in the second pass (Examples 13.6 to 13.12) demonstrate the dramatic significance of T_3, T_6, and T_9 with X and other pcsets; the interaction of the Example 13.5 space with text–music relations; the importance of X, Y, and Z to each adult's "explanation"; the different reasons behind simultaneous X_n tetrachords in Harry or Larry's and Stella's episodes; and the

Ex. 13.13 "The Singing Stage"

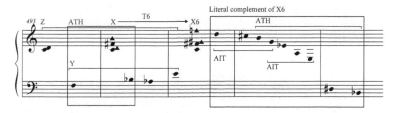

close relation between X, Kid, the English horn, and irony. To conclude, Example 13.13 depicts the final appearance of X in *What Next?*. It connects the end of episode 18 to the beginning of episode 19, an orchestral interlude titled "The Singing Stage," which features an English horn solo. In episode 18, the five adults depart the stage one by one, leaving Kid alone on stage for episode 19. Given the close association throughout the opera between the English horn, Kid, and X, the title "The Singing Stage" suggests that it is Kid who is "singing" during the interlude, with the English horn acting as his surrogate voice.

The concluding statement of X ties together several motivic strands that run through the explanation episodes. Example 13.13 shows that X overlaps with Y to form Z. In the process, X joins pcs ⟨5T⟩ to form the all-trichord hexachord {0256TE}. The union of X with ⟨5T⟩ is important in two respects. First, it forecasts the status of the all-trichord hexachord as the most prevalent set class in "The Singing Stage." Second, the moment is marked from a set-theoretical perspective: ⟨5T⟩ is the only dyad that X can merge with to form an all-trichord hexachord. Likewise, Z is the only pcset in [0124678T] that includes {0256TE}. Example 13.13 notes two further features of the excerpt. First, T_6 maps X onto X_6; both chords occurred with identical pitches at the opening of Stella's explanation episode. Second, X_6 is followed by its literal complement, composed to project two all-interval tetrachords and an all-trichord hexachord. As with Rose's episode, Carter uses an aggregate to mark a formal boundary.

Example 13.14 relates all of Kid's vocal statements in the opera to X and the space in Example 13.5. Kid's melodies draw on the ic 3 outer nodes of the space, while X uses the {C, F♯} inner node. In mm. 47–48, "Starve, I'm starving" presents C♯5–G♯4–C♯5–A♯4, which uses the {A♯, C♯} outer node and repeats G♯4 from the prior A♭4s (mm. 32 and 38). At "A big Mac" and "You're welcome," Kid sings pitches directly from X. Notably, these three melodies occur at the ends of their respective episodes, recalling the framing function performed by X. Kid's final melody is a soletto titled "A question" (episode 36, m. 923). It presents two all-interval tetrachords that invert around their shared pitches, G4 and D5. The melody draws on the outer

Ex. 13.14 Kid's vocal statements

nodes {G,B♭}, {A♭,B♮}, {B♭,C♯}, and {B♮,D}. In this view, the space in Example 13.5 provides the pitch material for Kid's melodies, X, and the X$_n$ tetrachords. Just as X gives voice to Kid, and thus is integrated with him, so too do X and Kid share a common pitch source.

By focusing on the explanation episodes through the lens of Kid and the music that represents him, I hope to have thrown light on one aspect of the rich and varied interaction of text, music, and irony in *What Next?*. As Shreffler notes, "because in [*What Next?*] two semantic layers – text and music – are present, the possibilities for different kinds of interaction are increased. Since these interactions are based on misunderstanding and incomprehension, multiple layers of irony result."[33]

[33] Shreffler, "Instrumental Dramaturgy as Humane Comedy," p. 162.

14   Words and music in *The Defense of Corinth*

Annette van Dyck-Hemming

Elliott Carter's 1941 composition *The Defense of Corinth* – for speaker, men's voices and piano, four-hands – is completely rooted in its time. Not only is it part of the Glee Club Tradition, it also deals with the question of whether or not America should enter the Second World War and what the average citizen, the artist included, may be able to contribute in such a critical situation. At the same time, this early vocal composition shows many characteristics that were to become general features of Carter's style: a rootedness in Renaissance culture; the influence of Stravinsky; a multi-layered, but formally straightforward concept realized using avant-garde techniques; and the serious desire to express a socio-political point of view (of course in a rather subtle way, and possibly even with a twinkle in the eye).

The historical context

1941, the year in which *The Defense of Corinth* was written, was a dark year in the world's history: people were dying in their millions on the battlefields, especially after Germany declared war on Russia in June and the extermination camp in Auschwitz-Birkenau was established in October. As the year drew to a close the war escalated: after the Japanese bombed Pearl Harbor in December, the United States, Britain, and China declared war on Japan. On December 11, Germany declared war on the United States, and on the same day the United States Congress declared war on Italy and Germany.

Despite the United States Senate agreeing to significantly increase funding for the army and navy in May of 1940 and Congress authorizing nationwide conscription in September of that year, by January of 1941 United States intervention in the war was still by no means a certainty. In his famous "Four Freedoms Address" to Congress, President Roosevelt drew an image of a world with fewer weapons and a free, peaceful society; at this time he still considered the United States to be a supporter of Hitler's enemies without becoming active participant in the war. Throughout 1941, while aggressive provocation by German submarines in the Atlantic continued, speculation abounded about the "when" and "how" as well as the economic consequences of America's entry into the war. The European experience was very different. Great Britain had been involved in the war since 1939. In 1940 the British endured the continuous bombing of their cities and were initially quite shocked at their inability to fight back effectively. They had to stand by and watch as Germany invaded the Netherlands, Belgium, and Luxembourg and attacked France in May. Moreover, they had to cope with the ineffectiveness of the British troops sent to help Greece, which had been attacked by Italy. On April 26, 1941 Corinth fell. Beginning in August 1941, after the so-called "Butt report" revealed the lack of direction and effectiveness of the British war effort, a plan for aerial bombardment of German cities was developed. Intensive bombing began in March 1942, both for strategic reasons and to demoralize the enemy.[1]

In his twenties, Elliott Carter had already learned to speak some German; he had toured Germany with his father shortly after the First World War;[2] and he had visited friends in Munich in the late 1920s. Carter and his friends had sworn never to fight in any war.[3] Carter had almost witnessed the anti-Semitic riots that followed the Stavisky affair in Paris in 1934, and after he returned home from his stay in France (1932–35), he followed the continuing rise of the Nazis in Germany and other developments in Europe.[4] During this time, Carter wrote for Minna Lederman's groundbreaking periodical *Modern Music* from 1936 on, and from 1937 to 1939 he worked as a musical director for Lincoln Kirstein's Ballet Caravan. Kirstein successfully staged Carter's ballet *Pocahontas* in May 1939 (though it was overshadowed by Copland's *Billy the Kid* premiered at the same performance).[5] Carter married Helen Frost-Jones in July 1939, and they received news of the outbreak of World War II in September.

It was during the early part of the war (1940) that Carter accepted a position as a tutor in music, mathematics, and ancient Greek at St. John's College in Annapolis, Maryland. The College was founded in the late seventeenth century and upholds the ideals of Humanism to this day. Together with Nicolas Nabokov, Carter established a curriculum for music.[6] However, in 1942 Carter left his position and completed *The Defense of Corinth*, which was premiered on March 12, 1942. Carter continued to compose, working on his Symphony No. 1. Fifty years later he described his feelings and reactions during those years as follows:

---

[1] Cf. Hynes (ed.), *Reporting World War II. American Journalism 1938–1946.*
[2] Edwards, *FW*, pp. 49–50.
[3] Restagno, *Elliott Carter in Conversation with Enzo Restagno*, p. 34; Edwards, *FW*, p. 50.
[4] Restagno, *Elliott Carter in Conversation with Enzo Restagno*, p. 14; Edwards, *FW*, p. 53n. With the help of French local politicians and

members of the French high society, Stavisky issued bonds that today would be classified as "toxic assets." When the swindle was detected, Stavisky (who was Jewish) was declared the main culprit by fascist groups.
[5] Schiff, *MEC*, 1st edn, pp. 97 and 99–100.
[6] Meyer and Shreffler, *ECCP*, p. 45.

When I saw that another war had broken out, it was a terrible disappointment. I would have liked to take an active part, so I volunteered for different kinds of service. I took a course in cryptography, to learn to decipher code, but I must not have been gifted or smart enough for it, and I couldn't pass the exams. I also saw that I wasn't suited for certain other kinds of service either. At the time we were living on East 85th Street, in a neighborhood with a large German community. I was instructed to go around the neighborhood and find out who had Nazi sympathies. I remember that once in a while I went into the shop of a German butcher to sound out his political opinions, but that really was not a job for me, so I decided to stick to my music.[7]

In 1943, Carter began to work for the Office of War Information, which had started to operate in July 1942, producing radio and motion picture series. Carter himself worked on news reports, musical programs and French-language broadcasts. He produced recordings which were sent to various fronts[8] and remembered in 1989 that "it was hard work, which took all day and sometimes part of the night as well," but that he "did it with great enthusiasm because [he] wanted to make [his] contribution."[9]

Even with the benefit of hindsight, the historical setting at the beginning of the 1940s appears as both significant and highly dramatic. Today, it is questionable to what extent any individual could have made a difference in those worrying times and it is all too easy to assume that nearly everything a person did in those years would acquire a special meaning in relation to its unique historical context. While this certainly applies to Carter's composing of *The Defense of Corinth*, a close look at this piece will reveal it to be part of a complex network of meanings, associations, and connotations. Analysis will provide an understanding of the composition not only as an "early work" of a "late bloomer," but as a significant part of Carter's early compositional output as well as an expression of his continuous concern for the composer's role in society.[10]

Classicism and Neoclassicism

The Defense of Corinth is the eighth of Carter's eleven compositions with choir, and the fourth of five pieces for men's choir (the last of which is

[7] Restagno, *Elliott Carter in Conversation with Enzo Restagno*, p. 34; see also Meyer and Shreffler, *ECCP*, pp. 45–49 and 51.
[8] Restagno, *Elliott Carter in Conversation with Enzo Restagno*, p. 32.
[9] Restagno, *Elliott Carter in Conversation with Enzo Restagno*, p. 34; see also Meyer and Shreffler, *ECCP*, pp. 51–52, and Winkler, *The Politics of Propaganda: The Office of War Information 1942–1945*.
[10] "Musical meaning" and "connotation" are used here in the sense of Leonard

B. Meyer (*Emotion and Meaning in Music*). He underlines that "meaning and communication cannot be separated from the cultural context in which they arise" (p. ix). Connotations are defined as "interpersonal" (p. 258), "intracultural" (p. 259) and as "the result of the associations made between some aspect of the musical organization and extra-musical experience" (p. 258). "Association is by contiguity . . ." (p. 259).

Emblems). The text is based on an anecdote about Diogenes of Sinope, living in his tub in the ancient Greek city of Corinth. The people there are busy preparing for a war with Macedonia, when Diogenes suddenly begins beating his tub vigorously. Asked why he was acting that way, he admitted that he did not want the Corinthians to think of him as lazy.

The Defense of Corinth was composed ten years before String Quartet No. 1 (1951), which marks Carter's turn away from regarding a hypothetical "broad public" as his audience. As such it belongs to a group of compositions written at the time when Neoclassicism was the "state of the art" in music composition. Carter's title already hints at this connection, which is further reinforced by the piece's deeply rooted extra-musical relations, musical connotations, and cultural context. Like *Tarantella* from 1936, *The Defense of Corinth* is set for speaker, men's choir and piano four-hands. Both pieces also share a reference to Antiquity as a subject, and both were premiered by the Harvard Glee Club under G. Wallace Woodworth. Enrolled as a student in Harvard from 1926 to 1932, Carter sang in a Bach Cantata Choir and was a member of the Harvard Glee Club himself.[11] At the time, it was an all-male chorus, conducted (until 1934) by Dr. Archibald T. Davison, who included Italian church music of the fifteenth and sixteenth centuries in the choir's repertoire. Moreover, Carter's education at Harvard University – which comprised "the study of German and Greek"[12] as well – was shaped not least by "the influence of Irving Babbitt and the 'New Humanism'."[13] Babbitt refers in his essay *The New Laokoon* (1910)[14] to Gotthold Ephraim Lessing's famous interpretation of the marble sculpture of *Laocoön and His Sons* (1766).[15]

As a new Lessing, Babbitt aims at a new distinction between different aesthetic traditions: Lessing criticizes "Schilderungssucht" (addiction to description) and "Allegoristerei" (allegorization)[16] – typical elements of late Baroque art – and advocates "Maß halten" (moderation) against the extensive striving for an alleged "Wahrheit und Ausdruck" (truth and expression).[17] Instead, Babbitt wants "to discriminate between the truly classic and the romantic"[18] and calls his point of view "Neo-classicism."[19]

---

[11] Edwards, *FW*, p. 48.
[12] Edwards, *FW*, p. 47.
[13] *Ibid.*
[14] Babbitt, *The New Laokoon: An Essay on the Confusion of the Arts.*
[15] Lessing, *Laokoon: oder über die Grenzen der Mahlerey und Poesie.*

The sculpture shows at its center the nearly naked muscular figure of a man (Laocoön) with curly beard and hair. Only his toes are touching the marble base, which has two steps. Laocoön is fighting with a snake, which tries to bite him in the hip as he tries to repel it

with his left hand. The snake winds itself tightly around two distinctly smaller figures on the right and left side of Laocoön (the sons). They obviously fail in repelling the snake, and they share the agonized and fearful facial expression of their father.

[16] *Ibid.*, chapter I.
[17] *Ibid.*, chapter III.
[18] Babbitt, *The New Laokoon: An Essay on the Confusion of the Arts*, p. x.
[19] *Ibid.*, p. xi.

Serge Koussevitzky, who led the Boston Symphony Orchestra from 1924 until 1949, also strongly influenced the kind of music the Harvard students got to know. For example, he conducted the American premiere of Igor Stravinsky's *Oedipus Rex* in 1928 with the Boston Symphony Orchestra and the Harvard Glee Club. Its piano score had already been printed in Koussevitzky's own publishing house Edition Russe de Musique. Koussevitzky chose programs with a lot of (notably American) contemporary music, although the audience at this time mostly preferred the canonical concert repertoire with music by "Beethoven and Brahms and Mozart."[20] Carter not only was enthusiastic about Koussevitzky's performance of *Le sacre du printemps* in 1924 but also took part in the performances of *Oedipus Rex*[21] at Harvard and New York in 1928, and praised "the revelation" of the *Symphonie de psaumes*, first performed in 1930.[22] Finally, when he studied with Nadia Boulanger in Paris (1932–35), Carter got to know Stravinsky personally as the latter regularly visited Boulanger's salon and gave previews of his latest works.[23] Through Boulanger's detailed "illuminations," Carter learned to understand Stravinsky's works on a technical level and for the first time grasped "why a given thing was what it was in a modern piece."[24]

In the first half of the twentieth century Stravinsky's transformation of antique and classic references into his style of Neoclassicism set the standard for many composers. Regarding *The Defense of Corinth*, Stravinsky's formal concept in *Oedipus Rex* might have served as a model for Elliott Carter.[25] Both compositions begin with a narrator's introduction, followed by a section for the male chorus, which – like the antique chorus in classical Greek tragedies – plays the role of the citizens commenting on the actions of the main character (or, in the case of *Oedipus Rex*, the four main characters). And, in both pieces the drama continues with the entrance of the protagonist, although the musical realizations are different: Oedipus is represented by a soloist, while Diogenes makes his first appearance as part of the narration presented by the chorus. On the other hand, the dotted rhythms

---

[20] Edwards, *FW*, p. 58; see also pp. 45–46, as well as Leichtentritt, *Serge Koussevitzky: The Boston Symphony Orchestra and the New American Music*, and Spalding, *Music at Harvard: A Historical Review of Men and Events*.
[21] Carter, "Soviet Music" (1967/94), in *CEL*, p. 332.
[22] Restagno, *Elliott Carter in Conversation with Enzo Restagno*, p. 22.
[23] Edwards, *FW*, p. 56.
[24] Edwards, *FW*, p. 51.
[25] In *MEC*, 1st edn, Schiff suggests several models for *The Defense of Corinth*

including Darius Milhaud's *Les choéphores* (1915), Stravinsky's *Les noces* (1923), and notably Milhaud's *La mort d'un tyran* (1933). In *MEC* (1998), he only mentions the Milhaud, but he does not explain his choice further. Indeed, there are similarities in all these pieces regarding the sound and rhythmic organization of the voices, but the differences prevail at least in the cases of *Les choéphores* and *Les noces*. Though, it would be of interest to compare the origin of the texts of *La mort d'un tyran* and *The Defense of Corinth*.

Ex. 14.1 Igor Stravinsky, *Oedipus Rex*, number 16, mm. 1–4 (page 13), excerpt with first and second E♭-clarinet, bassoon and part of Oedipe (tenor)

Ex. 14.2 *The Defense of Corinth*, mm. 88–103, excerpt

(see Example 14.1 and 14.2) are quite similar, and even their intervallic structure seems to be related. Stravinsky frequently used dotted rhythms in *Oedipus Rex* as a reference to classical music, as he pointed out in his conversations with Robert Craft.[26] It seems plausible that Carter adopted this technique from Stravinsky to characterize his protagonist in *The Defense of Corinth*: as can be seen in Example 14.2, Diogenes's entry is prepared in Piano II by a melody in dotted rhythm consisting mostly of fourths and seconds.[27]

Carter's composition differs from Stravinsky's in both the role of the chorus and the importance of the narrator. In *The Defense of Corinth*, the narrator is

[26] Stravinsky, *Stravinsky in Conversation with Robert Craft*, pp. 34–5.
[27] The first printed edition of *The Defense of Corinth* by Mercury Music/ Theodore Presser 1950 suggests two pianos but in the same edition the work's subtitle explicitly says "Piano, 4 Hands."

integrated into the piece using melodramatic techniques; rhythms are only partly set out in the score, and the speaker's voice is sometimes accompanied or briefly interrupted by the chorus and/or the piano parts. The role of the chorus in *The Defense* comes close to the idealized role classical philologists attribute to the early antique chorus. They follow Aristotle, who conceives the development of classic tragedy from Aeschylus to Sophocles as an enlargement of the cast: "Aeschylus innovated by raising the number of actors from one to two, reduced the choral component, and made speech play the leading role. Three actors and scene painting came with Sophocles."[28] Aristotle also declares that the chorus shall not be a "number" in a piece, nor a filler or decoration, but an interwoven and integral part of the action: "The chorus should be treated as one of the actors; it should be a part of the whole and should participate . . ."[29] These statements are supplemented by a critique of overacting.[30] According to Aristotle, an adequate protagonist does not need gestures at all if he addresses an educated audience.[31] He states that the literary composition in any case is the most important thing and does not really need naturalistic acting.[32] Despite these reservations, Aristotle ultimately defends an artistic representation on stage that has more effect than merely reading. Aristotle's aesthetic statements in his *Poetics* provide good reasons to let the chorus *and* the narrator represent both important actors in the story of the defense of Corinth: the people of Corinth *and* Diogenes.

The text

The anecdote about Aristotle's contemporary Diogenes of Sinope was originally passed on by Lucian of Samosate, who lived in the second century AD. He was a restless critic of human vanity and renowned for his satirical irony. In his Πῶς δεῖ ἱστορίαν συγγράφειν (*How to write history*), Lucian recounts as support for his own position the story of Diogenes's vain efforts to participate in the Corinthians' defense of their city. In this text, composed as a "letter to Philo," Lucian complains about the increase of amateurish history writing. He distinguishes among different genres of writing and argues for moderation and a refined, agreeable style of writing history. Lucian's aim of promoting one's own ideas and disregarding previous definitions corresponds to the

---

[28] "Καὶ τό τε τῶν ὑποκριτῶν πλῆθος ἐξ ἑνὸς εἰς δύο πρῶτος Αἰσχύλος ἤγαγε καὶ τὰ τοῦ χοροῦ ἠλάττωσε καὶ τὸν λόγον πρωταγωνιστεῖν παρεσκεύασεν. τρεῖς δὲ καὶ σκηνογραφίαν Σοφοκλῆς." (Aristotle, *Poetics*, chapter 4, 1449a, 15–18). The translations are by Stephen Halliwell (Wicksteed [ed.], *Aristotle*); see also Barnes (ed.), *The Complete*

Works of Aristotle: The Revised Oxford Translation.
[29] *Ibid.*, chapter 18, 1456a, 25–27.
[30] *Ibid.*, chapter 26, 1461b, 26, 1462b, 19.
[31] *Ibid.*, 1462a, 1–3.
[32] *Ibid.*, 1462a, 10–13.

self-consciousness of the above-mentioned Babbitt and Lessing. Carter, however, carefully hides this network of connotations behind the name of François Rabelais who is credited as the author of the text of *The Defense of Corinth*.[33]

In the second third of the sixteenth century, the French Renaissance cleric François Rabelais created a hedonistic and sardonic parody of medieval romances entitled *Gargantua et Pantagruel*, about a family of giants. Addressing an uneducated broad public, Rabelais wrote five very successful parts of the saga, each with an extensive introduction. In these introductions, he presented stories as well as authors and philosophers from Antiquity in a kind of humorous pedagogy. By thus making sure that his audience would understand any allusions and references to the ancient tradition that he used in his own narration, Rabelais was able to use the plot to greater effect and underline the authority of the narrator. Our Diogenes anecdote has its place shortly after the beginning of the third book, which was written in 1546. For Rabelais (as for Lucian) the brief story serves as an example – in a rhetorical sense – and is part of the "argumentatio" about the writer's role in society. While Lucian justifies the formal aesthetic approach of an historian, Rabelais extensively protests that, in a time of impending war, he cannot do any better than watch, lest his compatriots think of him as useless.[34]

> Therefore, by reason of my weakness and inability, being reputed by my compatriots unfit for the offensive part of warfare; and on the other side, being in no way employed in matter of the defensive, although it had been but to carry burthens, fill ditches, or break clods, either whereof had been to me indifferent, I held it not a little disgraceful to be only an idle spectator of so many valorous, eloquent, and warlike persons, who in the view and sight of all Europe act this notable interlude or tragi-comedy, and not make some effort towards the performance of this, nothing at all remains for me to be done …[35]

The wordy style is typical of the French original as well as the famous translation by Thomas Urquhart of Cromarty from 1693, which Carter chose as the text for *The Defense of Corinth*.[36] Urquhart's text[37] was more suitable to a choir's (or composer's) vocal-artistic ambitions than the ancient

---

[33] In a similar way, the text of Milhaud's *La mort d'un tyran* offers several layers of authorship. Aelius Lampridius, to whom the Latin excerpt of the *Historia Augusta* is attributed, might not have existed or his work might have been only the literary model for an unknown adaptor. In any case, a version by a writer other than Lampridius was translated by Denis Diderot, the important author of the Age of Enlightenment, in 1764. See Syme, *Emperors and Biography: Studies in the Historia Augusta*.

[34] The peace of Crépy of 1544 brought a short interruption to the Italian wars, but the French king Francis I was already preparing a new war against Spain and the Netherlands, when he died in 1547.

[35] Urquart and Motteux (eds.), *The Works of Rabelais*, p. 317.

[36] *Ibid.*, pp. 314–16.

[37] After his death Urquhart's translation was edited by Peter Motteux who completed the translation of all five books.

French and made it more accessible to the listener, while also preserving the original's archaic style. Carter, though, took the French original into consideration, as shown by some notes in the autograph.[38] A comparison of the texts gives an indication of the special challenges one would have to consider if setting them to music (see Table 14.1).[39]

With almost sportsman-like ambition, both texts compete in the physical performance of uttering words. A sense of breathlessness is achieved by adding many paraphrases once a main clause is completed. Urquhart even amplifies the effect by expanding the enumerations. Like Rabelais, he uses strings of only slightly varied words ("ting it, ring it, tingle it"); the sound effect and the rhythmic drive of the series seem to be more important than its meaning. Indeed, the translation reminds one of "today's rap poetry"[40] and probably shares some of its functions: impressing the listener/reader and gaining his or her respect, but also exploiting the sound of speech via endless paraphrases and lists. Combining this virtuosity with music, especially choral music, might suggest itself to a composer: in 1915, Maurice Ravel even created a text with all the linguistic characteristics just described[41] and set it to music as *Ronde*, one of *Trois chansons* and a showpiece for mixed *a cappella* chorus.

Words and music

Carter rose to the challenges posed by the text's volubility in different ways: he used interlocking texts (see Examples 14.3 and 14.4), juxtaposed different texts (see Example 14.4), and used a very fast succession of words in rhythmically spoken passages (mm. 49–50) or passages written in sixteenth notes (mm. 175 ff., mm. 277 ff.). Using the virtuosity and poetic richness of spoken language as a primary element in a composition was quite new in the 1940s. Since the eighteenth century, melodrama exemplified the combination of the speaking voice and music, but it was not until the early twentieth century that further possibilities for this combination were explored through the works of Arnold Schoenberg (*Pierrot lunaire*) and Darius Milhaud (*Les choéphores*). In the 1920s

[38] Meyer and Shreffler, *ECCP*, p. 45; whether this was for a possible performance in France as Meyer and Shreffler suggest, is still to be clarified.
[39] Rabelais, *Le tiers livre des faicts et dicts héroïques du bon Pantagruel*, excerpt from the *Prologue de l'autheur*, all sentences with paraphrases and enumerations are shortened except for one.
[40] Meyer and Shreffler, *ECCP*, p. 45.
[41] "N'allez pas au bois d'Ormonde, Jeunes filles ... : Il y a plein de satyres, de centaures ... Des ogres, des lutins, Des faunes, des follets, des lamies, Diables, diablots, diablotins ...." Ravel, *Trois chansons* (Paris: Durand, 1916); with an English translation by Mme. Taillandier: "Go not to the woods of Ormond, Maidens beware ... : They are full of grim satyres, and of centaurs ... Imps and ogres there hide, Will o'the wisps and fauns, roguish lamies, Flying devils, devilkins ..."

Table 14.1 Comparison of texts by Urquhart and Rabelais

Rabelais	Urquhart
Quand Philippe roy de Macedonie entreprint assieger & ruiner Corinthe, les Corinthiens par leurs espions advertiz, que contre eulx il venoit en grand arroy & exercice numereux, tous feurent non à tort espoventez, & ne feurent negligens soy soigneusement mettre chascun en office & debvoir, pour à son hostile venue, resister, & leur ville defendre.	When Philip, King of Macedon, enterprised the siege and ruin of Corinth, the Corinthians having received certain intelligence by their spies that he with a numerous army in battle-rank was coming against them, were all of them, not without cause, most terribly afraid; and therefore were not neglective of their duty in doing their best endeavors to put themselves in a fit posture to resist his hostile approach and defend their own city.
Les uns des champes es forteresses retiroient meubles ... Les autres remparoient murailles ...	Some from the fields brought into the fortified places their movables ... Others did fortify and rampire their walls ...
Chascun estoit au guet, chascun portoit la hotte. Les uns polissoient corseletz ... Les autres apprestoient arcs, fondes, arbalestes, glands, catapultes ... Esguisoient vouges, picques ...	Everyone did watch and ward, and not one was exempted from carrying the basket. Some polished corslets ... Others made ready bows, slings, crossbows, pellets, catapults ... They sharpened and prepared spears, staves, pikes ...
Affiloient cimeterres, brands d'assier, badelaires ... Chascun exerceoit son penard: chascun desrouilloit son braquemard. Femme n'estoit, tant preude ou vieille feust, qui ne feist fourbir son harnoys: comme vous sçavez que les antiques Corinthiennes estoient au combat couraigeuses.	They set edges upon scimitars, cutlasses, badelairs ... Every man exercised his weapon, every man scoured off the rust from his natural hanger; nor was there a woman amongst them, though never so reserved or old, who made not her harness to be well furbished; as you know the Corinthian women of old were reputed very courageous combatants.
Diogenes les voyant en telle ferveur mesnaige remuer, & n'estant par les magistratz enployé à chose aulcune faire, contempla par quelques iours leur contenance sans mot dire: puys comme excité d'esprit Martial, ceignit son palle en escharpe ... se troussa en cueilleur de pommes, bailla à un sien compaignon vieulx sa bezasse, ses livres, & opistographes, feit hors la ville tirant vers la Cranie (qui est une colline & promontoire lez Corinthe) une belle esplanade: y roulla le tonneau fictil, qui pour maison luy estoit contre les miures du ciel,	Diogenes seeing them all so warm at work, and himself not employed by the magistrates in any business whatsoever, he did very seriously, for many days together, without speaking one word, consider and contemplate the countenance of his fellow-citizens. Then on a sudden, as if he had been roused up and inspired by a martial spirit, he girded his cloak ... and, giving to one of his old acquaintance his wallet, books, and opistographs, away went he out of town towards a little hill or promontory of Corinth called (the) Cranie; and there on the strand, a pretty level place, did he roll his jolly tub, which served him for a house to shelter him from the injuries of the weather:
& en grande vehemence d'esprit desployant ses braz le tournoit, viroit, brouilloit, barbouilloit, hersoit, versoit, renversoit, grattoit, flattoit, barattoit, bastoit, boutoit, butoit, tabustoit, cullebutoit, trepoit, trempoit, tapoit, timpoit, estouppoit,	there, I say, in a great vehemency of spirit, did he turn it, veer it, wheel it, whirl it, frisk it, jumble it, shuffle it, huddle it, tumble it, hurry it, jolt it, justle it, overthrow it, evert it, invert it, subvert it, overturn it, beat it, thwack it, bump it, batter it,

Table 14.1 (*cont.*)

Rabelais	Urquhart
destouppoit, detraquoit, triquotoit, chapotoit, croulloit, elançoit, chamailloit, bransloit, esbranloit, levoit, lavoit, clavoit, entravoit, bracquoit, bricquoit, blocquoit, tracassoit, ramassoit, clabossoit, afestoit, bassouoit, enclouoit, amadouoit, goildronnoit, mittonnoit, tastonnoit, bimbelotoit, clabossoit, terrassoit, bistorioit, vreloppoit, chaluppoit, charmoit, armoit, gizarmoit, enharnachoit, empennachoit, carapassonnoit, le devalloit de mont à val, & praecipitoit par le Cranie: puys de val en mont le rapportoit, comme Sisyphus faict sa pierre: tant que peu s'en faillit, qu'il ne le defonçast.	knock it, thrust it, push it, jerk it, shock it, shake it, toss it, throw it, overthrow it, upside down, topsy-turvy, arsiturvy, tread it, trample it, stamp it, tap it, ting it, ring it, tingle it, towl it, sound it, resound it … And then again in a mighty bustle he bandied it … slid it down the hill, and precipitated it from the very height of the Cranie; then from the foot to the top (like another Sisyphus with his stone) bore it up again, and every way so banged it and belaboured it that it was ten thousand to one he had not struck the bottom of it out.
Ce voyant quelqu'un de ses amis, luy demanda, quelle cause le mouvoit, à son corps, son esprit, son tonneau ainsi tormenter? Auquel respondit le philosophe, qu'à autre office n'estant pour la republicque employé, il en ceste façon son tonneau tempestoit, pour entre ce peuple tant fervent & occupé, n'este veu seul cessateur & ocieux.	Which when one of his friends had seen, and asked him why he did so toil his body, perplex his spirit, and torment his tub, the philosopher's answer was that, not being employed in any other charge by the Republic, he thought it expedient to thunder and storm it so tempestuously upon his tub, that amongst a people so fervently busy and earnest at work he alone might not seem a loitering slug and lazy fellow.

Ex. 14.3 *The Defense of Corinth*, mm. 55–56, excerpt with voices

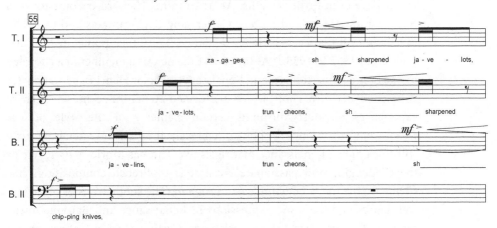

Albert Roussel and the nearly forgotten Maurice Emmanuel (teacher at the Paris Conservatoire from 1907 to 1936) again referred to the tradition of the melodrama. They – as well as Arthur Honegger and Stravinsky in the 1930s – combined it with antique plots, not least to make a point about the excessive

Ex. 14.4 *The Defense of Corinth*, mm. 195–98, excerpt with voices

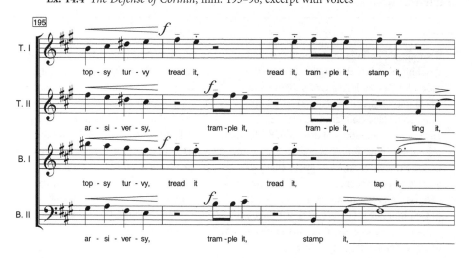

style and pathetic matter of Romantic opera. Other approaches stem from the Italian Futurists and the Dadaistic movement after about 1910, and also indicate a new consciousness of the sound quality of speech. Kurt Schwitters, for example, completed his famous *Ursonate* in 1932, the year in which Milhaud created *La mort d'un tyran*, which also contains rhythmic speech. Interestingly, one of the first examples of integrating fast, rap-like rhythmic speech in the Western art tradition dates from 1935, namely the dispute between Maria and Sportin' Life in the first scene of the second act of Gershwin's folk opera *Porgy and Bess*.

But the virtuosic use of speech in vocal works to which Carter refers might have even earlier origins. Apart from his Harvard encounters with European madrigals and motets, Carter sang Bach cantatas and pieces by Machaut with his teacher Nadia Boulanger and other pupils in his Paris years from 1932 to 1935.[42] At the same time he was a member of a choir led by the French musicologist and Renaissance-scholar Henri Expert and later conducted his own choir which performed Renaissance music.[43] These experiences obviously inspired certain elements of the style of *The Defense of Corinth* since the piece often recalls the vital and often humorous spirit of English Renaissance madrigals like Thomas Morley's *Fyre, fyre* or the challenging and passionate vocal style of French compositions like Clément Janequin's *La bataille de Marignan*. The subtle transfer of rhetorical figures and linguistic expressions in Renaissance and Baroque music seems to be particularly closely related to Carter's style of text setting. Of course, this does not imply the existence of an encyclopedia of musical

---

[42] Restagno, *Elliott Carter in Conversation with Enzo Restagno*, p. 19, and Edwards, *FW*, p. 55.

[43] Edwards, *FW*, p. 55.

denotations.[44] The link between music and text always works at a level of connotation and should be regarded from this perspective. As L. B. Meyer puts it: "Most of the connotations which music arouses are based upon similarities which exist between our experience of the materials of music and their organization, on the one hand, and our experience of the non-musical world of concepts, images, objects, qualities, and states of mind, on the other."[45] The kind of musical meaning that results is not stable, but floats in the course of time and changing cultural contexts. However, "if connotations are to be aroused at all, there will be a tendency to associate the musical motion in question with a referential concept or image that is felt to exhibit a similar quality of motion."[46] For example, Monteverdi's madrigal *Ecco mormorar l'onde* begins in the deep registers of each voice, thus underlining the dark vowels and vibrating consonants of the Italian words. In *The Defense of Corinth* a large repertoire of such relations also can be found. The structure of the relations as well as some of the musical means can be classified as typical of Carter's style of setting words to music.

Music and military sphere

At the beginning of *The Defense of Corinth*, there are several connotations of the military sphere: one of the pianos' entries is in the high register, appearing like a xylophone-and-piccolo alarm in a marching band in octaves and seconds accompanied by a drum roll-like tremolo in the lower piano part. A bi-tonal fanfare combining B and A major and some chords in purely A major prepare a recitative announcing the speaker who, briefly interrupted by the choir, explains the dramatic setting. After its next tentative spoken cue, the chorus (m. 23) is more and more vividly accompanied by percussion-like piano playing. While the tenor self-consciously repeats the section's quasi-title ("Every one did watch and ward"), the other voices describe the preparations for war in a military style with heavy accents on the first, second, third, and fourth beat of the measure, regardless of the poetic meter (mm. 35–45).

The dynamic change to *piano* in m. 46 marks a new undertone expressed through the voiced "sh" and "ss" sounds in "polish- - -," "sh- - -arpened," "ss- - -spears," "ss- - -staves" and "ss- - -scymetars," which sound like a "be quiet" hissing. The change refers to a remark the narrator made in his introduction: the spies have told about the impending war, there is no

---

[44] Carter points out in some remarks on Joseph Schillinger that he never regarded this as an option for himself. See Restagno, *Elliott Carter in Conversation with Enzo Restagno*, p. 18.

[45] Meyer, *Emotion and Meaning in Music,* p. 260.

[46] *Ibid.*, p. 261.

official information, so beware, the enemy is listening – a situation typical in times of war.[47] "And not one was exempted" (mm. 62 ff.) announces a homophonic part sung *forte*. Simultaneously the repeated praises of unity begin to sound overstated. However, except for a short modulation to C minor (mm. 73–79), the hollow fifth C–G is the harmonic center of the end of this part. It also shapes the chorus and piano parts and clearly expresses musical unity.

It is not uncommon for a drum roll to have a military association and Carter uses the drum roll again in this way in the song "View of the Capitol from the Library of Congress" from the cycle *A Mirror on Which to Dwell* (1976), when lines of the text refer to the "Air Force Band" (mm. 23 ff.). Furthermore, we also find the piano playing staccato in a high register (this time underlined by a real piccolo) and the harmonic structure also changing, culminating in a series of fourths in the piano (m. 28). Thirty-five years after *The Defense of Corinth*, Carter still relies on these same connotations, although, of course, the musical means are refined and the harmonic grounding is completely different. We can observe a semantic shift of connotation by comparing some measures of *The Defense of Corinth* (mm. 48 ff.) with the entry of the voices in Carter's opera *What Next?* (1997–98). In both pieces, Carter uses surprisingly similar musical means: in *What Next?*, the voiced "s"s and "sh"s of the six protagonists blend with the percussion, before they arise to distinct pitches and words, which are primarily connected through their sound-quality ("Star," "Starts," "Startle," "Starlings," "Starch," "Starkest," "Starve"). Here the words describe the different characters like titles. The pitchless sound of the words relate them to the "st"-arting point of the opera, a car-accident, musically accompanied by the percussion. In *The Defense of Corinth* voiced "s"s and "sh"s are part of the choir's rhythmic speech. The text – full of alliterations ("staves, skenes, spears, sabbles") – tells about the preparation for war ("sharpened … scymetars"). The "sh"s sound like a call for secrecy and the "s"s represent the ominous noise of the sharpening. What links both settings is their closeness to a catastrophe, which is no longer or not yet real. But beyond this, the connotations are quite different. In the first setting, the musical means relate to weapons, war, secret but united action; in the second, the musical means provide the only the ground on which the very different individuals meet. This shift of connotation confirms Meyer's statements about the threatened stability of text–music relations through the course of time. The comparison of these two pieces – separated by nearly sixty years – again throws light on the aspect of continuity and self-reference in Carter's work.

---

[47] Carter's use of the sound of consonants with no definite pitch represents a very early example of integrating noiselike sound into a musical composition.

Table 14.2 Musical differences between the many and the one in *The Defense of Corinth*

everyone	Diogenes
allegro	meno mosso
ff	mp
eighths, triplets, sixteenths	dotted patterns, halves
common time	$\frac{4}{4}$ signature, but sounding like a slow waltz
mostly staccato, accents	mostly legato
percussion-like, fanfares	easy going, "grazioso"
A/B major	around A♭/B♭ major

The many and the one

The tutti break in m. 89 marks an important change in the piece, as such breaks often do in Carter's music: "Diogenes's theme" – an easy-going, punctuated *meno mosso* with accompanying octaves on beats 1 and 3 – is presented in the pianos (see Example 14.2). In nearly every musical parameter this section differs from the preceding one. At the same time, the text establishes a semantic distinction between "everyone" and "Diogenes" (see Table 14.2). Here we already see a principle of musical organization Carter will use in many later compositions. In the Piano Concerto from 1965, the soloist (representing the "individual") ends up being completely isolated and ignored. Not only are the "individual's" elements in *The Defense of Corinth* musically separated from those of the "crowd," but the musical means of expression are more artificial, more original, and more challenging, despite the fact that the text is about the individual's assimilation of the general behavior of the masses. In musical terms this is countered by a kind of "overassimilation" as we shall see.

Assimilation

Diogenes's bustling activity after a time of contemplation is the result of his "serious" (m. 25) decision to adapt to the ways of the ordinary people in Corinth as much as he can. As a consequence, after his entrance and the exposition of his situation, his new efforts to assimilate are expressed as a double fugue (mm. 208 ff.).[48] In the fugue's quasi-prelude (mm. 127–208) we find numerous musical features which up to that point had been assigned to "the Corinthians": imitating and hocket-like as well as homophonic

---

[48] Cf. Schiff, *MEC*, 1st edn, pp. 83–85.

Ex. 14.5 *The Defense of Corinth*, mm. 208–212, excerpt with second Tenor

slid it down the   hill,   and pre-cip-i-ta-ted   it   from   the   ver - y height of the Cra - ne - um;

Ex. 14.6 *The Defense of Corinth*, mm. 227–34, excerpt with second Tenor

then from the   foot   to____   the top.____   like an - oth - er Sis - y - phus with____ his   stone,

passages, triplets and rhythmic accents, a dynamic range from *p* to *ff*, a motoric piano accompaniment in quarters and the piccolo-xylophone sound in the first piano part. Typically, the assimilation is not perfect, but always a little bit overdone: a *sforzando* is added to the dynamic range. The imitation also occurs as an echo and as carefully worked-out fugati. The harmonic sphere not only moves to A major, but is clearly stated as A major (for example mm. 140, 167, and so on). The double fugue finally leads to the climax of the composition and also of Diogenes's business. At this point we find the main themes in the chorus. The piano parts mostly support the vocal lines, except when their music is drawn from the piccolo-and-xylophone fanfares of the introduction. Two themes are presented and developed. The first theme (see Example 14.5 and labeled *th1* in Example 14.7) consists of three motives (*a*, *b*, and *c*) separated by rests, and recurs with different functions over the course of the double fugue. The second theme (see Example 14.6 and labeled *th2* in Example 14.7) is more lyric (moving slowly up and down) and presented with a 'Sisyphus'-connotation in its exposition.

   The two themes (*abc* and *th2*) and their respective counterpoints (*cp1* and *cp2*) correspond to two sections of the text: the first one describing the many ways the tub is being beaten, the second one summing up and commenting on an action ("like another Sisyphus") and placing a bet on the result. The themes are developed in an unusual and original fashion: the missing fourth entry of the second theme appears about thirty measures too late during the third development of the first theme. In fact, the third development consists of only two entries. With the common-time signature, one of the last differences between the spheres of "Diogenes" and "the Corinthians" is given up in favor of the musical elements attributed to the Corinthians. Technically the fugue turns to imitation at the point when the development of its second theme is expected. The musical process culminates in a homophonic arrangement in the high registers of the voices (mm. 306/307).

Ex. 14.7 Melodic and motivic structure of the double fugue in the voices in *The Defense of Corinth*, mm. 208–323

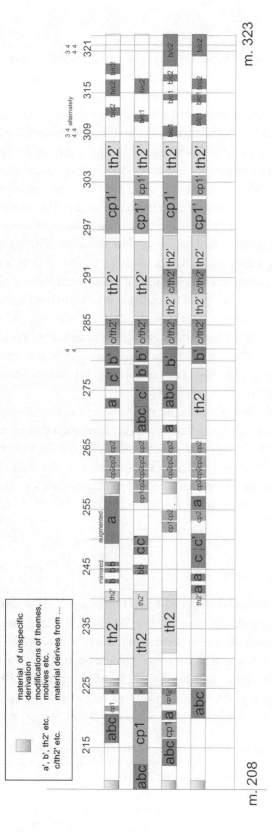

Compromise?

Only the last development (mm. 309–23) – in an idiom that merges both themes – shows some kind of compromise, paying respect to both parties, "Diogenes's" and "everyone's": $\frac{3}{4}$ and $\frac{4}{4}$ meters alternate at this point. The themes *b/c1* and *th2* consist of musical material taken from the first theme while the text relates to the second theme. At the end of the section, the usual structure of a double fugue is followed: themes 1 and 2 are combined and developed together. Augmentations decelerate the musical process and thus anticipate the close of the composition. It is not clear whether Diogenes will have to take a break from his exaggerated attempts at assimilation or whether the crowd will be too amazed by his actions to remain agitated. However, the tempo clearly is a reference to Diogenes's first entrance. The harmony remains in A major/B major, with somber allusions to minor. Does a compromise between the parties of Diogenes and everyone mean that the tempo of the crowd approaches the tempo of the individual, provided they can agree on the same underlying sound? Moreover, in the last measures, the choir again takes the role of the antique Greek chorus commenting on the action narrated by the speaker. The voices echo the narrator's words, adding a new nuance of meaning, in this case compassion for the consequences of Diogenes's wild behavior.

The music remains silent when the narrator proclaims the philosopher's answer but the piece ends with two octaves on A set in registers that are nearly (but not completely) as far apart as possible. The philosopher's charming answer and the unpretentious final staccato comment in the piano parts completely contradict the preceding homophonic statements and contrapuntal settings, and inevitably leave the listener smiling.

Hermeneutic summary

Before 1939, when *Pocahontas* was premiered, Carter was mainly acknowledged as a composer of choral music.[49] *The Defense of Corinth* shows an advanced and quite elaborate style of vocal composition.[50] The way the story is set is unusual, yet consistent with the context of ancient tradition. Parts are not assigned to individual actors. Instead the choir and narrator play all of the parts thereby creating a greater distance from the action. Leaving aside his incidental music, *The Defense of Corinth* is as close as Carter ever got to music

---

[49] Rosenfeld, "The Newest American Composers," 157–58.
[50] Even the Harvard Glee Club was unable to prepare the piece in a span of about four weeks as a letter by Wallace Woodworth shows. See Meyer and Shreffler, *ECCP*, p. 47.

drama until he wrote his opera *What Next?*. However, it is neither a music drama nor an opera. Instead both the formal conception and the cast refer to Antiquity. Carter borrowed from contemporary musical theatre, in particular from Stravinsky's *Oedipus Rex*, the aesthetic of emotional distancing. In *Oedipus Rex*, the resemblance to oratorio helps to de-emphasize the setting and the emotions. Carter chose a Renaissance text drawn from a parody of the romance of the Middle Ages. The text's translation, as well as its musical means – such as the double fugue – stem from the Baroque era. The imitative style of choral composition clearly suggests English Renaissance music. Numerous references to the Classical style and to contemporary music can be identified. In other words, the composition refers to many different musical traditions and periods, but one is conspicuously absent: *The Defense of Corinth* is anything but Romantic.

In *Oedipus Rex* Stravinsky illustrates a hopeless situation: a trapped political elite find themselves unable to relate to the people who follow them almost unconditionally. In *The Defense of Corinth*, as in many of his later works, Carter is concerned with the relation between the one and the many. He always focuses on the position, the work, the engagement of the subject with respect to an "other," in this case Diogenes's efforts to imitate "the Corinthians" preparing for war. And Carter describes Diogenes's assimilation musically as a crossing of harmonic and rhythmic bridges, a developing and merging of different themes and motives, and an adaptation of a certain style of composition. But the analysis also highlights an implicit characteristic of the figure of Diogenes, which typifies Carter's perception of the relationship between the individual and the mass. The individual is distinguished by striving for something beyond the social norm or by setting himself apart from it in some way. Diogenes exemplifies this trait, albeit not in relation to the subject matter at hand, as he is not able to better prepare himself for war than his fellow citizens. However, if he cannot prepare effectively for war then he can at least act unpredictably, more originally, fueled by greater knowledge, passion, and dedication. Diogenes can serve as an example: through a kind of modest and solemn humor he becomes so persuasive that he provokes the Corinthians to compassion and amazement.

In the context of the interventionist debates of the years 1939/40, the composition cannot stand as a "hurrah-for-war" piece. Rather, it sounds like a plea to stand together in spite of our differences and to employ all kinds of talent to overcome a difficult political situation. *The Defense of Corinth* can also be understood as a parody. However, it is not Diogenes who is ridiculed but the people he is imitating. By doing nothing in a very noisy way, Diogenes reveals the emptiness of their busyness. In this sense, *The Defense of Corinth* stands as a sharp critique of America's political chess playing at the time. The position and feeling of the individual (Diogenes) are worked out most thoroughly in *The Defense of Corinth*. He is assigned not only the larger part of the text, but also the most elaborate forms and musical means. Carter uses the relationship between Diogenes and the crowd as a metaphor for the relationship between the artist – isolated and ostensibly redundant – and society.[51] At the time *The Defense of Corinth* was premiered, Carter had "decided to stick to [his] music" and was writing his first symphony. However, like Diogenes, Carter had no wish to be considered "a loitering slug and lazy fellow." *The Defense of Corinth*, in which the hero's ostensible uselessness is counteracted by his will and energy, can be read as an expression of Carter's own position on the perceived ineffectiveness of the artist's work in a time of crisis. Artists have often identified themselves with Diogenes, as the examples of Lucian, Rabelais and even Urquhart show. When he wrote *The Defense of Corinth*, Elliott Carter was not only a practicing composer himself but he was also very familiar with the worlds of other artists: his wife was a sculptor, he was collaborating with dancers and authors, and he knew many artists who struggled to find a place in society in which to work. A pointed example is Hart Crane, whose text *Powhatan's Daughter* Carter turned into a ballet just before writing *The Defense of Corinth*. Crane committed suicide in 1932 after a restless life so clearly marked by being different, yet also by continuous attempts to assimilate. *The Defense of Corinth* might well be considered a parable on this theme.

[51] Schiff, *MEC*, p. 157.

Bibliography

Interviews with Elliott Carter are listed under the name of the interviewer

Albright, Daniel. "Elliott Carter and Poetry: Listening To, Listening Through." In *Music Speaks: On the Language of Opera, Dance, and Song.* University of Chicago Press, 2009, pp. 105–21.

Alsen, Eberhard (ed.). *The New Romanticism: A Collection of Critical Essays.* New York: Garland, 2000.

Arthur, Claire. "Cooperation and Other Unifying Processes in Elliott Carter's *Esprit rude/Esprit doux* Trilogy." MA thesis, University of British Columbia, 2008.

Auden, W. H. "In Memory of W. B. Yeats." In *Collected Shorter Poems.* London: Faber & Faber, 1950, pp. 141–43.

Aylward, John. "Metric Synchronization and Long-Range Polyrhythms in Elliott Carter's Fifth String Quartet." *Perspectives of New Music* 47/2 (2009): 88–99.

Babbitt, Irving. *The New Laokoon: An Essay on the Confusion of the Arts.* Boston: Houghton Mifflin Co., 1910.

Barenboim, Daniel. "Elliott Carter." In *Journal,* www.danielbarenboim.com/index.php?id=29.

Barnes, J. (ed.). *The Complete Works of Aristotle: The Revised Oxford Translation.* Corrected 6th edn. Princeton University Press, 1995.

Bauer-Mengelberg, Stefan, and Melvin Ferentz. "On Eleven-Interval Twelve-Tone Rows." *Perspectives of New Music* 3/2 (1965): 93–103.

Beck, Jeremy. "Elliott Carter's Tonal Practice in 'The Rose Family'." In James R. Heintze (ed.), *Perspectives on American Music since 1950.* New York: Garland, 1999, pp. 41–65.

Benadon, Fernando. "Towards a Theory of Tempo Modulation." In S. D. Lipscomb, R. Ashley, R. O. Gjerdingen, and P. Websters (eds.), *Proceedings of the 8th International Conference of Music Perception & Cognition, Evanston, 2004.* Adelaide: Causal Productions, 2004, pp. 563–66.

Bernard, Jonathan W. "Chord, Collection, and Set in Twentieth-Century Theory." In J. M. Baker, D. W. Beach, and J. W. Bernard (eds.), *Music Theory in Concept and Practice.* University of Rochester Press, 1997, pp. 11–51.

  "Elliott Carter and the Modern Meaning of Time." *Musical Quarterly* 79 (1995): 644–82.

  "The Evolution of Elliott Carter's Rhythmic Practice." *Perspectives of New Music* 26/2 (1988): 164–203.

  "An Interview with Elliott Carter." *Perspectives of New Music* 28/2 (Summer 1990): 180–214.

  "The Legacy of the Second Viennese School." In Bryan R. Simms (ed.), *Schoenberg, Berg, and Webern: A Companion to the Second Viennese School.* Westport, CT: Greenwood Press, 1999, pp. 315–83.

  "Poem as Non-Verbal Text: Elliott Carter's Concerto for Orchestra and Saint-John Perse's *Winds.*" In C. Ayrey and M. Everist (eds.), *Analytical Strategies and Musical Interpretation.* Cambridge University Press, 1996, pp. 169–204.

"Problems of Pitch Structure in Elliott Carter's First and Second String Quartets." *Journal of Music Theory* 37/2 (1993): 231–66.

"Spatial Sets in Recent Music of Elliott Carter." *Music Analysis* 2/1 (March 1983): 5–34.

"The String Quartets of Elliott Carter." In Evan Jones (ed.), *Intimate Voices: The Twentieth-Century String Quartet*. University of Rochester Press, 2009, vol. 2, pp. 238–75.

"Varèse's Space, Varèse's Time." In Felix Meyer and Heidy Zimmermann (eds.), *Edgard Varèse: Composer, Sound Sculptor, Visionary*. Woodbridge: The Boydell Press, 2006, pp. 149–55.

Bernstein, David W. "Nineteenth-century Harmonic Theory: The Austro-German Legacy." In Thomas Christensen (ed.), *The Cambridge History of Western Music Theory*. Cambridge University Press, 2002, pp. 778–811.

Boland, Marguerite. "The All-Trichord Hexachord: Compositional Strategies in Elliott Carter's *Con Leggerezza Pensosa* and *Gra*." MA dissertation, La Trobe University Melbourne, 1999.

"'Linking' and 'Morphing': Harmonic Flow in Elliott Carter's *Con Leggerezza Pensosa*." *Tempo* 60/237 (2006): 33–43.

Bons, Joël. Interview with Elliott Carter. In *Elliott Carter: Homages & Dedications* [CD recording]. Disques Montaigne compact disc MO 782089, 2003, pp. 16–20.

Boretz, Benjamin. "Conversation with Elliott Carter." *Perspectives of New Music* 8/2 (1970): 1–22.

Borio, Gianmario, and Hermann Danuser (eds.). *Im Zenit der Moderne. Die internationalen Ferienkurse für Neue Musik Darmstadt 1946–1966*. 4 vols. Freiburg im Breisgau: Rombach Verlag, 1997.

Botstein, Leon. "Gespräch mit Raphael Hillyer" [in English]. In Markus Grassl and Reinhard Kapp (eds.), *Die Lehre von der musikalischen Aufführung in der Wiener Schule*. Vienna: Böhlau Verlag, 2002, pp. 153–59.

Boucourechliev, André. *Essai sur Beethoven*. Arles: Actes Sud, 1991.

Boulez, Pierre. "Conférence sur *Anthèmes 2*" (Paris, 21 October 1997). Trans. in Jonathan Goldman, "Understanding Pierre Boulez's *Anthèmes* (1991): 'Creating a Labyrinth Out of Another Labyrinth'." MA thesis, University of Montreal, 2001.

Leçons de musique: deux décennies d'enseignement au Collège de France (1976–1995). Vol. 3 of *Points de repère*. Paris: C. Bourgois, 2005.

Orientations. London: Faber & Faber, 1986.

Buchler, Michael. "Dramatic Oppositions and their Musical Voices in *Guys & Dolls*." Paper presented at the University of North Carolina – Greensboro, February 6, 2008.

Capuzzo, Guy. "The Complement Union Property in the Music of Elliott Carter." *Journal of Music Theory* 48/1 (2004): 1–24.

Interview with Elliott Carter. May 22, 1996. New York, NY.

"Registral Constraints on All-Interval Rows in Elliott Carter's *Changes*," *Intégral* 21 (2007): 79–108.

"Variety Within Unity: Expressive Ends and their Technical Means in the Music of Elliott Carter, 1983–1994." Ph.D. dissertation, Eastman School of Music, University of Rochester, 2000.

Carter, Elliott. "American Music in the New York Scene" (1940). In *CEL*, pp. 48–53.

    Collected Essays and Lectures, 1937–1995. Ed. Jonathan W. Bernard. Rochester: University of Rochester Press, 1997.

    "Composer's Note." In String Quartets No. 1 and 5 [CD recording]. Pacifica Quartet. Naxos 8.559362, 2008: n.p.

    "Composer's Notes." In *Clarinet Quintet.* Boosey and Hawkes, www.boosey.com/ pages/cr/catalogue/cat_detail.asp?musicid=52832.

    "Composer's Notes." In *Mad Regales.* Boosey & Hawkes, www.boosey.com/cr/ music/Elliott-Carter-Mad-Regales/52613.

    "Composer's Notes." In *String Quartet No. 5* [score]. New York: Boosey and Hawkes, 1995.

    "The Composer's Viewpoint" (1946). In *CEL*, pp. 3–5.

    "Coolidge Crusade; WPA; New York Season" (1939). In *WEC*, pp. 39–47.

    "'Elle est la musique en personne': A Reminiscence of Nadia Boulanger" (1995). In *CEL*, pp. 281–92.

    "A Further Step" (1958). In *CEL*, pp. 5–11.

    Harmony Book. Ed. Nicholas Hopkins and John F. Link. New York: Carl Fisher, 2002.

    Liner notes for *What Next?* In *Elliott Carter: What Next? Asko Concerto.* ECM New Series 1817, 2003.

    "Mozart's Human Touch." *The Musical Times* 132 (1991): 549.

    "Music and the Time Screen" (1976). In *CEL*, pp. 262–80.

    "Music as a Liberal Art" (1944). In *CEL*, pp. 309–13.

    "Music of the 20th Century." In *Encyclopedia Britannica.* Chicago, 1953, vol. 16.

    "The Orchestral Composer's Point of View" (1970). In *CEL*, pp. 235–50.

    "Orchestras and Audiences: Winter 1938." In *WEC*, pp. 28–31.

    "Performance Notes." In *String Quartet No. 3* [score]. New York: Associated Music Publishers, 1973.

    "Preface." In *Night Fantasies* [score]. New York: Associated Music Publishers, 1982.

    "Program Note." In *In Sleep, In Thunder* [score]. New York: Boosey and Hawkes, 1981.

    "Program Note." In *Of Challenge and of Love* [score]. New York: Boosey and Hawkes, 1995.

    "Program Note." In *String Quartet No. 4* [score]. New York: Boosey and Hawkes, 1986.

    "Programme Note." In *Three Illusions for Orchestra.* Boosey and Hawkes, www. boosey.com/cr/music/Elliott-Carter-Three-Illusions-for-Orchestra/47675.

    "Season of Hindemith and the Americans" (1939). In *WEC*, pp. 60–63.

    "Shop Talk by an American Composer" (1960). In *CEL*, pp. 214–24.

    Sketches for String Quartet No. 1 (1950–51). Library of Congress, http://memory. loc.gov/diglib/ihas/loc.natlib.ihas.200155638/pageturner.html.

    "Sound and Silence in Time: A Contemporary Approach to the Elements of Music" (1957). In Meyer and Shreffler, *ECCP*, pp. 130–37.

    "Soviet Music" (1967/94). In *CEL*, pp. 331–35.

    "String Quartets Nos. 1, 1951, and 2, 1959" (1970). In *CEL*, pp. 231–35.

    "3rd String Quartet BBC Talk. Sept. 15, 1975." Unpublished manuscript, Elliott Carter Collection, Paul Sacher Foundation Basel.

    "The Three Late Sonatas of Debussy" (1959/94). In *CEL*, pp. 122–33.

    "The Time Dimension in Music" (1965). In *CEL*, pp. 224–28.

    "Time Lecture" (1965/94). In *CEL*, pp. 313–18.

"To Be a Composer in America" (1953/94). In *CEL*, pp. 201–10.

"Two Sonatas, 1948 and 1952" (1969). In *CEL*, pp. 228–31.

Untitled program note. In Double Concerto *Duo for Violin and Piano* [CD recording]. Nonesuch H-71314, 1975.

Untitled program note. In *Night Fantasies* Piano Sonata [CD recording]. Nonesuch H-79047, 1983.

Untitled program note. In *A Symphony of Three Orchestras A Mirror on Which to Dwell* [CD recording]. Columbia Masterworks M35171, 1980.

"Walter Piston" (1946). In *CEL*, pp. 158–75.

The Writings of Elliott Carter. Ed. Else Stone and Kurt Stone. Bloomington and London: Indiana University Press, 1977.

Carvin, Andy. "American Gothic: An Interview with Elliot[t] Carter" (February, 1994). www.edwebproject.org/carter.html.

Childs, Adrian. "Structural and Transformational Properties of All-Interval Tetrachords." *Music Theory Online* 12/4 (2006).

Cogan, Robert, and Pozzi Escot. *Sonic Design: The Nature of Sound and Music*. Englewood Cliffs, NJ: Prentice-Hall, 1976.

Cone, Edward T. *Musical Form and Musical Performance*. New York: W.W. Norton, 1968.

"Stravinsky: The Progress of a Method." *Perspectives of New Music* 1/1 (1962): 18–26. Reprinted in Benjamin Boretz and Edward T. Cone (eds.), *Perspectives on Schoenberg and Stravinsky*. New York: W. W. Norton, 1968, pp. 155–64.

Copland, Aaron. "Composer from Brooklyn: An Autobiographical Sketch." In *Our New Music*. New York and London: Whittlesey House / McGraw Hill Book Company, Inc., 1941, p. 229.

Cowell, Henry. *New Musical Resources*. New York: Alfred A. Knopf, 1930. Reprint, New York: Something Else Press, 1969.

Dahlhaus, Carl. "Schoenberg and Schenker." Trans. Derrick Puffett and Alfred Clayton. In *Schoenberg and the New Music*. Cambridge University Press, 1987, pp. 134–40.

Danuser, Hermann. "Spätwerk als Lyrik: Über Elliott Carters Gesänge nach Dichtungen von Elizabeth Bishop, John Ashbery und Robert Lowell." In Klaus Wolfgang Niemöller (ed.), *Bericht über das internationale Symposion "Charles Ives un die amerikanische Musiktradition bis zur Gegenwart," Köln, 1988*. Regensburg: Gustav Bosse Verlag, 1990, pp. 195–222. Reprinted as "Elliott Carter, Late Work as Lyric Poetry," trans. Matthias Truniger, *Sonus* 19/1 (Fall 1998): 53–66.

Downes, Olin. "Ives Music Played at Columbia Fete." *The New York Times*, May 12, 1946.

Drabkin, William. "Theme." In S. Sadie and J. Tyrrell (eds.), *The New Grove Dictionary of Music and Musicians*. 2nd edn. London: Macmillan, 2001, vol. 25, p. 352.

Dubiel, Joseph. "Observations of Carter's Clarinet Concerto." Unpublished paper presented at the Cardiff University Music Analysis Conference, September 4, 2008.

Duke, Vernon. *Passport to Paris*. Boston and Toronto: Little, Brown and Co., 1955.

Van Dyck-Hemming, Annette. "Diskurse zur 'Musik Elliott Carters.' Versuch einer Dekonstruktiven Hermeneutik 'Moderner Musik'." Ph.D. dissertation, Rheinischen Friedrich-Wilhelms-Universität, Bonn, 2002.

Edwards, Allen. *Flawed Words and Stubborn Sounds: A Conversation with Elliott Carter*. New York: W. W. Norton, 1971.

Eisenlohr, Henning. "Hören und Gesellschaft. Zur Ästhetik Elliott Carters," *MusikTexte* 76/77 (1998): 30–40.

   Komponieren als Entscheidungsprozess: Studien zur Problematik von Form und Gestalt, dargestellt am Beispiel von Elliott Carters Trilogy for Oboe and Harp (1992). Kassel: Gustav Bosse, 1999.

Epstein, David. *Shaping Time – Music, the Brain and Performance*. New York: Schirmer Books, 1995.

Esclapez, Christine. "Pour une herméneutique de l'analyse." In J. Viret (ed.), *Approches herméneutiques de la musique*. Presses Universitaires de Strasbourg, 2001, pp. 73–83.

Fink, Robert. *Repeating Ourselves: American Minimal Music as Cultural Practice*. Berkeley and Los Angeles: University of California Press, 2005.

Finscher, Ludwig (ed.). "Streichquartett." In *Die Musik in Geschichte und Gegenwart*. 2nd edn. Kassel: Bärenreiter, 1998, Sachteil, vol. 8 (1998), cols. 1924–77.

Folio, Cynthia. "An Analysis of Polyrhythm in Selected Improvised Jazz Solos." In Elizabeth West Marvin and Richard Hermann (eds.), *Concert Music, Rock and Jazz Since 1945*. University of Rochester Press, 1995, pp. 103–34.

Forte, Allen. *The Structure of Atonal Music*. New Haven and London: Yale University Press, 1973.

Foucault, Michel. *The Archaeology of Knowledge* (1969). Abingdon: Routledge Classics, 2002.

Garcia, Luis-Manuel. "On and On: Repetition as Process and Pleasure in Electronic Dance Music." *Music Theory Online*, 11/4 (Oct. 2005).

Goethe, Johann Wolfgang von. *Briefwechsel zwischen Goethe und Zelter*. 3 vols. Ed. Max Hecker. Frankfurt am Main: Insel-Verlag, 1987.

Goldman, Richard F. "Current Chronicle." *The Musical Quarterly* 37/1 (Jan. 1951): 83–84. Reprinted in Richard Franko Goldman, *Selected Essays and Reviews 1948–1968*. Ed. Dorothy Klotzman. Brooklyn: Institute for Studies in American Music, 1980, pp. 69–74.

Gollin, Edward. "Multi-Aggregate Cycles and Multi-Aggregate Serial Techniques in the Music of Béla Bartók." *Music Theory Spectrum* 29/2 (2007): 143–76.

Greenbaum, Matthew. "Debussy, Wolpe, and Dialectical Form." *Contemporary Music Review* 27/2–3 (2008): 343–59.

Griffiths, Paul. "Before *What Next?*." Paper presented to the Elliott Carter Symposium, University of Minnesota, March 9, 2006.

   "'Its Full Choir of Echoes': The Composer in his Library." In Marc Ponthus and Susan Tang (eds.), *Elliott Carter: A Centennial Celebration*. Hillsdale, NY: Pendragon Press, 2008, pp. 23–40.

   Libretto for *What Next?*. In *Elliott Carter: What Next?/Asko Concerto*. ECM New Series 1817, 2003.

   Modern Music and After: Directions Since 1945. New York: Oxford University Press, 1995.

   "String Quartet." In S. Sadie and J. Tyrrell (eds.), *The New Grove Dictionary of Music and Musicians*. 2nd edn. London: Macmillan, 2001, vol. 24, pp. 282–95.

Haimo, Ethan. "Developing Variation and Schoenberg's Serial Music." *Music Analysis*, 16/3 (1997): 349–65.

Hanson, Howard. *Harmonic Materials of Modern Music*. New York: Appleton-Century-Crofts, 1960.

Harvey, David I. H. *The Later Music of Elliott Carter*. New York: Garland Publishing, Inc., 1989.

Hasty, Christopher. "Broken Sequences: Fragmentation, Abundance, Beauty." *Perspectives of New Music*, 40/2 (Summer 2002): 155–73.

Heinemann, Stephen. "The American Premiere of Elliott Carter's Clarinet Concerto." *The Clarinet* 26/1 (Dec. 1998): 34–40.

    "Melodic Practice in Elliott Carter's Clarinet Concerto." *Mitteilungen der Paul Sacher Stiftung* 14 (April 2001): 19–22.

Hepokoski, James, and Warren Darcy. *Elements of Sonata Theory: Norms, Types, and Deformations in the Late Eighteenth-Century Sonata*. Oxford University Press, 2006.

Herzfeld, Gregor. "Carter, String Quartet, and the Idea of Musical Character." In Max Noubel (ed.), *Actes du Colloque "Hommage à Elliott Carter."* Le Vallier: Editions Delatour-France (forthcoming).

Holliger, Heinz. "Abseits des Mainstreams: Ein Gespräch mit dem amerikanischen Komponisten Elliott Carter." Trans. Siegfried Schibli. *Neue Zeitschrift für Musik* 152/3 (March 1991): 4–9.

Hook, Julian. "Why are there 29 Tetrachords?" *Music Theory Online* 13/4 (Dec. 2007).

Hynes, Samuel (ed.). *Reporting World War II. American Journalism 1938–1946*. New York: Literary Classics of the United States, 2001.

Jenkins, J. Daniel. "After the Harvest: Carter's Fifth String Quartet and the Late Late Style." Paper presented at the Society for Music Theory conference, Nashville, TN, 2008. Revised version, *Music Theory Online* 16/3 (August 2010).

Johnson, Stephen. "Elliott Carter at 100." Interview with Elliott Carter for the radio program "Discovering Music," broadcast December 14, 2008, BBC Radio 3.

Johnston, Robert. "Elliott Carter's Imagery Drawn from Modern Life." *Music Magazine* 8/5 (1985): 12–14, 33.

Johnston, Robert *et al.* "Elliott Carter in Conversation with Robert Johnston, Michael Century, Robert Rosen, and Don Stein (1984)." In Meyer and Shreffler, *ECCP*, pp. 252–58.

Kapp, Reinhard. "Shades of the Double's Original: René Leibowitz's Dispute with Boulez." *Tempo* 165 (1988): 2–16.

Keltner, D., P. Ekman, G. C. Gonzaga, and J. Beer. "Facial Expression of Emotion." In R. J. Davidson, K. R. Scherer, and H. H. Goldsmith (eds.), *Handbook of Affective Sciences*. Oxford University Press, 2003, pp. 415–31.

Kerner, Leighton. "Creators on Creating: Elliott Carter." *Saturday Review* (Dec. 1980): 38–42.

Kim, Yeon-Su. "Stylistic Analysis of Elliott Carter's String Quartet No. 5: Aspects of Character and Rhythm." DMA dissertation, Boston University, 2006.

Klumpenhouwer, Henry. "Dualist Tonal Space and Transformation in Nineteenth-century Musical Thought." In Thomas Christensen (ed.), *The Cambridge History of Western Music Theory*. Cambridge University Press, 2002, pp. 456–74.

Koivisto, Tiina. "Aspects of Motion in Elliott Carter's Second String Quartet." *Intégral* 10 (1996): 19–52.

    "Syntactical Space and Registral Spacing in Elliott Carter's *Remembrance*." *Perspectives of New Music* 42/2 (Summer 2004): 158–89.

Kolisch, Rudolf. "Democratic Principles of Ensemble Playing. Notes for a Seminar at Black Mountain College, Summer 1944." Kolisch Collection, Houghton Library, Harvard University, Cambridge, MA, 5 pages.

"Tempo und Charakter in Beethovens Musik." *The Musical Quarterly* 29/2 (1943): 169–87, and 29/3 (1943): 291–312. Reprinted in *The Musical Quarterly* 77/1 (1993): 90–131, and 77/2 (1993): 268–342. Critical edition of the German text, Regina Busch and David Satz (eds.), in *Musik-Konzepte 76/77* (Munich: Edition Text & Kritik, 1992).

Kramer, Lawrence. "Song as Insight – John Ashbery, Elliott Carter, and Orpheus." In *Music and Poetry: The Nineteenth Century and After*. Berkeley and Los Angeles: University of California Press, 1984, pp. 203–21.

Kummacher, Friedhelm. *Das Streichquartett*. 2 vols. Laaber-Verlag, 2003.

Kurth, Richard. "Suspended Tonalities in Schoenberg's Twelve-tone Compositions." *Journal of the Arnold Schoenberg Center* 3 (2001): 241.

Leibowitz, René. *Schoenberg and his School: The Contemporary Stage of the Language of Music*. Trans. Dika Newlin. New York: The Philosophical Library, 1949.

Leichtentritt, Hugo. *Serge Koussevitzky: The Boston Symphony Orchestra and the New American Music*. Cambridge, MA: Harvard University Press, 1947.

Lensing, George N. "Stevens' Seasonal Cycles." In J. N. Serio (ed.), *The Cambridge Companion to Wallace Stevens*. Cambridge University Press, 2007, pp. 118–32.

Wallace Stevens and the Seasons. Baton Rouge: Louisiana State University Press, 2001.

Lerdahl, Fred. "On Carter's Influence." In Marc Pontius and Susan Tang (eds.), *Elliott Carter: A Centennial Celebration*. Hillsdale, NY: Pendragon Press, 2008, pp. 15–22.

Lessing, G. E. *Laokoon: oder über die Grenzen der Mahlerey und Poesie*. Berlin, 1766. New edn: Werke und Briefe in zwölf Bänden, vol. 2. Frankfurt am Main: Dt. Klassiker-Verlag, 1990.

Lewin, David. *Generalized Musical Intervals and Transformations*. New Haven: Yale University Press, 1987.

Musical Form and Transformation: Four Analytic Essays. New Haven: Yale University Press, 1993.

Link, John. "Carter's Harmonic Context." Paper presented at the Cardiff University Music Analysis Conference, September 4, 2008.

"The Combinatorial Art of Elliott Carter's *Harmony Book*." In *HB*, pp. 7–22.

"The Composition of Carter's *Night Fantasies*." *Sonus* 14/2 (Spring 1994): 67–86.

Elliott Carter: A Guide to Research. New York and London: Garland, 2000.

Elliott Carter's Late Music. Cambridge University Press, forthcoming.

"Elliott Carter Talks about his *Harmony Book*." In *HB*, pp. 27–35.

"Elliott Carter's 'Late Music'?." *Tempo* 62/246 (2008): 2–10.

"Long-Range Polyrhythms in Elliott Carter's Recent Music." Ph.D. dissertation, City University of New York, 1994. http://www.johnlinkmusic.com/JohnLinkDiss.pdf

Lister, Rodney. "Boston, Symphony Hall: Harbison's *Requiem* and Carter's *Boston Concerto*." *Tempo* 57/225 (2003): 38.

Lochhead, Judy. "On the 'Framing' Music of Elliott Carter's First String Quartet." In Raphael Atlas and Michael Cherlin (eds.), *Musical Transformation and Musical Intuition: Essays in Honor of David Lewin*. Dedham, MA: Ovenbird Press, 1994, pp. 179–98.

Mailman, Joshua B. "An Imagined Drama of Competitive Opposition in Carter's *Scrivo in Vento*, with Notes on Narrative, Symmetry, Quantitative Flux, and Heraclitus." *Music Analysis* 28/2–3 (2009): 373–422.

Marx, Adolf Bernhard. *Die Lehre von der musikalischen Komposition, praktisch-theoretisch* (1837–47; 4th edn, 1868), excerpts. In Scott Burnham (trans. and ed.), *Musical Form in the Age of Beethoven: Selected Writings on Theory and Method*. Cambridge University Press, 1997.

Mayer, Patricius. Interview with Paul Griffiths. In program notes for *What Next?*, Miller Theater, Columbia University, December 7–11, 2007.

Mead, Andrew. "Fuzzy Edges: Notes on Musical Interaction in the Music of Elliott Carter." In Max Noubel (ed.), *Actes du Colloque "Hommage à Elliott Carter."* Le Vallier: Editions Delatour-France, forthcoming.

  "On Tempo Relations." *Perspectives of New Music* 45/1 (2007): 64–109.

  "Pitch Structure in Elliott Carter's String Quartet #3." *Perspectives of New Music* 22 (1983–84): 31–60.

Mehrabian, Albert. *Nonverbal Communication*. Chicago: Aldine-Atherton, 1972.

Messiaen, Olivier. *Technique de mon langage musical*. 2 vols. Paris: Leduc, 1944.

Meyer, Felix. "Elliott Carter in Conversation with Felix Meyer, New York, April 20, 2001." In *Lauds and Lamentations: Music of Elliott Carter and Isang Yun* [CD recording]. ECM New Series, 1848/49, 2003, pp. 26–31.

Meyer, Felix and Anne C. Shreffler. *Elliott Carter: A Centennial Portrait in Letters and Documents*. Woodbridge: The Boydell Press, 2008.

Meyer, Leonard B. *Emotion and Meaning in Music*. University of Chicago Press, 1956.

Montaigne, Michel de. *Complete Essays*. Ed. Donald M. Frame. Stanford University Press, 1958.

Morris, Robert D. "Compositional Spaces and Other Territories." *Perspectives of New Music* 33 (1995): 328–58.

  "Pitch Class Complementation and its Generalizations." *Journal of Music Theory* 34/2 (1990): 175–245.

Morris, Robert, and Daniel Starr. "The Structure of All-Interval Series." *Journal of Music Theory* 18/2 (Fall 1975): 364–89.

Newlin, Dika. *Bruckner, Mahler, Schoenberg*. New York: King's Crown Press, 1947.

Nichols, Jeff. "Mistaken Identities in Carter's *Variations for Orchestra*." Unpublished paper, presented at the AMS/SMT Joint Annual Meeting, Seattle, Washington, November 11, 2004.

Nolan, Catherine. "Combinatorial Space in Nineteenth- and Early Twentieth-Century Music Theory." *Music Theory Spectrum* 25/2 (Autumn, 2003): 205–41.

Norris, Geoffrey. "Minimalism is Death." *The Telegraph*, July 26, 2003, www.telegraph.co.uk/culture/music/classicalmusic/3599302/Minimalism-is-death.html.

Northcott, Bayan. "Affirmations of a Modern Master." Program note in *Symphonia* [CD recording]. BBC Symphony Orchestra, Oliver Knussen, cond. Deutsche Grammophon, 459 660–2, 1999.

  The Way We Listen Now and Other Writings on Music. Ed. Christopher Wintle. London: Plumbago Books, 2009.

Noubel, Max. *Elliott Carter ou le temps fertile*. Geneva: Éditions Contrechamps, 2000.

Olmstead, Andrea. *Juilliard: A History*. Chicago: University of Illinois Press, 1999.

Oteri, Frank J. "Elliott Carter Centenary: Video Interview Podcast." www.boosey.com/podcast/Carter-Centenary-Video-Interview-Podcast/12006.

  "In the First Person: Elliott Carter." Interview with Elliott Carter. *New Music Box*, March 2000, http://newmusicbox.org/page.nmbx?id=11fp06.

Paddison, Max. *Adorno's Aesthetics of Music*. Cambridge University Press, 1993.

Palisca, Claude. *Baroque Music*. Englewood Cliffs, NJ: Prentice-Hall, 1968.

Palmer, Larry. "Sylvia Marlowe." In *Harpsichord in America: A Twentieth-Century Revival*. Bloomington and Indianapolis: Indiana University Press, 1989, pp. 110–17.

Parks, Richard S. *The Music of Claude Debussy*. New Haven: Yale University Press, 1990.

Porter, Andrew. "Fancy's Rainbows, Wit's Momentary Fires." The *New Yorker*, December 23, 1991: 96–98.

Interview with Elliott Carter. Broadcast on WNYC radio, New York, New York, December 1986.

Poudrier, Ève. "Toward a General Theory of Polymeter: Polymetric Potential and Realization in Elliott Carter's Solo and Chamber Instrumental Works After 1980." Ph.D. dissertation, City University of New York, 2008.

"Local Polymetric Structures in Elliott Carter's *90+* for Piano (1994)." In Björn Heile (ed.), *The Modernist Legacy: Essays on New Music*. Aldershot: Ashgate, 2009, pp. 205–33.

Rabelais, François. *Le tiers livre des faicts et dicts héroïques du bon Pantagruel*. Paris: Michel Fezandat, 1552.

Rao, Nancy Yunhwa. "Ruth Crawford's Imprint on Contemporary Composition." In Ray Allen and Ellie M. Hisama (eds.), *Ruth Crawford-Seeger's Worlds: Innovation and Tradition in Twentieth-Century American Music*. University of Rochester Press, 2007, pp. 110–47.

Ravenscroft, Brenda. "The Anatomy of a Song." *Ex Tempore* 9/1 (1998): 84–102.

"Finding the Time for Words: Elliott Carter's Solutions to the Challenges of Text-Setting." *Indiana Theory Review* 22/1 (2001): 83–102.

"Setting the Pace: The Role of Speeds in Elliott Carter's *A Mirror on Which to Dwell*." *Music Analysis* 22 (2003): 253–82.

"Texture in Elliott Carter's *A Mirror on Which to Dwell*." Ph.D. dissertation, University of British Columbia, 1992.

Reis, Claire C. "Elliott C. Carter." In *Composers in America: Biographical Sketches of Living Composers with a Record of their Works, 1912–1937*. New York: Macmillan, 1938. Rev. and enlarged edn, New York: Macmillan, 1947.

Restagno, Enzo. *Elliott Carter in Conversation with Enzo Restagno for Settembre Musica 1989*. Brooklyn: Institute for Studies in American Music, 1991.

Roeder, John. "Autonomy and Dialogue in Elliott Carter's *Enchanted Preludes*." In Michael Tenzer (ed.), *Analytical Studies in World Music*. Oxford University Press, 2006, pp. 377–414.

"A Transformational Space for Elliott Carter's Recent Complement-Union Music." In Timour Klouche and Thomas Noll (eds.), *Mathematics and Computation in Music: First International Conference, MCM 2007*. Heidelberg: Springer Verlag, 2009, pp. 303–10.

"Voice Leading as Transformation." In Raphael Atlas and Michael Cherlin (eds.), *Musical Transformation and Musical Intuition: Essays in Honor of David Lewin*. Dedham: Ovenbird Press, 1994, pp. 41–58.

Rosen, Charles. *The Classical Style*. London: Faber & Faber, 1971.

"Elliott Carter: The Sustained Line." In Marc Ponthius and Susan Tang (eds.), *Elliott Carter: A Centennial Celebration*. Hillsdale, NY: Pendragon Press, 2008, pp. 59–64.

"Happy Birthday Elliott Carter!" *The New York Review of Books* 56/4 (March 12, 2009): 29–31.

"An Interview with Elliott Carter." In *The Musical Languages of Elliott Carter*. Washington, DC: Library of Congress, 1984, pp. 33–43.

"The Musical Languages of Elliott Carter." In *The Musical Languages of Elliott Carter*. Washington, DC: Library of Congress, 1984, pp. 1–19.

Rosenfeld, Paul. "The Newest American Composers." *Modern Music* 3/4 (1938): 153–59.

Rotella, Guy. *Castings: Monuments and Monumentality in Poems by Elizabeth Bishop, Robert Lowell, James Merrill, Derek Walcott and Seamus Heaney*. Nashville: Vanderbilt University Press, 2004.

Rothstein, Edward. "The Twilight Fantasies of Elliott Carter." *The New Republic* (Dec. 26, 1988): 23–28.

Rupprecht, Philip. *Britten's Musical Language*. Cambridge University Press, 2001.

Sallmen, Mark. "Listening to the Music Itself: Breaking Through the Shell of Elliott Carter's 'In Genesis'." *Music Theory Online* 13/3 (2007).

Schachter, Carl. "Motive and Text in Four Schubert Songs." In *Unfoldings: Essays in Schenkerian Theory and Analysis*. Oxford University Press, 1999, pp. 209–20.

Scheffer, Frank (dir.). *Elliott Carter: A Labyrinth of Time*. Alegri Film BV DVD, 2004.

Schiff, David. "Carter as Symphonist: Redefining Boundaries." *The Musical Times* 139/1865 (Winter, 1998): 8–13.

"Carter in the Seventies," *Tempo* 130 (Sept. 1979): 2–10.

"The Carter-Messiaen Project: Is the Music American? Or European?" In the program book for *The Carter Messiaen Project*, Chamber Music Northwest, 1998, www.cmnw.org/pdfs/schiff_carterEssay.pdf.

"Carter's New Classicism." *College Music Symposium* 29 (1989): 115–22.

"Elliott Carter's Harvest Home." *Tempo* 167 (Dec 1988): 2–13.

"Keeping up with Carter." *Tempo* 214 (Oct 2000): 2–6.

The Music of Elliott Carter. London: Eulenburg Books; New York: Da Capo Press, 1983. (MEC, 1st edn.) Revised second edn., London: Faber; Ithaca, NY: Cornell University Press, 1998. (MEC)

Schmidt, Dörte. "Emanzipation des musikalischen Diskurses. Die Skizzen zu Elliott Carters zweitem Streichquartett und seine theoretischen Arbeiten in den späten 50er Jahren." In Günther Wagner (ed.), *Jahrbuch des Staatlichen Instituts für Musikforschung Preußischer Kulturbesitz 1995*. Stuttgart: Verlag J. B. Metzler, 1996, pp. 209–48.

"Formbildende Tendenzen der Musikalischen Zeit. Elliott Carters Konzept der Tempo-Modulation im zweiten Quartett als Folgerung aus dem Denken Schönbergs." In Günther Wagner (ed.), *Jahrbuch des Staatlichen Instituts für Musikforschung Preußischer Kulturbesitz 1999*, Stuttgart: Verlag J. B. Metzler, 2000, pp. 118–36.

"Kammermusik mit Bläsern und der Umbau des Gattungssystems." In Sven Hiemke (ed.), *Beethoven Handbuch*. Kassel: Bärenreiter, 2009, pp. 495–545.

"*What Next?* oder: Ein Portrait des Künstlers als grand old man." In *Arnold Schönberg: Von heute auf morgen, Elliott Carter: What Next?: Zwei Einakter*. Frankfurt: Insel Verlag, 1999, pp. 150–74.

Schoenberg, Arnold. *The Musical Idea and the Logic, Technique and Art of its Presentation*. Ed. and trans. Patricia Carpenter and Severine Neff. New York: Columbia University Press, 1995.

Style and Idea: Selected Writings of Arnold Schoenberg. Ed. Leonard Stein. Trans. Leo Black. London: Faber & Faber, 1984.

Theory of Harmony. Trans. Roy. E. Carter. London: Faber & Faber 1978.

Schütz, Alfred. "Don Quixote and the Problem of Reality." In *Collected Papers II: Studies in Social Theory*. The Hague: Martinus Nijhoff, 1964, p. 136.

Schwartz, Lloyd. "Elliott Carter and American Poetry." *Sonus* 19/1 (1998): 12–25.

Scruton, Roger. *The Aesthetics of Music*. Oxford University Press, 1997.

Sessions, Roger. "Report on Black Mountain." *The New York Times*, September 24, 1944.

Sherry, Fred. Panel discussion with Oliver Knussen, moderated by Richard Dyer. Tanglewood Music Center, July 21, 2008. Video recording, bso.permissiontv. com/tanglewood.html.

Shreffler, Anne C. "Elliott Carter and his America." *Sonus* 14/2 (1994): 38–66.

   "'Give the Music Room': Elliott Carters 'View of the Capitol from the Library of Congress' aus *A Mirror on Which to Dwell*" (in German). In Felix Meyer (ed.), *Quellenstudien II*. Winterthur: Amadeus Verlag, 1993, pp. 255–83.

   "Instrumental Dramaturgy as Humane Comedy: *What Next?* by Elliott Carter and Paul Griffiths." In Hermann Danuser with Matthias Kassel (eds.), *Musiktheater heute*. Mainz: Schott, 2003, pp. 147–71.

Simms, Bryan. *The Atonal Music of Arnold Schoenberg, 1908–1923*. Oxford University Press, 2000.

Skulsky, Abraham. "Elliott Carter." *American Composers Alliance Bulletin* (Summer 1953): 2–16.

Slonimsky, Nicolas. *Thesaurus of Scales and Melodic Patterns*. New York: Schirmer Books/Macmillan, 1987; originally published by Charles Scribner's Sons, 1947.

Spalding, Walter Raymond. *Music at Harvard: A Historical Review of Men and Events*. New York: Coward-McCann, 1935; New York: Da Capo, 1977.

Steegmuller, Francis. *Blue Harpsichord*. New York: Dodd, Mead and Co., 1949. Paperback edn, New York: Carroll and Graf, 1984.

Stein, Leonard. "Playing in Time for Schoenberg." In Markus Grassl and Reinhard Kapp (eds.), *Die Lehre von der musikalischen Aufführung in der Wiener Schule*. Vienna: Böhlau Verlag, 2002, pp. 61–69.

Stockhausen, Karlheinz: "... how time passes ..." *Die Reihe* 3 (1957): 10–40.

Straus, Joseph N. "A Revisionist History of Twelve-Tone Serialism in American Music." *Journal of the Society for American Music* 2/3 (August 2008): 355–95.

   Twelve-Tone Music in America. Cambridge University Press, 2009.

Stravinsky, Igor. *Chronicle of My Life*. London: Gollancz, 1936. Reprinted as *An Autobiography (1903–1934)*, London: Marion Boyars, 1990. Reprinted, New York: W. W. Norton & Co., 1998.

   Poetics of Music. Cambridge, MA: Harvard University Press, 1942.

   Stravinsky in Conversation with Robert Craft. Harmondsworth: Penguin Books, 1962.

Street, Alan. "The Obbligato Recitative: Narrative and Schoenberg's *Five Orchestral Pieces*, Op. 16." In Anthony Pople (ed.), *Theory, Analysis & Meaning in Music*. Cambridge University Press, 1994, pp. 164–83.

Syme, Ronald. *Emperors and Biography: Studies in the Historia Augusta*. Oxford: Clarendon Press, 1971.

Szersnovicz, Patrick. "Le Temps restitué." *Le monde de la musique* 117 (Dec. 1988): 90–94.

Talbot, Michael. "The Italian Concerto in the Late Seventeenth and Early Eighteenth Century." In Simon P. Keefe (ed.), *Cambridge Companion to the Concerto*. Cambridge University Press, 2005.

Taruskin, Richard. "Standoff (II): Music in History: Carter." In *The Oxford History of Western Music*. Oxford University Press, 2004, vol. 6, pp. 261–306.

Thomas, Gavin. "Crashing Through the Picturesque." *The Musical Times* 136/1828 (1995), 285–88.

Tilmouth, Michael. "String Quartet." In S. Sadie and J. Tyrrell (eds.), *The New Grove Dictionary of Music and Musicians*. 2nd edn. London: Macmillan, 2001, vol. 18, pp. 276–87.

Tomlinson, Gary. *Metaphysical Song: An Essay on Opera*. Princeton University Press, 1999.

Truniger, Matthias. "Elliott Carter: *Esprit rude/esprit doux*." *Sonus* 19/1 (1998): 26–52.

Tusa, John. Interview with Elliott Carter. www.bbc.co.uk/radio3/johntusainterview/carter_transcript.shmtl.

[unattributed]. "New Carter Song Cycle: European Premiere in London." *Boosey and Hawkes*. www.boosey.com/cr/news/New-Carter-song-cycle-European-premiere-in-London/11405&LangID=1.

Updike, John. "Late Works: Writers and Artists Confronting the End." *The New Yorker* 82/24 (Aug. 7, 2006): 64–71.

Urquart, Thomas, and P. A. Motteux (eds.). *The Works of Rabelais*. London: Richard Baldwin, 1693.

Vermaelen, Denis. "Elliott Carter's Sketches: Spiritual Exercises and Craftsmanship." In Patricia Hall and Friedemann Sallis (eds.), *A Handbook to Twentieth-Century Musical Sketches*. Cambridge University Press, 2004, pp. 161–75.

Wagner, Richard. *On the Application of Music to the Drama*. Trans. William Ashton Ellis. In *Richard Wagner's Prose Works*. New York: Broude Bros., 1966. Original edn, 1895–1912: vol. 6, pp. 173–91.

Wallace, Helen. *Boosey & Hawkes: The Publishing Story*. London: Boosey & Hawkes, 2007.

Weston, Craig A. "Inversion, Subversion, and Metaphor: Music and Text in Elliott Carter's *A Mirror on Which to Dwell*." DMA dissertation, University of Washington, 1992.

Wheeldon, Marianne. "Interpreting Discontinuity in the Late Works of Debussy." *Current Musicology* 77 (2004): 97–115.

Whittall, Arnold. "Boulez et le classicisme moderne (Schoenberg, Berg)." In J. Goldman, J-J Nattiez, and F. Nicholas (eds.), *La pensée de Pierre Boulez à travers ses écrits*. Sampzón: Editions Delatour France, 2009, pp. 275–98.

"'A Play of Pure Forces'? Elliott Carter's Opera in Context." *The Musical Times* 149 (2008): 3–13.

Serialism. Cambridge University Press, 2008.

"Summer's Long Shadows." *Musical Times* 138/1850 (1997): 14–22.

Wicksteed, P. H. (ed.). *Aristotle*. 23 vols. Cambridge, MA: Harvard University Press, 1970–. New edn, 1995.

Williams, Alastair. "New Music, Late Style: Adorno's 'Form in the New Music'." *Music Analysis* 27/2–3 (2008): 193–97.

Williams, William Carlos. *Asphodel, That Greeny Flower and Other Love Poems*. New York: New Directions Publishing, 1994.

Winkler, Allan M. *The Politics of Propaganda: The Office of War Information 1942–1945*. New Haven: Yale University Press, 1978.

Index